A Commentary
on
the Minor Prophets

A
COMMENTARY
ON
THE MINOR PROPHETS

Homer Hailey

BAKER BOOK HOUSE
Grand Rapids, Michigan

Copyright © 1972 by
Baker Book House Company

ISBN: 0-8010-4049-3
Library of Congress Catalog Card Number: 72-80331

First printing, August 1972
Second printing, January 1973
Third printing, October 1973

PRINTED IN THE UNITED STATES OF AMERICA

To Lois, the mother of my children, whose faithful
and sacrificing care for the home made possible my hours of study, teaching, and
preaching through the early years
of life.

PREFACE

For many years the study of the prophets has been to me a challenging experience and a source of inspiration and information. During recent years friends have asked me to write a short, usable commentary on the twelve Minor Prophets. Lack of spare time has hindered my undertaking the task. Finally, however, I determined to make the effort before advancing age makes such a work impossible.

From the prophets I have derived an insight into God's work among the nations which has helped me to determine something of the principles on which He works among them. This has enabled me to look to Him, rather than to men, for the solution of modern problems; for He continues to rule in the kingdoms of men. This study has been of help in preaching to people of today, for the prophets preached to people in similar circumstances and under like conditions. Also, the study has strengthened my faith in Jesus as the Christ, as I have seen fulfilled in Him the glorious promises of the Lord spoken through these great men of God. In the light of what the prophets have meant to me, I have wished to share this rich blessing with others.

There are many excellent commentaries that have come from the hands of writers far more scholarly than I. These books examine in a critical manner the words and background of the prophets. I do not attempt to compete with them. My hope is that I may present in a brief and simple manner the thought of each prophet. I write for "the common people" who are not so much interested in a technical approach, but who earnestly desire to know more of this portion of God's great library.

Instead of following the arrangement of the books as found in our English Bible, I have decided to discuss them in their chronological order. The date of at least two of the books, Obadiah and Joel, is uncertain. I begin with these two because the evidence seems to place them early. However, I realize the evidence is not absolutely conclusive.

A general pattern is followed in presenting the material. Some observations are made which include the date, the background of the prophets, the message, and the lesson or lessons of the book. The design has been to help the student in understanding the particular book and its message and to encourage and aid teachers in directing studies in the twelve Minor Prophets.

I am indebted to a host of writers of other generations and of recent years for help in understanding the writings of the prophets. In a special way I am indebted to Mrs. Margie Garrett, head of the Development Office of Florida College, for her invaluable help in correcting sentences and for her suggestions toward their proper structure. She has continued to encourage me in the writing of this book. Likewise, I owe a debt of gratitude to Miss Mary Cannon, my efficient secretary, for typing and correcting the manuscript. Above all, I am grateful to our heavenly Father for the providence that made this study possible.

Homer Hailey
Temple Terrace, Florida

CONTENTS

INTRODUCTION

A study of the prophets will enrich the life of anyone who applies himself to learn their teaching; conversely, it will only add to the confusion of those who would use their writings as a basis on which to speculate about the future. An understanding of the prophets' teaching concerning Israel and Judah, the heathen nations of that day, and the Messiah who was to come will strengthen the faith of the one who sees the fulfillment of those predictions in history and in the New Covenant. An understanding of how the prophets dealt with the religious, political, social, and moral corruptions in their day will give courage to the Lord's faithful today. Studying the consequences of Israel's disobedience and understanding the principles on which God dealt with that disobedience will help one better to read the signs of the times. A knowledge of the writings of the prophets will make reading the daily newspaper and secular magazines and listening to news reports of present-day world events more meaningful. This is not to say that through the prophets God foretold any specific event of today, or pointed to any individual or nation of today. But by faith in the immutability of God and knowledge of the principles on which God dealt with the situations of that day, one will conclude that God will act in a like manner today. It is therefore with intent to learn more

11

about God and His methods of dealing with His people in sin and with sinful nations of the world that this study is approached.

In times of spiritual and moral repression and decay, God raised up men (prophets) in whose mouth He put His word and whom He sent to the people in an effort to turn them back to Himself. The prophets emphasized the sole deity of Jehovah, pointed out His majesty, holiness, righteousness, and justice, and made known the principles on which He would act toward people—both His own and the heathen. Jehovah used the prophets to point out the wickedness of His people in contrast to His infinite qualities and character. These servants of Jehovah declared that He is infinite in knowledge, in wisdom, and in understanding; therefore, He can declare the end from the beginning, and does not err in His actions. Also, He is infinite in power; therefore, He can carry out His divine purpose. In all His attributes God is immutable; His principles never change, nor does His application of these principles change. In this knowledge of God man can depend on Him to act and react at all times according to a definite pattern. Isaiah shows this part of the prophet's work as he summarizes Jehovah's claim to absolute and infinite deity when he quotes God as saying, "I, even I, am Jehovah; and besides me there is no saviour. I have declared, and I have saved, and I have showed" (43:11ff.); "I am the first, and I am the last; and besides me there is no God" (44:6); "I am Jehovah, that maketh all things; that stretcheth forth the heavens alone; that spreadeth abroad the earth; . . . that frustrateth the signs of the liars, and maketh diviners mad; that turneth wise men backward, and maketh their knowledge foolish; that confirmeth the word of his servant, and performeth the counsel of his messengers" (44:24-26), "declaring the end from the beginning, and from ancient times things that are not yet done; saying, My counsel shall stand, and I will do all my pleasure" (46:10).

Among the writings of the prophets are to be found some of the most beautiful, majestic, and artistic expressions of all literature. Although the prophet was inspired and spoke as the Spirit directed, Jehovah allowed the personality and background of each man to shine through his message, making the book throb with both the life of man and of God.

The reader may become acquainted with each and know them as individuals, rejoicing, sorrowing, praising, weeping, lamenting, and hoping, as he would come to know a man of his own age. The language of the prophets is in no way impoverished or penurious. It vibrates with the thunder of judgment as the lion roars or the earth quakes. On the other hand it may possess the tenderness of a mother for her babe as she takes it in her arms and calms its trembling fears. The prophet may make a direct appeal to the conscience; or he may speak in parables, metaphors, and similes. He may use hyperbole bordering on exaggeration that taxes the reader's credulity, or he may speak with such simplicity that one marvels at the failure of his audience to grasp his point. The prophet may speak of his message as having originated in a dream, a vision, or a direct word from Jehovah to his own soul; but always and by all means he is striving to make known the will of Jehovah to His people. Some of the words of the divinely inspired spokesmen fire the imagination of the reader and thrill his very soul. Consider the words of Obadiah as he describes the boast of Edom and Jehovah's reply, "Though thou mount on high as the eagle, and though thy nest be set among the stars, I will bring thee down from thence, saith Jehovah" (v. 4). The words of Amos bring before one the vivid picture of a mountain cataract as he says, "But let justice roll down as waters, and righteousness as a mighty stream" (5:24). Where can one find a fuller summary of Jehovah's requirement of man in fewer words than in Micah's classic question, "and what doth Jehovah require of thee, but to do justly, and to love kindness, and to walk humbly with thy God?" (6:8)? Nowhere is a deep and well-founded faith expressed more simply and fervently than in the words of Habakkuk as he sees all avenues of food taken away by the invading destroyer, then says, though it all fail, "Yet I will rejoice in Jehovah, I will joy in the God of my salvation. Jehovah, the Lord, is my strength; and he maketh my feet like hinds' feet, and will make me to walk upon my high places" (3:18 ff.). Wherefore, aside from the spiritual enlightenment through reading the prophets, one will find his study rewarding and enriching from a purely literary point of view. The writings of the prophets will ever stand as jewels of divine revelation and as classics among the giants of literature of all time.

Instructors Under
the Old Covenant

Under the law there were at least five classes of speakers: Moses, the lawgiver; the wise men, who gave counsel; priests, who taught the law; prophets, through whom God spoke His word; and psalmists, who were the singers or poets in Israel. Jeremiah and Ezekiel speak of three of these classes as being important to the instruction of the people:

> Then said they, Come, and let us devise devices against Jeremiah; for *the law* shall not perish from the *priest*, nor *counsel* from the *wise*, nor the *word* from the *prophet* (Jer. 18:18).

> Mischief shall come upon mischief, and rumor shall be upon rumor; and they shall seek a *vision* of the *prophet*; but *the law* shall perish from the *priest*, and *counsel* from the *elders* (Ezek. 7:26).

1. Moses: lawgiver

Since the law was given but once, there would be of necessity only one lawgiver, Moses, the servant of Jehovah (Neh. 8:1, 14; 9:13-14; John 1:17; 7:19).

2. Wise men: counsel

The function of these was to give sound advice on matters of life. The first mention of such persons is that of a *wise woman* (II Sam. 14:1-24); also, the second person to be characterized as wise was a woman (II Sam. 20:16-22). The most outstanding wise man of Israel's history was Solomon. The canonical books of wisdom are Job, Proverbs, and Ecclesiastes. Some include the Song of Solomon. As Eiselen has pointed out:

> The wise men did not appeal directly to the conscience as did the prophets, but rather to the mind through counsel and argument, though their ultimate aim was to reach the conscience and through it influence conduct and life.[1]

3. Priests: law

The special function of the priests was related to the law. Since the law was civil and ecclesiastical, their function was twofold: first, to declare, interpret, and teach the law;

second, to tend the sacrificial duties. Therefore when apostasy came, the priests were in a large measure responsible for it (see Lev. 10:8-11; Hos. 4:6; Ezek. 22:26; Mal. 2:7).

4. Prophets: word

The mission of the prophet was to communicate to Israel the divine word. Though they did predict, it may be said of them that so far as their work as a whole was concerned they were proclaimers rather than predictors.

5. Psalmists: poets

The poets or "sweet singers" complete the group after Moses. Posterity is indebted to these for the Psalms. In them are to be found expressions of the deepest emotions and feelings of the human spirit. Some reflect, others express, many foretell; but all seek to glorify God.

The Meaning of the Word "Prophet"

It is generally agreed that the etymology of the word presents difficulties; however, the use of the word in Scripture makes clear the meaning, since Scripture is its own best interpreter.

The word is defined as follows: "According to the uniform teaching of the Bible the prophet is a speaker of or for God. His words are not the production of his own spirit, but come from a higher source."[2] "To boil up like a fountain (Heb.). In both the Old and the New Testaments, [a prophet] is one who, under the influence of the Holy Spirit speaks the words and the thoughts of God, whether they relate to the past, to the present, or to the future."[3] "One who spoke in God's stead."[4]

The meaning of the word is more satisfactorily learned from its use in Scripture. God said to Moses that Aaron would be "thy spokesman . . . a mouth" (Exod. 4:16); also, He said that Aaron would be Moses' "prophet" (Exod. 7:1). Therefore as a prophet he was a spokesman, a mouth. The prophet of Jehovah then would be the mouth of Jehovah.

God said that when He should raise up a prophet, He would put his words in the prophet's mouth and that the prophet would speak them in His name (Deut. 18:9-22). The Hebrew prophet was an ambassador of Jehovah sent to make known the will and purpose of Jehovah to His chosen people (Amos 3:7, 8; Jer. 23:16; Ezek. 13:1-7). At other times as Jehovah's ambassador he was sent to the heathen; for example, Jonah was sent to Nineveh. As a spokesman for God he was more a "forth-teller" than a "fore-teller." To be sure, the prophet did foretell events, but this is not the basic meaning of the word.

Though "prophet" is the general term for God's spokesman used in the Old Covenant writings, other designations are used: Seer—this appears to have been the earliest term by which they were called (I Sam. 9:9); Man of God (I Sam. 9:6; I Kings 17:18); Servant of God (or, of Jehovah) (I Chron. 6:49; I Kings 18:36); Messenger of Jehovah (Isa. 42:19); and Watchman (Ezek. 3:17; 33:7). All these terms express the same fundamental idea—that of a mediator by speech between God and man.

From the prophets every preacher and teacher of the Word can learn. As Knudson has well expressed it:

> There are two classes of preachers—the good preachers who have something to say, and the poor preachers who *have* to say something. But there is yet another and higher class. It consists of those who both have something to say and who have to say it. Such are the prophets.[5]

Jeremiah well represents this latter class as he explains his feelings: "And if I say, I will not make mention of him, nor speak any more in his name, then there is in my heart as it were a burning fire shut up in my bones, and I am weary with forbearing, and I cannot contain" (20:9). He had something to say and he had to say it.

The Pre-Literary (Oral) Prophets

1. Period of the Patriarchs: Founders of the Hebrew Nation

a. **Abraham, Isaac, Jacob.** Abraham is recognized in Scripture as a prophet of God (Gen. 20:7, 17). Isaac and Jacob are probably referred to in Psalm 105:15, which includes them in the roster of God's spokesmen.

b. Moses. It is only natural that, as God's instrument, the deliverer and lawgiver of the Hebrew nation should have been a prophet. He would not necessarily be included with the pre-literary prophets who followed, for he stands in a class by himself (cf. Deut. 18:15-18; 34:10; Hos. 12:13).

c. Miriam. She is spoken of as a "prophetess," and in some way was used of God to assist Moses in his work, probably as teacher (Exod. 15:20).

2. Period of the Judges

a. Deborah. Deborah was a female judge as well as a prophetess (Judg. 4:4). During this period there was also an unnamed prophet whom Jehovah sent to the people (6:8).

b. The prophetic bands, or "sons of the prophets." The earliest reference we have to these prophets is during the time of Samuel, in the eleventh century B.C. (I Sam. 10:5-13). A similar company is mentioned in I Samuel 19:18-24. After the time of Samuel it was two centuries before the prophetic bands came again into prominence, this time in connection with Elijah and Elisha (I Kings 18:13; 22:6). These prophetic bands were probably religious individuals gathered around an outstanding prophet to study under him and to imbibe his spirit.

c. The "prophet-judge": Samuel (I Sam. 1:1—25:1). During these days two parties appear to have arisen in Israel, one political and the other religious. Saul chose—if he did not head—the political party, whereas Samuel cast his influence with the religious element. Peter indicates that Samuel's work marks the beginning of the prophetic era (Acts 3:24).

3. Period of the Kings

a. From David to the division of the kingdom. The prophets were Nathan, who rebuked David (II Sam. 12:1ff.), prophesied of the Messiah (II Sam. 7:1-17), and anointed Solomon (I Kings 1); Gad, who rebuked David for having numbered Judah (II Sam. 24:11ff.); Ahijah, prophet to Jeroboam concerning the division of Judah and Israel (I Kings 11:29 ff.); Shemaiah, prophet to Rehoboam with instruction not to go up and fight (I Kings 12:21-24); and an unnamed prophet, "a man of God" who was sent to Jeroboam to warn of the results of his apostasy (I Kings 13).

b. From the division of the monarchy to the time of Amos. There were Jehu, who declared the doom of Baasha (I Kings 16:1-7) and who rebuked Jehoshaphat for alliance with Ahab (II Chron. 19:1-3); Eliezer, who prophesied against Jehoshaphat, king of Judah (II Chron. 20:37); Micaiah, who stood against the false prophet Zedekiah (I Kings 22:1-36); Jonah (of the early literary prophets, who wrote the Book of Jonah), advisor to Jeroboam II (II Kings 14:25); and Elijah and Elisha, who prophesied in the days of Ahab and the period that followed (I Kings 16 through II Kings 13).

False Prophets

Along with the true there arose also false prophets (see Deut. 18:20-22; Jer. 28). These flourished from a very early period in the nation's history to the time of the close of the Old Testament writings. The false prophets fall into the two general classes, mercenary and political; some prophesied for money, others for political favor (see Mic. 3:5, 11). Oftentimes the false prophets were nationalistic—that is, they defended the national practices and rulers through ignorance; but whether false through ignorance or self-will, they and their messages were no less severely denounced by the true prophets. Albert C. Knudson has well said: "An ignorant conscientiousness may be quite as dangerous to a community as deliberate wickedness." When opposed by false prophets, the true prophets rise to their greatest heights of zeal and fearlessness.

The Literary Prophets in Chronological Order

Bible scholars differ widely on the dates of the literary prophets, and the dates of some are difficult to determine. Because of this a list of eight or ten various authors is included. In the dates ascribed to the prophets as given below, the first date is the one accepted in this study as the most probable.

In the first section, the "Ninth Century" prophets, the dates of the first two, Obadiah and Joel, are the most debatable. The problems faced and dealt with by these prophets are such as could fall into almost any period of the prophetic era. The principles laid down are timeless. Obadiah is placed by some in the period of Jehoram, king of Judah, when the Philistines, the Arabians, and the Ethiopians came up against Judah (II Chron. 21:8-10, 16-18). This would place the book early, about 845 B.C. Others place the prophet in the period of the fall of Jerusalem or shortly thereafter, approximately 586 B.C. This study follows Keil and Sampey in suggesting the earlier date, although it does so with considerable question. The date for Joel is equally uncertain. By various scholars he is placed from 830 to 350 B.C. Here again the early dating by the more conservative scholars is accepted. Jonah appears in the early part of the eighth century, but is placed in the ninth-century group with Obadiah and Joel because he prophesied before the rise of the Assyrian Empire under Tiglath-pileser.

1. Ninth Century—Early Assyrian Period

(The list of authors is arranged alphabetically.)

a. **Obadiah**, *ca.* 845 B.C. Davidson, uncertain; Driver, fifth century B.C.; Eiselen, after 586 B.C.; *I.S.B.E.* (Eiselen), 587 B.C.; Keil, *ca.* 845 B.C.; Knudson, *ca.* 460 B.C.; Pfeiffer, 460-400 B.C.; Sampey, *ca.* 845 B.C.; Young, before Jeremiah.

b. **Joel**, *ca.* 830 B.C. Davidson, after the restoration; Driver, fifth century B.C.; Eiselen, 400 B.C.; *I.S.B.E.* (R), 900-400 B.C.; Keil, before Amos and Hosea, during the reign of Joash (837-803 B.C.); Knudson, *ca.* 400 B.C.; Pfeiffer, *ca.* 350 B.C.; Sampey, *ca.* 830 B.C.; Young, *ca.* 830 B.C., during the reign of Joash.

c. **Jonah**, 790-750 B.C. Davidson, after restoration; Driver, fifth century B.C.; Eiselen, written 400-240 B.C., but Eiselen thinks the prophet lived *ca.* 770 B.C.; *I.S.B.E.*, 800-780 B.C.; Keil, early; Knudson, *ca.* 300 B.C.; Pfeiffer, *ca.* 350 B.C. or after; Sampey, *ca.* 800 B.C.; Young, 783-743 B.C.

2. Eighth Century—Assyrian Period

a. **Amos**, 755 B.C. All the above-mentioned writers are agreed in placing Amos in the decade 760-750 B.C. This study will consider 755 B.C. as the date.

b. **Hosea**, 750-725 B.C. The dates given by the above writers range from 786-734 B.C. From the internal evidence it appears that Hosea was later than Amos.

c. **Isaiah**, 740-700 B.C. Except for liberal scholars who place chapters 40—66 during the period of the Babylonian captivity, all are agreed on the date for Isaiah.

d. **Micah**, 735-700 B.C. With variations in their view as to when Micah began writing, all scholars consulted generally agree on this date.

3. Seventh Century—Chaldean Period

a. **Jeremiah**, 626-586 B.C. The exact close of Jeremiah's ministry as prophet is uncertain, for he spent some years in Egypt after the fall of Jerusalem, 586 B.C. All give this as the date except C. von Orelli (*I.S.B.E.*) and Young, who place the call of Jeremiah to the prophetic office in the year 627 B.C.

b. **Zephaniah**, 630-625 B.C. Davidson, 627 B.C. and after; Driver, before 621 B.C.; Eiselen, *ca.* 626 B.C.; *I.S.B.E.* (E), 630-626 B.C.; Young, early part of the reform of Josiah, and so generally do the others.

c. **Nahum**, 625-612 B.C. The date of this prophecy lies somewhere between the fall of No-amon, 663 B.C., and the fall of Nineveh, 612 B.C. Older scholars placed the fall of Nineveh at 606 B.C., and considered the prophet's work to date just before that event. Recent scholarship has established the fall of Nineveh as 612 B.C.; thus, the most probable date for Nahum is 614-612 B.C. However, this study will favor the one given above, 625-612 B.C. as sufficiently inclusive to cover the period of the prophet.

d. **Habakkuk**, 625-605 B.C. The Chaldean power began to rise in 625 B.C., and Jerusalem was brought under that power in 605 B.C.; so the prophet prophesied at some time between 625 and 605 B.C. Most scholars place him in this general period.

4. Sixth Century—the Exile

a. Ezekiel, 593-570 B.C. Some place the beginning of his ministry in 592 B.C., and some set the conclusion of his work in 572 or 571 B.C. The difference is minor.

b. Daniel, 605-536 B.C. Here there is great diversity of opinion. Davidson, late; Driver, late; Eiselen, 175-163 B.C.; *I.S.B.E.* (W), sixth century B.C.; Keil, Babylonian exile; Knudson, 165 B.C.; Pfeiffer, second century B.C.; Sampey, 605-536 B.C.; Young, sixth century B.C.

5. Sixth and Fifth Centuries—Post Exilic Period

a. Haggai, 520 B.C. All scholars are agreed on this date.

b. Zechariah, 520-518 B.C. Many scholars accept a later date for the latter part of the book, chapters 9—14; however, Farrar and others ascribe chapters 9—11 to the age of Isaiah before the fall of Samaria and chapters 12—14 to the time of Jeremiah before the fall of Jerusalem. Robinson thinks that chapters 1—8 record prophecies of the period 520-518 B.C. and that chapters 9—14 were spoken (and written) by the same prophet at a later time when, as an old man, he came forward to encourage his people during some Persian oppression.

c. Malachi, *ca.* 440 B.C. Various dates are given, from 460-432 B.C. On the basis of internal evidence, it seems safe to ascribe the work of the prophet to a period after Ezra's death and before the end of Nehemiah's governorship. The absence of Nehemiah may have given rise to the abuses exposed by the prophet. This would place his work in the general period suggested above.

There are three things one should keep constantly in mind as he studies a work of the prophets:

First, it is necessary to understand the political, moral, social, and religious conditions at the time in which the prophet lived and preached, and how he proposed to meet these conditions. It will be observed that whatever the conditions, the prophet endeavored to meet them by pointing the people back to God. Before reform could be effected, their

Table of Dates for the Literary

		Davidson	Driver	Eiselen
Prophets of Uncertain Dates				
	Obadiah	Uncertain	5th cent.	after 586
	Joel	after restoration	5th cent.	400
	Jonah	after restoration	5th cent.	400-250²
Eighth Century, or the Assyrian Period				
	Amos	760-750	760-746	755
	Hosea	750-737	786-734	750-735
	Isaiah	740-700	740-700	740-700
	Micah	724-?	Con. Isa.	735-700
Seventh Century, or Chaldean Period				
	Jeremiah	626-586	626-	626-586
	Zephaniah	626-?	bef. 621	*ca.* 626
	Nahum	610-608	664-607	*ca.* 608
	Habakkuk	605-600	bef. 600	*ca.* 600
Sixth Century, or the Exile				
	Ezekiel	593-573	592-570	593-570
	Obadiah—see above.			
	Daniel	late	late	175-163
Sixth and Fifth Centuries, or Post-Exilic Period				
	Haggai	520-	520-	520
	Zech. 1—8	520	520-518	520
	Zech. 9—14	late		aft. 350
	Malachi	460-450	458-432	*ca.* 450

* All dates are B.C.

1 Eiselen gives a choice between an early date, *ca.* 845, and 587, about the tim
of the destruction of Jerusalem by the Babylonians.
2 Eiselen says the book is the history of a prophet who lived *ca.* 770, but that i
belonged to a composition between 400-250.

Prophets — Chronologically Arranged *

I.S.B.E.	Knudson	Pfeiffer	Sampey	Young
586 (E)[1]	ca. 460	460-400	ca. 845	before Jeremiah
900-400(R)	ca. 400	ca. 350	ca. 830	ca. 830
800-780(S)	ca. 300	ca. 350	ca. 800[3]	783-743
ca. 760(E)	ca. 750	ca. 750	ca. 750	
750-735(E)	743-734	750-744	ca. 750	
740-700(R)	740-	740-	738-700	
722-701(vO)	bef. 722	Con. Isa.	Con. Isa.	Con. Isa.
627-ff.[4]	626-ff.[4]	626-586	626-ff.[4]	627-ff.[4]
630-626(E)	ca. 627	630-624	630-625	
663-607(E)	ca. 607	bef. 612	ca. 630	663-612
ca. 600(E)	ca. 600	605-600	609-598	609-598
593-571(M)	592-570	593-571	593-571	
6th cent.(W)	165	2nd cent.	605-536	6th cent.
520(R)	520	520	520	520
520-518(R)	520	520-518	520-	520-
	late	later		same
445-432(R)	450	ca. 460	ca. 440	

3 Just prior to Jeroboam's accession to the throne of Israel (Ephraim).
4 Knudson, Sampey, and Young all carry the date of Jeremiah beyond the destruction of Jerusalem.

hearts must be changed toward Him. The thunder along with their lightning flashes is heard at this point in all who dealt with Israel's sins and her reaction to Jehovah.

A second point of observation should be what the prophets consider is God's relation to the heathen nations with whom the Jewish people came in contact. It should be noted that God directs the destiny of these and that it is He who judges them. One could ask if God exercises such rule today. The testimony of both Old and New Testaments is that He does.

A final point that the student should particularly regard is the prophet's teaching of a future kingdom and king to be fulfilled in one who was to come. Whatever was the lot of Israel and its king of the prophet's day, a lasting kingdom comprised of a spiritual Israel and a spiritual King who should rule in righteousness was the true hope of the future.

With these three points in mind, the student of the prophets will find himself richly repaid for his labors in reading, searching, and studying these giants of spiritual and moral power in ancient times.

Political Background from Elisha to Amos

Shortly after the death of Solomon (932/31 B.C.), the empire built by David divided into two kingdoms, Judah and Israel. The years that followed were filled with bitterness, war, and the introduction of idolatry. Solomon had opened the door for idolatry to enter the national life by building altars for the gods of his foreign wives (I Kings 11:4-8; Neh. 13:26). After his death idolatry eventually became more and more a part of the religious life of the people of Judah. In the northern kingdom Jeroboam introduced calf worship, making it the national religion of Israel (I Kings 12:25-33). Added to this system of perversion of Jehovah worship, Ahab and Jezebel introduced pure idolatry into Israel in the form of Baal worship. This departure from Jehovah by both nations led to all manner of political, social, and moral corruption. In His intense desire to turn the people back to Himself, Jehovah raised up prophets with the special mission of pointing out to the people the contrast between their sins and His own holiness and the righteousness of His law. Although the prophetic era seems to have begun with Samuel (Acts 3:24), Elijah and Elisha stand out as the beginning of Jehovah's accelerated use of prophets in His effort to save His people from complete apostasy.

For further information on the background of conditions from the closing years of Elisha's career to the prophetic work of Amos, the reader should give careful attention to II Kings 8:1–15:7 and II Chronicles 21–26. In order that the reader may have before him a brief summary of the kings of Israel and Judah, the following list is given. Dates for the following material are based on Edwin R. Thiele's table, "The Dates of the Kings of Israel and Judah."[7]

1. Israel

a. **Jehu**, 841-814/13 B.C. (II Kings 9:1–10:28; Athaliah and Joash, rulers in Judah). Jehu was anointed at Ramoth-Gilead by a son of the prophets who was sent by Elisha for this purpose (9:1-10). The house of Ahab was smitten and Jezebel was slain by Jehu as had been predicted by Elijah (9:11-36). Ahab's seventy sons were subsequently slain (10:1-17); the priests and worshipers of Baal were also put to death (10:18-28). The sin of Jehu was his worship of the calves set up by Jeroboam.

b. **Jehoahaz**, 814/13-798 B.C. (II Kings 13:1-9; twenty-third year of Joash, king of Judah). Jehovah began to deliver Israel into the hand of Syria; Jehoahaz called for help from Jehovah, who hearkened to him because of His pity for Israel. However, Jehoahaz and Israel "departed not from the sins of the house of Jeroboam," leading ultimately to the downfall of the nation.

c. **Jehoash**, 798-782/81 B.C. (II Kings 13:10-25; Joash, king of Judah). Jehoash came to Elisha as he lay upon his deathbed and was told to take arrows and shoot them from an open window. The prophet made no explanation except that the arrows were Jehovah's arrows of victory over Syria's arrow. Jehoash obeyed the instruction. He was then told to take arrows and smite upon the ground; he did this three times. The prophet was displeased because he had smitten the ground no more than three times, and he announced that there would be only three victories over the Syrians. After the death of Elisha, Jehoash smote Syria three times, according to the prophecy of Elisha.

d. **Jeroboam II**, 793-753 B.C. (overlapping reign, 793/92-782/81 B.C.; II Kings 14:23-29; Amaziah, king of Judah). Jeroboam II restored the borders of Israel to the largest extent since the reign of Solomon. Jonah was the prophet of the period of his reign. Great prosperity was enjoyed under his leadership; but prosperity brought with it greed, corruption, and vices of many kinds. Toward the close of Jeroboam's reign, Amos began to prophesy.

2. Judah

a. **Jehoram**, 853-841 B.C., co-regent with Jehoshaphat, 853-848 B.C.; his independent reign, 848-841 B.C. (II Kings 8:16-24; II Chron. 21). As could be expected, Jehoram, son of Jehoshaphat and husband of Athaliah, the daughter of Ahab, was a wicked king. In his days Edom revolted. Jehoram made high places of idolatrous worship which led the people further into sin; for this he was rebuked by a letter from Elijah (II Chron. 21:11-15). The Philistines, Arabians, and Ethiopians were stirred up against him. According to the word of the prophet, he died of a terrible bowel disease. His character and the nature of his reign had been so revolting that the people were glad when he died.

b. **Ahaziah**, 841 B.C. (II Kings 8:25-29; II Chron. 22:1-9). Ahaziah, the son of Jehoram and Athaliah, walked in the way of Ahab, the idolatrous king of Israel. Death came within a year and cut short his reign.

c. **Athaliah**, 841-835 B.C. (II Kings 11; II Chron. 22:10—23:21). Athaliah, the daughter of Ahab and usurper of the throne, slew all the royal seed except Joash. Rescued from the hands of Athaliah by a daughter of Jehoram and daughter of Ahaziah, the infant Joash escaped. After reigning six years, Athaliah was slain by the people in an insurrection led by Jehoiada, the priest. Under Jehoiada worship of Jehovah was restored. These were stirring times!

d. **Joash**, 835-796 B.C. (II Kings 12; II Chron. 24). Joash was seven years old when he began to reign. He did that which was right while Jehoiada the priest lived, but upon the death of Jehoiada he became evil. He forsook Jehovah, restored the worship of the Asherim, and slew Zechariah, the son of Jehoiada. During his reign the Syrians took away the treasures of the house of God. Joash was slain by his own servants.

e. **Amaziah**, 796-767 B.C. (II Kings 14; II Chron. 25). It is said that this king did right, but not with a perfect heart. He put down Edom and brought their gods to Jerusalem "and set them up to be his gods, and bowed down himself before them" (II Chron. 25:14, 15). He warred against Joash, king of Israel, but was defeated. Joash broke down the walls of Jerusalem and took the gold, silver, and other valuables to Samaria. Amaziah reigned fifteen years after that.

f. **Uzziah**, 767-740/39 B.C. (II Kings 15:1-7; II Chron. 26). Uzziah is also called Azariah. He was sixteen years old when he began to reign, and he reigned for fifty-one years. He is named as one of the good kings of Judah; he did that which was right. He put down the enemies of Judah, promoted husbandry, and brought great prosperity to the people. But in the midst of success he became proud and offered incense to Jehovah (a responsibility of the priests only); for this he was smitten with leprosy and lived a leper until the end of his life.

---

1 Frederick Carl Eiselen, *Prophecy and the Prophets*, p. 14.

2 C. von Orelli, "Prophecy," *International Standard Bible Encyclopedia*, *IV*, p. 2459.

3 Robert Milligan, *Scheme of Redemption*, p. 298.

4 Albert C. Knudson, *Beacon Lights of Prophecy*, p. 30.

5 Albert C. Knudson, *The Prophetic Movement in Israel*, pp. 65 ff.

6 Knudson, p. 24.

7 Thiele, *The Mysterious Numbers of the Hebrew Kings*, p. 205.

1

OBADIAH

"Servant of Jehovah"

General Observations

1. Date: 845 B.C.

The date of Obadiah's work is ascribed to periods ranging from 845 to 400 B.C. However, the two most probable dates are 845 and 586 B.C. or shortly thereafter.

The prophet refers to an attack on Jerusalem which can well be narrowed down to two possibilities: the days of Jehoram when the Philistines and Arabians attacked the city (848-844 B.C.; see II Chron. 21:8-10, 16-17), and the destruction of Jerusalem by the Chaldeans (586 B.C.). Argument for the later date is made on the "we" of Obadiah 1, "we have heard tidings from Jehovah," which, in the mind of some, would include prophets other than Obadiah. This position is strengthened by statements from two additional prophets, Jeremiah (49:7-13) and Ezekiel (35:1-10), and by the words of an unknown psalmist in Babylon who said, "Remember, O Jehovah, against the children of Edom the day of Jerusalem; who said, Rase it, rase it, even to the foundation thereof" (Ps. 137:7). In his book, *The Minor Prophets,* F. W. Farrar presents a summary of arguments made for the later date (pp. 175-181).

Argument for the earlier date is based on the difference between the language of Jeremiah and that of Obadiah, which difference points to the conclusion that Jeremiah was later than Obadiah. This philological evidence is presented by Keil and others. The strongest argument for the early date, however, seems to rest on the text of Obadiah itself. Obadiah speaks of foreigners entering Jerusalem's gates, of Jacob's substance being carried away, of lots being cast upon the city, and of destruction and disaster. But his language is not inclusive enough to describe the destruction by the Babylonians. The destruction of the temple and the royal palace, the carrying away to Babylon of the king and the people, and the remnant that went into Egypt are not mentioned. Further, the language of the prophet implies that people were residing in the city at the time.

Keil, Deane, Laetsch, and Sampey all make convincing arguments for the earlier date that appear to outweigh the evidence for the later one. Sampey concludes his argument for the earlier date, however, by admitting that in his opinion the weight of evidence for the two is about even (see Keil: *Minor Prophets,* II, 335-349; Deane: *Pulpit Commentary,* "Introduction"; Laetsch: *The Minor Prophets,* pp. 201-203). Because of the weight of this evidence against the later date, and because of the philological evidence presented by Hebrew scholars, this study of the prophets accepts the early date and places Obadiah first.

2. Message

The message of Obadiah is twofold: the fall of Edom because of its pride and cruelty against Israel, and the exaltation of Zion when Seir, the Edomite counterpart of Zion, would be cast down. The rescued of both Israel and Edom will be in Zion, for in it the redeemed will be found.

3. Lessons

a. Pride is deceitful and "goes before a fall." Pride, which leads to vanity and a sense of independence from God, must be judged and exposed. Righteousness must be vindicated.

b. The injustice of cruelty, bitterness, and passion of one people against another must be avenged.

c. When one shares in the spoils of wrong-doing, though

he may not be an instigator of the crime, standing "on the other side" he becomes "even . . . as one of them" (v. 11).

d. As a people sows, so will it reap.

e. In time of divine judgment, God provides a means and a place of escape for those who will turn to Him. The place provided is His Mount Zion.

4. History of Edom

a. The early history of Edom begins even before the birth of Esau while the two brothers, Esau and Jacob, were in the womb of their mother, Rebekah (Gen. 25:22-26). At that time God chose the nation that would descend from the second son over the nation which should come from the first. Enmity prevailed between Esau and Jacob throughout their lives and between the two nations that sprang from them. Highlights in the history of Esau are: the securing of the birthright by Jacob from Esau (Gen. 25:27-34); the securing of the blessing by Jacob from Isaac (Gen. 27); and the meeting of the two brothers years later (Gen. 32—33). The conflict of the two nations began at the time of the exodus (Num. 20:14-21) and continued until the subjection of Edom under David (II Sam. 8:13-14). During the reign of Jehoram, son of Jehoshaphat, king of Judah, Edom revolted (II Kings 8:20-22). The writer of Hebrews sums up God's evaluation of the character of Esau as a profane person, "who for one mess of meat sold his own birthright" (12:16). And in the Book of Malachi He sums up this disposition toward Edom, the nation, when He says, "Esau I hated, and made his mountains a desolation, and gave his heritage to the jackals of the wilderness" (1:3). Throughout the writings of the prophets Edom stands as a symbol of the earthly, nonspiritual people of the world.

b. During their later history the Edomites were eventually overcome by the Nabataeans, a people who pushed in from the desert and drove the Edomites from their land. Pushed out of their own land at the south end of the Dead Sea, the Edomites were forced to occupy a territory just south of the land of Judah. Toward the close of the second century B.C. they were conquered by John Hyrcanus of the Maccabees, who forced many of them to be circumcised and accept the law. Thus, they became nominal Jewish proselytes. By 100 A.D. they had become lost to history.

For an account of the close of Edom's history, consult any good recent work, such as that of Joseph P. Free, *Archaeology and Bible History,* pp. 276-277; *International Standard Bible Encyclopedia:* "Edom or Idumaea"; Emil G. Kraeling, *Bible Atlas,* p. 343; Ernest Wright, *Archaeology and the Bible,* p. 230; *The Westminster Historical Atlas to the Bible,* pp. 69-70; and *The Biblical World,* edited by Charles F. Pfeiffer, pp. 206-207.

Outline of the Book

I. Utter destruction of Edom decreed, vv. 1-16.
   A. Announcement of the judgment, vv. 1-9.
   1. The decree, v. 1
   2. Condition: deceived by pride, despised and debased by Jehovah, vv. 2-4.
   3. Completeness of the destruction, vv. 5-6.
   4. Treachery of his allies, v. 7.
   5. Failure of his wisdom and might, vv. 8-9.

   B. Cause of the judgment against Edom, vv. 10-14.
   1. Violence and unbrotherly conduct toward Judah, vv. 10-11.
   2. Warning against such conduct, vv. 12-14.

   C. Terrors of the judgment: the day of Jehovah, vv. 15-16.

II. Exaltation of Israel: the kingdom of Jehovah to be established upon Mount Zion, vv. 17-21.

   A. A remnant to escape in Mount Zion, v. 17.

   B. Conquest of Edom (Mount Seir) and surrounding nations, vv. 18-20.

   C. Jehovah's universal sway from Mount Zion, v. 21.

Comments

Vv. 1-4. Judgment—to be executed by Jehovah against Edom—is decreed; the cause of the judgment is Edom's pride and cruelty.

v. 1   "The vision of Obadiah" serves as a title to the book and declares to whom the vision was made; but other than this we know nothing of the man Obadiah. "Vision" indicates what the prophet saw, the impression made on his inner senses, and what he was to communicate to his hearers. "Thus saith the Lord Jehovah concerning Edom"—the nation descended from Esau—establishes the authority of Obadiah's message and points to those to whom the prophecy pertained. "We have heard tidings." The "we" identifies the prophet either with the people of Israel or with other prophets. It is more probable that he identified himself with the people, for the tidings were for all to hear. "An ambassador is sent among the nations" refers to no particular individual who was sent, but it indicates that that which follows is of Jehovah and that He sends His angel or spirit among the heathen nations to arouse them against Edom (cf. I Kings 22:19-23; Jer. 25:15 ff; Dan. 10:13, 21). The nations will carry out Jehovah's purpose; the ambas-

v. 2   sador will stir them "up against her [Edom] in battle." In spite of Edom's arrogance and vaunting pride,

v. 3   Jehovah had made it small among the nations; it was greatly despised. The nation thought of itself as being completely secure in the mountainous stronghold of Seir—whether in a city, in the stronghold of Sela (the Rock), or in the general region surrounding what was later known as Petra. The country of Edom lay south of the Dead Sea in a rugged region known as the Arabah. The mountainous area on either side of the Arabah was noted for its steep canyons, impregnable mountain strongholds, and well-protected coves. In these the people felt themselves secure against their enemies. In the pride of his heart and the confidence of his supposedly invulnerable stronghold Edom had

v. 4   said, "Who shall bring me down to the ground?" Jehovah's answer to the boastful and swaggering pride of Edom's deceived heart is among the classics of literary beauty. "Though thou mount on high as the eagle," reach the loftiest heights of your rocky crags, "and though thy nest be set among the stars," a metaphor suggesting infinite security among the stars of sidereal space, "I will bring thee down from thence, saith Jehovah." The destiny, doom, and deliverance of nations are in the hand of God; it is He who determines "their appointed seasons, and the bounds of their habitation" (Acts 17:26). He alone has the power to build up or to debase and cast down.

Vv. 5-9. The destruction of Edom decreed by Jehovah is to be complete and final. His confederates will turn against him, the wisdom of his wise men will fail, and his mighty men will be dismayed. All will be cut off.

Edom took pride not only in his physical strength and strategic location, but also in his wealth. Possessing great ore deposits and being located as he was on the crossroads of caravan traffic, he had grown wealthy through trade, through duty charged the caravans that traversed his land, and through his disposition to plunder weak caravans that passed through. But Jehovah had decreed his destruction and it would be complete. As a general practice, if thieves or robbers break into a house they take only until they have enough. Likewise, gleaners of a vineyard leave a few isolated grapes; they do not search under every leaf. But not so with the plunderers of Edom! "How are the things of Esau searched! how are his hidden treasures sought out!" The prophet sees the nation cast down from its lofty height and its treasures ravaged. The hidden things of Edom would be thoroughly sought out and searched for. The wealth of the proud people would be completely confiscated, and the nation would be totally plundered; it would be helpless before its enemies. Edom had been deceived by his allies with whom he had made alliances, probably both trade and protective agreements and pacts. The men of these confederacies are not named, but it is easy to suppose that the neighboring peoples of Moab and Ammon would be included. Others embraced in treaties would undoubtedly be Gaza and Tyre, with whom Edom at some time had carried on

v. 5

v. 6

v. 7

slave traffic (Amos 1:6, 9). Doubtless, the traders of nearby Arabian tribes would seek some kind of agreement with such a rich and powerful neighbor. In time of need these confederates would fail; they would turn back the ambassadors whom Edom would send to them for help. Those who had likewise grown wealthy by their trade alliances with Edom would now "lay a snare under" him as they contribute to and partake in the fall of Edom and in sharing the plunder with others. "There is no understanding in him": Edom could not see what was happening; and with the desertion of his allies, he would not know what to do or where to turn. In general, the deceitfulness of confederates has been the experience of history, and is a lesson that nations of today would do

v. 8 well to learn. Not only would Edom lose his confederates, but he would also lose the counsel of his wise men. "Shall I not in that day, saith Jehovah, destroy the wise men out of Edom?" Edom had been noted for its wise men, but their wisdom would be confused and fail them in the day of need. By taking away their wisdom Jehovah would thereby destroy

v. 9 the wise men. "And thy mighty men, O Teman, shall be dismayed." Teman was the southernmost of Edom's two chief cities, possibly its capital, and was distinguished for its men of wisdom. It was from Teman that Eliphaz had come to comfort Job (Job 2:11). With God against him, his confederates gone, and his wise and mighty men made helpless, Edom was doomed. Ultimately Edom's destruction would be complete; all his mighty men would be cut off from the mount of Esau, their place of refuge and protection, and would be slain.

Vv. 10-14. Edom is severely condemned for the cruel attitude shown toward his brother Jacob. He had stood with the enemies whose aim was to destroy God's people.

v. 10 The cause of Jehovah's judgment upon Edom and the impending destruction was twofold: Edom's pride (vv. 3-5) and the cruelty and perpetual enmity against his kinsman Jacob. "For the violence done"—a strong word indicating violent wrong or wickedness done to Israel when she had been under extreme duress— "shame shall cover thee." As Edom had sown, so would he reap; as Edom had acted toward others, so would be his fate. When the judgment against Edom would be executed it would be "for ever": till the *v. 11* end of time. In the day of Israel's calamity and Jerusalem's plundering by her enemies, Edom had rejoiced. He had "[stood] on the other side," thus identifying himself with the enemies and becoming as one of those plundering the city. Foreigners had entered into the city and had "cast lots upon Jerusalem." This lends weight to the position taken in the introduction that the occasion was that of II Chronicles 21:8-18, where several nations were involved (vv. 16-17). When Edom should have felt sympathy for the humiliated and suffering kinsman, the Lord charges, "even thou wast as one of them," the enemies.

In the following three verses Edom is sternly *v. 12* warned as he is placed under three specific charges: "look not," "enter not," and "stand not," each followed by a second or third negative command. "Look not" with glee on the day of your brother's disaster, "and rejoice not" in the day of Judah's destruction; "neither speak proudly in the day of distress." Man cannot with impunity rejoice in the time of another's calamity nor flout the humane laws of God by aiding or abetting the cruel afflictions imposed by any on his fellowman. Nor can one afford to "speak proudly" of himself and his safety in contrast to the humiliating distress of his neighbor, for who knows what a day may bring forth? "Enter not into the gate of my *v. 13* people in the day of their calamity." In verse 12 Edom is forbidden to rejoice; now he is forbidden to share in the spoils of Jehovah's plundered people. "Look not" covetously, "neither lay ye hands on their substance" in the day of their evil lot. It is a travesty today on our society and its integrity that when disaster strikes a city or countryside the National Guard must be called out to protect the goods—not from the unfortunate people's enemies, but from the plundering hands of their own neighbors. Time changes little, and humanity not at all.

v. 14 "And stand not thou in the crossway": another negative command which indicates that the Edomites stationed themselves at the places where the roads forked or crossed that they might fall upon the hapless fleeing fugitives, either to rob or slay them or to take them captive to be sold as slaves (cf. Amos 1:6, 9). Edom was not to deliver up to their oppressors those who might otherwise have escaped.

> *Vv. 15-16. Every sowing brings its own harvest. Edom must now share in the judgment upon the nations, reaping the fruit of his sowing.*

v. 15 Edom would not escape the "day of Jehovah," a general judgment from God which was near upon all the nations. The expression "day of Jehovah" is used by the prophets to designate a judgment from God. It may be the introduction of judgment or the judgment itself. If the Book of Obadiah is early, as has been assumed in this work, then it is first used by him and subsequently by the prophets who followed (Joel 1:15; 2:1, 10-11; Isa. 13:9-13; et al.). The "day of Jehovah" is a day in which Jehovah manifests Himself in the overthrow of His enemies. It is a day of terror to the enemies of God but a day of deliverance to the people of God. In describing "the day of the Lord" in the destruction of Jerusalem, Jesus said, "But when these things begin to come to pass, look up . . . because your redemption draweth nigh" (Luke 21:28). The judgment that would bring destruction upon the enemies of God would bring deliverance and redemption to those who trusted in Him. Again the principle is laid down: Edom would reap as he had sown; "thy dealing shall return upon thine own head." As Edom had desecrated the holy mount of Jehovah, whether by a drunken carousal on its sacred precinct at the time the inhabitants were being carried away, or figuratively in the desecration of God's

v. 16

holy city and people by his violence done toward
Jacob (v. 10), so Edom would be swallowed up of his
own ungodliness. "They shall drink" of the wrath of
Jehovah and be as if they had never been—completely
removed from the face of the earth by His divine
judgment.

> *Vv. 17-21. Though judgment is pronounced
> upon the nations, Edom will be a partaker;
> escape will be found only in Mount Zion.
> Israel will possess her enemies.*

The second section of Obadiah's prophecy reveals   *v. 17*
the future exaltation and glory of Israel and the
defeat of all her enemies. The kingdom of Jehovah
would be established on Mount Zion and Mount Seir
would be abased. In contrast to the judgment on
Edom and all the heathen nations (vv. 15-16), "in
mount Zion there shall be those that escape." Mount
Zion represents Jehovah's stronghold, a place of protection (for Jehovah was there), and a place of worship, for there He had recorded His name. "And it
[Zion] shall be holy," made up of redeemed and
sanctified people. "The house of Jacob" refers not to
the physical descendants only, but to the future
house of the redeemed; for it was said of Jesus, "and
he shall reign over the house of Jacob for ever: and of
his kingdom there shall be no end" (Luke 1:33).
These would possess the possessions of their enemies   *v. 18*
whom the Edomites represented. "The house of
Jacob" and "the house of Joseph" indicate the unit-
ing of Judah and Israel who had been separated and
enemies since the death of Solomon. These, redeemed
and united, would be a devouring flame among the
house of Edom, which would be as stubble, wholly
consumed; for "there shall not be any remaining to
the house of Esau; for Jehovah hath spoken it."

Historically, Edom's destruction began with the
Chaldean invasion under Nebuchadnezzar but was not
completed by that nation. Between the sixth and the
end of the fourth centuries, Edom was invaded by
Arabs known as the Nabataeans, a highly gifted

people who drove the Edomites out of their land into a region south of Judea. The Maccabees brought them under subjection in the second century when Judas Maccabeus slew some twenty thousand of them. John Hyrcanus (134-104 B.C.) subjugated the remnant of the nation, forcing them to accept circumcision and nominally to accept the Jewish religion. Under the Romans some time during the first century after Christ the remaining Edomites were absorbed by the Arabs and their identity was lost completely. The Herods, descendants of the Edomites, were Edom's chief contribution to history; certainly, this is nothing of which to boast!

v. 19   "And they of the South [the Negeb] shall possess the mount of Esau." Mount Seir, the mount of Esau, was Edom's counterpart to Israel's Mount Zion. As Zion should be the conquering victor, possessing the territory of her enemies, Seir would become the conquered, the possession of others. The destruction of Edom and conquest by Judah is not the complete fulfillment of Obadiah's prophecy. The prophecy looks to the Messianic conquest fulfilled in Christ. In the prophecy of Balaam (Num. 24:15-24), it is said, "I see him, but not now; I behold him, but not nigh: there shall come forth a star out of Jacob, and a sceptre shall rise out of Israel. . . . And Edom shall be a possession, Seir also shall be a possession, who were his enemies; while Israel doeth valiantly." There is little doubt that this star and sceptre is the Christ and His power. It would be under Him that Edom and Seir would become a possession. Compare also Amos 9:11-12 with Acts 15:15-18, where Edom, as a remnant, was to become a possession and where James declares that the prophecy of Amos finds its fulfillment in Christ. The bringing in of the Gentiles by Peter's preaching fulfilled the predictions of Amos and Obadiah; consequently, the prophecy does not now look to the future for its fulfillment. This prophecy, therefore, looked to a Messianic fulfillment in which those of Edom who would escape would do so in Mount Zion under the Messiah.

The captives of Israel's host who had been carried *v. 20*
away into lands throughout the world would not be
forgotten. These would share in the redemption and
the possessing of their rightful heritage. This heritage
would be "from sea to sea, and from the River to the
ends of the earth" (Zech. 9:10). This deliverance *v. 21*
would be through "saviours," deliverers—that is, apostles or evangelists through whom the message would
be brought to them. The kingdom of these redeemed
is Jehovah's. The kingdom of Edom was destroyed;
and whatever remnant escaped did so in spiritual
Zion, the antitype of the ancient citadel of God
which they had sought to destroy. As Keil has well
expressed it, verse 21 points to the "dominion of the
people of God over the heathen." God's people are
triumphant, whereas the people of the world are
completely defeated.

2
JOEL
" Jehovah Is God "

General Observations

1. Date: 830 B.C.

Of the prophet Joel we know nothing except that he was "the son of Pethuel." This tells us little, and nothing more is known of him. His name means "Jehovah is God." From the internal evidence some have concluded that possibly Joel was a priest or the son of a priest, but this is purely conjectural.

The date of the book is as conjectural as the life of the man himself. It is variously placed from one of the earliest, *ca.* 900 B.C., to the period after the exile, *ca.* 400 B.C. Keil, Sampey, Young, and others—scholars of repute—defend an early date, about 830 B.C. Men of similar scholarship—Driver, Farrar, Pfeiffer, and others—contend for a post-exilic date. In this work the earlier date will be followed, placing the prophet in the period *ca.* 830 B.C. Although it must be admitted that the evidence for the late date is impressive, the balance falls in favor of the earlier. Though the date of its composition may be uncertain and beyond our ability to determine, the message of the book is immortal and timeless. It can teach us today as it did when it was spoken.

2. Occasion

The prophecy was occasioned by a calamity that befell the land from locusts and drought and from fires that followed in their wake. Some think the locusts were an invading army, and that the prophet used the terror of swarms of locusts, followed by drought and fire, as a figurative description of the devastation left by the invaders. The stronger possibility is that these were literal locusts from which the prophet draws his lesson and his strong call to repentance. Unless there is repentance and righteousness of life on the part of the nation, the locusts will be followed by a stronger and more severe judgment, an invasion by the nations.

3. Message

The message of the book is the doom of the nations and the ultimate glory of Jehovah's cause. The invading locust army is to be looked upon by the people of God as a warning to them, out of which came the urgent call from God for repentance. The locusts, drought, and fires heralded the "day of Jehovah," which could be averted only by genuine repentance. If they would repent, the "day of Jehovah" would be one of destruction upon the enemies of God and deliverance for those who trust in Him. Whether an army of locusts or a literal army, it was led by Jehovah; He was directing the campaign. The book is an appeal from Jehovah to the people to seek Him through repentance. Out of this repentance there would come material blessings followed by an outpouring of spiritual blessings. Although other prophets may have intimated or indicated the coming of the Holy Spirit, Joel is the one who makes a clear prediction of His coming, so graphically fulfilled in Jerusalem fifty days after the Lord's resurrection. Because of this prophecy, Joel is sometimes referred to as "the prophet of Pentecost." It may be said that though the book begins in gloom, with a dark and terrifying picture, it closes with the anticipation of a bright and glorious day to come.

The book falls into two distinct sections. In the first section (1:2—2:17) the prophet speaks. The locust invasion is the occasion for the prophet's call to repentance. Unless this is achieved through "rending the heart and not the garments," the locust invasion will be only the forerunner and warning of a greater judgment to follow. In the second division (2:18—3:21) Jehovah speaks. He assures the people of material blessings to be followed by spiritual blessings and the judgment of the nation's enemies. Joel presents a great world view of things to come, including the judgment of the nations and the coming of the Holy Spirit through whom all flesh would be blessed.

Outline of the Book

I. The harbinger of the day of Jehovah: the judgment of God and the prophet's call to repentance (the prophet speaks), 1:2—2:17.

A. Devastation of Judah: scourge of locusts, drought, and fire, 1:2-20.
1. Graphic description of the locust scourge, vv. 2-4.
2. Call to various classes to mourn (repent), vv. 5-14.
a) Drunkards—all luxuries are cut off, vv. 5-7.
b) Whole nation—means of the sustenance of life is lacking, vv. 8-12.
c) Exhortation to repentance, vv. 13-14.
3. The awful calamity: "day of Jehovah"—prayer for mercy, vv. 15-20.

B. A more urgent summons to repentance and prayer: for the scourge is a forerunner of the day of judgment, 2:1-17.
1. The urgent summons, vv. 1-11.
a) The trumpet of warning, vv. 1-3.
b) A more vivid description of the calamity, vv. 4-11.
2. A more urgent call to repentance, vv. 12-17.
a) Rend the heart, not the garments, vv. 12-14.
b) Sincerely repent and fervently pray, vv. 15-17.

II. The day of Jehovah: a day of blessing to Israel, a day of terror to her enemies (Jehovah speaks), 2:18—3:21.

A. Blessings promised to Israel, 2:18-32.
1. Repentance implied: Jehovah's gracious change, v. 18.
2. The removal of Jehovah's army; temporal blessings promised, vv. 19-27.
3. Outpouring of the Spirit and approaching judgment, vv. 28-32.
a) Outpouring of the Spirit, vv. 28-29.

      b) Judgment upon the wicked parallel to blessings on Israel, vv. 30-31.

      c) The escape of a remnant in Zion, v. 32.

B. Judgment on the nations, 3:1-16a.

    1. All wrongs committed against the people are to be avenged, vv. 1-3.

    2. Neighbor nations will suffer the severe judgment of slavery in a far land, vv. 4-8.

    3. Destruction of all heathen powers by a divine decree, vv. 9-16a.

C. Glorification of the people of God: Israel's final happiness and peace contrasted with the desolation of her enemies (the world powers), 3:16b-21.

Comments

Chapter 1

In the title of the book the prophet, whose name means "Jehovah is God," is distinguished from other men of the same name as "the son of Pethuel." According to Keil, "Pethuel" meant "the openheartedness or sincerity of God."   *1:1*

1:2-4. A graphic description of the locust scourge.

In any land locust invasions are dreaded by people of all classes; such invasions strike terror in their hearts. Through the years Palestine has been smitten many times by invasions of these devastating creatures. This one in the days of Joel is of unusual destructive force. It is so severe that the prophet bids the old men to call to remembrance any in the past similar to this one. They cannot; there had not been a locust invasion like this in the remembrance of any of them. The severity of this one is so great that they are instructed to tell it to their children from generation to generation, that the lesson be not forgotten.   *1:2*

      1:3

1:4   Four terms are here used to describe the invaders, but there is a question as to whether these describe four stages in the development of the locusts or the completeness of the devastation as the locusts come in waves. From the account of such an invasion of Palestine in 1915, it appears that Joel may be describing various stages of the insect development, as one stage is followed by another (John D. Whiting, *National Geographic Magazine*, December, 1915, pp. 511-550). First, there are the locusts that destroy much of the vegetation. The females lay their eggs in the hard soil, an estimated sixty-five to seventy-five thousand per square meter, hatching an estimated sixty thousand of these. Soon appear the larvae which continue the devastation. From the larva stage the locust passes through the pupa stage, in which small wings appear. These develop into full-fledged flying insects, which change into full-fledged locusts. In all, they pass through five molts (Conley, *National Geographic Magazine*, August, 1969, p. 211). At times the new broods move in the opposite direction to that from which the parents came. Whiting says they come from the northeastern direction, moving southwest, which accounts for Joel's calling them God's "northern army."

1:5-14. Desolation! Both luxuries and necessities are cut off. The picture of desolation is followed by a call to repentance.

1:5   The prophet begins by naming the luxuries and then proceeds to the essentials of life. All are affected. The drunkards and all drinkers of wine are called on to awaken out of their stupor, for the source of their drink is cut off. "The sweet wine," so desired by all, is the fresh grape juice; and with the vines destroyed by the army of locusts, the supply of

1:6   wine, both sweet and strong, would be cut off. Joel describes the invaders as a "nation . . . without number," strong to devastate the land. By an impressive metaphor the teeth of the invaders are described as

those of a lion or lioness, strong to destroy and   *1:7*
consume. Beginning with the leaves of the vines and
fig trees, the locusts do not stop; they eat the bark of
the trees, leaving them white and bare. In the article
referred to above, Whiting gives pictorial evidence of
this complete devastation, inserting pictures of trees
before and after the invasion. Joel's description is
vivid; the destruction is complete.

Passing from the plight of the wine-drinkers, the   *1:8*
prophet calls upon the priests to mourn and lament
because the offerings of worship are cut off. There is
nothing to bring before Jehovah. The lamentation of
a young woman for her husband lost in battle, or cut
off by some other calamity, is the deepest and most   *1:9*
poignant expression of grief. So now the grief of all
the people is great because of the invaders' effect on
the worship; especially great is the anguish of the   *1:10*
priests. The fields are left bare; there is no grain.
Vineyards are stripped; therefore there is no new
wine. The olive trees are barked; hence there is no   *1:11*
olive oil, essential as food for all. The husbandmen
along with the vine-dressers are called upon to join
the priests in mourning, for all share alike in the   *1:12*
desolation. With grain and all manner of fruit cut off,
the joy of fullness vanishes; hopelessness overwhelms
all strata of society.

This description of the invasion of the locusts and   *1:13*
the devastation of the land is followed by a call to
repentance and fasting before the Lord. The priests
are called upon to take the lead in this. Girding
themselves with sackcloth and lying all night before
the altar, they were to lament and mourn the nation's
condition. This should set before others an example
of genuine repentance. Sackcloth was a coarse, hairy
material uncomfortable to the skin, but worn next to
it, as symbolic of the misery of the soul of the
individual. The priests should be the most concerned
of all the people because of their relation to the altar   *1:14*
of God and to the people. This expression of humility
before God should be accompanied with a solemn
fast. The example in this fast, and in crying to Jeho-

vah, should be set by the old men (elders) and followed by all the people. In hours of calamity the people of God should be quick to turn to the Lord in solemn penitence and supplication. Better still, they should live in such a way that there would be no occasion for repentance.

> *1:15-20. The "day of Jehovah" was at hand. The locust devastation points to a universal judgment of God. All nature is affected by the evil. A prayer for mercy follows the description of devastation.*

1:15   The awful calamity had come upon the people as a warning of "the day of Jehovah" which was to come, the dawn of which was already breaking. For comments on "the day of Jehovah," see Obadiah 15. The destruction is "from the Almighty," a term describing God which is not often used in Scripture, but which, when used, indicates the mighty power of God. The judgment upon the world of the wicked is executed by His own omnipotence and controlling providence.

1:16   In order that the people would realize what was happening at the moment, the prophet calls attention to what had already taken place before their eyes: food had been cut off and misery was on every hand. In the consciousness that this condition was somehow related to their own former conduct, they could no

1:17   longer come before God with joy and gladness. They plant, but the seeds rot under the clods. There is nothing to harvest, the "garners," (granaries or storehouses) are laid waste, and the barns are collapsing.

1:18   That which does sprout withers. Not only are men and fields affected, but all the creatures of nature suffer: "How do the beasts groan!" The cattle and sheep in the fields and pastures groan and are perplexed as in their confusion they walk up and down the land. They hunger for food and pant for water, but to no avail. Thus sin indirectly affects all creation, causing it to groan, each in its own plight. This picture of desolation is followed by a fervent cry of

the prophet to Jehovah, "O Jehovah, to thee do I
cry," for the locust scourge had been succeeded by a
terrible drought. This, acting like a fire, or followed
by actual fires that break out, had dried up the
springs and streams and "burned all the trees of the
field"—those left by the locusts. Animal creation and
man suffer together because of man's sin which
brought on the judgment of the Almighty. This eco-
logical condition so vividly described sounds almost
like modern U.S.A. In his cry to Jehovah the prophet
acknowledges there was not at that time (nor is there
today) any other to whom one can turn in hours such
as this. In utter helplessness and in the consciousness
of his need for divine help, he cries to God.

1:19

1:20

Chapter 2

*2:1-11. Sound an alarm! The day of Jehovah
has arrived. There follows a vivid description
of the terrible day of visitation.*

The first warning and summons to look to God is
followed by a more urgent warning and call to repentance, for "the day of Jehovah" is near at hand;
therefore, "Blow ye the trumpet." The blowing of the
trumpet was used in Israel to call the people to the
door of "the tent of meeting," to start them on their
journey, to sound an alarm in the way, and to call
them to a holy convocation at the time of their
festivals (Num. 10:1-10). Here the trumpet is to
"sound an alarm," as the expression is used also by
Hosea (5:8; 8:1). "Zion" and "my holy mountain"
signify the same, the dwelling place of God among
His people. The sounding of the alarm from Zion
should direct the attention of the people toward the
Lord and His fortress, wherein alone safety is to be
found.

2:1

The "day of Jehovah" is now described in vivid
and somber terms: It is "a day of darkness and
gloominess, a day of clouds and thick darkness, as the
dawn spread upon the mountains." This language is

2:2

reminiscent of the darkness upon Egypt when the plagues came upon the land of the Pharaohs (Exod. 10:21-24), and of Sinai when God came to address His people (Exod. 19:16). Such a description of judgment was used by the prophets who followed (Isa. 13:9-13; Jer. 4:23; Ezek. 30:3; Amos 8:9). "As the dawn spread upon the mountains" refers either to the appearance of the locusts as they became visible in the dawn of the morning, with the early light reflected from their wings, or to the complete coverage of the judgment, pictured as the dawn breaking forth which covers the whole of the mountain. The latter seems to be preferable. This scourge was so unusual that there would probably never be another so severe; and if there should be, this one would continue to hold a place among the most harsh. Although subject to several interpretations, the devouring fire before and after probably refers to the locusts themselves. One group would be followed by another. What appeared as the garden of Eden in its beauty and promise was turned into a desolate wilderness, a picture of complete desolation and despair. All were affected by the destruction.

2:3

2:4 The prophet now makes the reader feel he is actually there, beholding the scene and experiencing the numbing sensation of helplessness, as in vivid and flashing language he describes the army of locusts.

2:5 Their appearance is as that of horses with their elongated heads and their forward march. The noise of their coming, gnawing, and moving on is described as the rumbling of chariots and the crackling flame of a

2:6 devouring fire in the midst of a field of stubble. The sinking heart, the anguished expressions, and the blood-drained faces express something of the terror

2:7 that took hold of the people as they stood helplessly beholding the ruin of their land. Nothing is able to deter the onward march of the invaders; as an indomitable army they march on! They climb the walls; they invade the courts and houses of the people; "they

2:8 break not their ranks." They do not interfere with one another, each fulfilling his mission, marching ever onward. No bulwark erected by man can stop them; "they burst through the weapons." In the *National Geographic* article mentioned earlier, Whiting has pictures of the locusts of the 1915 invasion clustered on and climbing the walls, as described by Joel. "They enter in at the windows like a thief." The description of the earth quaking, the heavens trembling, the sun and moon being darkened, and the stars withdrawing their light became the prophetic description of Jehovah's judgments used by the prophets that followed Joel (see under 2:2-3). Also, this was the language of Jesus in describing the destruction of Jerusalem (Matt. 24:29; Mark 13:25; Luke 22:25-28), and of John as he saw a vision of the crashing world in the judgment of the Roman Empire, the persecuting power of his day (Rev. 6:12-14). "Jehovah uttereth his voice before his army." The prophet sees this horde of locusts as the army of Jehovah, directed by Him and executing His will in carrying out His divine judgment. It is a terrible judgment, and who can abide it? But it is of Jehovah; it is an expression of His righteous indignation against a people who apparently had turned to ungodliness and wickedness. Surely, we can all learn a lesson from this experience of a people long since departed.

2:9

2:10

2:11

2:12-17. This more vivid description of the judgment is followed by a more urgent call to repentance.

In spite of the terrible judgment and destruction caused by the locusts, it is not too late. If the people will turn to Jehovah with a heart of genuine penitence, with unfeigned fasting and with weeping and mourning, rending the heart and not their garments, God will be merciful. This describes a sincere turning to the Lord. Rending the garment may be outward indication of a feigned repentance, but God requires more. He demands a true contrition of heart: "rend your heart"! As said David, "The sacrifices of God are a broken spirit: a broken and a contrite heart, O

2:12

2:13

God, thou wilt not despise" (Ps. 51:17). It was repentance of this character that God demanded then and requires now. The prophet makes his appeal on the ground of God's mercy and long-suffering, and on the ground of His readiness to forgive and to turn away from the evil that had been pronounced (cf. Exod. 34:6-7). God's repentance is a change of His will toward the people and is the result of a change of will

2:14 and conduct on their part. Their repentance would cause Him to pour out a blessing instead of judgment. By God's judgment they had been deprived of the things necessary to offer sacrifices to Him, but now out of the bounty of His outpoured blessings they would have the things needed for sacrifices, thank-offerings, and drink-offerings. They would be blessed and God would be praised.

2:15 This change of heart should be demonstrated by an assembly of the people and a fervent call upon God. "Blow the trumpet in Zion; sanctify a fast; call a solemn assembly." Here the trumpet blast is not an

2:16 alarm as in 2:1, but is a call to a solemn assembly. This assembly is to include all the people: the old men, young children, and even babes at the breast. It is to include the newly-married, who are to forget the

2:17 joys of the honeymoon that they may mourn. Led by the priests, God's ministers of the altar, let the cry be one of penitent supplication: "Spare thy people, O Jehovah, and give not thy heritage to reproach, that the nations should rule over them." This indicates that unless the people repent at the presence of the locust judgment, there would follow a more serious judgment, invasion by heathen nations and rule by them over the people of God. This would bring the name of Jehovah into disrepute, for the nations who would rule over them would look upon their rule as the result of weakness on the part of Israel's God. Why should it be said in a sneering manner, "Where is their God?" Why was He not able to save?

> 2:18-20. *Repentance is implied. Jehovah shows mercy upon His people; the northern army is removed.*

It is here implied that the people responded to   *2:18*
Jehovah's call by repenting and calling upon Him.
Touched by the change, Jehovah was "jealous for his
land." Deep and strong emotions for His nation
stirred within Him. He had pity—a divine compas-   *2:19*
sion—upon His people. This would be demonstrated
in two ways: first, He would send them the food they
so sorely needed that once more they might have   *2:20*
their hunger satisfied; and second, He would remove
the reproach brought on them among the nations by
driving out the locusts from their midst. Here He
speaks of the locusts as His "northern army." It
appears from this that they had come into Palestine
from a northeasterly direction; however, locusts are
known to have come from the northeast, east, or
southeast. They would be driven out of the land,
some into the "eastern sea," the Dead Sea, and some
into the "western sea," the Mediterranean. "Some
swarms inexplicably commit suicide," writes Cha-
pelle, "flying out to sea after veering away from good
feeding areas. Others blunder into cold or are shriv-
eled by intense heat" (*National Geographic Magazine,*
April, 1953, p. 556). The prophet here pictures complete and total destruction of the invaders. The putri-
fying insects in such immense quantities would cause
a terrible stench to fill the air. Truly, judgment brings
its dire consequences and leaves its reminders!

*2:21-27. Material fullness and plenty, glad-
ness, rejoicing, and freedom from the locust
scourge would follow the people's repentance
and their turning to the Lord.*

Jehovah had done great things. The people are now   *2:21*
called on to rejoice as before they had been called on
to weep and mourn. He had brought the judgment of
locusts upon the people that He could turn their
hearts back to Himself, and now He had driven the   *2:22*
locusts out of the land. Food for both beasts and man
would be amply provided; for as the beasts had suffered in the plague, so now would they be blessed. As
Jehovah had used the locusts to turn their Eden into

a desolate wilderness, so now He would restore their
2:23   plenty. "Be glad . . . and rejoice" would be the order
of the day, for Jehovah was now to pour out the
bounties of His great storehouse on them. The "children of Zion" were the inhabitants of Jerusalem, the
people of God. The "former rain" is the rain of
autumn that causes the grain to sprout; the "latter
rain" is the rain of late spring that causes the grain to
mature before the harvest. Instead of "the former
rain in just measure," as in the American Standard
Version, Laetsch translates and defends, "he will give
unto you the Teacher unto Righteousness." This
would make the passage, at least this phrase, Messianic, injecting here with the statement of material
blessing a reference to the future spiritual blessings.
This interpretation is doubtful. Pusey holds to the
same view. Keil translates it, "teacher for righteousness," though he does not make the passage refer
solely to the Messiah. It is true that the passage yields
to this translation; however, it seems best to accept
the Standard rendition which would make the statement introduce the blessing of rain which produced
the food, beginning with the fall rains and continuing
until the spring rains which mature the grain (cf. Lev.
26:3-5). This seems more consistent with the con-
2:24   text: "And the floors shall be full of wheat, and the
2:25   vats shall overflow with new wine and oil." The
abundance of the material blessings is further described as God assures the people that there will be
compensation for the devastation wrought by the
"great army," the locusts, which the Lord says He
2:26   "sent among you." The people are further assured
that they will eat in plenty and that out of this
experience they will praise Jehovah, who had dealt
wondrously with them. The locusts had been graciously used by Jehovah to turn the people to Him,
to be followed by His wonderful outpouring of material plenty. In their continued faithfulness to Him
2:27   they will never be put to shame. Further, the Lord
lays down the principle that He is in the midst of
them, that He is concerned for them, and that it is He

who sends the judgments, removes the offenders, and bestows the blessings on the people. He would have the people recognize Him as the sovereign ruler of the world as well as their own God: "I am Jehovah your God, and there is none else." And once more, as His people, they would never be put to shame. It is only when they turn away from Him that shame and reproach follow. This principle is universal and characteristic of God for that time and all time to come.

2:28-32. Not only material blessings but also the Spirit, and all blessings attendant to His coming, would be poured upon the people.

As the driving out of the locusts and the out-   *2:28* pouring of the abundance of rain would bring forth material blessings and plenty, so now would the outpouring of the Spirit and the judgment upon the ungodly world bring forth a spiritual harvest. The material blessings would be an indication that Jehovah had returned to His people. This return must precede the outpouring of spiritual fullness. "Afterward" indicates that the spiritual fullness would follow the material. The specific fulfillment is declared by Peter to have been on Pentecost following the resurrection of Jesus (Acts 2:16 ff.). "All flesh" seems to point to a world view; all shall be beneficiaries of the Spirit and His work. It is evident from Acts 2 that only the apostles received the outpouring of the Spirit on that occasion; and yet Peter quoted the passage from Joel, declaring "This is that which hath been spoken through the prophet Joel" (Acts 2:16). Later we find the gospel being carried to the Gentiles. The outpouring of the Spirit upon Cornelius and those gathered in his house (Acts 10) confirms the Gentiles' acceptance of the gospel and the Lord's acceptance of them. Philip had four virgin daughters who prophesied (Acts 21:9), and Paul tells of women who prophesied (I Cor. 11:5). This receiving of the Spirit would be without distinction of age—"old men and young men," without distinction of sex—"sons   *2:29* and daughters," and without distinction of social order—"servants and handmaids." Keil observes that nowhere in the Old Covenant period did God select a slave to be a prophet, one upon whom to put His Spirit. But here it is pointed out that there would be no distinction; the servant (slave) or handmaid (female slave) would not be disqualified. The New Testament recognizes this principle of no distinction (Gal. 3:28). The terms "prophesying," "visions," and "dreams" seem not to be completely distinct, but complementary. Prophesying stands for the whole of teaching by inspiration of the Spirit. Visions and dreams indicate two forms of revelation by which God would make Himself known to the prophet (Num. 12:6). It is concluded, therefore, that what took place on Pentecost marked the beginning of the complete fulfillment of Joel's word.

2:30   There would be forerunners of judgment before the great and terrible day of the Lord would come.
2:31   Joel pictures Jehovah as showing wonders: blood and fire and pillars of smoke in heaven and on earth. Blood suggests bloodshed; fire upon the earth suggests the burning of cities, during which the pillars of smoke billow heavenward. This figure, as here used by Joel, became a description of approaching judgment, and of the judgment itself, by writers who followed (Isa. 13:10; 34:4; Jer. 4:23; Ezek. 32:1-8; Amos 8:9; Matt. 24:29; Mark 13:24; Luke 21:25; Rev. 6:12-13). Jesus came not to judge the world but to save it (John 3:17-18); yet judgment became an inevitable result of His work (John 3:18-19). So, the outpouring of the Spirit and His work for the redemption and salvation of man would result in judgment on those who rejected His message. The rejection of the truth of the Spirit by the Jews, and their persecutions of Christians, became the forerunner of God's great judgment upon Jerusalem by the Romans, A.D. 70. The destruction of Jerusalem, which fulfilled the prophecy, in turn becomes a prophetic type of the ultimate end of the world and of the judgment of God on the world of the ungodly—

that is, on those who reject the Spirit of God in refusing to hear His Word.

In the midst of His judgments, God always provided a means of escape: "Whosoever shall call on the name of Jehovah shall be delivered." "Whosoever" indicates anyone. As the Spirit's work was for all, so the escape through His provision is for all. To call on the name of the Lord is to respond by obeying His command or revealed will. On Pentecost, in response to the question of the Jews, "What shall we do?" God's answer by His Spirit, through Peter, was "Repent ye, and be baptized every one of you in the name of Jesus Christ unto the remission of your sins" (Acts 2:38). This was in accord with Peter's quotation of Joel (Acts 2:21). Paul was to call on the name of the Lord by arising and being baptized, washing away his sins (Acts 22:16). The "mount Zion" and "Jerusalem" are used to indicate the spiritual dwelling place of God among His people. It is here that escape is found. Obadiah had also pointed out this truth (v. 17). It was to this spiritual Zion and heavenly Jerusalem that the Hebrew saints had come; it was here that they had come to God, the judge of all (Heb. 12:22-23). It was from among the remnant that escaped the divine judgments that God called His spiritual remnant "according to the election of grace" (cf. Rom. 11:5).

2:32

Chapter 3

3:1-8. While the people of God enjoy rich spiritual blessings, the enemies of His people are to be cut off. The more bitter the persecution, the more severe will be the judgment.

The prophet looks from the time of the outpouring of the Spirit, and of the judgment of the carnal Jews that was to accompany this great event, to the general judgment of the heathen nations that had opposed, and would yet oppose, His people. "For" connects the things following with what had been said above.

3:1

And "in those days, and in that time" identifies the judgment as being in the period of the outpouring of the Spirit, the dispensation following Pentecost. The use of the plural, "days," indicates a period of time rather than a specific point in time. This makes it impossible to identify the judgments at specific points in history. Also, it would be when Jehovah would bring "back the captivity of Judah and Jerusalem," or, "When I restore the fortunes of Israel" (G. A. Smith). Therefore, this cannot refer to the return from Assyrian and Babylonian captivity, for this bringing back referred to by Joel is to be in the time of the Spirit (cf. 2:28-31). Also, Amos uses the expression "I will bring back the captivity of my people Israel" (9:14) in a Messianic context (9:11-12); this is quoted by James and applied to the period under Christ (Acts 15:14-18), further strengthening the position that the judgments are after Pentecost. We must therefore look for the return of Judah and Jerusalem in a spiritual sense. Isaiah referred to this spiritual return as God's setting His hand "the second time to recover the remnant of His people" (Isa. 11:11). This statement also is in a Messianic context and is therefore fulfilled under Christ (see Rom. 11:5; 15:12). The entire chapter must be looked upon as a world view of things to come beyond the outpouring of the Spirit.

3:2   This judgment is to be a world judgment against those heathen peoples who had scattered Jehovah's heritage. The place of judgment is "the valley of Jehoshaphat," which, when translated, means "Jehovah judges." The literal valley of Jehoshaphat is thought by some to be a valley located southeast from Jerusalem near the wilderness of Tekoa. Others identify it as the north Kedron valley, northeast from Jerusalem. The location is uncertain. But the "valley of Jehoshaphat" is not to be thought of as a literal place in Palestine, but as an ideal place where judgment is to be executed. The point of emphasis is that it is to be a judgment by Jehovah on behalf of His "people" and for His "heritage Israel," whom the

heathen had "scattered among the nations." The
judgment is indicated as universal, on all nations that
had had a part in scattering His people, even to the
Roman Empire which God used to destroy Jerusalem.   *3:3*
The cruelty of the nations against God's people is
expressed in their disposition to scatter the people
among the nations, to cast lots for them to be used or
sold as slaves, and then to give a boy for the use of a
harlot, or a girl for a cup of wine. This low estimate
of the value of human life is characteristic of heathen
people who have refused to have God in their knowledge. Such a disposition and such conduct must be
judged.

The judgment is directed first to the Phoenicians,   *3:4*
located on the coast of Palestine northwest from
Judea, and to the people of Philistia, located in the
southwest coastal plain. To these God asks, "What are
ye to me?" They are nothing. He then asks, "Will you
repay me some wrong-doing which you fancy I have
inflicted upon you?" (Givens, *Pulpit Commentary*). If
so, God will return it upon them; they will fall into
the pit they have digged; they will reap as they have   *3:5*
sown. These peoples are charged with having carried
away God's silver and gold, His precious things, to
embellish their temples dedicated to heathen gods.   *3:6*
Also, they are charged with having sold His people
into slavery and having carried them into the islands
of Greece (Javan, see Gen. 10:2, 4). This charge of
selling the people into slavery was also leveled by
Amos against these same two neighboring countries
(1:6-10). As a result of this cruelty and as a vindica-   *3:7*
tion of God's righteousness, He would stir up against
these people the ones whom they had sold, bringing a
recompense upon the heads of the Phoenicians and   *3:8*
Philistines. "And I will sell your sons and your daughters [those of Phoenicia and Philistia] into the hand
of the children of Judah, and they shall sell them to
the men of Sheba" is difficult. Sheba, in southern
Arabia, is farther to the southeast than was Greece to
the northwest. The difficulty in looking for the fulfillment of this is twofold: (1) it could not be in the

time of Uzziah, of Alexander, or of the Maccabees, for these events are to be "in those days" (v. 1), the days of the Spirit; (2) it cannot be looked for in a literal sense after Pentecost, for there is no historical account of such an event. Neither could Jews after the flesh or spiritual Israel have done this, for it would be physically impossible for the one and morally impossible for the other. Therefore, the best conclusion seems to be that the prophet is here declaring a summary judgment upon all the neighboring peoples who had oppressed God's own people and sold them into slavery. Judgment against these is inevitable. "And I will sell your sons and your daughters into the hand of the children of Judah" would then indicate that the suffering inflicted on the children of Judah would be returned on the heads of the children of these heathen peoples. It would not be literal or physical selling, but an avenging by divine judgment of the shameful treatment inflicted on the people of the Lord.

> *3:9-17. Judgment of the nations is decreed by Jehovah; but in the midst of the execution of this judgment Jehovah's people will be secure in Zion.*

3:9   After referring to the judgment upon the neighboring peoples who had abused the people of God, the prophet resumes the thought introduced in verse 2, and brings into focus all the heathen nations and God's universal judgment against them. As God had judged those nations that had plundered, sold, and scattered His people, so will He judge the nations who oppose and seek to destroy His spiritual people, the church. A proclamation is issued to the nations to prepare war. Here God is declaring that the nations themselves will be the instruments of His judgment.

3:10   The seeds of destruction are sown in the forces of destruction. The implements and instruments of peaceful agricultural pursuits are to be converted into implements of war. This is opposite to the character of the kingdom of God, for in that kingdom its citizens are to convert the implements of war into instruments of peace (Isa. 2:4). The call is to all the nations; it is urgent: "Haste ye, and come, all ye nations round about, and gather yourselves together." With the call for all the mighty ones to become involved by their gathering together—a call of the nations to war—the prophet then utters a prayer to Jehovah, "Thither cause thy mighty ones to come down, O Jehovah." The prophet recognizes the destruction of mighty ones by mighty ones as a reckoning executed by the overruling providence and will of Jehovah, and calls upon Jehovah to use His mighty power in their destruction. The judgment of heathen nations is of God. Let them come to the valley of Jehovah's judgment, "for there will I sit to judge all the nations round about." Coextensive with the work of the Spirit in calling out God's spiritual Israel, there is the judgment by Jehovah on those who hearken not. The prophet uses two figures by which to impress this judgment: a harvest ripe unto threshing (cf. Isa. 17:5; Micah 4:12-13) and the harvest of a vineyard ready for the wine vat (cf. Isa. 63:1-6; Rev. 19:15). The two figures are combined in John's vision of the divine judgment against the enemies of God's spiritual kingdom. This judgment is being executed by His mighty ones (Rev. 14:14-20). The figure of a harvest or gathering of grapes is that of the nations ripe for judgment, gathered as grain to be threshed and winnowed, and as grapes gathered to the wine vat, with Jehovah treading them in the winepress of His wrath—the wine vat of His righteous judgment.

The prophet now teaches the lesson by a word picture of the hordes of the nations pouring into the valley of judgment. "Multitudes, multitudes" describes a noisy, tumultuous, diverse crowd gathering in "the valley of decision," equivalent to the "valley of Jehovah's judgment"; "for the day of Jehovah is at hand." Once more the dark day in which the sun and moon and stars give no light heralds the approaching day of utter doom. Jehovah's roaring from Zion and

3:11

3:12

3:13

3:14

3:15

3:16

uttering His voice from Jerusalem declares that the judgment is of divine determination. As He had led the army of locusts, so now He directs the judgment of the nations. The heavens and the earth shake as at Mount Sinai, as Jehovah sounds the call and doom of the nations in a merited judgment. In contrast to this scene there is again a bright light shining through the darkness and terror of the cloud of judgment. Jehovah will be a refuge and a stronghold to all who seek shelter beneath the shadow of His infinite wing.

3:17 Through times of judgment and of refuge men will know that Jehovah is God and that in spiritual Zion He reigns over the nations and over His people. All that He does will be consistent with the revelation He has made of Himself; men will know that it is He who directs and saves. Spiritual Zion is impregnable; strangers will not pass through her as they did through physical Jerusalem. The kingdom over which Jehovah reigns from Zion is one that cannot be shaken (Heb. 12:28); it will stand forever (v. 17; cf. Dan. 2:44; 7:13-14), finally to be delivered by His Son to Himself in glory (I Cor. 15:24-28).

> 3:18-21. The final picture: the happiness, permanence, and plenty of the people of God are contrasted with the desolation of the unregenerate world.

3:18 That which follows, verses 18-21, is identified with verse 17 by the phrase "And it shall come to pass in that day." "In that day" must be identified always with the context. The context describes spiritual Zion in the days of the Spirit. So the figure of the mountains dropping sweet wine, the hills flowing with milk, and the brooks flowing with water is a pictorial description of the spiritual plenty in the days of the Spirit. Paul summed it up by saying, "in whom ye are made full" (Col. 2:10), "filled unto all the fulness of God" (Eph. 3:19). A fountain of water from Jehovah's house will water the arid land to the east, the "valley of Shittim"—the valley of acacia trees. This valley lay east of the northern section of the Dead

Sea and was the last resting place of the Israelites before they crossed the Jordan. This land would be watered by the gracious Spirit of Jehovah. In contrast to the plenty provided by the Lord for those who will receive it is the picture of the utter desolation of Egypt and Edom, long-time enemies of God and His people. Their sin had been that of shedding innocent blood. Specific incidents are not related, but the Egyptians shed innocent blood when they ordered the slaying of Israel's male infants. No doubt there were other occasions that were in the mind of the prophet. Edom was accused of being guilty when, "in the day that they [you] stood on the other side" (Obad. 11), they were as those who carried their brothers away. Judah would be forgiven and would endure forever. Keil well expresses the fate of Egypt and Edom when he says that "the eternal desolation of the world-kingdoms mentioned here will wipe out all the wrong which they have done to the people of God, and which has hitherto remained unpunished." In contrast, God will cleanse the blood of Zion and dwell there, as He makes it His dwelling place among His people. Clearly, the message is that in the days of the Spirit God would establish His spiritual people and dwell among them. At the same time He would judge the world of the ungodly, bringing to a desolate end all who fight against Him.

3:19

3:20

3:21

3
JONAH
"Dove"

General Observations

1. The Man and the Date

The Book of Jonah gives us an unusual insight into the character of the man. His name and place of birth identify him as the prophet of Israel in the days of Jeroboam II (II Kings 14:23-25). There can be no doubt that Jonah played an important role in the exploits of this king, who restored the borders of Israel and brought great prosperity to the nation.

The home of Jonah is said to have been the village of Gath-hepher, located about four miles northeast from what was later the city of Nazareth, in Galilee. He is pictured in the book that bears his name as a narrow-minded, fiercely zealous patriot; he is jealous for Jehovah and desirous of seeing the enemies of His people destroyed. The expression of divine love for a heathen nation and of God's desire to spare it is magnified as it is shown in contrast to the spirit of the prophet. The prophet's disposition may be somewhat defended (at least excused) when one realizes that he knew of the suffering which had been inflicted by the Assyrians on the people of the world of that day and knew that this suffering would be imposed eventually on his own people by that great ruthless power. It would seem that instead of sparing the nation God should make this an opportune time to destroy it.

The date may be fixed at some time in the general period around 780 B.C. Thiele fixed the date for Jeroboam's reign from 793/92 to 753 B.C., and thus has the first few years of his reign overlapping that of his father (Edwin R. Thiele, *The Mysterious Numbers of the Hebrew Kings,* p. 205). The date would be some time during this period.

Geikie (Cummingham Geikie, *Hours With the Bible,* Vol. IV, pp. 183-184) points out that from shortly before 800 until 745 B.C., the time of Tiglath-pileser's accession to the throne, Assyria was torn with internal strife and by wars with revolting provinces. Thompson (J. A. Thompson, *The Bible and Archaeology,* p. 131) confirms this by the use of recent archaeological discoveries. He points out that not only were there revolts from within the empire but also the nation was at war with a powerful country (Urartu) near the Caspian Sea. No doubt this depressed state of Assyria contributed much to the readiness of the people to hear Jonah as he began to preach to them.

2. Interpretations

The Book of Jonah differs from all other books of the prophets. It is written primarily from the historical point of view—the history of a man, a nation, and God. There are three interpretations of the book taken by various schools of writers: the mythical, allegorical, and historical. The mythical school assumes that the story is a myth that grew up around some incident in the history of Israel. The allegorical view assumes that the story is an allegory of Israel's captivity, repentance, and restoration to its land. The historical conviction accepts the position that Jonah lived as a prophet of God, that he went to Nineveh and preached to the people of that city, and that God spared the nation. It accepts as historical fact that before going to Nineveh Jonah fled from Jehovah, that a storm arose at sea, that the prophet was cast overboard and was swallowed by a great fish, and that later he was vomited up on the land. Jesus placed His sanction on the story as historical fact by comparing it to His own death, burial, and resurrection (Matt. 12:39-41; Luke 11:29-32). Therefore, the historical interpretation is the only interpretation worthy of acceptance to all who believe that Jesus is the Christ. The book is essentially historical; and as history, it must be authentic. A book may be historically accurate and not be inspired, but it could not be inspired and historically inaccurate.

3. The Miracles

One should distinguish between "an act of God" and a "miracle." A miracle is an effect or deed in the physical world that surpasses all known human or natural powers and is therefore ascribed to supernatural agency or intervention. Neither the raising of a great wind on the Mediterranean Sea nor its ceasing would necessarily be a miracle; nor would the appearing of a fish of sufficient size to swallow a man be a miracle. But the preserving of the life of a man in the belly of the fish for three days and three nights and the ejecting of him upon the land would be a miracle. The growth of a vine to cover a shelter would not be a miracle, but the growth of such a vine in a night would be a miracle. The coming of a worm might or might not be a miracle. The appearance of miracles in the Book of God should cause no particular problem to anyone who does not assume that they are impossible. As the apostle John indicates, miracles are "signs" to the people; they are "works" of Deity. As suggested by McCartney, the ability or inability to accept a miracle depends on whether or not one spells his God with a capital "G."

4. The Message

The message of the book is twofold: (1) God is willing and anxious to save even the heathen nations if they repent. His love is infinite and universal; therefore, His concern is for all. (2) Jehovah is the one universal God, the God of the whole earth. As the one and only God, He is the God to whom the heathen must turn. In the book one sees a foreshadowing of the coming of Christ and the manifestation of God's love and desire to save all men. The death and resurrection of Christ are typified in the three days spent by Jonah in the belly of the great fish, from which he came forth in a new relation to his work with the Lord. The book is sometimes referred to as the forerunner of the universal gospel message which would be carried to all the heathen world.

5. Lessons

The lessons and preaching values of Jonah are many:

a. **National sin demands national repentance.** As this applied to Nineveh, so it applies to the nations of today. The book shows God's love for the heathen Gentiles and is a stern rebuke to the narrow exclusiveness of the Jews.

b. **One cannot run away from God** (cf. Ps. 139:7-11). McGarvey has well said, "Jonah learned, and through his valuable experience millions have learned, that when God enjoins a disagreeable duty, it is far easier to go and do it than to run away from it" (J. W. McGarvey, *Jesus and Jonah,* p. 54). Robinson has expressed a similar truth when he says, "When one sets out to baffle God, there is bound to be a storm" (George L. Robinson, *The Twelve Minor Prophets,* p. 71).

c. **God is able to use all incidents in the life of His servants for their good and His glory.** Some good can come even from mistakes such as Jonah's. In his flight from God and in the storm that arose, a tremendous impression was made on the seamen. They were caused to fear Jehovah, offer sacrifices, and make vows to Him. It is quite possible that these experiences at sea were related many times, so that the story had reached Nineveh before Jonah arrived there.

d. **Opportunity begets challenge.** According to Geikie and Thompson, as indicated above, Nineveh was dejected and depressed at the time. Opportunity comes to the people of God to offer a message of hope whenever the world is dejected. The people of God should be prepared to preach the message of hope when God opens such a door to them.

e. **The infinite concern of God for life is shown in contrast to the concern of man for the material.** Geikie has well summarized a weakness of human nature clearly brought out in the Book of Jonah when he says, "The withering of the prophet's gourd, with the regrets it excited, strikes home in all ages, as it must have done in Jonah's day, the contrast between the infinite love of heaven and the selfish coldness of man. The growth of a night can be pitied when it touches ourselves; but unspeakably higher claims too often awaken no tenderness where we are not personally concerned" (*Hours with the Bible*, IV, pp. 186-189).

Outline of the Book

I. Jonah's call and flight to Tarshish, 1:1-16. (Jonah's disobedience: "running away from God."—G.L.R.)

    A. Jehovah's charge to go to Nineveh, and the prophet's disobedience, vv. 1-3.

    B. The great wind and Jonah's confession, vv. 4-10.

    C. Jonah sacrificed—cast into the sea, vv. 11-16.

II. Jonah's miraculous preservation, 1:17-2:10. (Jonah's prayer: "running to God."—G.L.R.)

    A. The fish prepared by Jehovah, 1:17.

    B. Jonah's prayer from the deep, 2:1-9.

    C. Jonah's deliverance, 2:10.

III. Jehovah's second call; Jonah goes to Nineveh, ch. 3 (Jonah's preaching to Nineveh: "running with God." —G.L.R.)

    A. The call, response, and message to Nineveh, vv. 1-4.

    B. Repentance and Jehovah's gracious change, vv. 5-10.

IV. A narrow prophet vs. a merciful God, ch. 4. (Jonah's complaints: "running ahead of God."—G.L.R.)

    A. Jonah's anger at Nineveh's repentance, vv. 1-5.

    B. The gourd vine and the worm, vv. 6-8.

    C. Jehovah's rebuke and lesson of the gourd vine, vv. 9-11.

Comments

Chapter 1

1:1-3. Jehovah commissions Jonah to go preach to the people of Nineveh; but instead, he flees the opposite direction.

Jonah, the son of Amittai, has been introduced already as the prophet of Jeroboam II. Gath-hepher, his home, was a village about four miles northeast of Nazareth. His call was to "arise, go to Nineveh, that great city, and cry against it." More will be said about Nineveh in comments on Nahum; therefore, only a few characteristics will be pointed out here. The city is among the oldest of civilization, extending back to shortly after the great flood (Gen. 10:8-12), and estimated by archaeologists to have had its origin in the period between 5000-4000 B.C. It was located on the Tigris River approximately 225-250 miles north of Babylon and about 220 miles north and slightly west of the present city of Baghdad. The circumference of the city within the walls was about eight miles. Ancient writers believed that "Greater Nineveh" was a complex of several cities and their suburbs, in the shape of a parallelogram and about sixty miles in circumference. Modern writers think Greater Nineveh was in more of a triangular shape, but about the same distance around. At various periods of its history it shared with other cities the distinction of being the capital of Assyria; from the time of Sennacherib it remained the capital of the empire. Jehovah said, "Cry against it; for their wickedness is come up before me." Nineveh was long noted for the wickedness and cruelty of its people. The political and military temper of the city was at a low ebb at this time; therefore, it was a suitable time ·for the Lord to make an appeal for repentance.

Motivated by a fierce patriotism for his own country and the fear that Jehovah would spare Nineveh, Jonah fled in the opposite direction. He went down

1:1

1:2

1:3

to Joppa, Israel's only semi-adequate port, located on the Mediterranean shore, between fifty-five and sixty miles from Gath-hepher. From there he boarded a ship for Tarshish. Located in what is now southwestern Spain, Tarshish was a Phoenician outpost, a colony on the edge of Western civilization. He was fleeing from the presence of Jehovah—something no one can do. No doubt the prophet realized this; but out of his distaste for the work to which he was called, he was determined to make the attempt. He was "resigning his job" as a prophet.

1:4-10. Flight and storm! The prophet learns the hard way that no one can flee from Jehovah without arousing a storm.

1:4   Calamity overtook the fleeing prophet. A wind of unusual ferocity, sent by Jehovah, beat down on the ship. Wind and storm are ministers of Jehovah, sent by Him to accomplish His purpose (cf. Ps. 104:4). The ship was about to be broken up and smashed to pieces in the storm. This need not be considered a miracle, but rather an act of God; for severe storms

1:5   on the Mediterranean Sea are not uncommon. The mariners began to lighten the ship in an effort to save it, while each man cried earnestly to his god to save them. Jonah was the only "atheist" on board; he had left his God and "was gone down into the innermost parts of the ship," asleep. After the struggle within his soul, the decision to flee, and the journey from Gath-hepher to Joppa, no doubt the prophet was exhausted mentally and physically. Relaxation following the strain of such a decision may account for

1:6   the prophet's ability to fall into sound sleep in the midst of a raging storm. What a travesty on the religion of the true Jehovah this was: a heathen shipmaster rebuking a prophet of the Lord, a pagan calling to a prophet of God to awake and pray that

1:7   they might not perish! But such was the situation. The sailors decided to cast lots to determine who was the cause of this great storm, for there was yet no sign of its abating. Under the Old Covenant many issues were settled by the casting of lots. By this means land was divided, as in the case of the various inheritances of the tribes of Israel (Josh. 15—19); also by lot the selection of certain individuals was made (I Chron. 24). The use of the Urim and Thummim by the priests was a means of revealing Jehovah's will; however, the exact method of doing this is unknown. There is only one incident of a choice by lot in the New Testament—the selection of Matthias to take the place of Judas, which decision was of God (Acts 1:21-26). In the selection of Jonah as the culprit it could be said as in the proverb, "The lot is cast into *1:8* the lap; but the whole disposing thereof is of Jehovah" (Prov. 16:33). Seeing the lot had fallen on Jonah, the sailors shot a series of questions to the prophet in rapid-fire order: "Tell us, we pray thee, for whose cause this evil is upon us; what is thine occupation? and whence comest thou? what is thy country? and of what people art thou?" The men whose lives were endangered by the storm wanted a confession from Jonah as to why all of this had befallen them. Without hesitation Jonah confessed his *1:9* nationality: he was a Hebrew, the name his people called themselves and by which they were known by others. His faith was in God, the Creator of all; it was He whom he worshiped and from whom he was running. As God of land and sea, it was Jehovah who had sent the storm. What he told them in this one *1:10* breath left the sailors amazed, and made them exceedingly afraid. How could anyone run away from such a God? Though one could criticize Jonah for fleeing from a divinely given task, he cannot help admiring him for the honesty, the boldness, and the courage of his confession. However, his confession of Jehovah as the object of worship was most incongruous with his conduct in running away from Him.

1:11-17. After a strenuous but fruitless effort to save the prophet, the sailors were forced to cast him overboard; it was the only alternative to perishing.

1:11 The sailors were signally impressed by Jonah's fearless and courageous statement. They were willing to exert any effort at their disposal to save him. What should they do? Their own lives were in danger, and the sea grew more and more tempestuous. Not knowing Jehovah, yet fearful of offending Him, they asked Jonah this question, "What shall we do unto thee, **1:12** that the sea may be calm unto us?" Again Jonah's courage was clearly manifested. Realizing that his conduct was responsible for the endangering of their lives and that only by the sacrifice of himself could they be saved, he urged them to take him up and throw him overboard. In Jonah one sees likenesses and opposites of Him who was to come and of whom in some ways Jonah was a type. Like Jonah, Jesus was willing to be sacrificed for the sake of others; but unlike Jonah, who had brought the present storm on them by running from God, Jesus came to calm the **1:13** storm brought on by those whom He came to save. This courage and willingness on the part of the prophet to be cast overboard encouraged the sailors even more to try to save him by rowing to land. But it was a losing battle; the sea grew more tempestuous. It looked as if the God of Jonah was demanding that he **1:14** be given up to the sea. With a cry to Jehovah that the blood of this man not be upon them, and that they not be held responsible, they took him up and cast him into the sea. How unlike those who claimed to be **1:15** worshipers of God but cried, "His blood be on us, **1:16** and on our children" (Matt. 27:25). As they cast the prophet into the sea, the sea ceased from its raging. The mariners were deeply impressed and feared Jehovah exceedingly. They then offered sacrifices and made vows to the God of Jonah. What the vows were we are not told; nor are we told that they became worshipers of Jehovah as the sole deity. We learn only that they were deeply impressed with the power and being of Jehovah, the God of a fleeing Hebrew. Even the disobedience and flight of His prophet be-

came a means in the hands of God to glorify Himself.
God makes even the wrath of men to praise Him.

The chapter division here is unfortunate; chapter 2   *1:17*
should have begun here, as verse 17 introduces the
situation of Jonah that brought forth the prayer and
deliverance of chapter 2. Jehovah had further use for
Jonah and therefore made provision for the preservation of his life. The Scripture simply states, "And
Jehovah prepared a great fish to swallow up Jonah."
The Hebrew word translated *prepared* "does not
mean to create, but to determine, to appoint" (Keil).
There is no need to think that a fish was there created
on the spot to meet the need; but by an act of God
one was at hand to supply the need. The fish is
referred to by Jonah as "a great fish" and by Jesus as
a "sea-monster." It could have been one of several
varieties of sea creatures capable of swallowing a man.
The miracle is not that a fish was present, but that
Jonah survived the ordeal of the "three days and
three nights" in the stomach of the creature, living to
carry out the purpose of God. Too often in arguing
about the fish, whether whale or some other sea
creature, and about the possibility or impossibility of
one's surviving such an experience, men have focused
attention on this and forgotten God. Denial of the
historical fact of Jonah's experience becomes a forerunner of the denial of the resurrection of Jesus from
the dead. Accepting the latter would leave no difficulty in accepting the former. Rejecting the former
has led to rejecting the latter. Jesus declared to skeptical Pharisees that as Jonah had been in the belly of
the sea monster for three days and three nights, so
would He be in the heart of the earth three days and
three nights (Matt. 12:38-40). This would be the
supreme sign confirming His deity.

Chapter 2

*2:1-10. Jonah's prayer to Jehovah from the
Sheol of the fish's belly.*

Many commentators point out that much of the   *2:1*
material in chapter 2 is an echo of Scriptures found in

the Psalms. This appeal to the Psalms, or use of eloquent expressions found there, indicates the prophet's familiarity with that portion of Scripture. Where else but in the Psalms could one under circumstances such as this, or at any time, find more deeply meaningful words by which to express either his feelings in an hour of need or his cry to the Lord? In this psalm of Jonah one is made to feel the terror and helplessness of the prophet and to realize with him that if salvation is to be found it must be from Jehovah.

In the despair of this moment Jonah prayed. Here is the sinner who had been running from God but who is now running to God; there was no one else to whom he could go. What is here recorded probably reflects the thoughts and words of his heart put into this form after his deliverance. The psalm is more of thanksgiving than of petition. Out of the affliction 2:2 that prompted the cry God answered him. "Out of the belly of Sheol," that is, the unseen, he cried, for in the fish's belly he was truly in "the unseen." The earnestness of the prophet's cry is indicated by the fact that he was able to say, "And thou heardest my voice."

2:3   "For thou": although the sailors were the instruments used by the Lord, Jonah acknowledged that it was God who had cast him into the sea. "Thou didst cast me into the depth, in the heart of the seas." Someone has observed that there are times when we must be made to go into the lowest depths that we may regain a living faith. This was the experience of the prophet. The flood of waters was round about him; "all *thy* waves and *thy* billows" passed over him. These were from God. That which was sent upon the fleeing prophet, seemingly so terrible at the moment, was from the loving heart of the Lord and for the salvation of His servant. All of God's judgments necessary to accomplish the divine purpose are summed up in the words "*thy* waves and *thy* billows."

2:4   Both repentance and hope are expressed here. He was cast out from before Jehovah's eyes. This the prophet could not endure; this brought him to repentance. But the next word is one of hope: "Yet I will look again toward thy holy temple." The fact that he was yet alive in the belly of the fish assured him that he would again look toward the holy temple of God's presence. True penitence is always rewarded by hope.

"Even to the soul"—that is, to the very endangering of life—did the waters compass about him. As a turban, "the weeds were wrapped about" his head. One tries to imagine himself in the place of Jonah with seaweeds entangled about his head and face, and so pressed in from every side that he is helpless to move. He could not use his hands to brush them aside, thereby remedying this uncomfortable situation. Added to this discomfort, there would be about him the remains of whatever the fish had last eaten. Then there would be the impossibility of breathing, for there was no air; and added to this would be the exceeding great pressure of the waters about. Surely, death must come at any moment—a terrifying experience, indeed! Down, down, he was being carried to the bottoms of the mountains and to the valleys of the sea-bed. "The earth with its bars closed upon me for ever"; that is, shut him off from the earth. Thus entrapped, there was no hope of return apart from a divine intervention. This was "for ever," age-lasting; for so the word means, and so it seemed to the prophet. He was brought to the very gate of death and eternity—yet, he could not die! God had further use for him. "The pit" here is equivalent to "Sheol" (v. 2); he is brought up from death, from the unseen.

When his soul fainted and all hope had faded, Jonah then remembered Jehovah and prayed. As his prayer came up to Jehovah, the Lord heard him and graciously delivered him. From the very depth of Sheol the prayer had ascended to the throne of His holy temple, to the innermost sanctuary of God. This is reminiscent of the psalmist whose feet were almost gone and whose steps had well nigh slipped, until he went into the sanctuary of God. It was then that he could understand (Ps. 73:2, 17).

"Lying vanities" are the worthless and deceitful

2:5

2:6

2:7

2:8

idols of human invention. Those who follow the emptiness and impotency of idolatry do so at the price of their only source of mercy and kindness. Jonah had followed his own way instead of God's and

2:9 had come to a sad end. Instead of trusting to the empty creations of man's own imagination, the prophet would sacrifice with the voice of thanksgiving; he would give thanks and pay his vows to Jehovah. The only source of salvation is Jehovah; this the prophet had learned the hard way. From this Gethsemane of his experience he would now be better able to say, "Thy will be done." In our rejoicing over the rescue of the prophet and the prospect of Nineveh's being spared, let us not overlook the rebirth of the prophet—his conversion to the Lord.

2:10 Seeing the victory won over Jonah's disposition to run away from God, at least for the present, the Lord instructed the fish to release its prisoner. We are not told how God spoke to the fish, or where the fish vomited up its cargo. How long did it take Jonah to get home? Did he go home? How long before God called him to the task yet before him? We are left to wonder on all these questions. There could be no profit in our knowing, so these must be passed over in silence.

Chapter 3

3:1-4. To Jehovah's second call to go to Nineveh the prophet responded without argument; he had learned his lesson.

3:1 Once more the word of Jehovah came to the prophet, instructing him to arise and go to Nineveh and "preach unto it the preaching" that God would bid him. "The preaching" was to be the message that God would give to him. There is no remonstrance and no mention of Jonah's former call and flight. The Lord passes this over in gracious silence; the prophet had learned his lesson, and with this God is satisfied.

3:2 Again Nineveh is referred to as "that great city" (see comment under 1:2). Under the first charge it had been said "cry against" the city (1:2); this time it is "cry [preach] unto it." The prophet was to "preach unto it the preaching that I bid thee." This is the only preaching that will accomplish that which God wants accomplished. One of the tragedies of today—and of all time since the beginning of preaching—is that men are prone to substitute what their own wisdom dictates instead of preaching what God bids. Man can make no improvement on God's message.

This time, without hesitation or argument with God, the prophet arose to obey. The instruction "Arise" could suggest that he had returned to his home in Gath-hepher, although this is not certain. Again we are told that Nineveh "was an exceeding great city, of three days' journey." The expression "three days' journey" has long been debated by scholars. After considering a number of possible explanations, it seems best to think that the reference is to Nineveh itself, to the seven or eight miles of its circumference. This would mean that it would take the prophet three days to complete his mission, going from section to section where the crowds would be found, and preaching to them as they would gather about him. As "Jonah began to enter into the city a day's journey," that is, the first day, the day of the beginning of his preaching, "he cried, and said, Yet forty days, and Nineveh shall be overthrown." The message was simple, yet it was spoken in such a positive manner and with such conviction that the people were willing to give heed. Imagine a foreigner, probably rustic in appearance, entering into the capital city of the world and crying to the people that their city would be overthrown! Warnings of this nature are conditional; this should be understood. A principle of divine sovereignty was later recorded by Jeremiah: when God speaks to destroy a nation, if that nation turns from its wickedness, God will repent of the evil He had determined against it. On the other hand, if Jehovah speaks concerning a nation to build it up and it turns to do evil, God will repent Himself of the good He had thought to do (Jer.

3:3

3:4

18:7-10). This principle, though not specifically stated by Jonah, is implied.

*3:5-10. Triumphant evangelism rewards the
prophet's efforts, the results of which should
have been gratifying to the prophet. The
people of Nineveh repented and Jehovah
spared the city.*

3:5   "And the people of Nineveh believed God"! In-
credulous! This has been almost as difficult for the
skeptic to accept as has been the account of Jonah's
having been swallowed by the great fish. Jesus has
helped us at this point when He said, "For even as
Jonah became a sign unto the Ninevites, so shall also
the Son of man be to this generation" (Luke 11:30).
Jesus' resurrection from the dead would be the sign
to His generation, and to all generations since. So
Jonah was a sign to the people of Nineveh. This
indicates that the report of the experience of Jonah
at sea, being swallowed by the fish and released on
dry land, had preceded him to the great city. Here
was the man whom the God of the Hebrews had
commissioned to come to Nineveh; here was the man
who had fled from the task but, being thus repri-
manded and saved by his God, was now here in
Nineveh to carry out the commission. This would
have a tremendous effect upon the people. The man
who had been in "Sheol" and had been raised as it
were from the dead would be a tremendous "sign."
The people not only believed God, but the greatest to
the least of them demonstrated that belief by clothing themselves in sackcloth. Sackcloth was a rough
and scratchy material worn next to the body as a
symbol of humbling oneself. It was the symbol of
grief and penitence.

3:6   The effect of the prophet's preaching was electrifying. Tidings reached the king, who arose from his
throne, laid aside his royal robes, and donned sack-

cloth as had the lowest servant. He further demonstrated the humbling of himself before God by sitting in ashes. One could demonstrate the disposition of his spirit in no more impressive way than by putting on sackcloth and sitting in ashes. This practice seems to have been universal. The king further made decree by himself and his nobles that all persons, and beasts as well, put on sackcloth and fast and that the people pray to God. The covering of the animals was a custom practiced in mourning for the death of a great person. He further decreed that all turn away from their evil deeds. This indicates that the national conscience recognized that the overthrow of the city would be a just retribution on them for their wickedness. It would be the expression of the wrath of an angry God. It was an earnest plea in word and action that the wrath be turned away. "Who knoweth whether God will not turn and repent"—change His mind from destruction to deliverance? "And God saw their works"—here were visible demonstrations—"that they turned from their evil way." God's repentance indicates His change of mind or will toward Nineveh. He had said the city would be overthrown; their repentance would now avert this. Jonah said that the people turned; Jesus said that they repented (Matt. 12:41). Jonah said that "God repented"; the people desired that God would "turn away from his fierce anger." Repentance, both of God and the people, indicated a turning, a change of mind or will. God acted according to the principle stated above (see 3:4).

3:7

3:8

3:9

3:10

The chapter clearly and nobly portrays the love and compassion of God for even the greatest and most cruel of the heathen. If they will but turn from wickedness to Him, He will be merciful. It reveals His readiness to forgive and to spare; but it also gives us the other side of the picture which reveals God's fierce hatred for sin, cruelty, and corruption. Nations of today would do well to learn this lesson so graphically made known and so clearly declared by all the prophets.

Chapter 4

4:1-5. Instead of rejoicing over the deeds of his preaching, Jonah was exceedingly displeased. The true character of Jonah's spirit is demonstrated.

4:1   En route to Tarshish Jonah had shared with the sailors the threat to his life as they were endangered by the wrath of the storm. He had thanked God in a beautiful and poetic way for the sparing of his life and for his release from the belly of Sheol. Surely, we would expect him now to rejoice that Nineveh had been spared and that God had so wonderfully blessed his preaching. But not so! Instead, we find Jonah
4:2   exceedingly displeased, even angry with Jehovah for the mercy He had shown this heathen people. He now reveals the cause for his flight from Jehovah when he was first called to go to Nineveh: he had feared that God, in mercy and abundant lovingkindness, would spare the great city. He also discloses his own narrow spirit in revealing that this is what he did not want. In
4:3   contrast to the prayer and thanksgiving for deliverance (ch. 2), the prophet now prays that God will take from him his life; for he considered it better to
4:4   die than to live to see the city spared. Jehovah's reply seems to be that of a father chiding his child, even
4:5   with a sense of humor, "Doest thou well to be angry?" Piqued by the question of Jehovah, the prophet departed as a pouting child to prepare a booth where he would be protected from the sun, and where he could wait to see whether Jehovah would change His mind. There was still in the heart of the prophet the hope that the city would be destroyed.

In Jonah we see the narrow, sectarian spirit that has too often characterized the people of God. He reflects the very spirit and nature of the Jewish people: Jehovah was their God, and He was not to be shared with any other people. The Hebrew nation belonged to God, and upon the people of that nation alone were the blessings of Jehovah to be bestowed.

Farrar has well summed up the spirit of Jonah as the spirit of the three friends of Job who were willing to torture Job in order to save their own orthodox tradition. It is the spirit of the elder brother who was angry that his younger brother had returned home alive to enjoy the father's favor and forgiveness. It is the spirit demonstrated by the Pharisees in bringing the woman taken in adultery to Jesus to be condemned. It is the very spirit of the Pharisees who condemned Jesus for the mercy He manifested to sinners, publicans, and harlots (Farrar, p. 241). But further, it is the spirit too often unrecognized, but present, that manifests itself today in the lives and hearts of many who profess to be disciples of the Master. Judas's question, "Lord, is it I?" might be apropos to each today as he weighs in the balance of divine truth his own attitude before he condemns too strongly the fierce patriotic and jealous spirit of this prophet of the long ago.

> *4:6-11. The largeness of the heart of God and the smallness of the spirit of man are contrasted. A gourd, a worm, and a sultry wind are used to impress the lesson.*

A vivid contrast is again shown between the tender love of God and His mercy toward His servant, and the loveless and selfish nature of the prophet. Out of mercy for his lot, Jehovah made a gourd to come over Jonah to shade him from the intense heat of the sun in this Eastern land. What specific plant is indicated by "the gourd" is a matter of conjecture, for no one knows. To this point God has used the sea, the stormy wind, and the mighty creature of the deep to carry out His plan. Now He uses a plant of the vegetable kingdom, a worm of the lowly creeping order, and a sultry east wind to complete His divine purpose. He is Lord of all; all creation is at His disposal. In view of the fact that the gourd grew up in a night, it seems evident that a miracle was here involved. Jonah was exceedingly glad. Here is the first indication of joy manifested by the prophet. A small

4:6

4:7 thing like a protective plant could bring joy, whereas the sparing of a city could bring anger. As Luther suggests, God begins to play with the prophet in an effort to teach His lesson: a worm smote the gourd

4:8 and the vine withered. This was followed by a sultry wind that further withered the gourd-vine and added to the prophet's discomfort to the point that he fainted. Again he wished that he would die, saying, "It is better for me to die than to live."

4:9 Once more Jehovah chided the pouting prophet, asking if Jonah had done right in his anger. To this the prophet replied that he did well to be "angry, even unto death," thus "expressing the great excess of his anger." (Bewer, *International Critical Commentary*). His first anger had been because Nineveh was not destroyed; his present anger is because a vine was destroyed. Here is a contrast between the murmuring of Jonah and the voice of God as it speaks to the

4:10 conscience of the murmurer. There now follows the final word, spoken by Jehovah, which carries with it the true contrast between man and God. Man can become greatly concerned and disturbed when that which directly affects him is touched by the finger of providence; but he can be utterly indifferent, even hard, to that which may be of infinitely greater value when this does not affect him. He may murmur greatly over an immediate personal discomfort, but

4:11 wish for the destruction of those who may in time affect him. If man is so affected by the immediate, though ever so small, should not God be concerned over Nineveh with its teeming thousands? There seems to have been some one hundred and twenty thousand individuals not yet of accountable age, besides the multitude of adults for whom God was concerned. Keil, considering the one hundred and twenty thousand to have been those under seven and to have been one-fifth of the population, estimates the total population of the city to have been about six hundred thousand or more. God was concerned not only for the huge population, but also for the brute creation as well. Surely God cares for and is concerned about all of His creation.

4
AMOS
" Burden-bearer "

General Observations

1. The Man

From the obscurity of a shepherd's role Amos stepped out
for a few brief moments upon the stage of history, to go
down in its annals as one of its first and greatest reformers.
Having served the purpose for which he was called, he
stepped back into that same obscurity from which he had
come. His clear insight into the conditions of his day, his
indignation at the corruptions within a nation, and his courage and devotion to God have made him worthy of a place
among the great. Israel was corrupt from the top of its social
and political stratum to the bottom. Amos cried out against
these evils and pointed out to the nation its inevitable doom.

The prophet's background is clearly reflected in his preaching, and in his prophecies one hears the roar of the lion and
of the young lions and sees the spring of a snare or gin as a
bird is caught in it (3:4-5). As a shepherd he knows what it is
to rescue two legs (shin-bones) and a piece of an ear of a
beloved sheep from the lion that has slain it (3:12). At night
he has studied the constellations, Pleiades and Orion, in their
heavenly glory, and has watched the night turn to day as the
morning dawns (5:8). He has seen "the sun go down in the
clear day" as an eclipse swallowed the sun. He makes us feel

with him the despair of one who flees from a lion only to be met by a bear, and having escaped the bear, leans on the wall in the house to be bitten by a serpent (5:19). The folly of horses running on rocks, or of oxen plowing there (8:9), the sight of the wady as a raging torrent in the rainy season and as a dry wash in the dry season (9:5), and the separating of wheat from chaff (9:9)—all these were principles and scenes familiar to this man of the country.

a. **His Name.** "Amos" means "to bear," "to place a load upon" (Laetsch), or "burdened" or "burden-bearer" (Eiselen). He lived up to his name; for as Jehovah laid upon him the task of declaring His divine oracles to apostate Israel, he bore the burden and fulfilled his mission.

b. **Home.** The home of the prophet was the village of Tekoa, or the rugged environ of that village. Tekoa was located six miles south of Bethlehem and twelve miles south of Jerusalem. The surrounding terrain was rugged and uninviting. It was the type of country that develops hardy manhood in those who would draw their living from it. About eighteen miles east of Tekoa lay the Dead Sea. In the distance between were rocks, steep valleys, and rugged canyons. Also, there was the "Wilderness of Judea," or Jeshimon, where later Jesus spent forty days, and where, no doubt, John the Baptist spent some time. Across this wilderness swept the hot winds of the south; and from its hills could be heard the roar of the lion, the cry of the jackal, and the bleating of sheep as their sounds echoed from one canyon wall to the other. It was here that the prophet had grown up as a "herdsman of sheep" and "a dresser of sycomore-trees." This environment had prepared him well for the stern task to which he was called and is reflected most colorfully in the prophet's preaching.

c. **Occupation.** Amos tells us what his occupation had been: a herdsman and a dresser of sycomore trees. The particular word translated "herdsman" indicates that he was a herdsman of a peculiar, small, rugged type of sheep called "nakads." The wool of this special species was of superior quality and great value. The sycomore tree was found at a lower altitude than Tekoa, which suggests that Amos roamed from Tekoa eastward through the wilderness and toward the Dead Sea. The fruit borne by this tree is described as fig-like, slightly sweet and watery, and somewhat woody in its nature.

It was eaten by the poorer people and had to be pinched or bruised before it would ripen (George Adam Smith).

A quality of character developed in a background such as this would be a far cry from the type of society the prophet would face in Beth-el and Israel to whom God was sending him. From the frugal life of an out-of-doors man, accustomed to the wilds of nature and to hard, honest toil, Amos would have little sympathy for the luxurious and profligate life he would find among his northern kinsmen.

d. **Characterization.** Someone has described Amos as "the first Great Reformer." He was not of the school of the prophets, who by this time were disposed to cry what the people wanted. On the contrary, he was a man chosen of God, given a special message, and sent on a divine mission (7:14-15). There was not in Amos the sympathy, warm love, and feeling of the statesman or citizen, but a cold sense of justice and right. Not a sob is to be found in his book for the nation of wicked apostates, and there is only a sigh for the poor. Although of a common ancestry, in one way he was an outsider, having come from Judah. As an outsider he could view the situation in Israel more objectively than the local residents could. He was the stern prophet of justice and righteousness. His very attitude breathes the air of his life's rugged desert environment. "The lion hath roared; who will not fear? The Lord Jehovah hath spoken; who can but prophesy?" (3:8). In strong contrast to the spirit of Amos, Hosea was the prophet of sympathy, love, and compassion, speaking as one with a broken heart for those near and dear to him. Hosea's spirit was summed up in the word "loving-kindness"; Amos' is summed up in the one word "justice."

2. The Date

The date of Amos' prophesying and of the writing of his book is almost unanimously placed by scholars between 760-750 B.C. One will not be far amiss if he settles on the general date of 755 B.C. He prophesied in the days of Uzziah, king of Judah, and of Jeroboam, king of Israel. According to Thiele, Uzziah reigned in the period 792/91 to 740/39 B.C., a period of over fifty years. The date fixed by the same writer for Jeroboam was 793/92 to 753 B.C., a period of over forty years. It was somewhere near the close of Jeroboam's reign that Amos was called to preach to the decaying nation.

3. Background

During the ninth century B.C., Assyria had been increasing in power and in the exertion of that power in the east, gradually extending it into the west. However, for sixty years following 805 B.C., "the west was given a breathing space because the rulers of Assyria were not strong men" (*Westminster Atlas,* p. 73). It was during this period that Jonah had visited Nineveh. This sixty years' respite from the east gave Judah and Israel the opportunity needed to strengthen the power of each nation. Under the strong leadership of Uzziah and Jeroboam II, the borders of each nation were enlarged; and through trade, agriculture, and conquest each king was able to bring prosperity to the people. This prosperity brought equally great perils to both nations. With the accession of Tiglath-pileser to the throne of Assyria, 745 B.C., this picture was changed. Immediately the Assyrian monarch set out on a career of conquest that would include the west. It was during this period of Israel's prosperity and wealth prior to Tiglath-pileser that Amos was called to prophesy to the nation.

a. **Luxury.** The luxury of the wealthy class in Israel is clearly indicated by the prophet as he speaks of their "couches" and "silken cushions" (3:12), of their "winter-house" and "summer-house," and the "houses of ivory" (ivory inlay and ornamentation), and of "the houses of hewn-stone" (3:15; 5:12). The voluptuous women were spoken of as "kine of Bashan," who insisted that their husbands provide ample wine and other luxuries for their feasts, even if the poor had to be crushed in order to provide these (4:1-3). Their feasts were characterized by revelry, songs, music, choice meats, and the best of wines to satiate their lusts, and by cushions and silken tapestries upon which to recline (6:1-7). These luxuries were enjoyed by the wealthy, whose eyes were closed to the afflictions and needs of the poor (6:6). For this they would go away into captivity.

b. **Moral and Political Corruption.** The moral condition of the nation is clearly revealed by the prophet's shock at the cruel treatment of the poor by the rich, at the covetousness, injustice, and immorality of the people in power, and at the general contempt for things holy (2:6-8). Trampling on the poor, taking exactions of wheat (5:11), afflicting the just, taking a bribe, and turning aside the needy (5:12) stirred the indignation of the prophet and give us an insight into the morals of the day. They were ready to swallow up the needy and cause the poor of the land to cease, that is, to die (8:4). In political circles there was tumult and oppression, violence and robbery (3:9-10). There was the disposition to hate a judge who would reprove or speak uprightly (5:10); this indicates the character of those who would be selected to fill such offices.

c. **Religious Corruption.** Back of all moral, social, and political corruption there lies a basic cause: religious decay and apostasy. Jeroboam I had introduced the calf worship (I Kings 12:25-33), and Ahab and Jezebel had given emphasis to Baal worship. Cursed with two systems of false worship, the people's spiritual temper was exceedingly low. Extravagant religious ceremonies and rites were manifested on every hand. Tithes were offered every three days, that which was leavened was sacrificed, free-will offerings were abundant and the amounts advertised (4:4-5). God hated their feasts. He took no delight in their assemblies and demanded that they take away their songs and music, for it was just "noise." Religious fervor was high, but true spiritual devotion to God was utterly lacking. At the same time, the merchants were practicing dishonesty in trading. They observed the new moons and sabbaths, but chafed under the restraint of waiting until these had passed that they could return to their business (8:4-6). For all this God would bring them to judgment; therefore, "prepare to meet thy God!" (4:12).

4. The Message: Doom

The Lord had brought the people out of Egypt by His hand and had given them the land. He had driven out the inhabitants of Canaan before them. He had sent the blessings, the rain and the harvests, upon them. But in spite of all this, they had failed Him. Instead of worship, adoration, and righteousness, and instead of love and concern for one another, they had become cruel, selfish, and rebellious. They had been deceived by these things God had done for them, concluding that since He was their God and they His people, and since they had been so extravagant in their offerings and worship, surely He would favor them. Now they must be taught. They must learn that Jehovah is a God of righteousness and holiness, and that insulting such righteousness and holiness must result in a stern expression of justice. The doom of national exile was not the only remedy for their complete and flagrant apostasy. The full import of this judgment cannot be realized until one understands two important facts: (a) To the Jew the nation overshadowed the individual; it was through the nation and its relation to God that the individual entered into fellowship with Jehovah. (b) To the Jew every nation outside his own was unclean; in a foreign land he could not worship Jehovah acceptably. To him, therefore, exile would be far more serious than it would be to people of today. The doom of exile meant the collapse of all that was dear and glorious.

5. Teaching

The book emphasizes anew the principles that had long been announced to the people: "The wicked shall be turned back unto Sheol, even all the nations that forget God" (Ps. 9:17); and "Righteousness exalteth a nation; but sin is a reproach to any people" (Prov. 14:34). Also the book points out clearly that "it is an abomination to kings to commit wickedness; for the throne is established by righteousness" (Prov. 16:12). The nation had reached the point where there was a deep-rooted need for a vigorous and clear restatement of two fundamentals: (a) the true nature and character of Jehovah; and (b) the relation between Jehovah and the nations, and the proper basis of His relation to Israel. Amos and his contemporary prophets supplied this need.

a. **The Prophet's Conception of Jehovah.** Amos presents a world view of God and the nations. He never refers to Jehovah as "The God of Israel," a term familiar to them. Farrar has well expressed the prophet's view when he says, "His whole message centers in the common prophetic conviction that God is the sole and righteous Governor of the world, judging the people righteously, and when they rebel, dashing them to pieces like a potter's vessel." Amos clearly reveals the personality of God: He communicates with others

(3:7); He hates and abhors (5:21-22); He swears by Himself (4:2; 6:8); He repents (7:3); He commands (9:3-4).

Attributes of absolute deity are emphasized by Amos: (1) God's omnipotence may be seen in His acts of creation (4:13; 5:8), in His control over the forces of nature (4:6-11), in His supremacy over the nations (chs. 1—2; 5:9; 9:7), and in the titles by which He is called: "Jehovah," "the Lord Jehovah," "Jehovah, the God of hosts," "Jehovah, whose name is the God of hosts," "the Lord." (2) The omnipresence of God is plainly taught (9:2-4) or clearly implied (chs. 1—2). (3) His omniscience is indicated (9:2-4) and declared in His knowledge of man's thoughts (4:13).

The righteousness of Jehovah is constantly emphasized by the prophet; it stands out as one of the most important elements of his teaching. Mercy is not overlooked in the prophet's teaching, although it is not the supreme factor. One must search rather diligently to find it; however, he does make intercession for the people (7:2, 5) and pleads with them to "seek Jehovah" (5:4, 6, 8), promising them the possibility of graciousness from the Lord if they will meet certain conditions (5:14).

b. The Prophet's Conception of Israel. (1) The Israelites were the people of God, sustaining a special relationship to Him which involved responsibility on their part (2:9-12). (2) The people should reflect the character of God (5:14-15, 24). God had given His law to Judah and Israel (2:4); they had been His special people (3:2). (3) But Israel had failed in the divine purpose; therefore, judgment must come upon them as on any people who reject God. This judgment would be one of invasion and exile; but in spite of this, Jehovah would redeem a remnant through the house of David under whom the enemies should be conquered (9:11-12).

c. Permanent Lessons of the Book. (Eiselen) (1) Justice between man and man is one of the divine foundations of society. (2) Privilege implies responsibility. Israel had enjoyed special privileges; therefore, she had been given special responsibilities. (3) Failure to recognize and accept responsibility is sure to bring punishment. (4) Nations—and by analogy, individuals—are obligated to live up to the light and knowledge granted to them. (5) The most elaborate worship is but an insult to God when offered by those who have no mind to conform to His commands. "The distinguishing characteristic of heathenism is the stress which it lays upon ceremonial" (G. A. Smith).

Outline of the Book

Title and Preface, 1:1-2

I. The approaching judgment. The heathen's and Israel's sins, 1:3—2:16.

    A. Punishment of the nations bordering Judah and Israel, 1:3—2:3.
        1. Damascus—for their cruelty in war, 1:3-5.
        2. Gaza of Philistia—slave traffic, 1:6-8.
        3. Tyre—delivered up "brothers," 1:9-10.
        4. Edom—for implacable hatred for Israel, 1:11-12.
        5. Ammon—intense and uncalled-for cruelty, 1:13-15.
        6. Moab—vengeance even on a king's carcass, 2:1-3.

    B. Punishment of Judah—her sin was religious apostasy, 2:4-5. Note the difference between the accusations against the nations and against Judah: cruelty vs. apostasy.

    C. Punishment of Israel—the theme of Amos' prophecy, 2:6-16.
        1. Sins of Israel: injustice and oppression, shameless immorality, contempt for the Lord, vv. 6-8.
        2. Scornful contempt of the divine benefits bestowed, vv. 9-12.
        3. Inevitable consequences, vv. 13-16.
           In the accusations against the nations they are pictured as cruel, barbarous, etc.; against Judah and Israel the accusations are civil, religious, and charges of oppressions. This accusation becomes the thesis of the book; the remainder of the book is an elaboration of these charges.

II. Israel's crimes and her condemnation, chs. 3—6.

A. Condemnation of the wealthy ruling classes for civil and religious inequities, 3:1—4:5.
   1. Jehovah had known Israel, which makes her crime greater, 3:1-8.
      a) Because chosen for Jehovah, her sins must be visited, vv. 1-2.
      b) The prophet's right to speak: chosen of God, vv. 3-8.
   2. Civil oppression and inevitable judgment on the ruling class, 3:9—4:3.
      a) The ruling class: their sins, 3:9-15.
      b) The luxury-loving women: a special judgment against them, 4:1-3.
   3. Condemnation of their religious festivities— "which please you," not Jehovah, 4:4-5.

B. Unheeded chastisements—the prophet turns to the nation, 4:6-13.
   1. Chastisements from Jehovah, which have gone unheeded, vv. 6-11.
      a) General famine, "cleanness of teeth," v. 6.
      b) Drought, vv. 7-8.
      c) Blasting, mildew, locusts, v. 9.
      d) Pestilence, at the same time enemy attacks, v. 10.
      e) Earthquake, burning, v. 11.
   2. Final doom, for which prepare, vv. 12-13.
      They had looked upon God as a Being to be flattered; He looked upon them as children to be disciplined. Discipline had availed nothing; therefore, "Prepare to meet thy God."

C. Overthrow of the kingdom of the ten tribes, chs. 5, 6.
   1. Lamentations, denunciations, exhortations, and threats, 5:1-17.
      a) Lamentation—Israel is fallen, vv. 1-3.
      b) Seek Jehovah, forsake idolatry, and live, vv. 4-6.
      c) But Israel turns righteousness into unrighteousness, vv. 7-9.
      d) This unrighteousness God must punish, unless they seek Jehovah, vv. 10-15.

        e) The announcement of judgment, vv. 16-17.

    2. First woe—terrors of the day of Jehovah, 5:18-27.

        a) Terrors of the day, vv. 18-20.

        b) Their heartless worship will not avert the day, vv. 21-24.

        c) They have followed the steps of their fathers, vv. 25-27.

    3. Second woe—upon the careless heads of the nation, ch. 6.

        a) The luxury-loving wealthy rulers, vv. 1-6.

        b) Exile and destruction are certain, vv. 7-11.

        c) Cannot be averted by their foolish trust in power, vv. 12-14.

III. Five visions, which the prophet explains, 7:1—9:10.

    A. The vision of the locusts, in which the mercy of God averts the catastrophe, 7:1-3.

    B. The vision of the devouring fire—a severer judgment than that of the locusts, again averted by mercy of Jehovah, 7:4-6.

    C. The vision of the plumb line—destruction on the idolatrous nation of Israel, 7:7-9.

        An interlude: antagonism of Amaziah toward Amos, 7:10-17.

    D. The vision of the basket of summer fruit—the ripeness of Israel for judgment, ch. 8.

        1. The vision and its significance: the time of mercy is now past, destruction is at hand, vv. 1-3.

        2. The final eclipse of the nation—her sun sets at noon, vv. 4-14.

    E. The vision of the smitten sanctuary—destruction of the sinful kingdom, 9:1-10.

IV. Promise of a bright future—the Messianic hope, 9:11-15. This conclusion is the only optimistic note in the book.

Notice how each book directed to Judah or Israel has an optimistic note of future glory. Compare this passage with Acts 15:14-18.

Comments

Chapter 1

1:1-2. Title and preface to the book.

Amos speaks of himself simply as one "among the herdsmen of Tekoa" and as "a dresser of sycomore trees" (cf. 7:14; also see introduction to the book, under Occupation). Tekoa was a village twelve miles south and slightly east of Jerusalem. It was located on the edge of the Wilderness of Judah, described as a wild, semiarid, and rough section. "The words" are the words of the message "which he saw concerning Israel." The prophet indicates that the message was not from himself, but from Jehovah. He saw these words as they were revealed to his spiritual eyes. For the history of Uzziah in whose days Amos prophesied, see II Kings 15:1-7 and II Chronicles 26; for incidents in Israel's history during the days of Uzziah, see II Kings 15:8-28; and for the history of Jeroboam II, see II Kings 14:23-29. Although little mention is made of Jeroboam in the recorded history, he was a strong king and an excellent warrior and did much for the economic welfare of his nation. This earthquake in the days of Uzziah is also mentioned by Zechariah (14:5). Nothing is known of it more than the mentioning by these two prophets. It must have been of unusual significance. As the lion roars and his voice strikes terror in the hearts of those who hear, so Jehovah will roar from Zion, exciting terror in the hearts of the people. Zion was the fortress of David, located in the southeast section of Jerusalem. It was the site of the temple and was looked on by the people as the dwelling place of Jehovah among them. The thunder of His voice would be as the blast of a furnace, causing the pastures to mourn and the luxu-

1:1

1:2

riant growth of Carmel to wither. Located west of the Sea of Galilee, Mount Carmel juts out into the Great Sea.

Before pronouncing judgment upon Judah and Israel, the prophet scans the world of his day and selects six neighboring heathen nations upon whom he declares God's judgment. Three of these—Damascus, Gaza, and Tyre—were not related to Israel and Judah; the other three—Edom, Ammon, and Moab—were related. But whether related or not, or whether heathen or God's own people, the wicked and ungodly alike must receive the judgment of God. Sins of cruelty and inhumane treatment characterized the heathen; but it was for sins of unfaithfulness to God and His law that Judah and Israel were severely condemned.

Each judgment against the six heathen nations and Judah and Israel begins with the same declaration, "Thus saith Jehovah: For three transgressions of . . . , yea, for four, I will not turn away the punishment thereof." "Saith Jehovah" gives emphasis to the source of the judgment; it is from Jehovah and not from the prophet. "For three transgressions, yea, for four" is not to be taken literally, but signifies a full and complete number. It indicated that the wickedness that called down the judgment was growing from year to year (Farrar); it indicated repeated and cumulative guilt (G. A. Smith); the expression emphasized the multiplying of their sins (Keil). It indicated that the cup of their iniquity was filled to overflowing, and that now the cup of God's wrath must be mingled with it.

> *1:3—2:3. Punishment of the heathen nations bordering Israel. The judgment upon the six neighboring heathen peoples was for excessive cruelty. Edom, Ammon, and Moab were related to Israel; Damascus, Gaza, and Tyre were not.*

1:3   Damascus was the capital of Syria, located 135 miles north-northeast of Jerusalem. Gilead, the rich pasture land southwest of Damascus, was the ancient homeland of the half-tribe of Manasseh that had remained east of the Jordan when the people came in to possess the land. In their raids on the inhabitants of Gilead the Syrians had manifested an inhuman cruelty, even threshing the captives with iron instruments as grain would be threshed with heavy iron-spiked timbers. Hazael had murdered Ben-hadad I, king of Syria, and reigned in his stead (II Kings 8:7-15). He had a son also named Ben-hadad (II Kings 13:3, 22-25), who is not to be confused with the first king by that name. On this ruling house Jehovah would bring a fire of destruction. Breaking "the bar of Damascus" indicated the breaking of the city's "bolt" or arm of protection and security, leaving the city open for captivity. "The valley of Aven [vanity]" and "house of Eden" may indicate places now unknown to us; or "the valley of Aven" may suggest a place of idolatry and "house of Eden" a pleasure resort of the king. Definite knowledge of either is impossible at the present. "Kir" means "a walled place." Probably located to the north or east, it was the land from where the Syrians had come. However, the location is still unknown.

1:4

1:5

Gaza was a chief city of Philistia near the coast southwest of Jerusalem. The city probably stands for all of Philistia. The sin of Gaza had been that of slave traffic; they had taken the inhabitants of an entire village or group, probably Israelites, selling them to Edom. For this God would send a fire of divine judgment, bringing destruction to the city and its palaces. The whole of Philistia is included in the judgment, as four of the original five chief cities are specified. Gath is not mentioned; possibly by this time it had been destroyed. Uzziah had broken down its walls (II Chron. 26:6), and Amos mentions it as an example of divine destruction (6:2).

1:6

1:7

1:8

Tyre, the third of the nonrelated peoples, comes next under the divine judgment. Located on the coast of northern Palestine, Tyre was the chief city of sea traffic, having been forced to turn to the sea for its life because of its limited space between the moun-

1:9

tains to the east and the sea to the west. Isaiah, Jeremiah, and Ezekiel pronounced special judgments against it as the great commercial harlot of that time. Tyre had "delivered up the whole people to Edom"; whether this was people of Israel or their own people is debated by some. As was true of Gaza, their sin was that of slave trade with Edom. "[They] remembered not the brotherly covenant" refers either to the cove-

1:10 nant of David and Hiram, kings of Judah and Phoenicia, or to the attitude they should have had toward their own people. It is most probable that "the whole people" delivered up were those of Israel, and the covenant was that between David and Hiram. They had forgotten this covenant. For this her walls and palaces would be devoured. The fulfillment was literal, as witnessed by the ruins that may be seen today. The destruction of Tyre was undertaken by Nebuchadnezzar, but without success; the final destruction was by Alexander the Great.

1:11 Edom falls next under the fire of Jehovah's wrath. These were the descendants of Esau, the twin brother of Jacob; hence they were kinsfolk of Israel. Edom's habitation was south of the Dead Sea in what is called the Arabah, a semiarid country characterized by rock strongholds. Its strategic location made it ideal for collecting "duty" or customs from caravans traveling between the East and Egypt, as well as those from the Arabian Desert who would pass through Edom traveling to the sea coast. Also, Edom had an important seaport on the north shore of the Gulf of Aqabah, which added to the nation's economic advantage. From the beginning of their history there had been enmity between Israel and Edom. No particular sin is here named against Edom except an implacable and perpetual hatred for his brother Israel. This feeling had not been altogether one-sided, for David had subjugated Edom and placed garrisons there (II Sam. 8:14); and no doubt Israel maintained a similar atti-

1:12 tude toward the nation. For this God would send fire upon Teman, the chief city of southeast Edom and probably its capital, and upon Bozrah, another chief city and sometime capital of the nation.

The territory of Ammon was located on the border of the Arabian Desert, east of and adjacent to the ancient tribe of Gad, and north of what had been the land of Reuben. Ammon and Moab were descendants of Lot by the incestuous plot of his two daughters (Gen. 19:30-38). The crime of Ammon, like that of Damascus, was one of cruelty of the basest sort. They took delight in ripping up women with child as they invaded Gilead, a means to the end of enlarging their borders. Rabbah (Rabbath-Ammon) was the capital city of the nation. It was here that David had directed Joab to have Uriah killed in battle (II Sam. 11). It would now be destroyed by the fire of Jehovah's kindling, with shouting and tumult as in the day of battle when an enemy storms a city. It would be destroyed as with the tempest of a terrible tornado; her king and princes would be carried away into captivity.

1:13

1:14

Chapter 2

Moab lay south of ancient Reuben, between the river Arnon and the brook Zered, immediately east of the southern half of the Dead Sea. As his brother Ammon had demonstrated a spirit of cruelty in destroying the unborn, Moab demonstrated his fiendish spirit by burning the bones of the dead and making them into lime. The people could probably point to a building erected to their god and say, "The king of Edom is in here, his bones went to make up the lime in the mortar." Unable to capture him alive, the people had taken their vengeance on the king's carcass. Kerioth, one of the chief cities of Moab, singled out as representative of the whole land, would die amid the violent tumult of war and destruction. Her palaces of which she could have boasted would be no more. Her judges and princes would perish in the havoc and ruin to come. The judgment would be so severe that two later prophets wept as they contemplated its terribleness (see Isa. 15:5, 16:11; Jer. 48:36).

2:1

2:2

2:3

2:4-5. Judah's sin was religious apostasy. They had rejected the law of Jehovah and had turned to lies.

2:4   From these six heathen kingdoms the prophet turns to Judah, the southern kingdom, which had held firm to the Davidic lineage of kings after the division of the empire following the death of Solomon. What Amos said of Judah would continue to please the people of Israel, although the preaching may have been getting too near home to be comfortable. The same introduction of judgment used against the heathen nations is also used against Judah: "For three transgressions . . . , yea, for four. . . ." However, the difference in the accusations against the heathen nations and against Judah is striking. Judah's guilt or sin was that of religious apostasy: "they have rejected the law of Jehovah, and have not kept his statutes." "The law" was the sum of all God's principles and commandments revealed to the people. The "statutes" are the specific laws given by God which controlled the form of worship and regulated the moral conduct of the people. "Their lies have caused them to err." These were their false religious teachings and their false concept of Jehovah which
2:5   had led them into idolatry and which would now bring them to destruction. They had acted as heathens, and now God would treat them as heathens by sending the same judgment on them as He would send on the heathen. Jerusalem and her palaces would be devoured by the fire of Jehovah's wrath; however, through the efforts of Isaiah and Micah, prophets in Judah, and the influence of good King Hezekiah, the judgment was averted for 135 years after the fall of Samaria.

2:6-16. The burden of Amos' prophecy is begun here. Israel's sins were of a moral, social, and political nature, the result of idolatry and lawlessness.

2:6   At this point the prophet begins the real burden of his prophecy; he swoops down upon Israel as an eagle

upon its prey. The sin of Israel was that of apostasy, a
departure from God that had led to injustice, hardness of heart, and immorality, with no feeling for the
poor or regard for moral conduct. "They have sold
the righteous for silver, and the needy for a pair of
shoes" indicates their oppression of the poor. A
Hebrew who "waxed poor" could sell himself to
another of his people, but he was not to be considered as a slave. He was to be treated as a hired
servant (Lev. 25:39-46). This law was being violated.
There is no indication in the law that one could be
sold in payment for a debt. "The righteous" were
those of the people who were innocent of the crimes
charged against them. It is possible that through bri-
bery of the judges these were "being sold" without
receiving justice, thereby losing what they possessed.
The charge of injustice is followed by a charge of   2:7
oppression of the poor. The passage "they that pant
after the dust of the earth on the head of the poor" is
variously interpreted. Either they sought to crush the
poor so completely that they scattered dust on their
heads as an expression of anguish, or, more probably,
the prophet sarcastically refers to the greed of the
rich which was so strong that they begrudged the
poor even the dust that was on their heads. By
turning the meek man away, those in power would
hinder him in his desire to do the will of God. Their
flagrant immorality was demonstrated in their idolatrous feasts and worship where a man and his son
would go in to the same religious prostitute. They
further showed their contempt for the law of God by   2:8
keeping the garments taken in pledge, which were to
have been returned before night because they were
the poor man's covering (Deut. 24:12-13). Using the
money taken in fines to buy wine, or using the wine
given in lieu of money, they would drink in the house
of the golden calves. Idolatry, rejection of the law of
God, hardness toward the poor, greed, and immorality are the charges that summarize the sins of Israel.
Against these the prophet continued to cry throughout his ministry in Israel.

Yet it was God who had given them the land; it   2:9

was He who had driven out the strong inhabitants of Canaan, whose height was as the cedars and whose strength was as the oak, and in whose sight the ancient Hebrews had seemed as grasshoppers (Num. 13:33). In the presence of these mighty ones Jehovah had caused the sun and the moon to stand still in battle against them (Josh. 10:12, 13). He had used the forces of nature to aid His purpose and to demon-

2:10 strate His power (Judg. 5:20-21). It was Jehovah and not their idols who had brought Israel out of Egypt, had cared for and protected them in the wilderness,

2:11 and had caused them to possess the land. He had revealed Himself to them through their sons, the prophets; and He had honored many of their young men as Nazarites. The vow of the Nazarite was voluntary; he was to abstain from the grape and from anything derived from it, and he was to allow no razor to come on his head. The Nazarites were a symbol of separateness to Jehovah and of what was

2:12 holy. But the people had caused them to break their vow and to stumble; they had commanded the prophets not to prophesy. They showed a total rebellion against God and an utter contempt for all He had decreed as holy.

2:13 Having declared Israel's sins to him, the prophet now announces judgment. The difficulty of the illustration used by the prophet is indicated by the various translations and explanations offered by commentators. The text says, "I will press you in your place, as a cart presseth that is full of sheaves"; whereas the margin of the American Standard Version has it, "I am pressed under you, as a cart is pressed that is full of sheaves." Deane's suggestion seems more clearly accurate, "I will press you with

2:14 the full force of war, as a loaded wain (heavy cart) presses the earth over which it passes" (*Pulpit Commentary*). As the heavy forces of war roll over them they will be pressed down. Amos proceeds to specify the situations in which they will find themselves pressed: the swift will not be able to escape; the strong will have no strength; the mighty will be help-

2:15 less; the archer will find that his trusty bow fails him;

the swift of foot and the rider of the horse will be   2:16
unable to get away; the man of courage will find
himself a coward, fleeing from before the enemy. The
people will find themselves pressed in from every
side, unable to escape, regardless how strong or swift
they thought themselves to be. The terribleness of the
judgment would paralyze the strongest of them.

Chapter 3

3:1-8. Israel had sustained a special relation-
ship to God as His chosen people; and because
this had been violated, punishment must
come. The prophet defends his right to speak
to the point.

"Hear this word"—the prophet would get the at-   3:1
tention of the people—"that Jehovah hath spoken
against you." It is not the word of Amos but of
Jehovah. The word is addressed against "the whole
family" that God had brought out of Egypt, which
would include Judah, although the message is directed primarily to Israel. Of all the families of the earth   3:2
Israel had been Jehovah's chosen people. They were
His by right of choice and redemption; He had redeemed them from bondage. Because of this relationship and their sins He must punish them; He could
not be true to Himself should He let them go uncor-
rected. The greater the measure of grace, the greater
the responsibility incurred; therefore, the greater the
punishment for misuse or contempt of that grace.
Israel had failed to walk in the light God had provided. They had not walked with Him in agreement
with His will; therefore, judgment must be visited
upon the iniquities of the nation. Before proceeding   3:3
with the announcement of judgment, the prophet
declares his right to speak. "Shall two walk together,
except they have agreed?" The "two" are Jehovah
and the prophet. The prophet had been sent to Israel
to carry out a mission from Jehovah; it would be
Jehovah's judgment through the prophet's word. The
prophet's presence at Beth-el was by divine appoint-

3:4   ment. It is said that the lion roars when it has the prey in sight and before it springs, and that the young lion growls over its prey that has been taken. Jehovah has His prey in sight and is about to spring, and Israel is helpless before Him to deliver herself. From this

3:5   figure, so familiar to the prophet and the people, he moves to a second metaphor—a snare set for birds; however, the point is different. In this instance Israel had set the snare which was her sins and in which she was now to be taken. The net was set with a trap-stick, which when sprung would hold the victim captive. The thought is, "Can destruction possibly overtake you, unless your sin draws you into it?" (Keil). The snare catches what flies into it. Israel was flying into the trap she had set; she would be caught in the net of

3:6   her own sins. The trumpet blast was the sounding of an alarm. (For the purpose of the trumpet see Num. 10:1-10; Joel 2:1, 15; etc.) The voice of the prophet as the trumpet and voice of God should awaken the people out of their complacency, warning them of the imminent danger. Yes, it should do more than this; it should frighten them into immediate action. The "evil" that befalls a city is the judgment sent on it by Jehovah. In this instance the evil that was to befall the city is the inevitable consequence of the

3:7   city's wickedness. But Jehovah will not send the evil except first "he reveal his secret unto his servants the prophets," and except He warn the people through

3:8   the voice of His chosen messengers. "The lion hath roared": the mighty thunder of God's warning should cause the people to tremble and return to Him. "The Lord Jehovah," the God who rules in all realms, "hath spoken; who can but prophesy?" The secret of God's purpose having been made known to him, the prophet is left with no alternative but to declare it to the nation. Today God is no longer sending prophets directly to the people, but He continues to speak to nations through those of old. The principles violated by the people in those days are immutable and the character of God is unchangeable. Therefore, the principles and warnings set forth by the prophets in days long since gone have a message and a warning for today. On the ground of faith in the immutability of the divine character of Jehovah and of the principles revealed, one may expect God to act today as He did then. The Lord will not act except in accord with the divine principles revealed in the prophets.

> *3:9-15. The wealthy ruling class are the first to be condemned. Ashdod and Egypt are called to witness the confusion in Samaria. Beth-el will be visited.*

Amos begins his mission by condemning the wealthy ruling class of the nation. He calls upon those in the palaces of Ashdod, a city of the uncircumcised Philistines, and those in the palaces of Egypt, the land of their former captivity, to assemble on the mountains of Samaria that from there they may witness the wickedness of the city. "Tumults" denote the disorder and confusion of a greatly confused people where lawlessness prevails, and "oppressions" indicate the perversion of justice and the mistreatment of the weak. This is to say that the wickedness of Samaria rivals, if it does not surpass, the wickedness of the two heathen peoples called to witness. Samaria was the capital of Israel; therefore, this prophecy against Samaria would be directed against the nobles, the ruling class of the nation. "They know not to do right": they who take by violence and robbery have lost their sense of moral values. Their palaces were being used as storehouses for the plunder taken in this manner. The rulers were able to do this for it was in their hand to oppress the people. "Therefore" introduces a conclusion that follows the charge made or the proposition laid down. In consequence of their violence "an adversary" would be brought against the land to lay it waste. Amos nowhere specifies the nation to be used by Jehovah; however, it is brought out clearly by Hosea a few years later that Assyria was the adversary. The adversary would do three things: (1) surround the land, (2) bring down the nation's strength, and (3) plunder the palaces. The palaces which had been used as storehouses for plun-

3:9

3:10

3:11

der taken by force and corrupt means would yield these stored treasures of plunder to another violent plunderer. It was as if these valued possessions had been reserved as wages for the people used by Jehovah to serve His purpose of judgment. The severity of the judgment is announced: as a lion tears and devours a sheep, and the shepherd is able to rescue only a couple of "shin-bones" and a piece of an ear, a very meager remnant of Samaria will be rescued! Only a fragment, small and mean, would be left of the proud, wealthy people who were given to luxury and extravagance. "In the corner of a couch, and on the silken cushions of a bed" indicates their careless ease and extravagant tastes.

3:12

From the ignoble rulers of Samaria the prophet directs his judgment against Beth-el, the center of worship, and against the luxury of those dwelling there and in Samaria. "Hear ye" is a call to Ashdod and Egypt (see v. 9). Those who had been called to witness the violent wickedness of the nation are now urged to witness the judgment to be imposed upon it. "The Lord Jehovah, the God of hosts," is the God of the hosts of heaven and earth. Though the term includes more, it is used to designate Jehovah as the God of the armies, not of Israel's only, but of all. Therefore, He is the "God of battles," leading the armies of the world in executing His judgments through them. Beth-el was the religious center of the ten tribes of Israel. It was there that Jeroboam I had set up one of the golden calves (I Kings 12:25-33) which had become a snare to the nation. The altars of their idolatrous worship would be destroyed; and the horns, the symbol of strength, would be cut off. Complete devastation of their idolatry was determined! Extravagance, luxury, and excess come next under the sledgehammer blow of the prophet. There were those who owned summer-houses and winter-houses, and "houses of ivory," those decorated with ivory inlay. While some lived in this extravagant splendor, others of the nation were living in poverty and want. These palaces of luxury would be smitten, cast down and brought to an end.

3:13

3:14

3:15

Chapter 4

*4:1-3. The profligate women of Samaria,
called "kine of Bashan," are condemned with
their lords. Their luxurious homes shall be
broken down, and they shall go away captive.*

These verses are a continuation of the judgment   *4:1*
introduced in 3:9; the chapter division at this point is
unfortunate. The women of Samaria and Beth-el are
not to escape the ire of Jehovah. The "kine of Bashan" are the voluptuous women of Samaria, the
wives of the rulers and of the rich. These are addressed as "kine of Bashan," fat cattle of the rich
pastureland east of the Jordan. These women lent
their encouragement to their husbands, the rich and
oppressive rulers, to "oppress the poor" and to
"crush the needy," that by such oppression these
heartless wretches might have the luxuries of a satiated society. "Bring and let us drink" summed up the
heart of their interest. Jehovah "swears by his holi-   *4:2*
ness," the absolute righteousness of His being, because there is none greater by whom He can swear.
Inescapable judgment shall be brought upon these
sensuous, pleasure-loving fiends of a depraved generation. These lovers of luxury would be among the first
taken away captive, helplessly torn away from their
luxurious, profligate life, as fishes are haplessly taken   *4:3*
by the hooks of fishermen. "And ye shall go out at
the breaches," led out of their extravagant homes
through the breaks and gaps made in the walls by
battering. "Everyone straight before her," they shall
look neither to the right nor to the left. The identity
of "Harmon," the place to which they were to be
taken, is uncertain as no satisfactory explanation for
the term has yet been found.

*4:4-5. The apostate worship is condemned as
in irony the prophet calls upon the people to
multiply their transgressions at Beth-el.*

The voice of the prophet flashes with irony as he   *4:4*
calls upon the people to come to Beth-el and Gilgal,

headquarters for idolatry, and to transgress and multiply transgression in their worship. The bringing of sacrifices every morning and of tithes every three days indicates the extravagant emphasis placed on their religious cult. There was· an abundance of "religion" in the land, but no true piety and devotion to God. It is doubtful if they literally brought tithes every three days, although it is possible. In this charge the prophet sarcastically emphasizes the fact that their sacrifices and tithes were according to their own

4:5 ordering. "And offer by burning [margin, ASV] a sacrifice of thanksgiving of that which is leavened." To burn leaven in sacrifice was contrary to the law (cf. Lev. 2:11; 7:11). However, leavened cakes were to be offered with the sacrifice of peace-offerings and thanksgiving; but these were to be eaten by the priest who made the offering and were not to be burned on the altar (see Lev. 7:13-14). They proclaimed freewill offerings, yet these were not necessarily "freewill," or voluntary, but were forced. These were then "published" or broadcasted. All of this pleased them, but not the Lord. What the Lord saw was the rebellious spirit of a self-willed worship and not the quantity or quality that the worshipers offered.

> *4:6-13. Five chastisements are enumerated which had been sent by Jehovah on the people. But to no avail, for they had refused to be taught. Consequently, "Prepare to meet thy God, O Israel."*

4:6   In time past, God had chastened the people in an effort to bring them to repentance, but the chastisements had gone unheeded. First, He had "given [them] cleanness of teeth" and "want of bread"—

4:7   famine by which their hearts should have turned to Him. But Israel did not turn to God. Second, He had sent drought three months before the time of harvest

4:8   when the fields needed rain most. This meant that the rains of February and March had been withheld. Harvest time came from the last of April to the first of June, depending on the section, south or north. He had caused it to rain in spots, which resulted in the people congregating in one city or another in search of water to drink. But this too failed to turn their hearts to God. A third visitation was sent upon their gardens, fields, and orchards, smiting with blasting and mildew. "Blasting" was done by the scorching east wind, dry and hot, which withered the crops. "Mildew" was a blight that left the grain yellow and fruitless. At times these were followed or accompanied by locusts. This also failed to turn the people back to God. The fourth visitation from Jehovah was pestilence: sudden epidemics or plagues as those that came upon Egypt. This was accompanied by war and the sword. Their horses had been carried away, and those that had been killed had been slain in such quantity that the sickening stench of their decaying bodies filled the nostrils of the people. But all of this was to no avail! The fifth chastisement sent upon the nation is described as the overthrow and burning of cities, as the burning destruction of Sodom and Gomorrah. Some commentators consider this to have been by earthquake (e.g., Deane, Laetsch, Pussey), and others (viz., Keil) consider the ruin to be the result of wars and descriptive of the utter confusion of the people. Amos prophesied two years *before* the earthquake (1:1). If the overthrow of cities be by earthquake, and the earthquake be that of Amos 1:1, this would mean that Amos wrote his prophecies after the earthquake, and included this incident in his book. It is possible that he is referring to other earthquakes that are unknown to us. Earthquakes, accompanied by burnings, seem to be the calamities of which the prophet makes mention, rather than to wars as suggested by Keil. Amos has proceeded from the lesser to the greater visitation of judgment, none of which had accomplished the desired effect.

"Therefore," in the face of the failure of discipline they must "prepare to meet" their God in a more severe judgment. "Thus will I do unto thee" leaves the nation to wonder what must come, for God does not describe what will follow. In charging them to prepare to meet God, the Lord is insinuating that

4:9

4:10

4:11

4:12

there is at hand a final judgment more terrible than the chastisements sent in years gone by. The certainty of judgment is enforced by declaring the omnipotence of God: "He that formeth the mountains," and by appealing to His omniscience: "and declareth unto man what is his thought." Does the next expression continue the thought of God's creative power, or is Amos speaking metaphorically: "that maketh the morning darkness, and treadeth upon the high places of the earth"? It could be either, but more probably the prophet is speaking, as did Joel (2:2), of Jehovah's judgment that brings darkness to the nation's day as He treads upon the high places of earth. The prophecy is strengthened by an appeal to the eternal One who speaks—Jehovah, "the God of hosts," the God of battles.

Chapter 5

5:1-9. Facing the threat of judgment, Amos takes up a lamentation over the nation, followed by an urgent plea that the people "seek Jehovah."

In the next two chapters the prophet stresses the coming judgment. This judgment may yet be averted if they will seek Jehovah; the appeal to seek Jehovah is made twice (vv. 4, 6). However, in the light of their refusal two "woes" are pronounced upon the sinful nation: one was pronounced upon their mistaken concept of the day of Jehovah. They thought to avert any calamity upon themselves through their relation to Him in worship. The second was a denunciation of the revelers in Samaria who have no concern for the afflictions of the people. The revelers will be led away.

5:1   "Hear ye this word" indicates that a new discourse is being introduced. Because of the sin of Israel and the judgment to come, the prophet takes up a lamentation over the nation. A lamentation was a dirge

5:2   expressing extreme grief over death. "The virgin of Israel" does not indicate purity, but that the nation has continued unconquered, not having been cast down. But now that which has not been conquered is cast down. Amos speaks of the nation as already fallen, though the actual fall was several years in the future. "She shall no more rise," for there was none to raise her up. The kingdom would be brought to an end (cf. Amos 9:8; Hosea 1:4), for the judgment would be final. Israel would perish in war by a violent overthrow; only a very small remnant would remain. The cities, whether small or large, would suffer alike.

5:3

"Seek ye me, and ye shall live"—Jehovah offers a way of escape. The judgment could be averted, but it must be on the Lord's terms and not theirs. Escape cannot be found in Beth-el, the center of calf worship, in Gilgal, or in south Judah at Beer-sheba. Therefore, do not seek help in any of these centers; for these were chief cities of idolatry and would come to naught. Beth-el, "house of God," had become Beth-aven, "house of vanity"; and Gilgal, where the reproach had been rolled away (Josh. 4:19; 5:9), had now become a reproach itself; Beer-sheba, the city of patriarchal activity, had become a center of idolatry. Again the Lord calls upon the sinful people to seek Him. This time the call is accompanied by a threat of severe judgment: "lest [Jehovah] break out like fire," and both the house of Joseph, "house of Israel" (v. 1) of which Ephraim was the chief tribe, and Beth-el be devoured. For unless Jehovah turn away there will be none to quench the devastating flame. The prophet charges the ruling class with having turned "justice to wormwood." Justice (judgment, KJV) "used of man refers to right rule, right conduct, or to each getting his due, whether good or bad." (*Baker's Dictionary of Theology*, p. 308). "Wormwood" could be applied to all excessively bitter plants. This means that their justice or judgment, which should have dealt to each his due, had become the bitterest of injustice. "And cast down righteousness to the earth." Righteousness "signifies that which conforms to the norm. . . . [It] is a forensic term meaning judgment." (*Baker's Dictionary of Theology*, p. 461). Their righteousness failed to meet the divine standard

5:4

5:5

5:6

5:7

5:8   in their judgments; it was being cast down to the earth where it was trampled on. The words "justice and righteousness" are often joined by the prophets. For the third time the people are called on to "seek him," Jehovah, by whose power the two clusters of stars, Pleiades and Orion, were created. The Creator of these has power to turn the "shadow of death into the morning, and make the day dark with night." This declares the omnipotent rule of God, who could either turn the threatening judgment of death into a morning of hope, or turn their day into the night of destruction. Whether it would be morning or night was for them to decide. Jehovah's power is further indicated by His control over the immediate forces of nature, for it is He who brings the rain upon the earth. "Jehovah is his name" adds weight to the

5:9   claim. The use of this mighty power is now applied: it is He who "bringeth sudden destruction upon the strong, so that destruction cometh upon the fortress." However strong a nation may think itself to be, Jehovah rules and by His mighty power makes the strength of man appear exceedingly small. Let the nations of today take heed, for the Creator and Ruler of the universe yet controls the destiny of all—nature and nations.

> 5:10-15. The man who would judge fairly is hated by the rulers; therefore, only the corrupt are appointed. In such a state the poor receive no justice.

5:10   The prophet passes from rebuke of their idolatry and its inevitable consequence to reproof of court proceedings. In the ancient cities the seat of judgment was usually located near the entrance gate. The charge "they hate him . . . they abhor" does not refer to the people's feeling for the prophet who spoke in the gate, but refers to the people in power who hated a judge that reproved, or one that spoke uprightly. Judges were men appointed to decide matters of law between their brothers. They were to be located "in the gates": entrances to each city where they would

be easily accessible to the people. In discharging his
duties the judge was not to wrest justice due the
poor, show respect of persons, thereby "slaying the
righteous," or take a bribe. He was to keep himself
innocent of all false matters (Deut. 16:18-20; Exod.
23:6-9). Men of this character who would uphold the
law and reprove sinners were not wanted. Those "in
the gate" are severely criticized for their treatment of
the poor, for their flagrant violation of the law. They   *5:11*
trample the poor underfoot, exacting "gifts" or pay-
ments in wheat or other commodities before they
would hand down a judgment. With these bribes or
rewards they gratified their own sensuous desires by
building extravagant houses and planting pleasant
vineyards, reveling in these ill-gotten luxuries. But
they would not have the satisfaction of enjoying
these, for judgment would carry them away. These
transgressions of divine law and mighty sins of this   *5:12*
legal class were not hid from Jehovah; they were laid
bare before His eyes. Afflicting the just, taking a
bribe and turning away the needy from their rights
can but bring its just recompense of reward.

Because of the prevailing moral corruption, Amos   *5:13*
seems to sense the futility of going on with his
preaching or warning. "Therefore"—in the light of
such conditions—a prudent man, a wise man, will
refrain from speaking. But the prophet has a divine
commission and, like Isaiah, is to speak "until cities
be waste without inhabitant, and houses without
man, and the land become utterly waste, and Jehovah
have removed men far away, and the forsaken places
be many in the midst of the land" (Isa. 6:11-12).
Therefore he must speak on, for there is no place to
stop. Once more the earnest appeal is made to   *5:14*
"seek"; this time the exhortation is to "seek good,
and not evil." They had done the opposite, seeking
evil and not good; the reversal of their conduct is the
only hope of escape. "As ye say": they made un-
founded claims of Jehovah's being with them which
would not stand. The people were putting their trust
in the false confidence that they were the people of
God and that therefore He would not allow such   *5:15*

judgments to come upon them. There are two sides to the coin: while seeking the good (v. 13), they must also "hate the evil, and love the good, and establish justice in the gate." With the same intensity that one loves the good, he will hate the evil. They must demonstrate this quality of character by establishing justice in the gate instead of the injustice condemned above. When this is done, it may be that Jehovah will be gracious to "the remnant of Joseph." Two points are emphasized: "it may be," indicating that the cup of Ephraim's iniquity was so full that the nation may be beyond the point of no return; second, "the remnant of Joseph" suggests that if mercy is shown, it will be only a remnant that is spared.

> *5:16-20. For such wickedness God must punish the nation. Wailing will be heard on every hand, for "woe" to them when the day of the Lord comes.*

5:16   "Therefore" introduces another conclusion about to be revealed. The seriousness of what is to be said is indicated by the title of the Lord used by Amos: "Jehovah, the God of hosts, the Lord." "Jehovah" is His personal name; "the God of hosts" points to His rule in the affairs of judgment as He leads the armies in battle; and "the Lord" indicates His sovereign rule. It is this majestic One who now speaks. In the country and in the city, on the broad highways and in the narrow paths, mourning for the dead is heard. "Alas! alas!" is a cry of despair, the death wail. The "husbandman," the farmer or man of the soil, together with the skillful or professional mourner, alike will be

5:17   wailing and mourning over the death and destruction seen on every hand. In the vineyards, usually associated with rejoicing and thanksgiving, the same mournful sound would be heard. Instead of "passing over" as Jehovah had done in Egypt when He called His people out of bondage, He would "pass through" the midst of them as the destroyer.

5:18   Two woes are introduced, 5:18 and 6:1. The first is "woe unto you that desire the day of Jehovah!"

The people yearned for "the day of Jehovah," but why? It would not be as Israel thought, a day of darkness and judgment on their enemies and of blessing on themselves. But it would be a day of judgment and terror, of darkness and night, on their own ungodly nation. The prophet uses a figure of speech familiar to both him and those he addressed as he vividly pictures their effort to escape. A man flees from a lion and is met by a bear; he flees from the bear, and reaching the house he breathlessly leans against a wall to be bitten by a serpent. So it would be to the house of Israel. They would flee from one terror to be met by another until at last death strikes home. Amos continues the figure of the darkness of night: the day of Jehovah would be to them a day of extreme darkness with no light or brightness at all, and with no possibility of escape.

5:19

5:20

5:21-27. *The emptiness of Israel's worship is again condemned. The nation is charged with having never been completely faithful to God.*

Amos returns to the emptiness of their worship, which to Jehovah was an abomination. The language is strong: "I hate, I despise your feasts," your outward formal worship. That which should have been a delight to the Lord was now an abomination to Him which He could not accept. "Your solemn assemblies" were the great annual festivals or convocations. He includes and rejects all phases of their ritual—the feasts, solemn assemblies, burnt-offerings, meal-offerings, and peace-offerings. It is not to be inferred from this that God had not ordained these, for He had. But the people had so corrupted the worship by their departure from the law and by their introduction of idols that Jehovah could not and would not accept their offerings. Their music had become nothing more than "noise" in the ears of the Lord. The "viols" were a kind of harp (described by Josephus as having twelve strings and played by the fingers) played without true devotion from the heart; songs accompanied by the viol were empty. Instru-

5:21

5:22

5:23

5:24

mental music, which had been introduced by David with the sanction of Jehovah (II Chron. 29:25), had now been desecrated by idolatry. God wants not the empty songs and music of apostate children; He wants justice, which has to do with the rights of others, and righteousness, the will to do right in oneself. In this plea Amos rises to the lofty height of one of Scripture's most majestic utterances. As the prophet says, "Let justice roll down as waters, and righteousness as a mighty stream," one can envision a beautiful mountain stream as it rolls and tumbles, cascading toward the thirsty plain below, becoming a mighty, rolling river in its march.

5:25

At this juncture God points back to the experience of the fathers in the wilderness. He would have Israel know that even from the time of the wilderness wandering, to an extent, they had been essentially idolaters. The implied answer to the question, "Did ye bring unto me sacrifices, etc.," is "No, for your worship was mingled with idolatry even then." The following verse is admitted by all commentators to be difficult. The most probable thought is suggested by Keil: "The king whose booth, and the images whose stand they carried, were a star which they had made their god, i.e., a star-deity. . . . The booth and the stand were the things used for protecting and carrying the images of the star-deity" (p. 292). He concludes, "The prophet therefore affirms that, during the forty years' journey through the wilderness, Israel did not offer sacrifices to its true King Jehovah, but carried about with it a star made into a god as the king of heaven" (p. 296). This could not be said of all individuals, for there were at all times some who were faithful to the Lord. But in Egypt the seed of idolatry had been sown and it was carried with them through the wilderness, to bear its full fruit in the land to which they had been led. "Therefore": another determination is revealed: they would be carried "into captivity beyond Damascus." The judgment is again pointed out to be from Jehovah, the God of hosts; "beyond Damascus" indicates Assyria as the place of

5:26

5:27

their captivity, though the prophet never names that country specifically.

Chapter 6

6:1-6. A second woe is announced, this time against the revelers in Samaria. Their luxurious feasts are described and condemned.

By now false worship had produced the fruit of debauched character and false standards of conduct. The second "woe" is pronounced upon the revelers who felt secure in their mountain-surrounded city and in their perverted idea of God and their relation to Him. The prophet includes those "at ease in Zion," Jerusalem, as well as those "secure in . . . Samaria." The rulers of both cities were guilty of a false sense of ease and security. Neither realized the imminence of danger. "The notable men of the chief of the nations" were the rulers and nobles of Israel, which was in God's sight the chief of all nations because it was His. To these rulers the house of Israel came for judgment and leadership. But woe to them! They are no longer worthy of such honor. The people of Israel are urged to consider three strong cities, Calneh and Hamath to the north and Gath to the south, and are asked the question, Have these been blessed more than Israel and Judah? Hamath was north of Jerusalem and Samaria on the Orontes River, approximately seventy miles south of Antioch. The location of Calneh is uncertain. Older scholars located it in Babylon or Assyria, but more recent scholars locate it just north of Hamath. Gath had been one of the five chief cities of the Philistines, taken by Uzziah some time earlier. Calneh and Hamath were destined to suffer at the hands of the Assyrian power, if they had not already suffered. "Are they [Calneh, Hamath, and Gath] better than these kingdoms [Israel and Judah]?" Have they received greater blessings and larger borders than have you? The implied answer is No. If, in their strength, they fell, can Samaria expect

6:1

6:2

6:3   anything better unless she proves herself better? Because of this false sense of security the people had
put the day of accounting far into the future. They
had caused the "sitting" (margin, ASV), or the "seat

6:4   of violence," to come near. They had enthroned
violence in their midst, and there it ruled. Their
luxury and revelry are revealed in their lying on ivory
inlaid beds, lolling on couches, banqueting on the

6:5   best of fatted lambs and calves, having their depraved
spirits lulled and soothed by lascivious songs and

6:6   music, drinking their wine from large sacrificial
bowls, and anointing themselves with the choicest of
fine oils. But their debauched spirits were "not
grieved for the affliction of Joseph," the poor of their
brethren. The coming ruin of the nation, as it was
being heralded by the rising power of the conquering
Assyrians and by the warnings of Amos, struck no
responsive chord in their hearts that were satiated by
revelry and carousing. The inventing of "instruments
of music" "like [those of] David" did not refer to
the instruments used in worship; nor can this passage
be used as an argument against the use of such instruments in worship today as is done by Adam Clarke.
They invented musical instruments to be used in the
sordid revelry of their feasts and banquets of that
day.

> 6:7-14. *Jehovah swears by Himself that the
> revelers must go. He declares His hatred for
> that of which Israel boasted. A nation will be
> raised against the people to execute the
> Lord's judgment.*

6:7   "Therefore shall they"—the revelers described
above—"now go captive with the first that go captive": they will be at the head of the line of captives.
Then will the noise of their songs and music and their

6:8   boisterous merriment be at an end. All will be subdued and somber. Again the Lord swears by Himself,
the God of battles, declaring His feeling against the
palaces and cities of His rebellious and corrupted
people. As He had despised their worship (5:21), so

does He now "abhor the excellency of Jacob," that
of which Jacob is proud; and He hates his palaces, of
which he has made a vainglorious display. Jehovah $6:9$
will deliver up both city and people to destruction.
Every household will become extinct; though there
be "ten," a full and complete number, "they shall
die." If any escape the sword, they will die of famine
or in the captivity. The complete desolation and $6:10$
despair of the people that remain is described in the
statement that the "uncle," near kinsman, must burn
the bodies instead of burying them. The cemetery of
a city was usually located outside the city and therefore could not be reached in time of such calamity.
This necessitated the burning of the bodies, a custom
not commonly practiced by the Jews. Inasmuch as
they had rejected Jehovah and He had brought upon
them this great distress, the response from within
would be, "Hold thy peace; for we may not make
mention of the name of Jehovah." The answer was
prompted either by a feeling of complete despair,
indicating that they had failed their opportunity and
now there is no need to call on Jehovah (Pusey), or
by fear that if His name was mentioned He would
find them and His wrath would fall on them (Keil). It
is uncertain exactly which of these two meanings is
correct. The destruction is of Jehovah; it is at His $6:11$
command that the houses are smitten and the breaches made. There is no cause to believe that judgments
of this nature are not of Jehovah even today.

Men may call their sins by whatever softening $6:12$
terms they choose, but the end of sin against God is
disaster. Will horses run over rocks without exposing
themselves to the danger of stumbling, or of becoming "tender-footed"? Do men plow there with their
oxen? The answer to both is No. To act in such
manner would be sheer stupidity. It is equally as
stupid and contrary to nature and its consequences to
act as the people of Israel had in turning justice into
gall and the fruit of righteousness into wormwood,
and in having turned from God to dumb idols. They
had with equal imbecility thought they could take $6:13$
things into their own hands and make themselves

6:14   horns of power by their own strength. The prophet
closes this section of his preaching, pleas, and threats
with one more warning: Jehovah will bring against
them a nation that would afflict them from Hamath,
their northernmost boundary, to the Arabah, the
southernmost boundary. The Arabah is a gorge or
valley south of the Dead Sea, extending to the Gulf
of Aqabah. To reject Jehovah is to invite inevitable
destruction.

Chapter 7

*7:1-9. A new section is introduced. Amos is
shown a series of visions. The execution of
the threat of the first two is averted by the
prophet's intercession.*

7:1   The declaration of Israel's sins and of their punishment is followed by five visions and their interpretation shown to the prophet by the Lord. "Thus the
Lord Jehovah showed me." The vision therefore was
no inner feeling on the prophet's part, but it was a
revelation from God by His Spirit. The vision portrayed locusts formed by the Lord for judgment. This
probably was not a literal locust invasion as in Joel,
but was symbolic of threatened destruction. The time
was the beginning of the latter growth of the grass
after the king's mowing. There is no indication in
Scripture of a practice where the king takes the first
mowing for the horses and mules of his army, though
such may have been the practice. If this was the case,
7:2   there would have been nothing left for the cattle that
belonged to the people. In the vision, when the locusts had finished eating the grass, a complete devastation of the land is averted by the intercession of the
prophet. He prays for the forgiveness of the people
and pleads for them on the basis that Jacob is small
7:3   when compared to the power of Jehovah. Jehovah
heard and gave heed to the prayer of the prophet;
destruction was averted for the time. Probably the
lesson intended was that thus far Israel's destruction

had been averted by the intercession of Jehovah's
righteous prophets and by the prayers of others who
may have been among the righteous.   7:4

The first vision is followed by a second vision—a
great fire that devoured the Great Sea and threatened
to devour the land. The devouring of "the great
deep" was a symbol of total destruction by the fire of
Jehovah, and "would have eaten up the land" indicated the threatened destruction of Israel. Again
calamity is averted and the people are saved by the   7:5
intercession of the prophet. The appeal is on the same
ground and with the same result: Jehovah repented,   7:6
changed His will, and spared them. "This also shall
not be, saith the Lord Jehovah." Again, the power of
the intercessory prayers of the righteous is clearly
demonstrated and cannot be overstressed in any age.

The third vision is that of Jehovah standing by or   7:7
on a wall with a plumb line in His hand. The plumb
line, with a plumb bob on the end, is used to determine the vertical perfection of a wall. Another line
may be stretched horizontally with the base to deter-   7:8
mine its straightness. Israel had been formed by the
plumb line of the Lord, His law, and the principles of
right by which He had sought to build the nation.
Now, with a plumb line in His hand, He is going to
show how far out of line the nation is, how far it is
from being upright, and how completely crooked and
unbalanced it has become. This time there was no
need for the prophet to pray, for Jehovah would not
"pass by them any more." But as He had said earlier,
He would "pass through" them (5:17). "The high   7:9
places of Isaac" and "the sanctuaries of Israel" are
used synonymously. This double expression was to
emphasize the certainty of the destruction that was
to come on their places of worship. Also, God would
bring the sword of destruction on the ruling family of
Jeroboam. Because his father Jehu had not followed
Jehovah but had followed in the sins of Jeroboam I,
Jehovah had said that his descendants would reign to
the fourth generation of sons (II Kings 10:30). After
the death of Jeroboam, his son Zechariah—the fourth

generation—served six months and was slain (II Kings 15:12). This fulfilled the promise of Jehovah and brought to an end the dynasty of Jehu.

7:10-17. Amaziah, the priest of Beth-el, warns Jeroboam of Amos' danger to the royal sanctuary, and interrupts Amos, urging him to return to Judah. Amos' classic response is that his mission and message are from Jehovah.

7:10   With this threat against the house of Jeroboam, Amaziah the priest of Beth-el came into action. He sought to show strong loyalty to the king by sending word to Jeroboam that Amos had conspired against

7:11   him in the midst of the people; his words upset the status quo. Amaziah did not misrepresent the proph-

7:12   et, for Amos had said these things reported by Amaziah. The priest seems also to have been deeply concerned for his own position and that of the national shrine of worship. For though he urged Amos for his own good to flee to the land of Judah and "eat bread, and prophesy there," it is doubtful if he was concerned with the prophet's welfare. The expression ". . . and eat bread" insinuates that Amos was prophesying for hire; therefore, like many of his day, he was a hireling-prophet or seer. "Seer" was another word used in earlier days for "prophet" (I Sam. 9:9), inferring that he saw visions or that he had insight

7:13   into the unseen. Beth-el was not the place for Amos to prophesy, for it was "the king's sanctuary, and . . . a royal house." In this he spoke truly, for it was not Jehovah's; it had been founded by Jeroboam I and was human to the core. But it was here that the true prophet of God needed to be, prophesying in the very heart of apostasy.

7:14   This charge from Amaziah, the priest of the false worship at Beth-el, brought from the prophet a retort of indignation worthy of his noble calling. Amos soared to another pinnacle of true greatness as he replied to the priest of falsehood. He had never been a prophet prior to his call to go to Beth-el, nor was he of the school of the prophets. His occupation had been that of a herdsman and a dresser of sycomore trees. (See Introduction for a discussion of the syco- more.) Consider the prophet's appeal to Jehovah as the source of his mission and message. It was Jehovah who had called him; it was Jehovah who had said, "Go, prophesy unto my people Israel." "Therefore hear the word of Jehovah." The priest had insulted the Lord by saying to Amos, "Prophesy not against Israel, and drop not thy word against the house of Isaac." "Israel" and "the house of Isaac" are used synonymously. The prophet makes a final appeal to the source of his authority, "Therefore thus saith Jehovah." His mission was not of his own choosing, nor was his message that of his own wisdom; it was of Jehovah. Before his death Amaziah would see his own wife plying the trade of a harlot, his sons and daugh- ters fall by the sword, and his land divided. He would die in an unclean land; and Israel, the people whom he had sought to shield from the words of Amos, would be led captive out of their beloved land. This reply of the herdsman of Tekoa to the sophisticated but servile priest of Beth-el has since that day warmed and thrilled the hearts of all who have loved God, and who have stood for the things that originate from Him.

7:15

7:16

7:17

Chapter 8

8:1-10. The fourth vision: a basket of summer fruit, which the prophet interprets. The wicked practices of the merchants are ex- posed and condemned. The nation's sun shall go down at noon. The end is near.

After the interruption of his preaching by Amaziah, the prophet sees another vision. "The Lord Jehovah showed me: and, behold, a basket of summer fruit." Summer fruit indicates ripeness. Under this symbol Jehovah shows the prophet that the harvest is past and that the nation is ripe for destruction. The end is come upon the people. Jehovah repeats the threat of the third vision (7:8), "I will not again pass

8:1

8:2

by them any more." He will "pass through them," but not "by them" (cf. 5:17). "The songs of the temple [palaces, marginal note, A.S.V.] shall be wailings in that day." If "palace" be correct, then God is referring to the songs of the revelers (6:6) which are now become mournful songs of pain and grief. Instead of the joy of harvest, another harvest would have come. Dead bodies will be in every place and will be cast forth with silence, for there will be neither time nor place to bury them. What a tragic end to a great people who had been the chosen of Jehovah!

8:3

8:4 The prophet points out and condemns practices which further reveal that the nation was ripe for destruction. In the beginning of his preaching the prophet had introduced their sin of swallowing up the needy and oppressing the poor and had shown that Jehovah would "not turn away the punishment" from these (2:6-7). In their greediness, though they desisted from doing business on the new-moons and the sabbaths, they longed for the special religious day to end that they might return to their corrupt business practices. Their "religion" was pure hypocrisy. These practices consisted of "making the ephah small," short-selling the people by using measures smaller than standard, and "making the shekel great," overcharging them. And together with their fraudulent practices they also used false balances, dishonest scales. By following such false ethics and tactics they were so impoverishing the poor that they were being forced to sell themselves to these unscrupulous traders for very small sums. In return for all this the poor received only the "refuse of the wheat," that which was of inferior quality and unfit for human food. "The excellency of Jacob," by which Jehovah swore, was Jehovah Himself. As He had sworn "by his holiness" (4:2) and "by himself"—that is, by His life (6:8)—so now He swears "by the excellency of Jacob," by that which He should have meant to Jacob and the esteem in which He should have been held by him. He would not forget their works; the sins of the nation must be punished. Jehovah would

8:5

8:6

8:7

not be true to Himself and to His infinitely holy
character were He to pass over or ignore their iniquities and transgressions. In consequence of the oath,   *8:8*
"Shall not the land tremble for this?"—the punishment of their sins will be such as to cause the earth to
tremble and its inhabitants to mourn. Following his
use of the figure of an earthquake, "making the land
to tremble," the prophet uses a second simile of a
river heaving and overflowing the land and subsiding
as the Nile in times of flood and of receding. The
adversary would cover the land as a great flood (cf.
Isa. 8:7 ff.). The third figure used to indicate the end   *8:9*
is an eclipse. "I will cause the sun to go down at
noon, and I will darken the earth in the clear day."
As the sun is swallowed and the earth darkened in an
eclipse, so Israel's sun will go down at noon. At the
very meridian of what should have been her "golden
age" and when she should have been at the peak of
her glory, Israel's day would come to an end. The
earth would be darkened in the clear day as Jehovah
enshrouded it with the black mantle of His judgment.   *8:10*
Again the gloom of that day is predicted as the
prophet declares that the feasts will be turned into
mourning and their songs into a wailing lamentation
as for the dead. With sackcloth upon the loins and
baldness upon the head, each self-imposed as a sign of
deep grief, they would mourn as for an only son; and
the Lord would make the end of their history as a
bitter day. This is a terribly black picture, but one
painted by divine brush and palette from oils and
pigments provided by the people themselves. How
sorely do nations of today need to get the message of
Amos!

> *8:11-14. A famine of the word of God is
> predicted. They had rejected the message, but
> the day will come when they will seek it.*

Added to the extreme terribleness of the judgment   *8:11*
described is a famine of the word of God. As they
had now rejected and trampled underfoot His word,
in the hopelessness of their future condition God will

not respond to their cry for a message from Him.

8:12 Though they would seek for it, they will be unable to find it. "They shall wander from sea to sea," from one extremity of the earth to the other. "From the north even to the east" would they seek for it, but they would be left to stumble in their own self-

8:13 created darkness. The young maidens and the young men would faint for thirst: not for waters of the well-springs of Israel, but for the refreshing and heal-

8:14 ing water of God's word. Without it they would die. The cause of all this was their idolatry! "They that swear by" the calves of Beth-el and Dan will fall, "never [to] rise up again." Beer-sheba in southern Judah, the ancient home of the patriarch Abraham, had become a shrine to idolatry, to which some in Israel made pilgrimages, and is also included in the condemnation. All who look to these idol deities and swear by them as gods will be forever cast down. One of the great lessons of the prophets and of history is that back of a nation's decay in moral, social, and political life there is first a decay in its religious life. Doctrinal decay leads inevitably to decay in all phases of life. This principle was declared when the psalmist said, "The wicked shall be turned back unto Sheol, even all the nations that forget God" (Ps. 9:17).

Chapter 9

9:1-4. The fifth and final vision is shown to Amos. The house of Israel will crash about his own head. The people cannot hide from Jehovah, but will be sought out and punished.

9:1 The Lord reveals to His prophet the last of the five visions. This time the Lord does not ask, "What do you see?" for the prophet sees the people buried beneath the ruins of the house they had built upon the sands of falsehood and lies. Amos saw the Lord, the ruling One of all creation, standing beside the altar. But what altar is intended—the one at Beth-el erected by Jeroboam I (I Kings 12) or the altar of Jehovah at Jerusalem? Scholars are divided in their views. At first reading one would conclude that it is the altar at Beth-el; this seems to be supported by the context. But the fact that there were many altars at Beth-el, not just one (3:14), and that Jehovah roared "from Zion" and uttered His voice "from Jerusalem" (1:2), has, in the minds of many, indicated that the altar was more probably at Jerusalem. Whether one concludes that it is Beth-el or Jerusalem, the point is that at the command of the Lord the house of Beth-el is smitten from the top, the capital crumbling and crashing on the heads of the people. The "capital" is the uppermost member of a column or pilaster and crowns the shaft. The "threshold" is the timber or stone that lies under the door, the sill of the door. The smiting would result in destruction "from top to bottom." None would escape; all will have become victims of their own folly. But the judgment is of Jehovah. The prophet now uses a strong hyperbole to emphasize his point. Though they dig to the lowest depths, even into Sheol, the unseen, or ascend to the highest heights, even to heaven, Jehovah would bring them to judgment. They could not hide on the top of rugged and wooded Carmel or find escape in the bottom of the deepest sea; for even there God would command the serpent, His sea-slayer, to bite them. At the same time those carried into captivity could not escape, for there the sword would slay them. There was no escaping the searching eye of God. If this seems to put God in a bad light in the eyes of an effeminate generation, let all realize that here is a people who had enjoyed the manifold favors of God and had received His word, His love, and His chastisements, but all to no avail. Corruption had mounted upon corruption, and iniquity upon iniquity. Now there was nothing remaining but judgment commensurate with the infinite holiness of God and the heinous sins of the people.

9:2

9:3

9:4

9:5-10. The people will be swept away; the kingdom will be brought to an end. However, the righteous, if there are such, will not fall.

The threat of destruction is confirmed by an appeal to the omnipotence of God: "the Lord, Jehovah

9:5

of hosts," has spoken. The figure is vivid; this "Lord, Jehovah of hosts," touches the land and it melts before Him; and all that are there mourn at the great distress. Like the Nile of Egypt (cf. 8:8) that rises and falls, so the land is pictured as tossing about like an

9:6   upheaval of mighty waters. Such an upheaval is determined by the Lord, whose habitation is in the heaven and who stores the waters in the chambers of His firmament to be poured upon the face of the world of ungodly men when, in His own counsel, that time has come.

9:7   The children of Israel, God's chosen people, were now become to Him as the Ethiopians! Israel is no more to me, says the Lord, than the far-distant heathen nation of Ethiopia. Lest the people would boast that God would not act toward them in an evil way, the Lord points out that, although it was He who brought them up out of Egypt, it was also He who had brought the Philistines from Caphtor, the isle of Crete, and the Syrians from Kir (the location of which is unknown). It is He who directs all the nations, who builds them up and casts them down.

9:8   One of the prophet's strongest statements is now made, "The eyes of the Lord Jehovah are upon the sinful kingdom," which He finds to be no better than the Ethiopians or the Philistines or the Syrians. "And I will destroy it from off the face of the earth." Here is a plain and positive declaration of Jehovah that the kingdom of Israel would be destroyed, cease to exist, and be brought to an end. And if it is destroyed from off the face of the earth, it could never again be restored. However, as a people the house of Jacob would not be destroyed. This fact is attested to by Jehovah through Jeremiah, "I will make a full end of all the nations whither I have scattered thee, but I will not make a full end of thee" (30:11; 46:28). Israel, the nation, has long since ceased; but the Jews

9:9   as a people have ever continued. The people were to be sifted and scattered among the nations; yet not a

9:10 kernel, the good element, would fall, but only the chaff would be consumed. The prophet now makes clear what he meant by the sifting and the kernels:

"All the sinners of my people shall die by the sword" refers to those who have had a mistaken idea of God and of their sin and who had said, "The evil shall not overtake nor meet us." Their blindness had led them into the pit of destruction.

> *9:11-15. From the crash and ruin of the kingdom the prophet looks to the glorious future under the Messiah. Spiritual promises fill his closing word.*

To this point the prophet has painted an exceedingly dark picture, as of a world enshrouded in a cloud of blackness and of hopelessness, with scarcely a ray of light breaking through. But as is characteristic of the prophets who prophesied of Israel and Judah to give hope in the midst of disaster, so also the Book of Amos contains a ray of hope as it closes with an optimistic promise of future glory. These verses are like a beam of sunlight streaming through an opening in the dark clouds of a storm, as Amos looks beyond his time to a brighter day under a descendant of the house of David. "In that day," the day of the scattered people and the destroyed kingdom, when the blackness of despair has taken hold of them, Jehovah would "raise up the tabernacle of David that is fallen." The "tabernacle of David" was the house or tent of David, the rule of David's house which will have long since fallen into decay, or have become a mere "hut." The rule of David's house had ended for Israel when they left the theocracy; it ended for Judah with the carrying away of Coniah into Babylon (Jer. 22:24-30). It would be built "as in the days of old," as when David ruled over the combined houses of Judah and Israel. "That they may possess the remnant of Edom, and all the nations that are called by my name": Edom had been brought under subjection to the kingdom by David (II Sam. 8:14; I Chron. 18:13), but later Edom had revolted under the reign of Jehoram (II Chron. 21:8-10). Although the people of Edom were related to Israel, they were Israel's bitterest enemies. These

9:11

9:12

were to have the name of Jehovah called on them and thereby become the possession of the new David. This declaration of the prophet is clearly Messianic, to be fulfilled under the Christ. This is confirmed by James's use of it at the council in Jerusalem, to justify the bringing in of the Gentiles by the gospel (Acts 15:14-18). For further confirmation of this, see Luke 1:67-79 and Acts 3:18, 21, 24-27. The prophecy looked to the present dispensation or era, and not to a future millennial reign of Christ on earth.

9:13   In the Messianic period the fulness of spiritual blessings would be enjoyed by those under the Messiah. Planting and harvest would overtake one another, therefore continue simultaneous one with the other. The joy of a constant fulness, as the hills drop sweet wine, is indicated (cf. Joel 3:18-21; John 9:14   4:36 ff.). The misery which the people have suffered will be repaired; the blessings will compensate for the punishments inflicted. The passage is metaphorical, the fulfillment of which is not to be looked for 9:15   literally but spiritually. "They shall no more be plucked up out of their land which I have given them," which land is not that of Canaan, but the "fatherland" under the Messiah. Under Him the citizenship or homeland of the new Israel is "in heaven" (Phil. 3:20); His dominion is "from sea to sea, and from the river to the ends of the earth" (Zech. 9:10). The kingdom of the prophets has now been received, one that cannot be shaken (Heb. 12:28). The entire passage, verses 11-15, is Messianic and has been fulfilled under Christ.

5
HOSEA
"Salvation"

General Observations

1. The Man

a. Name. The prophet's name indicates "salvation," "deliverance," or "help." Hoshea (salvation) was the name of Israel's great military leader and successor to Moses before his name was changed to Joshua (salvation is of Jehovah) (Num. 13:8, 16).

b. Home. From his sympathetic understanding of the people it is generally thought that Hosea was a native of the north, possibly of Samaria. Nothing, however, is said of his early life or his native home. He speaks as a native and not as an outsider. His keen insight into the religious, social, and political conditions of his day indicates that he knew in an intimate way the things of which he spoke. His tender love for Israel argues for his being a citizen of the nation whom he addressed.

c. Occupation. Of this nothing is known with certainty. Because of his high estimation of the duties and responsibilities of the priesthood and his insinuation that they were largely responsible for the morals of the people, some have concluded that he was of the priestly order. Hosea recognized the important position of the priests, but because they were derelict in their duty he charged them with having con-

127

tributed greatly to the decay in national morals. All that can be concluded is that he occupied some position or place of distinction, but it is not revealed whether it was the priesthood or some other occupation.

d. **Marriage.** Hosea was directed to marry "a woman of whoredom"; that is, a daughter of the age, one brought up under the influence of idolatry and in whose character would have been planted the seeds of immorality. She was not unchaste at the time of the marriage but was a maiden of such background that in later conduct the fruit of idolatry was fully borne. Out of his experience with Gomer, Hosea came to understand as none other could the feeling of Jehovah for Israel. The real key to the book is the parallel between Hosea's experience with Gomer and Jehovah's experience with Israel. This experience "puts back of his words a bleeding heart, and this gives to them a new power" (Knudson, *Beacon Lights of Prophecy*, p. 85). To the question of why God would place this heavy burden on anyone, "reply may be made that it appears to be a universal law of this sin-stricken world that God makes perfect through suffering; that redemption is wrought through sacrifice" (Eiselen). Through his own broken heart over the conduct of Gomer and the realization that his children were actually not his own, Hosea could see God and Israel through tear-dimmed eyes and a broken heart in an experience not unlike that of the Lord.

e. **Characterization of Hosea and Amos.** Two men could hardly have been more different. Amos was a man of stern character who saw Jehovah as the God of justice and whose background set him apart from the world of men of his day. Hosea was one of keen sympathy, whose message was filled with "lovingkindness." He had a deeply emotional nature, a nature which by instinct could enter into the lives of others. However, there is in Hosea a conflict of feelings. Along with his sympathy there was a keen sense of righteous indignation at sin; and while pleading with the people to turn away from sin, he could at the same time see the justice of God's righteous judgment. Amos points out the stern justice of divine judgment; Hosea gives emphasis to the love that demanded such a judgment. Yet in the face of strong individual differences, the two men had much in common. Each held an exalted view of Jehovah; each saw Israel as God's people; each realized that punishment and destruction of the nation were inevitable.

2. Date

Hosea prophesied during the reign of Jeroboam II, apparently after Amos and probably about 750 B.C. Some place the period of his preaching between 750-725 B.C. However, there are others who think Hosea could not have prophesied as late as 725 B.C. because of certain historical events he does not mention or consider, such as the invasion by the Assyrians. A safe date would be from 750 B.C. until some years later. For a fuller discussion of the date one may consult various Introductions. The date suggested above fits into the content of the book, and is the one most generally held.

3. Background

a. **Religious.** By this time the excesses in religion and government had become more marked than in the time of Amos. Hosea summed up the indictments against Israel in the one word "whoredom." Israel had done worse than adultery; as a harlot she had prostituted herself before the baalim of the land for hire (2:12-13). The people were without knowledge (4:6; 5:4), and as a result they were ignorant of God and His laws (8:12). Nominally they paid homage to Jehovah, but in reality they honored the baalim. This sin brought Hosea's most severe rebukes (4:11-13; 8:4; 9:10; 10:1-3; 13:1, 2). The people were victims of two systems of false religion: the calf worship introduced by Jeroboam I, and Baal worship stressed by Ahab and Jezebel. Each was completely foreign to the revealed religion of the Lord Jehovah. Each was the fruit of apostasy.

b. **Moral.** Their conduct was the very opposite to that which God desired and demanded. The people were guilty of swearing, breaking faith, murder, stealing, committing adultery, deceit, lying, drunkenness, dishonesty in business, and other crimes equally abominable before Jehovah (4:2, 11, 12, 18; 6:8-9; 10:4; 13:1-2; etc.). The picture painted in the Book of Hosea is truly that of a nation in decay.

c. **Political.** The period of Hosea's prophesying was one of political upheaval in Israel. Upon the death of Jeroboam, his son Zechariah reigned for only six months, being unable to maintain his throne for a longer period. He was slain by Shallum, who reigned in his stead (II Kings 15:8-12). Shallum reigned for only one month, and was slain by Menahem, who assumed the throne and ruled for ten years (II Kings 15:13 ff.). During the reign of Menahem, Tiglath-pileser (Pul), king of Assyria, came up against Israel and exacted heavy tribute from the nation. At the death of Menahem, Pekahiah, his son, succeeded him (II Kings 15:17-22). Pekahiah reigned two years and was slain in Samaria by a conspiring captain, Pekah. During the reign of Pekah, Tiglath-pileser (who reigned over Assyria from 745 to 727 B.C.) began his conquest of northern Israel (II Kings 15:29). During the reign of King Ahaz in Judah, Pekah, king of Israel, and Rezin, king of Syria, conspired against Judah because Ahaz would not join them in an alliance against Tiglath-pileser (II Kings 16:1-9; Isa. 7). Hoshea, who became the last king of Israel, conspired against Pekah and slew him (II Kings 15:30). Hoshea also conspired against Shalmaneser, king of Assyria, by sending messengers to Egypt for help. Shalmaneser then lay siege against Israel, carrying away many of the people into Assyria as captives (II Kings 17:1-6). Shalmaneser died during the siege of Samaria (722 B.C.), and was succeeded by Sargon, who completed the siege. The city fell to Assyria in 721 B.C. This brief summary of the declining years of Israel will help one to understand better the political situation found by Hosea as he prophesied the doom of his nation and its people. These were trying years of political conniving and intrigue, of anarchy and rebellion, of treachery and murder. God was completely left out of the people's thinking. The prophet's task was to turn the thinking of the people back to God, but they were too deeply steeped in their idolatry to heed his warning. They had passed the point of no return; they refused to hear.

Their faithlessness was manifested in a twofold manner: (1) in rebellion against all constituted authority, a rebellion demonstrated in the assassination of various kings and princes (7:1-7; 8:4; 13:10); and (2) in their dependence upon human defenses and foreign alliances, rather than upon the power of Jehovah (5:13; 7:11-13; 10:13; 14:3; etc.). For this they would go into captivity. But compare 7:16; 8:13; 11:5. The cause for this widespread immorality and faithlessness toward Jehovah has been summarized as twofold: (1) the corruption of the priests, with whom the false prophets were in league; and (2) the corruption of worship (Farrar). Calf worship and baal worship were bearing a full harvest.

4. Message

a. **Hosea's message emphasizes the righteousness of Jehovah: God is love.** This great principle is emphasized throughout his prophecy. A favorite expression of the prophet is "lovingkindness." He has been called the prophet of love (Knudson), as well as the prophet of the broken heart (Sampey). God loved His people, and time upon time He had demonstrated this love. Love is the mainspring of God's actions. Hosea had come to grasp this aspect of the character of the divine Father which motivated Him in His actions toward His wayward children. Hosea expressed it as none before him had done.

b. **The doom of the nation is inevitable.** Although his message is that of the righteousness of Jehovah, it is also a message of the doom of Israel. Hosea stressed the imminence of danger and divine judgment. Hosea's appeal to the threat of this danger was intended to arouse the nation to a religious consciousness. "A religion which makes no appeal to the sense of danger has no edge to it. It has no power to grip the basal impulses of life. It is simply a meaningless sentiment, a worthless survival of some vital religious movement of the past." (Knudson, p. 109). "I will cause the kingdom of the house of Israel to cease" (1:4) was Jehovah's threat of doom to the nation in spiritual and moral dissolution.

5. The Teaching of Hosea (Frederick Carl Eiselen, *Prophecy and the Prophets,* pp. 66-68, a summary)

a. **Jehovah, His nature and character.** The prophet considers a lack of the knowledge of Jehovah responsible for the corruptions of Israel, and knowledge of Him fundamental to her well-being. (1) Monotheism. There is but *one* God, and that God is Jehovah (2:5 ff.; 8:4 ff.; 13:2; 14:3). (2) Omnipotence. Although the passages are not so numerous as in

Amos, the prophet assumes that all power belongs to Him. (3) Righteousness. At this point Hosea parallels Amos, showing that God will always punish sin, even in Israel. Righteousness alone can win His favor (8:13; 9:9). (4) Love—God is love. This perhaps is the distinguishing element in Hosea's conception of Jehovah. Jehovah is pictured as both a loving husband to his bride and a loving father to his child. In one, He tries to save a fallen wife; in the other, He tries to restore a wayward son.

b. The covenant between Jehovah and Israel. (1) From the beginning to the end Hosea sees Israel as the chosen of God, His peculiar people by His own choice. The union was cemented by the national covenant from the beginning of the nation's history (8:12; 9:10; 11:1-4; 12:9; 13:4). (2) The intimacy of this covenant relation is described under two figures: (a) a marriage (chs. 1—3), and (b) a father and son relationship (11:1; cf. Exod. 4:22). (3) A covenant always involves mutual obligations. Jehovah obligated Himself to provide the temporal and spiritual needs of His people; the people were to be faithful to Him. God kept His part of the covenant; Israel failed to keep hers. (4) Israel's faithlessness to the covenant is a glaring fault of the nation, for Israel repeatedly transgressed the covenant (6:7; 8:1). "Faithlessness" and "whoredom" sum up the whole, as a wife disloyal (2:5), and as a son disregarding the will of the father (10:9; 13:2). The covenant thus disregarded, Jehovah is compelled to set it aside: "I will drive them out of my house" (9:15; 2:9 ff.).

Outline of the Book

I. Israel's adultery, chs. 1—3.

    A. Hosea and Gomer—Jehovah and Israel: Israel the adulteress and her children, 1:2—2:1.

        1. The prophet's marriage to Gomer by divine command, and the three children who are given prophetic names, 1:2-9.

           a) Hosea charged to take a wife of "whoredom," vv. 2-3.

        b) Jezreel symbolizing the overthrow of Jehu's dynasty, vv. 4-5.

        c) Lo-ruhamah—Jehovah will no more have mercy upon Israel, vv. 6-7.

        d) Lo-ammi—the utter rejection of Israel, vv. 8-9.

    2. Restoration of children of Judah and Israel, 1:10—2:1.

  B. Chastisement of idolatrous Israel, conversion, and final restoration, 2:2-23.

    1. The threat of punishment, vv. 2-13.

        a) Condemnation of sinful conduct, vv. 2-7.

        b) Punishment more fully developed, vv. 8-13.

    2. Conversion and final restoration, vv. 14-23.

        a) The promise of their conversion, vv. 14-17.

        b) The renewal of a covenant and mercies, vv. 18-23.

  C. The prophet's second symbolic marriage, ch. 3.

    1. The symbolic action of the prophet, vv. 1-3.

    2. The application to Israel, vv. 4-5.

II. Prophetic discourses: The ungodliness of Israel and its inevitable punishment, chs. 4—13.

  A. Jehovah's controversy with Israel, chs. 4—6.

    1. The controversy: over the national guilt, ch. 4.

        a) Moral corruption in everyday life, vv. 1-5.

        b) Lack of knowledge—failure of the priests, vv. 6-10.

        c) Immoral religious practices, vv. 11-14.

        d) Ephraim joined to his idols—but let Judah be warned, vv. 15-19.

    2. Corruption in all phases of life, ch. 5.

        a) Guilt of priests, people, and princes, vv. 1-7.

        b) Judgment must follow—all to suffer the consequences; destruction slow, but sure, vv. 8-15.

    3. Insincerity—an abomination before Jehovah, ch. 6.

    a) Israel's return, but without heartfelt repentance, vv. 1-3.

    b) Jehovah is not deceived—there is no sorrow for sin on Israel's part, vv. 4-11.

B. Israel's corrupt political condition and consequence, chs. 7—8.

  1. The national government internally—moral degradation and anarchy, 7:1-7.

  2. The nation's corrupt foreign policy—her appeal to foreign nations is to end in destruction, 7:8-16.

  3. Judgment—national corruption and its consequences, ch. 8.

    a) Judgment has become inevitable—idolatry is an abomination: as have sown, so shall reap, vv. 1-7.

    b) Appeals to the nations will not save Israel, vv. 8-10.

    c) Multiplied idolatry—its harvest: condemnation and judgment, vv. 11-14.

C. Israel's religious and moral apostasy—its punishment, exile, and destruction, chs. 9—11.

  1. The degeneracy of Israel and ruin of its kingdom, ch. 9.

    a) The apostasy and its punishment: exile, vv. 1-9.

    b) As God found Israel and as they became, vv. 10-17.

  2. Guilt in rebellion against God, ch. 10.

    a) The guilt and the imminent destruction, vv. 1-8.

      (1) Puppet kings and puppet gods, vv. 1-3.

      (2) Their righteousness now becomes poison, vv. 4-5.

      (3) Assyria is now named, the instrument of judgment, vv. 6-7.

      (4) The terror of the judgment, v. 8.

    b) Israel's persistence in rebellion, vv. 9-15.

  3. Jehovah's love for prodigal Israel vs. Israel's ingratitude, ch. 11.

a) Israel's ingratitude (back to Israel's history a third time, see 9:10; 10:9; 11:1), vv. 1-7.
   (1) Love vs. ingratitude, vv. 1-4.
   (2) Ingratitude demands punishment, vv. 5-7.
b) Deserved utter destruction—but love of God tempers judgment with mercy, vv. 8-11.

D. Israel's apostasy and God's fidelity, chs. 12—13.
  1. Israel's degeneracy into Canaanitish ways, 11:12—12:14.
     a) Worldliness—Ephraim deceitful; Judah unsteadfast, 11:12—12:6.
        (1) Faithlessness of Ephraim brings punishment on all posterity, 11:12—12:2.
        (2) Example of forefather should have led to faithfulness, vv. 3-6.
     b) But Israel has become Canaan, 12:7-14.
  2. Israel's deep fall, ch. 13.
     a) Idolatry, the basis of Israel's destruction, vv. 1-8.
        (1) Idolatry, the curse, vv. 1-3.
        (2) Jehovah, their benefactor and judge, vv. 4-8.
     b) Distrust in Jehovah—this was the destruction of Israel, vv. 9-16.

III. Israel's conversion and pardon, ch. 14.

A. God's grace once more to those who turn to Him, vv. 1-8.
  1. Call to repentance, vv. 1-3.
  2. The promise of healing, vv. 4-8.

B. Epilogue, v. 9.
   Israel cries to Jehovah; He hears their cry and responds by an outpouring of rich blessings.

Comments

Chapter 1

Like other prophets, Hosea declares that his message was the "word of Jehovah" which came to him.   *1:1*

The word was communicated directly to the prophet by God, who had said of any prophet He would raise up, "I will put my words in his mouth" (Deut. 18:18-19). His father was Beeri, of whom nothing but his name is known. For the history of the rule of the kings who reigned during the days of Hosea, both in Judah and in Israel, see the Introduction, and read II Kings 14:23—18:8 and II Chronicles 26:1—29:11. It is probable that Hosea began prophesying in the last days of Uzziah and continued into the first part of Hezekiah's reign. Since Amos names only Uzziah and Jeroboam, and Hosea names three kings who followed Uzziah, it is concluded that Hosea prophesied after Amos.

1:2-9. The prophet's marriage to Gomer by divine command, and the birth of three children to whom were given prophetic names. The picture is one of apostasy and whoredom.

1:2   Jehovah's first word to the prophet instructed him to take a "wife of whoredom and children of whoredom." Does this mean that she was a harlot with children by whoredom when Hosea married her, or was she a woman reared in the environment of Israel's idolatry which would lead her into whoredom after her marriage? From the parallel between Hosea and Gomer and between Jehovah and Israel, it is more probable that she was not a harlot at the time of Jehovah's instruction to him, but a typical daughter of the age, who, after marriage, was so influenced by her surroundings and environment that she became immoral. This is further verified by the statement, "for the land doth commit great whoredom, departing from Jehovah." "The land" by metonymy stands for the people; "great whoredom" summarizes their unfaithfulness to Jehovah. In like manner Gomer committed great whoredom in departing from Hosea.

1:3   Of Gomer and Diblaim we know nothing more than that recorded in the first three chapters of Hosea. There is no indication that their names had any symbolic significance. To this union of Hosea and

Gomer three children were born, and to each a pro-   *1:4*
phetic name was given. The first was a son who was
named Jezreel, which meant "God will scatter," or
"God will sow." God would "scatter" the people
from Him, and later He would "sow" them unto
Himself. Also, God would "avenge the blood of Jezreel upon the house of Jehu." Jehu had written
letters to the elders of certain cities in Samaria, instructing them to slay the seventy sons of Ahab. The
order was carried out as directed, and the heads of
the seventy were sent to Jehu at Jezreel (II Kings
10:1-8). The valley of Jezreel is the fertile valley of
Esdraelon southeast of Mount Carmel, northeast and
east of the mountain of Megiddo, and west of the Hill
of Moreh and Mount Gilboa. In this valley a number
of decisive battles had been fought, which had given
the vicinity its significance. The slaughter of the
house of Ahab had been by divine decree (II Kings
9:1-10), and for carrying out this command of the
Lord Jehu had been commended by God (II Kings
10:30). Why, then, was this blood to be avenged
upon the house of Jehu? Jehu had obeyed the command of Jehovah in slaying the house of Ahab at
Jezreel; therefore, it was not for this that he was
condemned, for God had commanded the deed. But
this judgment was pronounced upon the house of
Jehu because, though he had carried out the command of God, he had been motivated by selfishness
and an unholy aim and desire on his part. He had no
concern for the will of God, but only for his own
will. He walked in the ways and sins of Jeroboam I,
and "took no heed to walk in the law of Jehovah, the
God of Israel" (II Kings 10:31). One may do the
command of the Lord and yet be in rebellion against
Him, doing the thing commanded because it is what
the individual desires and not because it is what God
desires. This was the case with Jehu. God further
declared that "the kingdom of the house of Israel"
should cease; it would be brought to an end. It is
folly to talk about the restoration of the house of
Israel and of the restoration of the kingdom at some
future time when God has declared He would bring it

1:5 to an end. The political house of Israel will never be restored. "At that day" God would break the military power of the nation, indicated by "break[ing] the bow of Israel in the valley of Jezreel." "At that day" is not the day of the end of the house of Jehu, but points to the day of the breaking up, or bringing to an end, of the kingdom of Israel.

1:6 Although Hosea may have considered the first child born to Gomer to have been his own, the name given to the second indicates doubt in the prophet's mind whether this one, a daughter, was his. To her

1:7 was given the name Lo-ruhamah, meaning "no pity," or "no mercy," "that hath not obtained mercy." God would no longer have mercy on the house of Israel, but on the house of Judah He would have mercy to save them. However, the salvation would not be by physical means or by military might, but by His own power. This He did at the gates of Jerusalem when the forces of Sennacherib were destroyed by the angel of Jehovah: one hundred eighty-five thousand were slain in a night (Isa. 37:36). Likewise when the remnant was brought back from Babylon, it was accomplished by Jehovah's power and not by military might (see Ezra 8:22, 31). To complete the picture, so also the salvation in Christ is brought about by His own divine power. God here made a distinction between Judah and Israel, but it was a distinction based on the difference in righteousness found in the two. Although the prophecies of Hosea were directed primarily to the house of Israel, he nevertheless utters warnings, threats, and asides, with promises, to the house of Judah. The house of Israel would be brought to an end, but God would have mercy on the house of Judah to save it. However, the salvation would be of Jehovah and not by military might. Though Israel play the harlot, let Judah be warned; let none from there follow Israel by making pilgrimages to Gilgal nor to Beth-aven, nor let any swear lightly by the name of Jehovah (4:15). Evidently Judah did partake of Israel's sin, for Judah stumbled with her (5:5; cf. Micah 1:13). Judah's princes became boundary movers, changing Jehovah's established boundary between right and wrong by partaking of Israel's sin of idolatry (5:10). Therefore Jehovah would be to the house of Judah as rottenness, which consumes and destroys (5:12); and as a young lion He would tear and go away (5:14). There was a harvest appointed for Judah; that is, a judgment, when God through judgment would destroy the sinners and bring the penitent to Himself (6:11).

Judah had put her confidence in fortified cities instead of in Jehovah. This was a false security which Jehovah would destroy (8:14). Judah had proved unsteadfast with Jehovah, with the Holy One who was faithful (11:12; compare the margin, ASV); therefore, Jehovah had a controversy with Judah as well as with Israel (12:2). Judah would suffer the judgment of God as did Israel, and for the same type of sins. Her judgment came 135 years later when Nebuchadnezzar destroyed Jerusalem (586 B.C.). However, God fulfilled the promise of mercy (1:7) by bringing back the remnant, and by bringing into the world through that remnant the Christ under whom those of both Israel and Judah were redeemed.

The third child was born, another son, to whom   *1:8* was given the name Lo-ammi, "not my people." God   *1:9* would no longer claim them as His own, nor be their God; they were to be rejected. In the prophet's own experience it is likely that by this time he realized the unfaithfulness of Gomer, and he knew this son was not his.

1:10—2:1. Restoration of the children of Israel and the children of Judah to Jehovah. Ammi: "my people"; Ruhamah: "that hath obtained mercy."

In spite of this rejection and scattering of Israel by   *1:10* Jehovah, "the number of the children of Israel shall be as the sand of the sea, which cannot be measured nor numbered." The children of Israel, the ten tribes, are before the prophet's mind. Whereas it was said at that time, "Ye are not my people" because God would cast them off, it would come to pass that they would at some time be called "sons of the living God." When would this be? The words of this passage are used by Peter with reference to the redeemed, "the elect who are sojourners of the Dispersion" (I Peter 1:1), "who had not obtained mercy, but now have obtained mercy," thereby becoming the people of God (I Peter 2:10). Paul appealed to this same passage in defending the right of the Gentiles, with the Jews, to be called by the gospel (Rom. 9:26). The Gentiles had long since ceased to sustain a relation to God. And now with Israel cast off, "not my people," Israel and the Gentiles would stand on equal ground before Jehovah. Each branch, Jew and Gentile, were now not His people; therefore, each could and would be called and saved by the same mercy of God, thus

1:11 becoming His people. Under one head (cf. 3:5) they, Israel and Judah, would "go up from the land." That is, as they had gone up out of the land of Egypt into their land of promise, so now, under one head, they would go up out of their land of scattering and captivity into the true fatherland. "Great shall be the day of Jezreel" refers back to 1:4; for inasmuch as the kingdom had been brought to an end, now Israel and Judah (and the Gentiles) could be brought together as one.

Chapter 2

2:1   The chapter division here is unfortunate, for the thought of this first verse of chapter 2 concludes that of chapter 1. They who had been "not my people," Lo-ammi, who had been "without mercy," Lo-ruhamah, would now be Ammi, "my people," Ruha-mah, "who have obtained mercy."

> *2:2-7. Jehovah addresses the sinful nation, charging it with spiritual whoredom, having played the harlot. Judgment is threatened.*

2:2   Jehovah now addresses the nation. That it is Jehovah speaking, and not Hosea, is clear from "I" (v.

2) and "saith Jehovah" (v. 13). That which Hosea had experienced in his unfaithful wife, Gomer, Jehovah had experienced in the unfaithful nation, Israel. Jehovah is the husband; Israel is the wife; and the children are the individuals of the nation. "Contend with your mother." Let the individuals not addicted to idolatry—the better minded among them—contend with the mother, the nation, that she change her ways. Jehovah renounces the relationship as husband and wife because of Israel's whoredom. He cannot be to her a husband nor she to Him a wife under these conditions. If a relation is to be sustained between them she must put away her adulteries, which were her idolatries, from between her breasts. Unless she *2:3* turns from her idolatry, Jehovah will strip her of all that He had given her and will let her be as when He had found her, desolate as a wilderness. When stripped of Jehovah's gracious beneficence, a nation or an individual is desolate, doomed to death from spiritual thirst. The individuals, like their mother, are *2:4* given to whorish idolatry. Therefore upon them Jehovah will have no mercy; for they are children of whoredom, the offspring of an unholy union. Instead *2:5* of holding fast to Jehovah in faithfulness as a wife to her husband, Israel had played the harlot after "her lovers," the baalim, bearing children of wickedness. She had praised the baalim as the source of her blessings. She had served them for the hire of material prosperity, as a harlot sells herself for the luxuries of her carnal desires. For this Jehovah would hedge up *2:6* her paths with thorns, making it impossible for her to escape. He would build a wall against her so that she is not able to find her way. She would seek after the *2:7* baalim but would not be able to find them; for they are nonentities, and a nonentity cannot be found. Completely baffled, she would be ready to return to her first husband, Jehovah, realizing that it was better with her when she served Him than now; for now she was reaping the ultimate result of serving idols. It was tragic that Israel as a wife had to learn her lesson after it was too late, but such is the fate of the transgressor.

2:8-13. Jehovah's address continued: The nation will be put to shame before her paramours. The days of the baalim will be visited upon her.

2:8   Israel had refused to recognize Jehovah as the source of her blessings and wealth and had used the riches bestowed upon her in praise to Baal. "Baal," meaning "lord" or "master," was the name of the chief god worshiped by the Canaanites when Israel entered the land, and was considered the father of the gods. The worship of the baalim was associated with certain fertility rites, very licentious in their nature. This worship had appealed greatly to the Israelites from the time of their entrance into Canaan, and had
2:9   contributed immeasurably to their apostasy. Because of this unfaithfulness to Himself, God would take back that which He had bestowed upon the nation.
2:10   This would leave the nation destitute. Stripped of her wealth and left naked in the presence of the idols and the world whose favor she had courted, the nation would be put to great shame. At that time the gods in
2:11   whom she had trusted would be helpless to aid or to hinder. The mirth of her festivals, annual feasts (cf. Exod. 23:14-17), monthly feasts of the new moon, and weekly sabbaths (cf. Num. 28; II Chron. 8:12-13) would be no more; mirth would cease among the
2:12   people who should have been living joyously before their God. Her beautiful vineyards and orchards, for which she had praised the baalim as her hire for playing the harlot, but which were from Jehovah, would be as a forest and as a field for animals. Jehovah had given and Jehovah would take away. Her
2:13   sin had been twofold: worshiping the baalim and forgetting Jehovah. "The days of the Baalim" (plural for baal) are the days dedicated to their worship. These days and deeds will not be forgotten; they will be recompensed.

2:14-20. In spite of rejection and punishment, God would bring Israel back to Himself.

*Under a new covenant He would betroth her
to Himself in righteousness and truth.*

Israel had wandered far from God in pursuit of her   *2:14*
lovers (v. 5); her land had become a desolation (v.
12); God had cast her out. Now He would allure her
back to Himself. "Therefore" indicates transition
from the punishment inflicted (vv. 9-13) to the
blessings of grace to be bestowed (vv. 15 ff.). God
would "allure her" to Himself with words of persua-
sion, demonstrating love and mercy beyond merit.
"The wilderness" of Israel's fathers had been Sinai,
which had meant deliverance from the bondage of
Egypt and a place of discipline and special blessings
from God. It was there that He had entered into
covenant with Israel, had given them the law, and had
led them and provided for their needs for forty years.
The present bondage of Israel was enslavement to the
baalim. Delivered from this servitude, Israel would be
brought by Jehovah into a new "wilderness" of spiritual discipline, guidance, and blessing. To her heart
He would speak a message of love. They would have
their blessings restored. "The valley of Achor" (of   *2:15*
troubling), a barren and desolate area west of the
north end of the Dead Sea, where Achan and his
family had been stoned, would be to them a door of
hope. The judgment through which she must pass and
the captivity in Assyria (11:5) would be a door
through which she must enter into the new life with
God. Once more the right relation between Jehovah
and Israel would be restored, as when Israel came up   *2:16*
out of Egypt. At that time Israel would call Jehovah
"Ishi," "my husband," not "Baali," "my master"; for   *2:17*
in calling Him "Baali" they had put Him on an
equality with the baalim. God would take away the
names of the baalim out of their mouths, "and they
shall no more be mentioned by their name." "And in   *2:18*
that day" identifies what follows with that which
God had just promised (vv. 14-17). A New Covenant
would restore the relation between God and His
people; a spirit of peace would characterize them. In

this new relationship through the New Covenant the animal nature of men would be brought under subjection to the Spirit of God. Isaiah's description of that relation is more complete (11:1-11). Implements of war would be abolished, for the nature of the new relationship and of the nation under this covenant

2:19 would be spiritual. God would be their protection and peace. God's people would be betrothed to Him forever in an uninterrupted betrothal. The betrothal here indicates a new marriage based on the New Covenant. Five words describe the divine basis on which the betrothal should rest: "in righteousness, and in justice," the very foundation of His throne (Ps.

2:20 89:14; 97:2-3); "in lovingkindness, and in mercies," expressions of His divine character. This betrothal should be "even in faithfulness"—God's faithfulness—the guarantee of the permanence of the relationship.

> *2:21-23. The new nation will be sown to Jehovah in the earth, filled with all fulness in Him. Those who were not His people, who had not obtained mercy, will now be His people, having obtained mercy.*

2:21   There can be no valid question that the above promises have reference to the present dispensation under Christ. They have been fulfilled in Him, and are not deferred to some future dispensation. "In that day" refers to the day of the covenant and betrothal discussed above. (cf. v. 18).

2:22   So what follows is identified with the blessings of the preceding verses. The passage therefore applies to spiritual fulness under Christ. Prayers will come through to Jehovah, and He will answer. The blessings are not to be thought of as material, though these may be provided (cf. Matt. 6:30), but as the fulness and completeness in Christ in whom "ye are made full" (Col. 2:10); in whom "ye may be

2:23 filled unto all the fulness of God" (Eph. 3:19). Again there is a play on the word "Jezreel." God's people would be "sown" unto Him (v. 23a), as before they had been "scattered" from Him (1:4). The Messianic import of the passage is confirmed by the application made of it by Paul and Peter. Paul quotes verse 23b and 1:10b, applying both to the present dispensation under Christ (Rom. 9:25-26); Peter also applies the words of the same two passages to the people of God under Christ today (I Peter 2:10). Therefore, there can be no question but that the prophecy has been fulfilled: God brought His people back into Canaan, then brought them to Himself under a New Covenant, bestowed all spiritual blessings on them in Christ, sowed them to Himself in the true fatherland (Phil. 3:20) and kingdom, showered mercy on them, and made them His own.

Chapter 3

3:1-5. The prophet tells of his second symbolic marriage in which he buys Gomer back to himself. As Israel would be without the essentials of true worship for a period, so Gomer would not enjoy conjugal relations for a time.

God directed Hosea to go again and love a woman   *3:1*
"beloved of her friend." The woman, "an adulteress," was evidently Gomer; and the "friend" of whom she was beloved was the prophet himself. This he was to do, "even as Jehovah loveth the children of Israel." In spite of their idolatry and love for "cakes of raisins," the reward in their minds for worshiping the baalim, Jehovah still loved Israel. Here is resumed the analogy between Hosea and Gomer and between Jehovah and Israel, dropped at chapter 1, verse 9. As Jehovah had continued to love Israel though she was unfaithful to Him, it is here indicated that Hosea had continued to love Gomer however deeply she had sunk in the mire of moral degradation. The prophet bought her for the   *3:2-3*
equivalent of thirty pieces of silver, the price of a wounded slave (see Exod. 21:32). Whether he bought her off a slave block for this amount, or whether this was an amount provided for her livelihood until she

would be restored to the full status of wifehood, is not divulged. But until she proves herself she would not be to him as a wife, nor would he be to her a husband; there would be no conjugal relation between them. There is division among scholars as to whether the woman purchased was Gomer or another woman. Unless the woman was Gomer, the parallel 3:4 between Hosea and Gomer and between Jehovah and Israel breaks down. The fact that Jehovah redeemed Israel, although for many days they were without the essentials of worship, and that He made not another "marriage," indicates strongly that the woman re- 3:5 deemed by Hosea was Gomer. As Israel had gone so far from God and had sunk so low, so Gomer had gone so far from Hosea and had sunk so low that she was no longer desired and had become a slave to be bought from a master. After the children of Israel would go through the long experience of being without the essentials of worship, they would return to Jehovah and to David their king. This would be "in the latter days," which identifies the promise as looking to the present dispensation. The "David" of the passage is David's illustrious descendant, Jesus the Christ.

These three chapters are very important. The parallel between Hosea and Gomer and between Jehovah and Israel is clear and striking. Hosea's experience with Gomer was parallel with Jehovah's experience with the nation. The nation's sin was that of idolatry, by which she had committed spiritual adultery and "whoredom." The kingdom would be destroyed, the nation scattered (Jezreel); they would be without mercy (Lo-ruhamah), not God's people (Lo-ammi). But the time would come when they would be gathered together, sown to Jehovah (Jezreel), become God's people (Ammi), having obtained mercy (Ruhamah). For many days they would be without true worship. But the time would come when they would seek Jehovah under David (Christ), and in Him find their fulness of all spiritual blessings "in the latter days" (the Messianic, or present dispensation). These chapters stand out in the Book of Hosea as of special importance.

Chapter 4

4:1-5. Jehovah has a lawsuit against His people. National guilt is exposed. Moral corruption has infiltrated everyday life on every hand. The people will be carried away.

With a burdened heart and burning indignation because of the sins of the nation, the prophet steps from the moral ruin of his own wrecked home into the atmosphere of a degenerate people—into that of a crashing world. Because of his experience with Gomer he was better prepared to see the nation and its whorish behavior toward Jehovah. All about him he saw the kingdom falling apart, its ideals gone, and the doom of captivity facing the nation. It was a nation in decay! The address is directed to the ten tribes of Israel. Jehovah has a controversy, a lawsuit, a case at law with "the inhabitants of the land." The charge before the court was "there is no truth"—that is, truthfulness—either in their speech or in their actions; there was no "goodness," love for one's fellow man, or "knowledge of God," a knowledge of Him imprinted on their hearts and directing their lives in His ways and steps. But on the contrary, "there is nought but swearing and breaking faith, and killing, and stealing, and committing adultery." In "swearing and breaking faith" they were violating the third and ninth commandments; the oath was not considered sacred. An oath taken before Jehovah was lightly esteemed. "Make it and break it" was the flippant attitude of the people. In killing, the sixth commandment was violated, the violation of which carried with it the death penalty (Exod. 21:12). This they had ignored, so now God would have to execute it Himself. In stealing, the eighth commandment was transgressed. The property right of others was lightly esteemed. Committing adultery transgressed the

4:1

4:2

seventh commandment. The sanctity of the home was defiled; God's moral standard was flouted. The violation of this law also carried the death penalty (Lev. 20:10-12). Crime followed crime until "blood toucheth blood." The controversy was a case of law before Jehovah's court; it was His law that had been contemptuously violated and now they must be tried

4:3   before the Judge of final appeal. "Therefore": because of this moral decay desolation would come on the land, a desolation so terrible that even all nature would be affected by it—the land, the people, and the living creatures. Such is the consequence of sin.

4:4   There was no need to "strive" or "reprove," for the people were beyond the point of anyone's reasoning with them; "the people are as they that strive with the priest." The priests were the teachers of the law (Lev. 10:10-11; Deut. 17:8-11), and the people should hearken to their interpretation of the law. To "strive with the priest" was to reject the word of the

4:5   Lord at his mouth. This sin also incurred the death penalty (Deut. 17:12). This attitude added to the guilt of the people. Both the people and the false prophets would stumble, and the mother—the nation—would be destroyed. The expression "false prophet" is not found in the Old Testament; however, the prophets who spoke against the true prophets were utterly "false" and were condemned by the true prophets.

> *4:6-10. "Lack of knowledge" was the stumbling block of the people. The priests are charged with "feeding on the sin of the people"—encouraging sin that the priesthood would prosper through sacrifices for sin.*

4:6   The prophet lays the blame for this condition upon the priests; they, primarily, were responsible. As those responsible for the instruction of the people they had failed. For this the people were being destroyed. Knowledge of Jehovah and of His ways is

essential to the life of any people. Because the priests
had forgotten the law of the Lord and had failed to
teach it, they would be rejected as priests and their
children would be forgotten by the Lord. In the next
statement, "As they were multiplied," there are dif-   *4:7*
fering ideas on the word "they"; Keil refers it to the
people, Harper (*I.C.C.*) to the priests. It could be
either, for as the population increased, so did the
priests increase. Verse 8 indicates that Hosea is speak-   *4:8*
ing of the priests. Either way, as the population
increased so their sins increased. As God blessed them
they went farther from Him. The priests fed themselves on the sins of the people; for the more the
people sinned the more were the sacrifices offered for
sin, and the more the sacrifices, the more the benefit
to the priests. Their heart was set on this type of
iniquity. What a parody on the religion of Jehovah!
Those responsible for the teaching of righteousness
were encouraging sin that they themselves could profit. As the people had sinned, so had the priests; and as   *4:9*
the people would be punished, so would the priests.
Each would reap his own reward. There would be   *4:10*
scarcity of food in the land. As they would "play the
harlot"—that is, appeal to the idols to which they had
ascribed praise for their blessings—they would continue to fail in obtaining blessings. The cause would
be, "they have left off taking heed to Jehovah."
Either ignorance of the law or willful indifference to
its practice is fatal to any people.

*4:11-14. Gross immorality has characterized
their idolatrous worship until now. Therefore,
they will be overthrown.*

"Whoredom"—both their idolatry and the licen-   *4:11*
tious acts that were a part of the worship—combined
with intoxication takes away the ability to think
clearly. They take away the understanding. "Wine
and new wine" indicated both the fermented and the
newly extracted grape juice. However, since in that
country the juice began fermentation early, it seems

4:12   that in this instance the term "new wine" indicates
fermented wine with the ability to intoxicate. The
taking away of the understanding by whoredom and
wine turned the hearts of the people to a full and
complete devotion to idolatry by seeking guidance
from "the stock" and "the staff." "The staff" seems
to indicate the use of rods in the practice of witchcraft or magic as they sought guidance and answers to
questions from their deities. The rods, held upright,
would be released after magic formulas were said over
them. The direction in which the rod fell indicated
the answer to the question posed. "The stock" is the
carved wooden image or idol. This disposition of
spiritual whoredom had led them to depart "from

4:13   under" Jehovah. The altars to false gods were usually
erected on the tops of high elevations and hills, and
under trees of heavy foliage on the plains or level
sections. Here worship of a terribly immoral and
depraved nature was practiced. In such places of
worship their daughters and brides committed adul-

4:14   tery, a practice that resulted from their base concept
of religion. The daughters and brides would not be
held responsible to the same extent as were the
fathers and husbands who set the example. Instead of
"under the shadow of the Almighty," it was under
the thick foliage of trees; instead of a spiritual worship to Jehovah, it was adultery with prostitutes
dedicated to false deities. For this their understanding
had been taken away, and with the understanding
gone the nation would be overthrown.

> 4:15-19. Ephraim (Israel) is joined to his
> idols, but let Judah be warned by the example
> and not follow such a course.

4:15   Jehovah directs a warning to Judah: let her people
learn and take warning from Israel. Let not the
people of Judah join those of Israel in going to Gilgal.
According to many, the Gilgal spoken of here was
located on the border between Manasseh and
Ephraim, between Shechem and Joppa, northwest
from Jerusalem. This had come to be a center of

idolatry. Others think it to have been the Gilgal near the Jordan River where Israel had camped when she crossed the river to enter the land (Josh. 4:19-20). This latter seems the more probable of the two, though it remains indefinite. Nor let them come to Beth-aven, "house of vanity," formerly called Beth-el, "house of God." Beth-aven is an expression used by Amos, and now repeated by Hosea. The "house of God" had become a "house of vanity—emptiness." Nor let them swear falsely by Jehovah as did those of Israel, for this was to profane the name of Jehovah (Lev. 19:12). Instead of acting as a lamb that follows, Israel had acted like a stubborn cow that refuses to yield to the yoke put upon her by Jehovah. She would not be trained. And because of this Jehovah would feed them "as a lamb in a large place," as a lamb unprotected out on the hills, a prey to wolves and lions. Ephraim, who stands for the nation, is hopeless; he is joined, or mated, to idols as a wife is joined to her husband. He is so hopelessly united with them that recovery now seems impossible. "Let him alone," give him up to abandonment. This case is desperate, there is no hope. The degeneracy that is on every hand and the consequential destruction are now described. Their wine is become sour, turned in their stomach, and has left them sick from its inflaming effects. But this does not deter them. They continue in their debauchery and idolatry; "they play the harlot continually." Her rulers, "shields," or princes join in the shameful practices, notwithstanding that "it is an abomination to kings to commit wickedness; for the throne is established by righteousness" (Prov. 16:12). They go straight ahead into the chaos of utter ruin. Destruction must come; and when it comes it will come as a tornado, wrapping the nation up in its wings and carrying the people away. This shameful end is the ultimate fruit of their idolatry.

4:16

4:17

4:18

4:19

Chapter 5

5:1-7. The deep-seated nature of Israel's revolt is exposed. The spirit of whoredom is its

cause. God would rebuke them. Their hypoc-
risy would devour them.

5:1   "Hear this" points back to chapter 4, and relates
the following to what has been said. Corruption is
discovered in all phases of life and makes punishment
inevitable. Idolatry is found not only among the
people of the nation, but among the priests, in the
house of the king, and among the princes of his
household. These, the priests and the house of the
king, who should have led the people in the right
way, have themselves become a snare at Mizpah, east
of the Jordan, and a net on Mount Tabor, west of the
Jordan. The people had been trapped in these snares
and nets as birds in a cage. To these rulers belongs the
5:2   sentence of judgment. These revolters against God
had gone to great excesses in carrying out their will
against God's will. "In making slaughter" probably
applies to their leading the people into slaughter.
However, it could be taken literally in application to
their willingness to slaughter in order to carry out
their purposes. But they must deal with God who
rebukes with severity, commensurate with the crime.
5:3   Any attempt to hide from God would be ridiculous.
Ephraim, the ruling house, and Israel, the people, in
all their idolatry and defilement are ever before His
eyes. The ruling house had led the way and now the
5:4   nation was defiled. Their actions and conduct have so
seared their hearts that they cannot turn to Jehovah.
The spirit of whoredom (idolatry) had so turned
5:5   them away that they knew Him not, nor were they in
a condition of heart to be taught. "The pride of
Israel" or "excellency of Israel" (cf. margin, ASV) is
interpreted by Keil to mean Jehovah, who should
have been their pride, Israel's excellence, as in Amos
8:7, but who would testify against them. However,
others think that "the pride of Israel" was the
nation's arrogance, combined with the worldly
wealth, false power, idolatry, and accomplishments of
which she was so proud (Deane, Laetsch, Harper,
Huxtable, Pusey, and others). Either is admissible, for
it is Jehovah who would humble Israel and Samaria;

and it was because of those things of which she
boasted that she would be brought down. Since the
context deals with Israel's arrogant idolatry, the latter
position seems the more probable. This view com-
ports with the LXX, Chaldee, and Syriac versions.
Judah would stumble with them; however, it was over
a century later that Judah fell. When Israel went up   5:6
out of Egypt they took with them their flocks and
herds to meet Jehovah (Exod. 10:24-26)—and they
found Him. Now they will go forth with their flocks
and herds to seek Him, but will be unable to find Him
for He will have withdrawn Himself from them; their
search will have come too late. In their idolatry they
had borne strange children, children that did not   5:7
belong to Jehovah. As Gomer had borne children of
whoredom to Hosea, so Israel had borne strange children to Jehovah. If "new moon" is correct, then the
prophet is saying that the sacrifices to their gods at
the time of the new moon would bring full and
complete destruction and not deliverance. If the
translation "a month" (see margin, ASV) is correct,
then he is saying that destruction will come shortly.
Both positions are defended by able scholars. The
first is preferable.

The prophet sees judgment beginning to fall on the   5:8
nation. He sees destruction coming from without and
within. Warnings fall like hammer blows. "Blow the
cornet," a horn made from a curved ram's horn, and
"the trumpet," an instrument usually made of brass
or silver. These were to sound an alarm at "Beth-
aven," house of vanity, not Beth-el, house of God.
Why are Gibeah and Ramah, both located on the
border of Judah, indicated? Probably because the
prophet sees in vision the destruction of the northern
tribes, as if the Assyrians had already swept over the
land to the border of Judah. The enemy is now
behind Benjamin invading Judah, on her very border
ready to strike deeper. In the day of Jehovah's rebuke   5:9
Ephraim will be made desolate. God was making
known what He would do. Amos had said, "Surely
the Lord Jehovah will do nothing, except he reveal
his secret unto his servants the prophets" (Amos 3:7).

5:10   Jehovah was making known this purpose in ample time to avert the judgment. Judah, likewise, would experience the wrath of Jehovah, for her princes had removed the landmarks that distinguished between right and wrong. For this Jehovah would pour out His

5:11   wrath in full measure. As the women of Samaria had "oppressed" and "crushed" the poor and needy in carrying out their intemperate desires (Amos 4:1), so now is Ephraim oppressed and crushed by the heathen who are executing the judgment announced (cf. v. 9). The cause for this crushing of Ephraim, who "was content to walk after man's command," probably refers to the command of Jeroboam I who had introduced the calf worship in Israel (I Kings

5:12   12:28-33), after which Ephraim had walked from its beginning. Moth and rottenness work slowly, but they destroy completely. God would be as these to Ephraim and Judah, bringing both to nothing. When

5:13   Ephraim realized his condition he should have turned to Jehovah for help, but instead he sought to make an alliance or covenant with Assyria. This alliance was doomed to failure. "King Jareb," king striver, or contention, apparently was a symbolic name for the king of Assyria who would add only woes to Ephraim's present troubles. "King Jareb" will be helpless to aid; the only hope is a turning back to

5:14   God from within the nation itself. The moth works as silently as the lion tears fiercely. Jehovah will be as a lion, even a young lion, as He tears Ephraim and Judah, using Assyria as the instrument of His judg-

5:15   ment, who will carry them away as booty. Jehovah will leave them until they are ready to seek Him, acknowledging their offenses as they return. He will return to His place as the lion returns to its den.

Chapter 6

6:1-11. Insincerity is an abomination to Jehovah. He sees their "goodness as a morning cloud" that vanishes quickly. Their crimes stand out before Him as the fruit of spiritual whoredom. A harvest is inevitable.

The thought of these verses is considered by many *6:1-3*
to be very closely connected with that of 5:15. If so,
the chapter division is unfortunate. It is thought by
others that verses 1-3 are more closely related to verse
4. The prophet's words in verses 1-3 have been subjected to two very different interpretations. (1) There
are those who interpret the exhortation to be a
prayer of the people in an earnest and urgent appeal
to one another that they return to Jehovah, saying
that since it is He who has smitten and torn He will
also bind up and heal. The time, "After two days . . .
on the third day," indicates a brief period; "two or
three days" as we would say. There are some among
older commentators who thought this had reference
to Christ's period in the tomb, and to His resurrection
on the third day. But this is completely foreign to the
context and is to be discounted. He will heal us; He
will bind us up; He will revive us; He will raise us up;
and we, the people, will live before Him. All of these
statements refer to what God would do for the penitent sinners. The people now recognize that they
must know and follow Jehovah; repentance and
knowledge of Jehovah are bound together. God,
seeing repentance effected through knowledge, will
heal, revive, and raise up. Not only will He bestow
these favors, but He will also come to them with
blessings as of the heavy rains of winter and the latter
rain before harvest. (2) There are others who would
interpolate the word "saying" after 5:15, following
the LXX, making it read, "In their affliction they will
seek me earnestly, *saying,* Come, and let us return to
Jehovah. . . ." This would indicate an attitude lacking
in deep and genuine repentance, suggesting that in
their minds they need only to intimate a disposition
to return to Jehovah for Him to readily accept them.
This would reveal a low estimate of the demands of
Jehovah on His people. This interpretation associates
verses 1-3 with 4 ff. and is in harmony with this latter
passage. Jehovah is not deceived by the shallowness
of their conduct; for as a morning cloud that soon
evaporates, so their goodness is represented as quickly
passing away. Scholars are divided as to which view is

correct. Be reminded again that the view taken depends on whether verses 1-3 are to be connected directly with 5:15, or whether they are to be more directly associated with verse 4 and those that follow. Two things are certain: since they were destroyed for lack of knowledge (4:6), if the people would now sincerely "follow on to know" Him (v. 3), He would surely return to bless them. On the other hand, if they took a smug attitude toward themselves and God's willingness to return to them, He would not now be deceived but would see through their hypocrisy as He had in the past. He would not return to them. Although it necessitates adding the word "saying" at the conclusion of 5:15, the second interpretation is more consistent with the context, and is to be preferred.

6:4   If one accepts the first interpretation above, the prophet here introduces a new point; but if one accepts the second, then this is a continuation of verses 1-3, indicating the shallowness of their repentance. The suffering and grief of Jehovah is vividly expressed as He says, "O Ephraim . . . O Judah," manifesting a deep hurt as He beholds the evanes-

6:5   cence of their goodness: it is as a morning cloud and as the dew which quickly vanishes before the scorching sun. What should He do? Because their love has been in the past as a transient cloud, He has condemned them by the prophets; He has slain them in

6:6   His divine judgments, which have been as visible to all as the light of the clear day. "For" connects the judgments of verse 5 with the fervent desire of Jehovah expressed in verse 6. The prophet summarizes the true desire of Jehovah to be goodness on the part of His people; that is, loyal and faithful love toward God and toward one's fellow man, and not sacrifice. True love is rooted in the knowledge of God and grows out of that knowledge of Him. He desires this goodness and knowledge more than sacrifices and burnt-offerings. The sacrifices and burnt-offerings initiated by Jehovah at Sinai were now being abused by the people. They thought that by these outward tokens of devotion, void of true piety, all their wick-ednesses were taken care of.

"But they like *men* have transgressed the cove-nant" (KJV); "But they like *Adam* have transgressed the covenant" (ASV). The latter is preferable. For as God had placed Adam in Eden, making with him a covenant which he had violated, causing him to be expelled from his Eden, so God had placed Israel in this good land and made with them a covenant which they had broken. Now they must be expelled from their Eden. They had dealt treacherously against the Lord and now must pay for their folly. No such city as Gilead is mentioned in the Old Testament, nor have the remains of such a city been located. Gilead is a mountainous district east of the Jordan and served as a haunt or retreat for wicked men. Because of its nature the prophet speaks of the district as a city. The whole land of Israel had become as a haunt for wicked men, stained with the blood of their crimes. Again an indictment is brought against the priests. They are charged with conduct characteristic of gang-sters who lie in wait to murder and rob. They commit great deeds of lust and wickedness. Shechem was a city of priests, as also it was a city of refuge for the man-slayer (Num. 35:9-15; Josh. 20:7). But instead of being a city of refuge, Shechem had become a sanctuary for murderers—and priests at that! Jehovah seems to stand aghast at the horrible fruits of idolatry He finds in Israel. A moral defilement for which Ephraim must bear the chief blame is discovered in the nation. Again the prophet looks toward Judah, for Jehovah has a harvest laid up for them. Their wickedness must bear its own reaping as must that of Israel. There is no respect of persons with God. Keil seems to express the correct view when he says, "When God shall come to punish, that He may root out ungodliness, and bring back His people to their true destination, Judah will also be visited with the judgment."

6:7

6:8

6:9

6:10

6:11

Chapter 7

In the following two chapters the prophet exposes Israel's corrupt political conditions and the consequences that must follow.

7:1-7. Thieves and troops of robbers collaborate with the king in carrying out his wicked plots.

7:1   The wickednesses of Israel seem endless. Israel the nation, Ephraim the ruling tribe, and Samaria the capital are all involved. As God would heal one, the wickedness of another is brought to light. Lawlessness
7:2   and confusion, gangsterism and basic dishonesty seem to be the order of the day. When God would heal Israel, the wickedness of Samaria, the ruling class, breaks out. Weakness within the house of state encouraged violence throughout the land. They had left God out of their hearts and their thinking, refusing to acknowledge Him; consequently, He was left out of their actions. They consider not that God takes cognizance of all that they do. Their sins are ever before His face (cf. Amos 5:12; 8:7), but they refuse to acknowledge this.

7:3   "They," the wicked of Samaria who conduct themselves as a troop of robbers (v. 1), make the king glad with their wickedness and lies. These collaborate with the king in carrying out his wicked desires; each is in league with the other. The next four verses are admittedly difficult; all commentators seem to have trouble with the text. However, the thought seems to be this: The wicked companions of the king plot his overthrow. "They are all adulterers," unfaithful to God and to the king. As a baker prepares the dough, waits for it to rise, then stirs the fire for the baking, so the plotters lay their plan and wait for the opportune
7:5   time to carry it out. "On the day of our king," either his birthday, an anniversary, or the day of a feast in which the plotters plan to strike, they heat themselves with wine until they are ready to carry out their shameful purpose. The king is pictured as

stretching out his hands to them—that is, opening the way for them by becoming involved in their disregard for God—but it is to his own destruction. Having let the plot mature, they carry it out when the proper moment arrives. All are inflamed with the spirit of anarchy, greed, and lust. They devour their judges and kings. The picture is one of complete moral and political chaos. During the last few years of Israel's history kings were plotted against, murdered, and replaced by others. Four of the last six were murdered (II Kings 15). The saddest part of the picture is seen in the statement of Jehovah, there is "none among them that calleth unto me." All their deeds were of their own wicked designing and conniving, which brought the downfall of the nation upon their own heads.

7:6
7:7

> *7:8-16. Cursed with a corrupt foreign policy, Ephraim was as a silly dove flitting from Egypt to Assyria. He was playing both ends against the middle.*

In addition to the internal moral corruption of the people, the nation was cursed with a corrupt and destructive foreign policy. The strength of Israel was to have been the people's trust in Jehovah and their separateness and seclusion from all other nations. Ephraim, the ruling tribe, had mixed himself with the peoples of heathen nations, adopting their ways and making himself one with them. "A cake not turned," burned on one side and uncooked on the other, was fit for nothing. They were "cooked" by heathenism but "uncooked" or raw in their relation to God. "Strangers have devoured his strength": the heathen nations from without and the heathen spirit from within had destroyed his power, and yet he was ignorant of what was taking place. "Gray hairs are here and there upon him": he is growing old. Like men who have dissipated their strength in youth and have become prematurely old, yet realize it not, so is Ephraim's plight. "The pride of Israel"—either Jehovah who should have been their pride, or vanity,

7:8

7:9

7:10

wealth, and wicked deeds of which Israel was proud—now testifies against him (see discussion under 5:5). But in spite of all that their wickednesses have brought upon them, or that God has done to bring

7:11   them to judgment, they have refused to give heed. Like a silly dove that flits from one water-hole to another where the hunter lies in wait, so Ephraim has flitted from Egypt to Assyria, calling upon each for

7:12   help. He is guilty of playing both ends against the middle. The nation cannot escape the consequence of such rejection of God. As they flit here and there He will spread His net upon them; He will bring them down; He will chasten them; they will be taken as birds in His net. "Their congregation hath heard": they had been warned of this by Amos earlier, and now over and over again by Hosea.

7:13   Therefore, woe unto them! Their wandering far from Jehovah is bringing destruction upon them. This destruction explains the woe. Though God was seeking to redeem them through His prophets, they lie

7:14   about Him. They deny His sole deity by turning to idols, and they lie to Him in word and action. They deny Him the opportunity and privilege of redeeming them. Instead of coming to Him, the fountainhead of all help and blessings, and crying to Him from the heart, they "howl upon their beds." In their distress they work themselves into a frenzy. There was no repentance; they howl because the physical blessings are being taken away. Their concern is for the material, not the spiritual. In this they rebel against God and the true good He would give to them. God's

7:15   goodness toward them had been manifested by instructing them in righteousness and in the skills that should have made them strong. But instead of accepting this and using it to His glory, they had used it

7:16   against God by devising mischief against Him. "They return": they leave the impression of returning to Jehovah, but they do not return. Their disposition toward God is like a deceitful bow—it misses the mark; it will be as a boomerang returning to them. The princes, who were greatly responsible for the current conditions, "shall fall by the sword for the rage of their tongue." The "rage of their tongue" had been their arrogant boasting, their defiance of God, and their lies against Him. The people were led astray. For this they would fall by the sword. Their fall by the sword in the fall of their arrogant rejection of their God would be "their derision in the land of Egypt." Egypt, in whom they had trusted and to whom they had appealed for help, would only mock them in their fall by the hands of Assyria.

Chapter 8

8:1-7. Inevitable judgment! False gods and kings unsanctioned by Jehovah have wrought their havoc. The calf must go. They have sown the wind; they will reap the whirlwind.

The marginal reading (ASV) suggests two exclama- *8:1*
tions: "The trumpet to the mouth! As an eagle against the house of Jehovah!" The trumpet sounds the alarm of war; the threat is that of Assyria swooping down as an eagle on the "house of Jehovah"—the people of Israel, Jehovah's congregation or family—bent on its destruction. The cause was sin! The people had transgressed the covenant Jehovah had made with them at Sinai, and had trespassed against the law He had given them. God had made a covenant with Israel that had made them His people; He had given them a law to govern them in the land of promise (Exod. 19:5-6). These they had lightly esteemed. A second covenant was made at Moab, this one pertaining to their retention of the land after they would possess it (Deut. 28—30; cf. 29:1). Both covenants had been violated. In contrast to their past *8:2* conduct (7:14), they would cry to Jehovah, saying, "We . . . know thee"; but the knowledge was superficial. In reality, they did not know Him. They had cast off Jehovah, their only true good; and now the *8:3* enemy would pursue them. It was too late to cry. His "good" is only for those who respect Him and keep His covenant. Their conduct contrary to the covenant

into which they had entered had brought this on them.

8:4   The setting up of kings and the making of princes, but not of Jehovah, goes back to the very beginning of the establishment of the monarchy (I Sam. 8:4-7). Although God selected Jeroboam I, the division of the kingdom was because of sin and therefore contrary to God's choosing. From the beginning of the kingdom under Jeroboam I, there had not been one king in Israel who had worshiped Jehovah; all had served the calf, or the baalim, or both. With their silver and gold they had made and sustained the idols and idol worship which would lead to their being cut off. Idolatry and rebellion were their downfall. God
8:5   had determined that the calf erected at Beth-el by Jeroboam I would be cut off, destroyed. He speaks as if the destruction had taken place already. His anger is against the people who had erected it and against the people of Samaria who worshiped it. Their guilt was that of setting up kings by murder and plotting and idolatry in the rejection of Jehovah. How long would it be before they would "attain to innocency," be clear of their guilt? This question is not answered.
8:6   "The calf of Samaria," the calf of gold erected at Beth-el, had come from the hands of Israel. It was a product of human creation, and as such it was not God nor could it represent God. The calf would be broken in pieces; it will not be able to deliver itself, much less the people.
8:7   A further declaration of their destruction is revealed: they sow the wind, nothingness; they will reap the cyclone, destruction. There is no grain for food and no growing stalk to produce food. Should something grow voluntarily, the invading strangers will devour it.

8:8-10. Israel's appeal to the nations will be futile; it will only add to his present burden.

8:8   The nation is practically ruined; it is being swallowed up. The ambassadors of Israel are going among the nations, seeking help; but instead of being re-

spected, they are despised. They are gone up to   *8:9*
Assyria seeking assistance. This appeal to Assyria further indicates their unfaithfulness to and contempt
for Jehovah. "Like a wild ass alone by himself." A
wild ass maintains its independence by staying alone;
but Ephraim has given up his independence by going
to Assyria, seeking help from that heathen power. He
sought to hire his "lover," or give to them "love-
gifts" for their favors. Though they prostitute them-   *8:10*
selves before the nations by their effort to buy affection through gifts, it will not avail. "Now will I gather
them": whom will He gather? God will not gather the
nations among whom Ephraim has gone; but He will
gather Israel, who has gone among the nations for
help. He will gather them before Him in judgment to
carry them into Assyria. They will be diminished by
the very king of princes, Assyria, whose help they had
sought.

*8:11-14. Altars for sinning had been multi-
plied and Jehovah's law had been rejected.
They must now go into "Egypt," that is, into
captivity.*

God had decreed that His people should have one   *8:11*
altar and that it should be where He would record His
name (Deut. 12:5 ff.). But Ephraim had multiplied
altars to the calf and to the baalim. This sin of
idolatry had multiplied his sins in every aspect of life.
The "ten thousand things of my law" indicate the   *8:12*
complete fulness of God's law in the covenant He had
made with the nation. But these had been accounted
as strangers to the people; they knew them not. As
for the sacrifices which they offer, they are nothing   *8:13*
more than the eating of flesh; for there is no com-
munion with Jehovah, no true worship of Him. Their
iniquities will not be forgotten; they will go into
"Egypt." Egypt here stands for bondage; for they
would not return to physical Egypt, but would be
carried into Assyria (11:5). "Israel hath forgotten his   *8:14*
Maker"; he had put Him out of his plans. He had
built palaces or temples that gratified his own lust for

personal pride and glory. Judah had followed in Israel's steps in forgetting Jehovah; he had built fortified cities, looking to these for protection instead of looking to the Lord. Now God would send a fire that would devour the fortified cities of Judah and consume the castles of Israel. The devouring fire would be Assyria. As Israel had sown, so will he reap.

Chapter 9

9:1-9. Premature rejoicing. The people were rejoicing over their material prosperity. But it was premature; they would eat the bread of mourning in Assyria.

9:1   The people were enjoying a period of temporary prosperity that led them into premature rejoicing. It is possible that for a moment the Assyrians had lifted their threat against Israel (cf. II Kings 15:19-20). This gave occasion for the joy now being expressed. The people were making material gain the reward of worship; it was a gift from the gods of the land. They had departed from their God, Jehovah, and now they were accepting the harvest as a harlot's hire for their
9:2   spiritual prostitution before the baalim of the Canaanites. But that which Israel had sought as a compensation from the baalim for worshiping them
9:3   would fail. Exile in a foreign land now faced the people. They would not dwell in "Jehovah's land," the land of His choice, in which He had put His name and in which He had agreed to bless His people. Ephraim, who had been born in Egypt and had come out of that land, would now "return to Egypt" and "eat unclean food in Assyria." The return to Egypt would not be literal, but Israel would be returned to the bondage which Egypt signified. The captivity would be in Assyria. This is made clear by what follows. "They would eat unclean bread," for anything outside of "Jehovah's land" was considered unclean. Their increase could not be sanctified by the offering of first-fruits and proper sacrifices to Jehovah; therefore it would be unclean. Instead of

being able to pour out wine-offerings to Jehovah and $\quad$ *9:4*
to offer sacrifices of joy to Him, their sacrifices
would be as the bread of mourning. Bread of mourning is bread eaten in mourning for the dead, or as one
shares grief with others over the sorrow of death (see
Jer. 16:7; Deut. 24:16). Their food would be eaten
for the satisfying of the appetite and not in com-
munion with Jehovah. "What will ye do in the day $\quad$ *9:5*
of . . . the feast of Jehovah?" for they will have been
carried into exile. "It shall not come into the house
of Jehovah"; for there would be no "house of
Jehovah" in which to bring the offerings, and no altar
to Jehovah upon which to offer burnt-offerings. They
would go into "Egypt," captivity, from the destruc- $\quad$ *9:6*
tion of their own land. The beautiful and pleasant
things in which they had rejoiced would become the
possession of their captors, and in their stead there
would be the constant pricking and misery of nettles
and thorns in their habitation. Again Egypt stands for
their captivity and Memphis, a chief city of Egypt,
represents a burying ground for their luxuries. "The
days of visitation," or recompense, were already upon $\quad$ *9:7*
them; they were even then suffering the consequences
of their folly. Israel would be made to realize that the
prophet, the man who claimed the Spirit of God and
who had aroused false hopes in the hearts of the
people, was a fool (cf. Mic. 2:11). The deceitfulness of
the prophet (false prophet) and the iniquity of the
people go hand in hand. With the blind leading the
blind, both were falling into the pit. However, there is
another interpretation of the passage: Ephraim would
realize that it was only in the minds of the people
that the true prophet was a fool and that he was mad.
In reality it was their own iniquity that led them to
such a conclusion. In the light of the context it seems
that the first suggestion is correct. They had been
deceived by false prophets and would realize this.
Their prophets had been fools. The following verse is $\quad$ *9:8*
quite difficult. Was Ephraim a "watchman *with* my
God" or "*against* my God," as in the margin (ASV)?
The use of *my* God and *his* God indicates that
Ephraim was a spy or watchman against God and that

his (Ephraim's) prophets were a snare in the way of the people. In the house of *his* god he was an enemy to the *true* God. God did appoint prophets to be watchmen *with* Him (Ezek. 3:17), but the prophets of Ephraim were watchmen *against* Him. When Hosea looked for an experience in the history of the people with which to compare the depth of their present corruption, he appealed to the conduct of their fathers in the days of Gibeah, when one of the tribes was all but exterminated because of its wickedness (Judg. 19—20). Ephraim had now become as abominable as in those days. God would remember their iniquity and visit their sins with a comparable judgment.

9:9

> *9:10-17. God had found Ephraim as one greatly to be desired; but he had corrupted himself beyond God's ability to claim him. He would cast them away, and if children should be born to them they would be slain.*

9:10

The prophet reverts to the early days of Israel's history as he does in 10:1 and 11:1. In the freshness of Israel's youth Jehovah had found them, "your fathers," but they had corrupted themselves at Baalpeor. As in the wilderness one comes upon a vine laden with clusters of ripe grapes which gladden the eye, so Jehovah had found Israel. And as one delights in the first ripe figs of the early summer after a long season of no fresh fruit, so Jehovah had looked upon His chosen ones. It was a pleasant picture indeed. But at Baal-peor they had prostituted themselves before the idols, committing sin against Jehovah by joining with the people of Moab in the worship of Baal of Peor (see Num. 25:1-9). Lust for the material and the physical which seduced them to idol worship had been their downfall from the beginning. A person becomes like what he worships. The glory that God had so graciously bestowed upon Ephraim, meaning "double-fruit," would be taken away; it would fly away like a bird. This "double-fruit" would become double barrenness. The women would be barren; to

9:11

9:12

the Jews this was a mark of divine disfavor. And if they should conceive and bear children, God would bereave them of these until there would be none remaining. Only woe could be expected when Jehovah would depart from the people. Tyre was a **9:13** powerful and prosperous city located on the beautiful Mediterranean coast. With the sea to the west and mountains to the east, Tyre should have been secure. God had selected a soil like Tyre in which to plant Ephraim where he, too, could have become strong and prosperous, beautiful in the divine sight, protected in a secluded spot. But instead of enjoying prosperity Ephraim would bring out his children to be slaughtered by a foreign power. Standing in the indig- **9:14** nation of Jehovah's righteousness, the prophet excitedly appeals to Jehovah to give them—but what will He give them? For what will he pray? "Give them a miscarrying womb and dry breasts." Let the judgment be complete; let the nation be brought to an end by lack of offspring brought to maturity. This would be preferable to bearing children and rearing them for the slayer. From "double-fruit" to "double-barrenness" was now to be their lot.

Gilgal, located in the Jordan valley northeast from **9:15** Jerusalem, had been the scene of many of Jehovah's blessings. It was there that Israel camped and ate the first of the produce of the land when they came out of Egypt, and it was there that stones had been set up in memory of their passing over Jordan (Josh. 4:19-20). There the reproach of their failure to circumcise, keeping the covenant of Abraham, had been rolled away (Josh. 5:9). At Gilgal the covenant of the divine appointment of Saul as king had been renewed, and there he had been anointed (I Sam. 11:14-15). It was at Gilgal that the blessings of Jehovah's deliverance from Egypt had been culminated (Mic. 6:5). But now, idolatry of the basest sort had been found in Gilgal; and for this the people would be cast out of Jehovah's congregation. Instead of being His people, enjoying His mercy and favor, they had become "Loruhamah," without a father's mercy, and "Lo-ammi," not my people. Again a play is made on the word **9:16**

Ephraim. From "double-fruit" they should become fruitless, dried up, bearing no fruit; and what would be born would be destroyed. They would be cast off by Jehovah; they would be wanderers among the nations. And all of this was come to pass because they did not hearken unto Jehovah in the day in which He had called to them. What a warning this should be to all men for all time!

9:17

Chapter 10

10:1-3. Puppet gods and puppet kings had led the people away from God into utter confusion.

10:1

Israel is described as a luxuriant vine, a running vine that puts out its shoots and bears abundant fruit. As such a vine it should have filled Jehovah's land and should have borne a satisfying harvest to Jehovah. But instead, according to its fruitfulness, the nation had multiplied altars and obelisks to the baalim, acknowledging them as the source of their fruitfulness.

10:2

Their heart was divided, "smooth," deceitful; their altars (plural) testified to their guilt before Jehovah. They had given lip service to Jehovah, but in their hearts they had worshiped the baalim. And now Jehovah will "break the neck" (Harper) of their idols and statues (see Ps. 80:8-19). To fear Jehovah is to reverence Him, and to reverence Him is to serve Him. And now, because there was not this reverence for Jehovah, He would not help them but would be against them. The king could do nothing for them. Therefore, being without God and having only an impotent king, they would be brought to the realization of their utter helplessness as the judgment for their guilt fell upon them. Puppet kings and puppet gods are helpless to save in time of need.

10:3

10:4-8. The calf of the "House of Vanity" will be for terror to the people. It will be

*carried away to Assyria. Terror and destruc-
tion reign.*

Hypocrisy is exposed and condemned! The rulers   *10:4*
who speak empty words, swearing falsely (cf. 4:2) in
making covenants which they do not intend to keep,
as with Assyria (5:13) or with Egypt (7:11), are
condemned. The "judgment" which springs up "as
hemlock in the furrows of the field" is not that of
divine punishment, but rather it is "justice" or
"right" which is perverted into wrong and becomes
bitter or poisonous. Their "right," which was "unrighteousness," and their "justice," which was "injustice," have now become as hemlock (cf. Deut.
29:18), a bitter and poisonous herb. Because of this   *10:5*
condition the people of Samaria will be in terror for
the calves (plural, for one was at Beth-el and the
other at Dan), and will mourn over it (singular, the
one at Beth-el), for its glory was now departing. Beth-
el, "house of God," has now become Beth-aven,
"house of vanity," for it is the essence of emptiness.
The *chemarim* (see II Kings 23:5; Zeph. 1:4), the
priests of the idols who with the people had rejoiced
over the calf, will now mourn with the people over it.
When it is carried away, its glory will go with it. The
calf will be unable to save itself and will be carried as   *10:6*
a present to "king Jareb," combat, striver, warrior,
king of Assyria. Ephraim and Israel will both be
ashamed of the counsel to which they had listened in
worshiping the calves, for it has brought them to
nothing. Samaria's king will be cut off as a chip or   *10:7*
twig on the water. The destruction of the monarchy
indicated here is the destruction of the nation. "The   *10:8*
high places also of Aven," the places of vanity or
idolatry, which was the sin of Israel, will be destroyed. And on the altars before which they once
worshiped will come up thorns and thistles, symbols
of desolation. In their fright the people will cry for
the mountains and the hills to cover them and to fall
upon them. The people of Judah would seek a similar
refuge at the threat of destruction by her enemies

(Isa. 2:19). Centuries later there would rise from the inhabitants of Jerusalem a similar cry as the Romans threatened them with destruction (Luke 23:30). The enemies of God's people will seek the same protection as their world crashes about them (Rev. 6:16).

10:9-11. Israel's persistency in sinning from her early history till now shall bring severe chastening.

10:9 Again the prophet introduces the incident at Gibeah (cf. 9:9), as he charges that they have "sinned from the days of Gibeah," or, "more than in the days of Gibeah" (margin, ASV). The text of the American Standard Version is followed instead of the footnote. The text is difficult and writers have given various interpretations to it, which, except one, are passed over. Pusey, accepting the text, offers a probable and acceptable explanation when he suggests it means that "not a battle like that in Gibeah, terrible as that was, shall now overtake them; but one far worse. For although the tribe of Benjamin was then reduced to six hundred men, yet the tribe still survived and flourished again; now the kingdom of the ten tribes, and the name of Ephraim, should be utterly cut off."

10:10 This judgment or chastening will be only when God wills it: "when it is my desire." And this chastisement will be by Jehovah's bringing heathen nations against Israel, "when they are bound to their two transgressions." Scholars are divided in their opinions concerning the two transgressions. Some think the prophet refers to the calves at Dan and Beth-el, but most reject this. Others hold that the two transgressions are the same as those of Jeremiah's day, the forsaking of Jehovah, the fountain of living water, and turning to idols (Jer. 2:13). Others suggest "idols and man-made kings" (G. A. Smith); "apostasy from Jehovah and the royal house of David" (Keil); "apostasy from the house of David, and the true worship of the Lord" (Laetsch); "the cult and . . . the establishment of the kingdom" (Harper). Most probably the "two transgressions" are the rejection of Jehovah as their King, when they asked for a king like those of the nations around them (I Sam. 8), and their rejection of Him as their God, when they introduced idolatry. Ephraim, *10:11* standing for Israel, is like a young cow that is taught to thresh, and that loved to thresh the grain because of the advantage to herself. The animal threshing the grain should not be muzzled; therefore, she could eat while doing the work (Deut. 25:4). But this would all be changed: Jehovah would put a heavy yoke upon her fair or beautiful neck and a rider would drive her. This will be when Israel is carried into "Egypt," the bondage that lay ahead. Again Judah is introduced: The two, Judah and Jacob (Israel), would do the hard, servile labor of slaves, as plowing and harrowing the sod in the field of their enemies.

10:12-15. The prophet calls the people to return to righteousness, but with little hope of response. They have gone too far.

This threat of judgment is followed by a call to *10:12* repentance announced or given by the prophet in the form of three commands: (1) "Sow to yourselves in righteousness," for before a harvest can be reaped there must be a sowing; therefore, to reap the good of righteousness one must sow in righteousness. (2) "Reap according to kindness," or "love"; for reaping according to love will have to be preceded by sowing in righteousness. (3) "Break up your fallow ground": land that has lain idle and untilled, which would represent righteousness and faithfulness toward God. That this had been long neglected is indicated by the call to seek Jehovah that he would come and rain righteousness on the people. In apposition to what *10:13* God calls on them to do, He points to what they have been doing—"ye have plowed wickedness, ye have reaped iniquity." For instead of trusing in Jehovah, they had trusted in lies and in the strength of a multitude of men. Eating the fruit of lies would be to *10:14* experience the consequence of idolatry. And now a tumult as a rushing of mighty waters will rise against the people; this had been threatened by Amos against

Moab (Amos 2:2). Fortresses, the objects in which they had trusted, will be destroyed. "Shalman" is uncertain, but probably refers to Shalmanezer, king of Assyria. The occasion of the destruction of Beth-arbel is unknown, as well as the location; but whenever or wherever it occurred, the incident was terrible *10:15* and well known to the house of Israel. Mothers and children were dashed in pieces by their destroyers. So will Beth-el bring destruction on you, inasmuch as it has been the seat of your idolatry and is now the cause of Israel's destruction. At daybreak, or at what appeared to be the dawning of a better day, the destruction will come. The king will be utterly cut off; he will rise no more.

Chapter 11

11:1-4. Jehovah persists in His love for the ungrateful nation. As a father teaches an infant son to walk, so had Jehovah led Ephraim, only to be paid back by ingratitude.

11:1   Once more the prophet looks back to the beginning of Israel's history (cf. 9:10; 10:9). When Israel was but a child God had called him out of Egypt. Although so richly blessed by God's benevolence and affection bestowed from his childhood, Israel's ingratitude is now Jehovah's remuneration from the ungrateful nation. In its context the passage seems to have no direct reference to the Messiah (see Matt. 2:15). But as Keil so aptly puts it, the passage was quoted by Matthew "because the sojourn in Egypt, and return out of that land, had the same significance in relation to the development of the life of Jesus Christ, as it had to the nation Israel. Just as Israel grew into a nation in Egypt, where it was out of the reach of Canaanitish ways, so was the child Jesus hidden in Egypt from the hostility of Herod." In Egypt Jehovah had claimed Israel as His son, His first-born (Exod. 4:22-23), and from there He had called him to Himself. Jehovah had found Israel as "grapes in the wilderness," to be greatly desired. But the more He blessed them the more they had sinned (cf. 9:10; 10:1). The more God sent prophets to warn and call the people to Himself, the more had they served the baalim and burned incense to the images. This was an expression of sheer ingratitude to Jehovah. As a tender father, Jehovah had taken infant Israel by the arms and supported him as He taught him to walk. Taking him into His arms, close to His great heart, He had healed the people of their hurt in stumbling; He had been a Father-physician to them. "I drew them with cords of a man." As a devoted father would lead his young son with cords and bands of love, God had led them. From the beginning Jehovah had been concerned for their faithfulness to Him, and had been solicitous for their comfort and good. As one moved by sympathy would lift up the yoke and set food before a weary animal, so Jehovah had been moved by divine compassion and concern for the welfare of His chosen people. But what had He received in return? His reward was ingratitude toward Himself and a disposition on their part to turn from Him to dumb idols.

11:2

11:3

11:4

11:5-7. The prophet clearly reveals that the "Egypt" of their bondage will be Assyria.

For this spirit of ingratitude and contempt for Jehovah, the people will go into captivity. The prophet now declares clearly where that captivity will be: it will not be Egypt, but Assyria. Egypt was the symbol or type of bondage, and so into Egypt they will go (8:13; 9:3, 6). Yet they will not be taken into Egypt literally, but into bondage in the land of Assyria. They will return to bondage because they had not returned to Jehovah; the Assyrian will be their king because they had refused to have Jehovah as King. Because of the false counsel to which they had listened, the sword of destruction will ravage their cities. The branches—more correctly, bars—by which the gates were secured against entrance by others, will be devoured. That upon which they rested for security will melt away under the onslaught of Assyria. The

11:5

11:6

11:7

people had their heart set on backsliding from
Jehovah; they were completely bound to their transgressions. "Though they call" ("they" being either
the prophets, v. 2, or a very few among the people
who saw the impending ruin coming upon them,
probably the prophets), there were none who looked
above or who sought to lift themselves to a higher
plane of life.

> *11:8-11. How could God give them up? This
> is one of the most emotional passages in the
> book.*

11:8   This threat of judgment and captivity (vv. 5-7) is
followed by one of the most deeply emotional passages in the book: how will God give them up? How
will He cast them off? How can God destroy Israel as
He destroyed Admah and Zeboiim, cities of the plain
with Sodom and Gomorrah, which He destroyed in
11:9   His wrath because of their wickedness (Deut. 29:23)?
Jehovah's heart is represented as being heavy within
Him; His compassions were deeply kindled. He will
not completely exterminate Israel. Though they be
brought to the brink of destruction as Benjamin had
been (Judg. 19—20), or as the people in the wilderness had been (Exod. 32:10), Jehovah would not
execute the fulness of His wrath by annihilating them
as their deeds deserved. After the execution of the
judgment now at hand in which they would not be
completely destroyed, Jehovah would not destroy
them again. Is God here showing fickleness by saying,
"I will utterly destroy," and "I will not destroy"?
God answers this by declaring that He is not man, but
God; that the judgment will be the expression of the
wrath of a Holy God; and that the mercy shown will
likewise be of a righteous and infinite One. Once the
wrath has been poured out, He will have mercy on
11:10   the remnant. This is verified by what follows: "They
shall walk after Jehovah," which is the remnant who
give heed. To walk after Jehovah is to be obedient to
His will. God will roar, make His voice to be heard,
11:11   and the meek will come trembling from the west, or

from the sea. Likewise as a bird will they come trembling out of Egypt, the bondage into which they had been carried; as a dove seeking its resting place will they come out of Assyria. God will make them to dwell in their house, their place of protection under Him. Nothing is here said of their returning to Palestine. This word is a ray of hope to be realized under the Messiah, through whom they would be called by the gospel to peace and protection in Him. In fulfilling this prediction Hosea's earlier predictions will be fulfilled (1:11; 2:23; 3:5). They will have come to spiritual Zion (Heb. 12:22-28), to a heavenly fatherland (Phil. 3:20).

Chapter 12

In chapters 12—13, Israel's apostasy and God's fidelity are set forth in contrast.

11:12—12:6. Ephraim's infidelity and weakness are contrasted with Jacob's devotion and strength.

Jehovah now speaks. He charges Ephraim with *11:12* having surrounded the Lord with falsehood, and the house of Israel with having compassed Him with deceit. Repeatedly this had been Jehovah's charge against them (4:2; 6:7; 7:1, 3, 13; 10:4, 13). Again the Lord turns to Judah, but is it to commend or condemn him? The marginal reading (ASV) seems to give the correct thought, especially when compared with verse 2: "And Judah is yet unstedfast with God, and with the Holy One who is faithful." Judah is unbridled toward God. Ephraim grazes on the wind; *12:1* or as a hunter, he seeks the east wind, the terrible, dreaded sirocco which blows with scorching and devastating heat from the desert. Instead of seeking Jehovah in truth, Ephraim had surrounded Him with lies in his effort to court Assyria and Egypt. A covenant made with Assyria was not intended to be kept; for while in the process of making the covenant Ephraim had sent presents of oil to Egypt in an effort

12:2 to buy their help. Nor is Judah innocent. Though not so guilty as Israel she "was yet unstedfast with God" (cf. 11:12), and therefore should not escape the punishment for her sins. Jehovah has a controversy, a lawsuit, with Judah and will visit upon both peoples ("Jacob" includes both Israel and Judah) a judgment commensurate with their sins.

12:3 At this point the prophet looks back to the historical Jacob, the ancestor of both nations, and appeals to him as an example of one who had had power with God. In his birth his hand had held Esau's heel, which prophetically indicated that he would supplant his brother (Gen. 25:23-26). His high regard for the birthright and his desire to obtain it as his own was demonstrated in the hard bargain he drove with Esau in order to possess it (Gen. 25:27-34). Later he received the blessing from his father Isaac by deception

12:4 (Gen. 27:5-29). On his return from Padan-aram, Jacob met the Lord at the ford of the Jabbok and there wrestled all night with His angel and prevailed. His name was then changed from Jacob to Israel (Gen. 32:22-30). It was to this period of the patriarch's history that the prophet appeals, holding before the descendants of Israel the example of their illustrious ancestor who had so earnestly sought the birthright. And likewise, he presents Jacob as one who through weeping and supplication had found strength and favor with God. From the Jabbok Jacob moved to Beth-el where Jehovah spoke with him, instructing him to build an altar to Him (Gen. 35:1-15). There at Beth-el Jehovah had spoken to Jacob and through him to the descendants. The

12:5 power of Jacob to prevail was the power for Israel of Hosea's day if they would but avail themselves of it. This power was in the name of Jehovah, the God of hosts, and was to be laid hold on by weeping and making supplication before Him, as in the case of

12:6 Jacob. Having called to remembrance the power of their highly esteemed and venerable ancestor, the prophet makes an appeal to the people to turn to the God of their father Jacob, the God in whose name he had prevailed, and in Him find their power to live.

This power to prevail must be realized by turning to Him with the whole heart, demonstrated in showing kindness and justice toward their fellow men and in waiting "for thy God continually." To wait for Him is to put one's trust in Him and let Him lead the way. This they must do; it is the only way to salvation.

12:7-14. Instead of being an "Israel" the nation had become a "Canaan"—a fraudulent trafficker. Jacob and the nation are contrasted.

Instead of following the pattern of Jacob's intense leaning on Jehovah, Ephraim had become a "Canaan," a trafficker with false balances in his hand. He loved to defraud; it had become ingrained in his very nature. In trafficking with false balances and defrauding the people, Ephraim boasted that in his acquisition of wealth and riches he had committed no sin. He had gained his wealth independently of God; therefore, there was no sin against God. In this he had acted completely contrary to God's will as expressed in verse 6. But the Lord would assure Ephraim that he is not dealing with man, but with Jehovah who sees and knows all. He had been Ephraim's God from the days of Egypt; therefore, it was He who had blessed him. But because of their corrupt practices God would drive the people out of their land, and they will dwell in booths as in the wilderness of Sinai, the memory of which had been kept before them continually by the feast of tabernacles. *12:7* *12:8* *12:9*

They had no excuse for their ignorance of Jehovah, for He had spoken to them through prophets, through multiplied visions, and by the use of similitudes through which they should have learned. Again Gilead is singled out (cf. 6:8) as representing all that is false and wicked. At Gilgal where they had insulted Jehovah by worshiping Him in that city of idolatry, their altars would become as piles of rocks in a field—forsaken and desolate. What would happen at Gilgal would also be the lot of the nation. *12:10* *12:11*

Again the prophet appeals to the example of *12:12*

12:13   Jacob. He had fled into the land of Haran where he had served many years for his wife and where he had kept sheep for Laban. The prophet contrasts this with the lot of Israel. Jehovah had brought Israel out of Egyptian slavery by a prophet, Moses, and had given them the land of Canaan as a gracious gift. In contrast, Jacob had served as a slave for his wife, serving Laban for seven years without other remuneration; but the nation had been given its good land as a gift.

12:14   Instead of being grateful to God for what He had done, Ephraim had provoked Jehovah to bitter anger against him. Therefore his blood will be upon him; the blood-guilt for his crimes could be expiated only by the blood of the guilty. Punishment for his crimes was imperative.

Chapter 13

13:1-3. Israel's deep fall and the causes of that fall are set forth. Ephraim had been exalted, but in Baal he died.

13:1   From the height of favor with God and man Ephraim had fallen to the lowest depth. Blessed by Jacob above Manasseh (Gen. 48:18-20), Ephraim had stood tall among the tribes in the days of the judges (Judg. 8:1-3; 12:1 ff.), and was the tribe from which the first king of the ten tribes had been selected (I Kings 11:26 ff.). The prophet points to this exalted position held by Ephraim and the respect in which he was held by the other tribes; when he spoke, "there was trembling" and the people listened. But Ephraim's death warrant was sealed when he introduced idolatry. Calf worship was introduced by Jeroboam I, and pure Baal worship was given prominence by Ahab and Jezebel (I Kings 12:25 ff.; 16:29-33).

13:2   From the introduction of idolatry, Ephraim had accelerated the pace of sinning against Jehovah. From a perverted worship of Jehovah through the figure of the calf they had come to worship the idol itself; and from the calf-worship they had progressed to the introduction of a pure Baal cult. These were of their own understanding; God was left out. Kissing the calves, or kissing the hand toward the calves or idols, was an act of homage or devotion expressed toward the false deity. The practice of "kissing the hand toward" is found as early as Job and later in the days of Elijah (see Job 31:27; I Kings 19:18). The Spirit instructs kings of the earth to kiss the Son, that is, to do homage to Him (Ps. 2:12). The prophet followed this charge with four figures that illustrate the passing of Ephraim: They who worship idols (1) will pass away as the morning cloud that appears for a short time and vanishes; (2) will be as the dew that soon disappears under the rising sun; (3) will be as chaff that is driven away from the threshing-floor by the wind; and (4) will resemble the smoke of the chimney that is seen for a moment and then is gone. These four figures express in homely but vivid metaphors the disappearing of the idolaters.

13:3

13:4-8. It was Jehovah whom the nation had offended. He had blessed them in the wilderness; now He would tear them as wild beasts of the forest.

The tragedy of Ephraim's conduct was that Jehovah had been their God from Egypt, and had charged them over and over that they should have no other gods than Himself. It was He who had delivered the people; He alone is God. As the only God, he alone could save; besides Him there was no Saviour. In the great and terrible wilderness He had revealed Himself to them time upon time. "In the land of great drought" He had amply provided for their needs. Therefore they should have known no other god, for no other god had exerted good over them. "According to their pasture so were they filled." But God's people had been unable to abide prosperity, for the richer the blessings from Jehovah the farther they went from Him. Their hearts were exalted; they became proud, worshiping the creatures of their own imagination rather than the true God. As Moses had predicted, so it had come to pass: "But Jeshurun

13:4

13:5

13:6

waxed fat, and kicked. . . . Then he forsook God who made him" (Deut. 32:15). In their prosperity they forgot God. This tragic example has been emulated many times since by the people of God's favor.

13:7 Another "therefore" is introduced. In verse 3 a "therefore" had introduced the passing of Ephraim; now it introduces the power which brings that de-

13:8 struction. God would be to them as a lion, a leopard, a bear. God would treat them as a lion treats its prey; He would be as the leopard that watches by the way; as a bear bereaved of its cubs, He would rend the caul of the hearts of the people. The caul is the covering, cap, or enclosure of the heart. As these wild beasts of the forest or mountain tear and rend, so God would bring them to complete destruction by the judgment that had already begun. Who would be able to help them? No one, for they had rejected the Lord, and their idols would be utterly helpless to rescue them.

> *13:9-14. Distrust in God's kingship had led to their asking for a king. And now the king whom they had requested would be helpless to save them. However, through travail and sorrow there would come a new birth. God would redeem them.*

13:9 The only help for Israel had been Jehovah; now that they had rejected Him there was none. Their destruction was being wrought by their refusal to recognize Jehovah as God and by their rejection of Him. Why is this lesson so difficult to learn? Early in

13:10 their history they had asked for a king, which Jehovah had granted (I Sam. 8:4, 5); and at the division of the kingdom He had given them Jeroboam, the son of Nebat, of the tribe of Ephraim (I Kings 12:20). Instead of leading them in the way of truth, their kings had led them into idolatry and rebellion against God. The kings were weak and with-

13:11 out faith; they could now do nothing to save the people. God had given them a king in His anger; He would now take him away in His wrath. For God to restore the old political kingdom at some future date would be to restore what was in rebellion against His will from the beginning. However, Hosea is here speaking especially of the kings of the ten tribes. These all had been idolaters; from Jeroboam to Hoshea, the first to the last, there had not been a true worshiper of Jehovah among them. The cup of Ephraim's iniquity was now full. As men count money and put it away in a bag, so Jehovah had counted the sins of Ephraim and was holding them all for reckoning. They were laid up before Him for judgment. The figure of a travailing woman is common to the Scriptures. The sorrows and pains as of childbirth are upon the nation; however, the picture is that of a woman unable to perform the act. When the birth is retarded, the life of both mother and child is endangered. The prophet then shifts from the woman in pain to the child in the mouth of the womb about to be born. He should not tarry long at the opening of the womb because of this danger. Out of the pains of this experience there would be a new birth; a new nation would come forth. Is verse 14a to be interpreted as a threat, "Shall I ransom?" (Harper), or as a promise, "I will ransom, etc." (Keil, Deane, and others)? It is a promise of God to the doomed nation that though they go into captivity and there suffer the pangs of travail and sorrow, yet God will redeem them; He will deliver them from their captivity. Their restoration would be as a birth; also it would be as a resurrection from the dead (see Ezek. 37). The pestilences and destruction of Sheol would be overcome. Hosea looks not to Christ's resurrection or to ours, but to the restoration of the people. However, the true significance of death's destruction and of Sheol's defeat was not made clear until Christ's resurrection, and the complete defeat of death will be consummated in our own resurrection from the grave (I Cor. 15:54, 55). "Repentance shall be hid from mine eyes": God will not change His mind; He will fulfill His purpose of redemption. As the judgment against Ephraim was irrevocable, so the redemption and deliverance from Sheol was unchangeably determined.

13:12

13:13

13:14

13:15-16. "Double fruit" will now become a
dry waste. Irrevocable doom is decreed.

13:15   Ephraim, whose name meant "double-fruitful-
ness," would now become "fruitless." An east wind,
Assyria, would sweep them away as the terrible sirocco from the Arabian desert often dried up and destroyed the fields and orchards of the people.
Ephraim would become dry. He, the Assyrian, would
make spoil of all that Ephraim had counted precious.

13:16   Samaria, the capital where the treasures of Ephraim's
wickedness were stored, would become desolate. The
cause was that he had rebelled against his God; this
was his supreme sin. The picture of his end is one of
terror and destruction such as only the cruel
Assyrians could execute. "They shall fall by the
sword; their infants shall be dashed in pieces, and
their women with child shall be ripped up." The sun
would set upon the rebellious and wicked nation in
the midst of the storm of heaven's divine wrath and
anger.

Chapter 14

*14:1-9. Israel's conversion and pardon. As
Israel comes to Jehovah with words of true
repentance, Jehovah pardons and restores to
His own favor those who had wandered so far.*

14:1   From the dark picture of judgment and destruction
of the sinful kingdom, the prophet looks with hope
to the future when the faithful few will return. After
the first three chapters of this book, the prophet
seems to make only one allusion to the Messianic
hope (11:10-11) until this point is reached in his
prophecy. The call is to repentance and to a complete
conversion. By their iniquity they had fallen, and
now by genuine repentance they would be restored.

14:2   "Take with you words": not empty, half-hearted
words, but words expressing the deep penitence of
the heart. Their words should be pleas for forgiveness,
such as express the fervent desire that Jehovah will

accept their plea as genuine. The offerings brought to the Lord would not be offerings of animals, but those of praise and thanksgiving, the melody and joy of the heart. Repentance will be expressed in a complete trust in and dependence on God. No more would reliance be placed on Assyria and Egypt, the powers of evil; nor would they trust in military might or in the idols of their own creation, but in God. For in Him alone do the helpless find mercy.

14:3

In response to this plea from the penitent remnant Jehovah replies indirectly through the prophet. Their sin of apostasy will be considered as a terrible disease which Jehovah will heal. Their reward will be His great love which He will bountifully bestow upon them; at the same time His anger will be turned away. Jehovah will be to His people as the refreshing dew, copiously distilled upon them, preserving and nourishing life. Israel, in turn, will blossom as the lily, which suggests beauty, purity, sweetness of odor, and erectness in its growth. "Cast forth his roots as Lebanon" suggests the strength with which he will be able to withstand the tempests that may beset him, for the "roots of Lebanon" go deep into the heart of the earth. Beauty and strength are indicated by the two similes. "His branches shall spread"; that is, his influence will be extended to and felt by others. "His beauty shall be as the olive tree," fruitful and precious, highly prized by the people of the land. "The smell of Lebanon" indicates the constant freshness and fragrance as of the trees and herbs of the mountain. "They," those who dwell under the shadow and influence of the new Israel, will be so influenced by him that they will be caused to live and bear fruit also. This should impress the people of God with the power of a good influence over others. Ephraim, now the fruitful one, will have nothing more to do with idols. He will have learned his lesson. To this determination on the part of Ephraim Jehovah answers that He will be to him the source of his protection, and that from Jehovah will his fruit be found.

14:4

14:5

14:6

14:7

14:8

As suggested by Keil, "this verse contains the epi-

14:9

logue of the whole book." Who is wise? As the wise man said, "The fear of Jehovah is the beginning of wisdom" (Prov. 9:10). The wise man is one who fears the Lord, and the prudent man is one who can make a practical application of wisdom. These wise ones come to know the things which Jehovah has spoken—the things Hosea has written. The ways of Jehovah are right; those that walk in them stumble not, but transgressors stumble therein. God had made an earnest plea that His people hear and walk in His ways, but they did not listen; therefore, they had stumbled and must suffer the consequence. But a better day would come.

Retrospect. Hosea had deeply loved a maiden in Israel who, because of the influence of her idolatrous surroundings, had proved untrue to him. Though she bore him three children, he could not take these to his heart; for he did not know whether they were his. From adultery Gomer had gone into whoredom, selling herself to her lovers, which brought her to shame and the breaking of her husband's heart. Time took its toll. Finally she had lost her beauty and the charm of youth had faded. Her paramour put her on the slave block and sold her for the equivalent of the price of a gored slave. Out of the depth of a heart of love for this one who had been so dear to him, the prophet bought her. But she would not be a wife to him; she could only sit by the hearth of the home she had wrecked and there, in the depth of her conscience-stricken memory of what might have been, come to repentance.

Out of this terrible experience in his own life Hosea came to see more clearly than any prophet before him the depth of God's divine love for Israel. God had taken Israel to His heart, brought the people into a good land, and bestowed on them His love and the bounty of His great storehouse of material blessings. But for all this Israel had shown ingratitude and had gone whoring after the idols. Falling deeper and deeper into sin, she must learn the utter folly of her ways and be made to drink of the dregs of her cup. God cast her off but never ceased to love her. Though she must go for a time without a place of worship and experience a separation from her rightful husband, He would buy her back to Himself, redeem her, and make her once more His own. This the prophet saw clearly. Jehovah accomplished this redemption under the Messiah, and today the spiritual Israel of prophecy enjoys the favor of Jehovah and acts as the leavening influence for good in a world of wickedness. Hosea magnified the great and infinite love of God to its rightful place before man.

6
MICAH
" Who Is Like Jehovah "

General Observations

1. The Man

a. Home. Micah identifies himself with the village of Moresheth-gath (1:1, 14), a small town on the border between Judah ānd Philistia, twenty-two to twenty-five miles southwest of Jerusalem. It is thought that modern Beit-Jebrin now occupies the site of ancient Moresheth-gath. The fertile and richly productive soil with its fields, olive groves, and flower-covered hills stands in marked contrast to the home of Amos, seventeen miles to the east. But like the home of Amos, Moresheth-gath was sufficiently detached from Jerusalem to produce men of courage and independence of thought.

b. Occupation. Nothing is known of Micah's occupation. From his book one can surmise that Micah lived close to both the people and the soil and possessed a keen sympathy for both.

c. Characterization. Micah was the prophet of the poor and downtrodden. The reader immediately detects in him the courageous and fearless spirit of one who is indignant over the corruption and heartlessness of inhuman rulers and time-serving religionists. In clear and forceful tones he denounces the wrongs of his day. J. M. P. Smith (*I.C.C.*) has well summarized his relation to two contemporary prophets when he says, "He had Amos's passion for justice and Hosea's heart for love." Micah saw clearly the conditions and needs of the hour, and he met these by fearlessly attacking and condemning the sins of the people and by pointing them back to God. He summed up the source of his power when he said, "But as for me, I am full of power by the Spirit of Jehovah, and of judgment, and of might, to declare unto Jacob his transgression, and to Israel his sin" (3:8).

In many ways Micah and his contemporary, Isaiah, were alike; in other ways their differences are clearly discernible. Micah was a simple country man of unknown parentage, possessing deep compassion for those being oppressed. He took no interest in the political affairs of the day but gave himself to the concern of spiritual and moral problems. Isaiah, on the other hand, was of the city, in close contact with world affairs, and was the associate of kings and princes. He was the leader of the "Jehovah party," the loyalists of his day, standing in opposition to the pro-Assyria and pro-Egypt parties. However, there was one special thing these two great men shared in common: each saw Jehovah as the infinite ruler of nations and men. Each recognized the absolute holiness and majesty of their God, and each pointed out that to violate the principles of His divine sovereignty and holiness would bring inevitable doom. Jehovah's favor could be obtained only by the faithfulness and righteousness of the people as they leaned on Him for help, and not on the strength of men.

2. The Date: from about 735 B.C. to 700 B.C.

Micah began prophesying before the destruction of Samaria (1:5) and continued into the reign of Hezekiah (Jer. 26:18-19). He was a younger contemporary of Isaiah, as Hosea had been of Amos. Though contemporary with Isaiah, he appears to have begun prophesying a few years later (cf. Isa. 1:1; Mic. 1:1).

3. Background

a. **Political.** Through unusual leadership in successful wars and in the revival of commerce and the development of agriculture, Uzziah had brought a degree of prosperity to the people of Judah that had not been enjoyed since the days of Solomon. This prosperity brought with it the usual attendant social evils and spiritual falling away from Jehovah. Uzziah was succeeded by his son Jotham (740-736 B.C.), a good man who followed the policies of his father. Ahaz (736-716 B.C.), an unusually wicked king when compared to other kings of Judah, ruled after Jotham's death. Ahaz was succeeded by Hezekiah (716-687 B.C.), one of Judah's exceptionally good kings.

In the days of Ahaz, Judah was threatened by the coalition of Israel and Syria, whose two kings, Pekah and Rezin (Isa. 7), were indignant toward Ahaz because he would not join them in an alliance against Tiglath-pileser III, king of Assyria. While Tiglath-pileser III was at Damascus, Ahaz appealed to him for help; this proved costly to Judah both in tribute and in its independence. During the days of Hezekiah, Sargon II (722-705 B.C.), successor to the throne of Tiglath-pileser III and a ruler of unusual cruelty, invaded Judah 712/711 B.C. Following the death of Sargon II, Sennacherib became ruler of the Assyrian Empire. To secure his western provinces he invaded Judah 702/701 B.C., besieging Jerusalem and shutting Hezekiah up in Jerusalem "like a bird in a cage." According to the claims of Sennacherib's movements, he captured and claimed as booty forty-six Judean cities, which would no doubt include those spoken of by Micah (ch. 1). Among those captured was Lachish, considered by him to be of such significance that a bas-relief of the capture was made on one of the walls of his palace.

These were trying days, constantly overshadowed by the threat of invasion and foreign rule. Had it not been for the rule of the good King Hezekiah and the diligent and fearless preaching of Isaiah and Micah, it is probable that Judah would have gone the way of Israel. However, by the providence of God enough spiritual "salt" was found to save the land and the people from ruthless destruction by Assyria.

b. Social. Socially and morally Judah presented a dark picture during the latter part of the eighth century. Rulers sold the rights of men and vested interests gained control of the lands, taking away the privileges of the people. The wealthy coveted the lands (2:1-2) and robbed the poor (2:8), casting women out of their possessions (2:9). Corrupt business ethics were practiced (6:11). The people were under the powerful control of false prophets (2:11) who prophesied for reward (3:6, 11) and priests who taught for hire (3:11). Rulers in their greed were as cannibals (3:1-3, 9), and judges judged for a bribe (7:3). The corrupt concept of Jehovah held by the people was little different from the heathen concept of their gods (3:11b); they kept the statutes of Omri and walked in the counsels of Omri and Ahab (6:16). These conditions fanned the indignation of the prophet Micah into white heat, and he held not back from declaring to the nation their sins and to the people their transgressions (3:8).

c. **Religious.** Great religious reforms were initiated by Hezekiah (II Chron. 29—31). The priests sanctified themselves and cleansed the inner part of the house of God. In Jerusalem altars erected to heathen deities were destroyed, and the true worship of Jehovah was restored. The feasts and sacrifices were kept. The singers and players of instruments were once again employed as in the days of David. The altars and pillars were broken down not only in Jerusalem, but throughout the land of Judah and Ephraim and Manasseh. Also destroyed was the brazen serpent which was set up by Moses, but which had become an object of worship as an idol.

Micah seems not to have been very deeply impressed with these reforms. Religion had become a matter of form with the people; ceremonial observances were thought to meet all religious requirements. The reform was not from the deep recesses of the heart. There was widespread misapprehension that as long as the external acts of worship were scrupulously performed the people were entitled to the divine favor and protection. True, things were not as bad as in Israel, for Judah endured another 135 years after the fall of Samaria; but the religious fervor was too superficial to bring permanent results.

4. Teaching

a. **Jehovah.** The holiness of Jehovah and the righteousness of His government are stressed by Micah. His teaching at this point, as at others, is forceful and simple. As long as Jehovah's people do right they will enjoy His favor; when they turn away from Him and His standard they must suffer punishment. The good will of Jehovah cannot be obtained by carefully observing ritual, but by observing His divine principles of right in manner of life. A living fellowship with God must be maintained by a spirit of humility toward Him and by recognizing one's brotherly relation to his fellows. The prophet combats the heathen practices that had entered in. The social injustices are sternly rebuked as the people are brought before the bar of Jehovah in a spiritual lawsuit.

b. **The Messiah.** Micah's clear presentation of the Messianic hope is among the most outstanding to be found in all the prophets. He sees the mountain of Jehovah's house as above all other powers and kingdoms; he beholds Jehovah, in His righteousness, ruling and judging among the nations. But this would be accomplished through a ruler born in Bethlehem who would be coeternal with Jehovah. The enemies would be beaten down, and in contrast the Messianic kingdom would shine among all the nations of earth. The picture is graphic and glorious.

c. **Ethical Teaching.** It has been pointed out by others that Micah took the cardinal teachings of Amos, Hosea, and Isaiah and bound them into one embracing statement which includes all. Amos gave emphasis to the need of justice, "Let justice roll down as waters, and righteousness as a mighty stream." Mercy as shown in the lovingkindness of Jehovah was the great theme of Hosea. Isaiah pleaded with the people to have humble fellowship with God. Micah brings all of these together in his striking declaration, "What doth Jehovah require of thee, but to do justly, and to love kindness, and to walk humbly with thy God?" (6:8).

Outline of the Book

Title: Author and date of Micah's labors, 1:1

I. Judgment on Samaria and Judah—salvation of a remnant, chs. 1—2.

A. Judgment on Samaria and judgment on Judah, 1:2-16.
  1. Samaria—her destruction, vv. 2-7.
     a. General announcement of judgment, vv. 2-4.
     b. Destruction of Samaria, vv. 5-7.

      2. Lament over the destruction of Judah, vv. 8-16.

  B. Causes that make the judgment inevitable, 2:1-11.
      1. Arrogance and violence of the nobles, vv. 1-5.
      2. False prophets who would silence the true prophet, vv. 6-11.

  C. Eventual restoration of a remnant, 2:12-13.

II. Contrast between present devastation and future exaltation, chs. 3—5.

  A. The sins and crimes of the heads of the nation, ch. 3.
      1. Civil rulers—outrages committed by them, vv. 1-4.
      2. False prophets—condemnation of their mercenary practices, vv. 5-8.
      3. Rulers, prophets, and priests—renewed condemnation, vv. 9-12.
         a. The accusation against them, vv. 9-11.
         b. Consequence: Jerusalem to be plowed as a field, v. 12.

  B. The Messianic hope in contrast to present destruction, chs. 4—5.
      1. The glory of the latter days, 4:1-8.
         a. The glorification of Zion—the center of universal religion of Jehovah, vv. 1-5.
         b. The restoration of "the former dominion"—healing of the dispersed, vv. 6-8.
      2. Distress and captivity before restoration, "now," 4:9—5:1.
         a. Distress—into Babylon before restoration, 4:9-10.
         b. Deliverance of Zion and destruction of the enemy—Jehovah's purpose, 4:11—5:1.
      3. The Messiah and the Messianic era, 5:2-15.
         a. The Messiah who shall arise out of Bethlehem, shall feed the flock, vv. 2-4.
         b. The Messiah to be the peace of His people, vv. 5-6.
         c. The Messiah provides power to His people, vv. 7-9.

           (1) The remnant to be as dew among the peoples, v. 7.
           (2) To be as a lion, v. 8.
           (3) To triumph over their enemies, v. 9.
       d. In this strength and power Israel is to triumph, vv. 10-15.

III. Jehovah and Israel in controversy (judicial contest)—the way to salvation, chs. 6—7.

    A. The case against Israel, ch. 6.
       1. Israel's ingratitude for blessings bestowed, vv. 1-5.
       2. Not outward sacrifice, but righteous conduct, is God's requirement, vv. 6-8.
       3. Jehovah's threat of judgment—denunciation of prevalent crimes, vv. 9-14.

    B. Penitential prayer and divine promise, ch. 7.
       1. Confession of the nation's guilt (people, or prophet), vv. 1-6.
       2. Confession of faith—prayer of the penitent, vv. 7-13.
       3. Prayer for renewal of grace, v. 14; and the Lord's answer, vv. 15-17.
       4. Doxology: praise to Jehovah who alone is God, vv. 18-20.

Comments

Chapter 1

1:1   "The word of Jehovah that came to Micah" introduces the entire prophecy as having come from Jehovah. It was God's word through the prophet. Moresheth-gath was a village about twenty-two to twenty-five miles southwest of Jerusalem on the boundary between Judah and Philistia. Three kings of Judah are named because the prophet was sent primarily to Judah. The omission of Uzziah's name indicates that Micah's prophetic work began shortly after Isaiah had begun to prophesy. As Hosea had prophesied to Israel but had included Judah, so Micah prophesied to Jerusalem and Judah and included Samaria. Although the prophet's preaching was directed to Jerusalem, it was confined to the villages out from Jerusalem. The inclusion of both Israel and Judah clearly indicates that God considered them as one people, His people.

1:2-7. The nations are called to witness the judgment of Jehovah on Samaria and Jerusalem. The severity of the judgment is described.

The prophet begins by calling the nations of earth to behold the judgment of the Lord against the people of His wrath and to learn a lesson from this. His judgment against Israel and Judah should be a warning to all heathen nations. The "holy temple" is not Jerusalem, but heaven; it is from there that the judgment emanates. "Jehovah cometh" indicates the nearness of the judgment as He "cometh forth out of his place," the heavenly temple. The throne from which He descends is higher than the highest of the high places, for He comes to tread upon these. All nature is thrown into convulsion at His presence. The figures of volcano and earthquake are used by the prophet as he pictures melting hills with lava flowing like water down into the valleys. This figure of speech is not to be taken literally but as a figurative illustration of the terribleness of the judgment. "For the transgression of Jacob is all this." Jacob stands for both houses, Israel and Judah. "Israel," in the latter part of the verse, is the northern ten tribes. This seems preferable to making Jacob and Israel synonymous for the whole covenant people. "For all this" points to the judgment announced in verse 4. The crimes of the ten tribes of Israel are found in Samaria, and the transgressions of Judah are found in the high places of Jerusalem. "The high places" in Jerusalem are the shrines to idols found there. The capitals and the rulers of the two nations are held responsible for leading the two peoples into apostasy and ruin.

1:2

1:3

1:4

1:5

1:6   Samaria, proud and corrupt, formerly at ease in her mountain fortress (Amos 6:1), is to be cast down, becoming an utter waste. The stones of her magnificent buildings and supposedly impregnable walls would be rolled down into the surrounding valley. She would be cleared of these as one clears a place for

1:7   planting a vineyard. "All her graven images," the objects of her adoration and trust, "shall be beaten to pieces." This will clearly reveal their impotence and inability to save others or themselves. "All her hires shall be burned with fire." The hires were her wealth which she considered to have been given her by the baalim which she worshiped. "For of the hire of a harlot hath she gathered them." Jehovah looked upon the idol worship of His people as spiritual harlotry; the people had sold themselves as prostitutes to the baalim for the hire of material blessings (see Hosea). All these objects of her worship and symbols of her spiritual prostitution would be beaten in pieces. Her wealth and golden images for which she had worshiped the baalim and for which she had given them credit, would perish. "And unto the hire of a harlot shall they return." Israel had looked upon her prosperity as the pay for her spiritual service to the baalim. The idols were built from her wealth. Though beaten down, these idols and Israel's wealth would be carried into a foreign nation and there be offered by the conqueror before his idols as further wages in religious harlotry.

> 1:8-16. *The seriousness of the coming judgment is emphasized by the prophet's dress and by the paronomastic play on the names of the villages involved.*

1:8   Because of the terrible judgment to come on Samaria the prophet would lament and wail in a dirge-like utterance characteristic of oriental peoples in times of great grief. He would strive to impress on the sinners about him the terribleness of this judgment and to warn them of its imminence by going barefoot and wearing the garb of a captive. "I will go stripped and naked," not nude as we would think of being naked, but stripped of his ordinary clothes and dressed as a captive. He would wail with the mournful sounds of the jackal and the fearful and doleful screech of the ostrich, familiar sounds to the people he addressed. Micah realized that the wounds of Samaria were incurable; she had gone beyond hope of redemption. From the sins of Samaria and the judgment about to befall her, he looks to his own beloved Judah in his deepest grief. The sins and the consequent judgment of Samaria have reached to Jerusalem. "The gate of my people" points to Jerusalem as the meeting place of the people.

1:9

In a unique and mournful dirge, the prophet pictures the desolation that is to sweep the country. Making a play on the names of villages and towns in the section of country about him, he expresses his grief in a series of paronomasias. All commentators recognize and give special attention to this. In spite of the possibility that he may have exaggerated the translation and application in some instances, Farrar's translation is inserted here because it emphasizes the thought so clearly:

1:10

> In Gath (Tell-town) tell it not;
> In Akko (Weep-town) weep not!
> In Beth-le-Aphrah (Dust-town) roll thyself in dust.
> Pass by, thou inhabitress of Shaphir (Fairtown) in nakedness and shame!
> The citizen of Zaanan (March-town) marched not forth.
> The mourning of Beth-ezel (Neighbor-town) taketh from you its standing-place.
> The inhabitress of Maroth (Bitter-town) is in travail about good,
> Because evil hath come down from Jehovah to the gate of Jerusalem.
> Bind the chariot to the swift horse, thou inhabitress of Lachish (Horse-town);
> She was the beginning of sin for the daughter of Zion,

> For the transgressions of Israel were found in
> thee.
> Therefore will thou (Oh, Zion) give dismissal
> (farewell presents) to Moresheth-Gath
> (The Possession of Gath).
> The houses of Achzib (False-spring) become
> Achzab (a disappointing brook) to Israel's
> kings.
> Yet will I bring the heir (namely, Sargon, king
> of Assyria) to thee,
> thou citizen of Mareshah, (Heirtown).
> Unto Adullam (the wild beasts' cave) shall the
> glory of Israel come!
> Make thyself bald (Oh, Zion) for the children
> of thy delight.
> Enlarge thy baldness as the vulture,
> For they are gone into captivity from thee
> (1:10-16). (F. W. Farrar, *The Minor
> Prophets,* pp. 130-131.)

"Tell it not in Gath" may have become a proverb (cf.
II Sam. 1:20), for by this time it is quite probable
that Gath had been destroyed. Beth-le-aphrah, "a
house of dust," "I have rolled," or "roll thyself" in
the dust, was an indication of sorrow or shame. In
1:11 Shaphir, "beauty-town" or "fair-town," nakedness
and shame would be substituted for beauty or fair.
They are not marching from Zaanan, "march-town,"
for apparently they shut themselves up behind the
1:12 walls of the city. Beth-ezel, "neighbor-town," will no
longer stand by as a neighbor. Maroth, "bitterness,"
waits anxiously for good, but only bitterness and evil
from Jehovah come down to it, even to the gates of
1:13 Jerusalem. Lachish was an important post on the
border of Judah toward Egypt. "The paronomasia
here is in the similarity of sound (in the Hebrew HH)
between chariot and Lachish" *(I.C.C.).* "Bind the
chariot to the swift steed": make preparation to flee
before the enemy. "She was the beginning of sin to
the daughter of Zion." In what way Lachish was the
beginning of sin to the daughter of Zion is unknown.
G. A. Smith offers the best suggestion: "As the last

Judaean outpost towards Egypt, and on a main road thither, Lachish would receive the Egyptian subsidies of horses and chariots, in which the politicians put their trust instead of in Jehovah." If he is correct, in this was the sin of Zion found in Lachish. Zion will now lose one of her towns, Moresheth-gath, and not only will she lose it, but she will also be giving a parting gift to the Assyrian conqueror as he takes the town. Achzib, "false-town" or "lying-fountain," will prove true to its name, for it will become a false possession to the kings of Israel as it passes to their enemies to become their possession. Mareshah is to be distinguished from Moresheth-gath. Mareshah, "heir-town" or "hereditary city," that which possesses, will become the possession of another. "The glory of Israel shall come even unto Adullam." All of which they had been proud will be brought to Adullam, "the wild beasts' cave," even to captivity and shame. "They are gone into captivity." The prophet speaks as if the people are already gone into bondage for he sees little to encourage him otherwise. As a mother deprived or bereaved of her children, let Zion make herself bald as a vulture, whose neck and head are almost completely bare. Let the people mourn, for they and their children are destined to be led away. Captivity! Exile! Terrible word, but such do the people face who fail to give God His rightful place.

1:14

1:15

1:16

Chapter 2

2:1-11. The judgment is made necessary by the arrogance and corruption of the rulers. These would add to their sins by forbidding the true prophets to prophesy.

The judgment announced in chapter 1 is made necessary by the arrogance and wickedness of the rulers and the wealthy class in whose hand is the power to oppress. "Woe to them that devise iniquity and work evil upon their beds!" Their wickedness is planned and deliberate. "Woe," sorrow or affliction, be upon them; for instead of retiring at night to sleep, they lie awake scheming and devising evil plans. When

2:1

it is morning they are able to carry these out because it is in the power of their hand; they control the judges and have power over the lower classes. The

2:2 prophet passes over the intermediate "how" their nefarious plans are accomplished, but he sees them no sooner planned than executed. In the excessive avarice of the rulers, the fields, houses, and heritage of the poor are swallowed up greedily; they show no concern for the resultant suffering brought on the poor. When wealth is centered in the hands of a few, they are able to buy property at their discretion and thereby control the economy. The concentration of ownership of the land forces the population to move into congested cities, which leads to further moral

2:3 decay. The lessons of history are preserved for following generations and should teach men today. "Therefore thus saith Jehovah": the Lord raises His voice against the evil. Jehovah now speaks; because of this ruthless exercise of power He will devise and bring evil against "this family," the people of Judah; there will be no escape from this calamity. Instead of walking haughtily as in the past, they will now be humbled as the yoke of disaster "which I devise" will come upon them. "For it is an evil time": the Assyrians were pressing westward, carrying destruc-

2:4 tion in their wake. They seemed to be invincible. "In that day," the day of judgment and disaster, the opponents and enemies of Judah will take up "a parable," a taunt-song against these wealthy oppressors who will have been brought low. The doleful lamentation of the people, "It is done," "We are ruined," is wrung from their hearts as God takes away the portion or inheritance belonging to His people and gives it to the enemies. The people's cry of lamentation and ruin is taken up by the conquerors in a taunting and sneering mockery of their misery. The mockery heaped on the heads of the poor by the wealthy when it was in their power to rob, is now heaped on the heads of the wealthy as their inheritance is divided among the conquerors. Micah now

2:5 addresses the individual oppressors who have so ruthlessly oppressed the poor. Because of their having robbed the poor they will have no inheritance; there will be none to measure by line an inheritance for them. The inheritance had been measured and divided by lot when Israel came into the land, but the rich had removed the landmarks. Now the boundaries of their own lands would melt away. They will be cast out of their heritage as they have cast the poor out of theirs.

"Prophesy ye not, thus they prophesy." There is division of opinion whether the speakers here are the wealthy oppressors whom Micah has condemned, or the false prophets. It is probably the wealthy speaking through their representatives, the false prophets, who shared with the rich their indignation at the words of Micah. The passage is difficult, but Deane seems to have the best explanation as he suggests that the great men and the false prophets accuse the true prophets of preaching misfortune and denunciations, pointing constantly to judgment. They insist that the true prophets desist from such prophesying (P.C.). "Shall it be said, O house of Jacob, Is the Spirit of Jehovah straitened?" Are these the words of the speaker or speakers of verse 6, who question Jehovah's doing anything but good to His people? They are saying such an idea is absurd! God will do only good to His people (G. A. Smith). On the other hand, is not this the reply of the prophet himself? Most commentators hold to this latter view. Jehovah's Spirit is not shortened or impatient; He seeks their good. His words, whether of instruction or of warning and judgment, are intended for the good of the people; but they do good only to those who walk in them. The prophet charges that instead of walking uprightly in His words, the people have become the enemy of God and of those who would walk uprightly. "Ye strip the robe," the outer garment, "from off the garment," the under garment, "from them that pass by." Men who would live at peace and are averse to violence and corruption became the targets of the violent. Those stripped are probably debtors who can walk peacefully in neither the country nor in the city without being molested,

2:6

2:7

2:8

2:9

2:10 but who desire such a tranquil climate in which to live. The enmity of this aristocracy toward their own people is further shown by their disposition toward the women and children when they cast them out of their own homes. Making them homeless does not worry the heartless rulers. In thus destroying their nation, the people of God, they were depriving them of their rightful glory and the glory due God through them. "For ever" indicates that their practice was continual. Such practices demand their removal from the land, "Arise ye, and depart." As they had displaced the poor and the women and children, so now will they be displaced as they are driven out of the land. Their land would no longer be their resting place, for their uncleanness had made it fit only for purging and cleansing. The prophet has now answered

2:11 their objection to his prophesying and is ready to point out to them the kind of prophet they want. The prophet who will tell them the things they want to hear, speaking of prosperity, luxuries, and strong drink, "he shall even be the prophet of this people," and the one to whom they would listen.

2:12-13. *The dark cloud is penetrated by a Messianic promise: a remnant will be saved.*

2:12 The prophet interrupts his message of judgment with a word of hope and encouragement. Although this people will be cast out of their land, there to perish for their sins, yet Jehovah will bring back the faithful remnant. "Jacob" and "the remnant of Israel" stand for all who will return, those of the ten tribes and of the tribe of Judah. "As the sheep of Bozrah" indicates a large group. Bozrah was a chief city of Edom, noted for its large flocks of sheep. Although a remnant, yet the noise of their rejoicing

2:13 will be as of a great multitude of men. "The breaker is gone up" is thought to be the Messiah who breaks down the wall of sin that separated them from the Lord and made them bondsmen. As they go out their King, the Messiah, leads them, with Jehovah at the head. It is conceded by most commentators that these two verses present a Messianic picture. The "breaker" is the liberator, one who breaks through the gates of their bondage; the king is Jehovah, working through the Messiah. The whole work is of Jehovah. This glorious hope in the midst of a prophecy of judgment and doom is the prophet's answer to his critics who would accuse him of preaching only adversity.

Chapter 3

3:1-12. Micah utters three oracles against the leaders of the nation: (1) against the rulers, vv. 1-4; (2) against the false prophets, vv. 5-8; and (3) against the rulers, priests, and prophets, vv. 9-12.

"And I said" is thought by some commentators to   *3:1* resume the message of doom interrupted at the end of 2:11. Instead, it seems to introduce a fresh prophecy (ch. 3) which serves as the background and introduction of the great Messianic message of chapters 4 and 5. It presents a contrast between the old and the new, the present and the future. Micah directs his shaft at the rulers, "ye heads of Jacob, and rulers of the house of Israel," rulers over Judah in general and over Jerusalem in particular. It is their responsibility to know and practice justice in their rule, but they have betrayed their trust in a disgraceful way. The utter corruption of these leaders is indicated by the   *3:2* charge, "ye who hate the good, and love the evil." The prophet charges them with being cannibalistic in their very nature. Instead of ministering justice, they pull the skin off the people and cut the flesh from off   *3:3* the bones. The description becomes more forceful: they eat the flesh; they skin them alive; they break the bones, chopping them up and boiling them in the great kettle! They act like cannibals. There are no stronger similes found anywhere else in Scripture; there could be none more expressive than these. In this highly exaggerated figure Micah expresses the white heat of his indignation at the treatment dealt

3:4   the common people by the rulers. Therefore when judgment falls on these heartless rulers and they cry to Jehovah, His face will be hid from them. As they have sown, so will they reap. They have destroyed the people without mercy, and so without mercy will their destruction come.

3:5   The prophet proceeds from the rulers to the false prophets, who likewise have made their contribution to the miserable condition of the nation. These false religious guides make the people err; they lead them astray. They "bite with their teeth"; that is, they inflict suffering and harm as the biting of a serpent. This is preferable to Keil's interpretation, which makes "bite with their teeth" parallel with "whoso putteth not into their mouths," making both refer to food. They cry "Peace," creating in the people a sense of security when there is neither peace nor security. They prophesy for material benefits; and when these are not provided, they declare war on all who refuse to reward or support them. Condemna-

3:6   tion is pronounced upon these false teachers. Because of their time-serving practices and disregard for truth, the night of divine judgment will engulf them. When they desire it most there will be no vision to them. Complete darkness will be their lot, and they will no longer divine. "The verb 'to divine' is never used of legitimate prophetic activity, but always of the arts of magic, soothsaying, necromancy, the like" (J. M. P. Smith, *I.C.C.*). The prophet further emphasizes the

3:7   darkness of their day when he says that "the sun shall go down upon" them, "and the day shall be black over them" (cf. Amos 8:9; Jer. 15:9). All will be darkness. "Seer," one who sees, an early word for "prophet" (I Sam. 9:9) which implies visions, is here used synonymously with one who "divines." "They shall all cover their lips." The covering of the lip was used by the leper to indicate that he was unclean (Lev. 13:45); it was also used to indicate mourning (Ezek. 24:17). The expression is probably used here of trouble and shame, for there was no answer from God. God refuses to reveal His will to any who will

3:8   not hear or see. In contrast to the character and spirit of the false, time-serving prophets, Micah declares the source of his own insight and preaching. He was full of power by the Spirit of Jehovah; and by this power had come the revelation of the divine will, and with the revelation had come might to declare to the nation their sins and transgressions. The difference between the false prophets and Micah was that a false prophet derived his right and power from his own will and the desires of the people; Micah derived his from God. Micah here lays down a principle which determines the difference between the true and the false teacher. It is not enough to preach platitudes, even when true; for unless one declares the things a people need to know, and unless he condemns the sins of which they are guilty, he is as much a false prophet as one who declares untruths or that which contradicts truth.

At this point the prophet reaches the climax of his *3:9* prophecies of doom. Again he directs his address to the ruling class as in 3:1. He lays the blame for the coming judgment at the feet of the rulers, prophets, and priests. He repeats his charge that the rulers abhor justice and pervert all equity; they stand in opposition to all that is right. Instead of fulfilling the position and mission for which they were appointed, they had acted in a completely opposite manner. Zion and Jerusalem are here used as equivalents. The *3:10* rulers build the house of state and their magnificent buildings by blood service of the people or with money gained by extortion. Possibly they gained their end by literal blood shedding, and certainly they gained it by their disregard for what is right. The prophet now brings the three classes of rulers to- *3:11* gether: the heads or rulers who judge for a bribe, the priests who teach for hire rather than for the reward of divine favor and the love of truth and its dignity, and the prophets who divine for money and for the food put into their mouths. This disposition reveals a materialistic concept of service and confirms the adage that "money answereth all things" (Eccl. 10:19). Adding insult to their perversions of right, they place their reliance on Jehovah, claiming they

3:12

are His people and He is in the midst of them; therefore, He will let no evil come on them. It is difficult to imagine a more perverted concept of the God of heaven. The prophet lays down a conclusion that falls as a thunderbolt from heaven: "Therefore shall Zion for your sake be plowed as a field"; it is a figure of total destruction. The temple stood on Mount Zion; therefore, with the plowing of Zion it would be destroyed. The entire city, the pride of the nation, would fall. Where once had stood houses and centers of business there would be only heaps of stones. The mountain on which the house of Jehovah had so majestically reigned will be grown up with trees and become as a forest. The fulfillment of the prophecy was averted until the time of the Chaldeans, but it did come. To the nation and to Jerusalem the razing of their temple would be the climax of all destruction.

Chapter 4

The following two chapters present one of the clearest Messianic prophecies to be found.

> *4:1-8. In these verses we are told what will come in the latter days: the new Zion, new law, new spirit of the divine subjects, and restoration of the Davidic dominion.*

4:1

The announcement of Jerusalem's destruction and the plowing of Zion as a field (3:12) is followed by a glorious Messianic promise. "In the latter days" (variously translated "in the issue of the days," "at the end of the days," "in the end of the days," "the last days," "in the days to come"), when used by the prophets, always refers to the time of the Messiah. It points to the end of the Jewish age and the introduction of the new era under the spiritual ruler. The temple-mountain, that on which Jehovah's spiritual temple would rest in the latter days, would be at the head, or above all other powers. It would be permanently established, never to be destroyed (cf. Dan.

2:44; 7:13-14; Heb. 12:28). There would be a constant stream of people flowing unto it. This new Zion   *4:2*
would be the stronghold and center of worship for
people of all nations. This spiritual mountain would
be the resting place of the "house of the God of
Jacob"; that is, the new spiritual center for all the
tribes. It is from this spiritual center that the word of
the Lord would proceed, and it would be the center
of all learning unto salvation. No word of instruction
would proceed from any other source. Jesus was
referring to this fact when He declared that repentance and remission of sins should be preached to all
nations, beginning from Jerusalem (Luke 24:47). In
this new society of many peoples and nations who   *4:3*
respected the word and law of the Lord, Jehovah
would be the arbiter and judge in all matters. It is He
who would decide all questions. Those who come
would devote their instruments and energies of war to
peace and useful pursuits; they would learn war no
more. The prophet is here describing the nature and
character of the kingdom ruled from this spiritual
Zion. The kingdom of "the latter days" would not be
established, defended, or extended by carnal weapons
and means. Force can have no place in a spiritual
kingdom. Jesus made this clear when He said, "If my
kingdom were of this world, then would my servants
fight, that I should not be delivered to the Jews: but
now is my kingdom not from hence" (John 18:36).
Instead of war and the dreadful consequences that   *4:4*
lead to fear and destruction, "they shall sit every man
under his vine and under his fig-tree." Sitting under
one's vine and fig tree was a symbol of peace, security, and safety (cf. I Kings 4:24b-25). There would be
none to make them afraid; for this spiritual Zion, the
dwelling place of Jehovah, would be their permanent
stronghold. The certainty of the fulfillment of this
promise is that Jehovah, by His mouth, has declared
it. All the heathen, the enemies of the Lord's people,   *4:5*
walk in the name or strength of their god; but these
who come to the mountain of Jehovah will walk, live,
and conduct themselves in the strength of Jehovah
forever.

The fact that this promise is now fulfilled in Christ, and is not to be fulfilled in some future time, is abundantly clear from the New Testament. The Hebrew saints had come to Mount Zion, to the city of the living God, the heavenly Jerusalem. They had come to God, the Judge of all, to a New Covenant that had had the beginning of its announcement from Jerusalem, and to the blood that could speak peace to their souls (Heb. 12:21-24). The things of the old order were being shaken and removed that the spiritual verities of the new may remain. The saints of the Hebrew letter were receiving a kingdom that could not be, and has not been, shaken (Heb. 12:28). The citizenship of these is in a heavenly fatherland (Phil. 3:20), where no force can ever drive them out or destroy them (John 10:28-29). Through the Spirit whom he claimed to possess, Micah saw clearly what would come in the latter days. The old Zion—Jerusalem with its temporal kingdom and house which was subject to decay and destruction—would be succeeded by a new Zion, which, in its spiritual quality, would never be destroyed. The prophet certainly did not envision a time when God would dominate and control the world by force, or an age when all men of all political kingdoms would live at peace on this earth. Only in God's spiritual kingdom established by Christ would this blessed experience be realized.

4:6   "In that day" indicates that the things which follow are related to the same period as that which has preceded; hence, it looks back to the expression "in the latter days" of verse 1. "In that day" is therefore the Messianic age of "the latter days." At that time God will gather into one those that limp, the lame who had been cast off in the divine judgment, whom

4:7   Jehovah had afflicted. This is the remnant of "the house of Judah" of 2:12. These lame ones will be the remnant of the redeemed, the elect under Christ according to divine grace (Rom. 11:5). Those cast off in the wrath of Jehovah will, under grace, become a strong nation, a nation which no force from without can destroy. As they are reinstated in the favor and service of the Lord, He will rule over them from the spiritual Zion from which His law had proceeded. This rule and reign will not be brought to an end, for it is a kingdom and rule that can never be destroyed. Returning to the figure of a flock, introduced verses 6-7a, the prophet emphasizes the royal power that will be restored over the flock. The "tower of the flock" is an expression taken from the practice of building towers from which to watch over sheep or cattle (II Chron. 26:10). The reference here is to the spiritual watchtower from which Jehovah would watch over His flock. To the hill of this tower, Zion, would the former dominion come. At this point the prophet introduces the Messiah who would come and through whom Jehovah would exercise the rule thus far discussed. The "former dominion" refers to the rule of the house of David which should be restored. Amos had told of the fall or decay of the house of David and of its being raised again (9:11-12). This return of the former dominion, the ruler of the house of David, would come to the kingdom of the daughter, the people, of Jerusalem. In the next chapter the prophet develops the character and rule of this restored dominion of the house of David.

4:8

> *4:9—5:1. From "the latter days" the prophet looks at the "now." Before the future glory would come, there will be humiliation, captivity, and return.*

"Now why dost thou cry out aloud?" At this point the prophet interrupts his message of the Messianic hope to consider the present, the immediate future of the nation, and the captivity that would precede the Messianic rule. He hears, as it were, the cry of the people for their king who is carried into captivity. The nation will be thrown into the sorest and most painful of mourning because of this loss. Pains and travail, as of a woman in childbirth, will take hold of the people. The people who have dwelt in Zion will now dwell in the field, away from the protection of the walled city, with neither walls nor covering to

4:9

4:10

protect. The prophet names the captor: it will not be Assyria, the dominant power of that day, but Babylon, who was at that time a vassal of Assyria. Both Micah and Isaiah had this truth revealed to them (cf. Isa. 39:1-6). It would be from Babylon that the Lord would redeem them and bring them back to their land. However, Babylon did not become an independent power until a century after Micah's prophecy.

4:11   "And now," at that time, there were assembled against Zion the "many nations" that made up the Assyrian army. It is probable that the neighboring nations wished to see Zion destroyed at that time; this was the thing they desired their eyes to see. But

4:12   they, the nations, did not know the thoughts of Jehovah. They wished the complete destruction of Jerusalem; Jehovah thought only to punish Judah through the instrumentality of these nations gathered against her. He had gathered them as sheaves are gathered to the threshing-floor. The people governed

4:13   from Zion are called upon to arise and thresh, for God will give them the strength and instruments with which to tread and destroy the enemies. The substance and gain of these would-be destroyers will be devoted as Jehovah directs. Whether this prophecy had reference to the destruction of Sennacherib's army at the gates of Jerusalem (Isa. 37:36-38) or to the ultimate destruction of Assyria and the triumph of God's remnant, is uncertain. The destruction of both was accomplished.

Chapter 5

5:1   Again the chapter division is unfortunate, for verse 1 is a continuation of 4:13. The people of Zion are pictured as gathering themselves together in a besieged city. "He," the Assyrian, had gathered himself against them in a siege. "They shall smite the judge of Israel with a rod upon the cheek." The "judge" is the king of Judah, who would be insulted by the besieger as the nation is humbled before the oppressor. But though humiliated, the true Israel will come forth triumphant.

5:2-9. The ruler of the new Zion: He will be born in Beth-lehem, rule in the strength of Jehovah, and give victory to His people. The invader would be defeated.

From the immediate future the prophet returns to 5:2
the Messianic hope to take up the coming of the
"former dominion" (4:8). Whereas the king had suffered severe humiliation (v. 1), the one to come
would lead the people in victory. The ruler would
come out of "Beth-lehem Ephrathah," though it was
of small account among the thousands of Judah.
Beth-lehem, "house of bread," and Ephrathah, "fruitfulness," referred to Beth-lehem, the ancestral home
of David, located five miles south of Jerusalem. From
here would come the one through whom the "former
dominion" would be restored. "Whose goings forth
are from of old, from everlasting" indicates more
than that He descends from an ancient lineage; it
relates Him to God, the eternal One. His rule reaches
back into eternity. The priests and scribes of Herod's
day recognized that the Messiah would be born in
Beth-lehem (Matt. 2:5, 6). "Therefore," in the light 5:3
of verse 2 which says that the ruler is to come from
Beth-lehem and not Jerusalem and is to be "from
everlasting," related to the infinite, God will "give
them up, until the time that she who travaileth"
brings forth. But who is "she who travaileth"? Some
identify her with the virgin of Isaiah 7:14, hence,
Mary. But this is unlikely. Considered in the light of
the context, it seems that the prophet is speaking of
the remnant of Jehovah's faithful of 4:10, who, in
their captivity, would be like a woman in travail.
Therefore, the woman in travail who gives birth to
the ruler is the faithful remnant who would go
through the Babylonian captivity before the ruler
would come. This is consistent with Isaiah who, in
speaking of Zion, said, "Before she travailed she
brought forth; before her pain came she was delivered
of a man-child. . . . Shall a land be born in one day?
Shall a nation be brought forth at once? For as soon
as Zion travailed she brought forth her children"

(66:4-8). The prophet was looking to the birth of the Messiah and the kingdom that began on Pentecost. The "great sign" seen by John on Patmos, a woman arrayed with the sun, having the moon under her feet and a crown of stars upon her brow, who gave birth to the man-child, is this same woman (Rev. 12:1-6). She is the remnant of the spiritually faithful through whom the Christ came, fulfilling the prophecies of Micah and Isaiah. Under this ruler the residue or remnant of the ruler's brethren would return to the family of Israel.

5:4   He, the ruler, will be a shepherd to the flock of the Lord and will feed them in the strength of the Lord. As a divine provider He will supply all their needs. His greatness will be recognized from one end of the

5:5   earth to the other. The peace of this new Israel will be in Him. Isaiah refers to Him as the "Prince of Peace" (Isa. 9:6), and Paul looks to Him as "our peace" (Eph. 2:14). The "Assyrian" is here used to symbolize the enemies or deadliest foes of the Messiah and the people of God. When an enemy will threaten the new spiritual Israel, "then shall we raise against him seven shepherds," the perfect number to meet the emergency, even eight princes, a number beyond that absolutely necessary. "Shall we raise" indicates that these will come from among the

5:6   people. Under the divine ruler these seven or eight undershepherds will be able to repel the enemy, even laying him waste with the sword. This is not a carnal sword, for these will have been beaten into plowshares (4:3). Spiritual weapons will be used (cf. II Cor. 10:3-5; Eph. 6:17). "He," the ruler, will deliver this spiritual Israel through those whom He will raise

5:7   up, who will fight in His strength and not under the weak and frail leadership of man. The Assyrian had laid waste their land, but under the heavenly King this will not be. This new spiritual Israel, the remnant of Jacob, will possess two exceptional qualities: (1) They will be in the midst of many nations as dew, exercising a refreshing spiritual and moral influence as does the morning dew and the welcome showers in a

5:8   parched world. (2) They will be among the same

group of nations as a lion among the beasts of the forest, exercising a kingly strength and power as they mingle with men. They will be able to tread their enemies underfoot, conquering and overcoming them by the spiritual strength provided through their relation to God and the ruler who would come forth from Beth-lehem. In Him no power can conquer them. "Let thy hand be lifted up above" the hand of their enemies to conquer and overcome. In this new strength let their enemies be cut off. In these promises God gives to His people a tremendous hope and promise of victory as they face the threats of immediate destruction and future captivity.

5:9

> *5:10-15. The instruments of carnal warfare, all classes of wizards, and the idols of the land will be cut off. God's vengeance will be on those who hearken not.*

"In that day" identifies what follows with the preceding thoughts; it is a continuation of the Messianic prophecy. The cutting off of the horses and chariots indicates that in the Messianic kingdom these symbols of force and war will have no place. The introduction of these had been forbidden by God through Moses (Deut. 17:16); the people were to trust in Jehovah and not in physical power (Deut. 20:1). Isaiah charged that the land was full of horses and chariots (2:7); Hosea foretold the extinction of these in the Messianic period (14:3); and Zechariah likewise declared that these would be cut off (9:9-10). Under the Messiah offensive and defensive war would be waged through the power of truth. Cities that were centers of wickedness, power, and pride, and strongholds that served as places of protection and defense would be abolished, for Jehovah would be their defense. In the new spiritual kingdom witchcraft, magic, and sorcery as practiced by the Canaanites would be abolished. "The exact content of this term (witchcraft) is uncertain; it is apparently a general designation of all sorts of magical rites" (J. M. P. Smith, *I.C.C.*). Soothsayers, "cloud-interpreters,

5:10

5:11

5:12

or cloud, i.e., storm makers" (Keil), persons who either interpreted by cloud shapes or professed to exercise power over storms, would be cut off. With

5:13   these practicers of magic must also go the various images, the creation of human hands, graven out of stone or wood and dedicated to false deities. These images and pillars—objects that marked the places dedicated to false gods—had been forbidden by the

5:14   law (Deut. 16:21-22). The "asherim," or posts, must also go. Although the exact origin and nature of these is not known (Smith, *I.C.C.*), they appear to have been the representations of a Canaanitish goddess, the worship of which was characterized by the grossest form of licentiousness. The people had been commanded to break these down (Exod. 34:13); but instead, they had adopted them into their own worship (II Kings 23:6). Even the cities in which these were found would be destroyed. In the Messianic kingdom there would be no place for the relics of

5:15   paganism. Vengeance and wrath would be executed upon the nations who reject the Messiah and refuse to hearken to the message of truth and to submit to Him. No nation can with impunity reject the Christ and His truth and survive; all who do come under the wrath of the Almighty.

Chapter 6

6:1-5. Jehovah calls upon the people to present their case against Him in the court He has called. What is their charge?

6:1   From the glory of the future the prophet returns to the present and immediate future. Farrar has well said, "In the earlier chapters (4—5) we have the springtide of hope, we have in these (6—7) the paler autumn of disappointment" (p. 137). The case against the people has been presented. Let the people now present their case before Jehovah. Like Hosea, his senior contemporary, Micah calls the nation to come before Jehovah in a court of law. As the mountains and hills have witnessed the whole of Israel's history, so now Jehovah calls upon the nation to present their cause before these as before a jury. They have witnessed both the nation's ingratitude and Jehovah's goodness; let them now hear the case. The prophet opens his address by appealing to the mountains and to the "enduring foundations," parallel with "mountains." These were thought to be the foundations of the earth. Jehovah has a controversy, a lawsuit, and will "contend with Israel" as the counsel for the prosecution. Before this jury Jehovah makes an impassioned plea to Israel, now on trial, calling upon him to testify against the Lord. What has Jehovah done? When has He wearied Israel? Where has He failed? Israel has fallen away; let him now tell why. God has done His people no harm, only good. He brought them up out of Egypt; He redeemed them out of bondage by His own power; through the wilderness He had provided adequate leadership for them. He had given them Moses, the prophet and law-giver, Aaron, the high priest, and Miriam, a prophetess. They provided for their spiritual guidance. When Balak, king of Moab, devised evil against the infant nation by sending to Mesopotamia for Balaam to curse them (Num. 22), Jehovah had turned the would-be curses into pronouncements of blessing (Num. 23—24). Shittim, "The Acacia meadow," was the last resting place of Israel before crossing the Jordan (Josh. 3:1). Gilgal was the first camp after crossing the river (Josh. 4:19). God calls upon Israel to remember His deeds between the two: the battle with the Midianites in which Balaam was killed (Num. 31:8), the conquest of the land east of Jordan, and the crossing of the Jordan at flood period. Call to mind all the righteous acts of Jehovah, and then find one thing of an evil nature that could be charged against Him. This is Jehovah's challenge before the court.

6:2

6:3

6:4

6:5

6:6-8. The people's response: What must they offer for their sins?

The people are convicted before the Lord and recognize their guilt. Micah personifies the nation as

6:6

an individual and addresses Jehovah in search for a solution to their sinful condition. In their reply through the prophet they reveal an ignorance of the true nature of Jehovah and of what He requires. Their question is, How must they come before Him? Must it be with burnt-offerings and calves a year old, the choicest of their animal possessions? They have forgotten the law of their God so far that they are

6:7 ignorant of how to approach Him. Quantity is the essence of the next question: Must they come before Him with thousands of rams, or with ten thousands of rivers of oil? Or must the offering for their sin be the most precious possession that one has, his son or daughter? Certainly not this last! This would be an abomination. In these rhetorical questions the people are ascending from the minimal, the burnt-offering, to the most precious gift, the greatest they could offer. But in all these questions they indicate a willingness to do anything except what Jehovah required.

6:8 Sacrifices such as these are not what God wants (cf. Ps. 51:16, 17); what He desires is the penitent heart of the individual, toward Him and one's neightbor. The "good" that He requires is the doing of His will. To "do justly" is to act toward God and man according to the divine standard of righteousness revealed in His law. To "love kindness" or mercy is to show a compassionate warmheartedness toward man. And "to walk humbly with thy God" is to recognize the absolute holiness and righteousness of God, and to walk in humble and submissive obedience to His desire and will. This verse is considered by many to be one of the most comprehensive and all-embracing statements in the Old Testament.

> *6:9-16. They could find no charge to make against Jehovah. In rebuttal, Jehovah presents His case against the people.*

6:9 "The voice of Jehovah crieth unto the city." The prophet emphasizes the solemnity of what he is about to say by declaring that it is the voice of Jehovah they are about to hear. "The city" addressed is Jerusalem, the capital of Judah. Although the bulk of the population could hear the words spoken, it is only the wise who will give heed to what is said. "The rod" is the chastisement or judgment about to be made known to the people; and "hear ... who hath appointed it" signifies it is God's appointment. The judgment is to be determined by the answers to a series of questions. Are there "treasures of wickedness," ill-gotten gains, in the house of the wicked? **6:10** Are they continuing to gain their wealth by corruption? Do they gain their wealth by a scant measure and by the use of short weights and measurements? In those days there were no civil laws to enforce the proper business weights and measures; business was to be conducted fairly on the ground of basic integrity. In the absence of this basic honesty crookedness prevailed. The real judgment would be against their heart, so far from God and right. Who asks the following question, "Shall I be pure with wicked **6:11** balances, and with a bag of deceitful weights?" Keil would supply, "Let every one ask himself," "Shall I be pure, etc.?" The answer would be: No, I cannot be pure in business transactions with wicked balances and a bag of deceitful weights. Retaining the present reading, Deane thinks "we must consider the question as put, for effect's sake, in the mouth of one of the rich oppressors" (*P.C.*). Smith makes it Jehovah's question, "Can I treat as pure him with the wicked balances, etc." (*I.C.C.*) Keil's explanation seems preferable. "The rich men thereof," of the city, Jeru- **6:12** salem (v. 9), "are full of violence." Besides the corrupt business practices charged against them they are also guilty of violence, the practice of oppression and injustice in their dealings. To these sins they add lies and deceit with their tongue. In no way can they be trusted!

Such abominable wickedness and corruption can- **6:13** not go unpunished. "But I, indeed, will begin to smite thee" (J. M. P. Smith); "So also now do I smite thee" (Keil); "Will I make thee sick in smiting thee" (Deane). Her grievous wound is the complete desolation that God will bring upon her because of her sins. Because of the excessive wickedness of the wealthy ruling merchant class, the whole population suffers.

6:14 "Thou": the wicked city continues to be addressed. The people will come to want and humiliation; they will put away but not to save, for what they put away will be consumed by others as it is given up to the

6:15 sword. The field, the olive yard, and the vineyard are brought before them. They will sow but not reap; they will tread the olives but not anoint themselves with its oil; they will gather the grapes but not drink of their vintage. All they could have used to satisfy

6:16 their own needs is given up to another. The reason for all this is that the people exchanged the worship of God for the false baalism of Omri and his son Ahab. Omri was the founder of one of the strongest dynasties in Israel's history. Ahab, his son, and Jezebel, Ahab's wife, had given emphasis to the worship of Baal. This corrupt and licentious worship, conjoined with the corrupt calf worship at Beth-el, had led to the destruction of Israel. And now Judah had succumbed to this false worship which had led to false life and practice. No specific statutes are under consideration, but rather the violation of principles that inevitably follows the acceptance of false standards. Desolation would come to Judah as the ultimate fruit of this corruption found among the leading class who had followed in this evil and wicked way.

Chapter 7

7:1-6. The prophet speaks for Jerusalem-Zion, confessing the sins of the people and bewailing the lack of righteousness.

7:1 "Woe is me!" The prophet speaks, but for whom? Are these the words of Jerusalem (6:9) in response to the judgment declared upon her? Or, is it Zion, bewailing the absence of all righteousness within her walls? Or, is it the voice of the penitent remnant that remains among the people? Probably the prophet represents Jerusalem-Zion bewailing the absence of any righteous ones within her ranks, for which cause the judgment has come. The harvest is past and there are no gleanings; she hungers for the first-ripe fig of spring, the return of righteousness. The following verses indicate that this is the correct view. The "godly" man, the pious man who respects God, and out of that respect has a proper regard for his fellow men, has perished out of the earth. Instead of the upright life that shows kindness and concern for one's fellow, there are only those who lie in wait to take the life and possessions of another. They spread the nets of their plans to take their brothers captive. Their greed knows no bounds. Having it in their power to do evil, they do it diligently with vigor and zeal. The men of power who are in a position to carry out their wicked schemes work together. The prince or man of political power asks a favor of the judge, and the judge grants the request for a reward or bribe. The great man, the man of power through wealth or position, makes his desire known, and the three—the prince, the judge, and the great man of wealth—then weave it together as one twists cords, carrying out the plan. "The best of them is as a brier": he pricks, hurts, and injures, but is of no value. "The most upright is worse than a thorn hedge," so woven and tangled together with plans and schemes that it would be impossible to unravel the entanglement. These are sharp in business but bear no fruit; they are as a hedge, obstructing righteousness and justice. "The day of thy watchmen," the fulfilling of the word of the prophets whom God had sent to warn the people (cf. Ezek. 3:17; 33:7), has now come. The day of "thy visitation" is the day of judgment visited upon them. In the midst of these hopeless social and political conditions, the perplexity of the people and the impossibility of correcting matters will devour and destroy them. The state of affairs is such that one knows not in whom he can place his trust; as a matter of fact, there is no one. Neither one's neighbor, his friend, nor his wife can be trusted. Truly, it is an evil day that the prophet is called to face. One's enemies may be found among those of his own house; the son

7:2

7:3

7:4

7:5

7:6

dishonors his father, the daughter her mother, and the daughter-in-law her mother-in-law. A condition of this sort is utterly contrary to the law of God and the natural relations that should exist. It manifests a time of complete social rebellion against constituted authority and natural relations. The paragraph reads almost like the daily newspaper of twentieth century United States.

7:7-17. The prophet now speaks for the spiritual remnant. He confesses their sins and calls upon Jehovah to receive them.

7:7 The prophet now speaks for the spiritual remnant who recognize the hopelessness of the hour and turn to Jehovah. This is indicated by his words, "But as for *me, I* will look unto Jehovah." Deliverance can come from no other source; the penitent remnant will wait for God who will hear and save. To "wait for Jehovah," an expression popular with Isaiah, is to put one's trust in Him, depend on Him and let Him lead the way. In the midst of an otherwise hopeless despair the spiritual remnant turns to the Lord. The rejoicing of the enemies of Judah at her immediate **7:8** calamity is premature. For though Israel fall, Jehovah will not forsake her; and though she sit in darkness, her God will be a light to guide her to a better day. He will lift up the fallen, and He will be a guiding **7:9** light to all who trust in Him. The remnant recognize and confess that they have sinned against Jehovah; they will humbly bear the indignation of the judgment imposed upon them. They have the faith to believe that out of calamity will come blessing. God will bring them forth to the light of salvation; He will plead their cause; these will behold the righteousness of God in all His ways. Even the severe judgment that has been executed against them will be acknowledged **7:10** as a righteous judgment. Jehovah will vindicate His people and sustain them through their shame. The enemies who had desired to see the shame of Israel and had ridiculed, saying, "Where is Jehovah thy God? Mine eyes shall see my desire upon her; now shall she be trodden down" (cf. 4:11), will now be put to shame. They who had gone into Babylon, whom God promised to rescue (4:10, 12-13), will now be rescued. Her walls will be rebuilt and the decree of shame and judgment will be removed. Howbeit, these walls will not be of stone and mortar, but will be the wall of Jehovah's presence round about His people (cf. Zech. 2:4, 5). "In that day," the day of the return of Zion's glory, the true Zion citizens will come from Assyria, the east, from Egypt, the west, from sea to sea, and from mountain to mountain; they will come from all directions to build in the new Zion. The prophet here looks beyond the desolation of his day and the return from captivity to the Messianic age, when men of all races and nationalities will come and build (cf. 4:5-6; Isa. 11:10-16; Zech. 9:9-10). While from all parts of the earth the spiritual ones come to Zion, in which is the presence of God, the rest of the earth remains bleak and desolate. A contrast between the new spiritual Zion and the desolate earth is before the prophet. This desolation is the fruit of the world's behavior and its rejection of Jehovah and His Messiah (cf. 5:15).

7:11

7:12

7:13

In response to the wonderful promises of God that there would be a glorious return to a new Zion, a prayer goes up to God from the heart of this penitent remnant. The prayer is that as God is the shepherd of His people He will feed or rule them by His rod, the rod being the symbol of His shepherd role. The people of His pasture are here pictured as dwelling solitarily apart, separate from the world of the heathen. This separation was a requirement of God in both ancient times (Num. 23:9b) and now under the Messiah (II Cor. 6:17). "In the forest in the midst of Carmel," the wooded mountain that juts into the Mediterranean Sea, indicates their protection and separateness as they find their pasture in the lush pastureland of Bashan and Gilead, east of Jordan. "As in the days of old" refers to the time either in the days of Moses and Joshua or of David and Solomon; more probably the Lord points back to that of David and Solomon (cf. I Kings 4:20-25). Jehovah responds

7:14

7:15

to this prayer by giving assurance that He would show them marvelous things. The redemption of His people from Egypt was a type of the redemption under the Messiah (cf. I Cor. 10:1 ff.). As He had redeemed their fathers out of Egypt by unrivaled demonstrations of His power, so would He redeem the remnant by showing "unto them marvellous things." These marvelous things were demonstrated in the Christ and His works for the salvation of the new Israel. In the

7:16 presence of this demonstration of Jehovah's marvelous power, the nations would see and be ashamed of their might. Their own power would appear exceedingly insignificant in comparison to that of the Lord. Laying their hands upon their mouth would signify that they were speechless in the presence of such power; they would have nothing to say. Their hands upon their ears indicates the thought of Job, "But the thunder of his power who can understand?"

7:17 (26:14); it is deafening. Like the serpents and other crawling creatures, they will "lick the dust—prostrate themselves before Jehovah. With fear and trembling they will reverence Him, for in the presence of His great power and mighty deeds they will recognize that "in none other is there salvation: for neither is there any other name under heaven, that is given among men, wherein we must be saved" (Acts 4:12).

> 7:18-20. With a doxology of praise to such a wonderful God, the prophet brings his message to a close.

7:18 How glorious are these promises of blessing and goodness from Jehovah! All of these are given in spite of the ingratitude and wickedness on Israel's part. The prophet stands in awe at the presence of such infinite love and greatness. In this awe he closes his message with an ode of praise to the Lord. "Who is a God like unto thee?" There is none to compare, for Jehovah passes over iniquity, the grossest and basest of sin, and pardons transgressions, the going over or beyond His law. He does all this because He is God who retains not His anger forever, and because He delights in demonstrating lovingkindness. Because He is God and delights in lovingkindness, He will again have compassion; He will repeat over and over this quality of His Godhood. Sin is the great enemy and destroyer of mankind, but by His power it will be triumphed over and trampled underfoot. The casting of sins into the depth of the sea indicates that they will be put completely out of His sight, "as far as the east is from the west" (Ps. 103:12); remembered no more (Jer. 31:34); "blotted out" (Acts 3:19). God will show His faithfulness by fulfilling in their descendants the promises and oaths made to Jacob and Abraham. These promises have found their complete fulfillment in Christ. Thus the prophecy of judgment and promise, of travail and birth, of gloom and hope, "ends with the glow of faith and happy hope."

7:19

7:20

7
ZEPHANIAH
"Jehovah Hides"

General Observations

1. The Man

a. Name. Zephaniah means "Jehovah hides," or "Jehovah has hidden," or "treasured." This meaning of the prophet's name has led some to conclude that he was born in the trying time of Manasseh, the wicked son of Hezekiah, who filled Jerusalem with blood (George Adam Smith); however, this is purely conjectural.

b. Ancestry. The prophet traces his ancestry back four generations to Hezekiah. This is unusual and indicates that the good king of the days of Isaiah and Micah was the great-great-grandfather of Zephaniah. This would make the prophet of royal blood.

c. Occupation and Home. Nothing is known of the prophet's occupation, nor is there anything in his book that indicates what it might have been. His reference to Jerusalem as "this place" (1:4) suggests that Jerusalem was his home. His acquaintance with the conditions of the city (3:1 ff.) further confirms this point.

2. Date

Thiele concludes that the reign of Josiah was from 641/640 to 609 B.C. Others place it from 639 to 608 B.C. It was during his reign that Zephaniah prophesied (1:1). Eiselen places the date at 626 B.C.; Robinson places it at 625 B.C. It would be safe to suggest 630 to 625 B.C. as the probable date of his work. If 626 B.C. is accepted, then the ministries of Jeremiah and Zephaniah began in the same year. Scholars are divided over the occasion that gave rise to his prophesying. Some think it was provoked by the invasion of the Scythians, who poured south from the northern steppes about this time. These ruthless hordes invaded the Assyrian empire and followed the Mediterranean coast south to the border of Egypt where they were turned back. Others think that his prophesying was prompted by the rise of the Chaldean power, which Zephaniah saw as the ultimate threat of a general world judgment. The weight of evidence lends greater credence to this latter view.

3. Background

a. **Political, in Judah.** Hezekiah was succeeded by his son Manasseh, a lad of twelve years. It is doubtful that at any period of its history Judah had a more wicked ruler than Manasseh. He sought to undo all the good his father had done. He rebuilt the high places, reared altars to Baal and Ashtoreth, and built altars to the host of heaven. He committed the abomination of making his son pass through the fire, practicing augury and enchantment, and dealing with familiar spirits. To all this he added the sin of bloodshed, filling Jerusalem with innocent blood (see II Kings 21; II Chron. 33:1-9). Under his reign the heathen party gained control of the government. Later Manasseh tried to correct the wickedness of his earlier years, but apparently without success (II Chron. 33:10-20). Ammon, who succeeded Manasseh, followed in the steps of his father; his reign was likewise one of great wickedness (II Chron. 33:21-25).

Josiah, who came to the throne at the age of eight, was the last good king to reign over Judah. At the age of sixteen he began to seek after Jehovah, the God of his fathers; and at the age of twenty he began to purge Judah. His reforms were among the most sweeping of any that were attempted by the kings who reigned over the southern kingdom. Altars and images were alike destroyed, and the bones of priests who had offered sacrifices on the altars of the false gods were gathered and burned. In the process of cleansing the temple a copy of the law was found and read before the young king. Alarmed at what he heard, he sent to a prophetess, Huldah, for a word from God concerning what he had learned. The young king caused the newly found Word of God to be read in the hearing of the people, great and small. Why he sent to Huldah and not to Jeremiah, Zephaniah, Nahum, or Habakkuk, all prophets of the period, is unknown. The cleansing of the temple was followed by a passover such as had not been observed with like enthusiasm in many years (see II Kings 22—23: II Chron. 34—35). It was in the time of the reign of this king that Zephaniah prophesied.

b. **Political, in the East.** War clouds, dark and foreboding, were hovering over the horizon to the north. In the period from Isaiah and Micah to that of Zephaniah, Assyria had been able to maintain supremacy over the world of that day. Revolts throughout the empire were frequent; however, at the cost of her resources and the shedding of much blood, her kings had been able to retain Assyria's place at the head of the world empires. It seems that Josiah remained loyal to the Assyrian king. Ashurbanipal, who died ca. 633 B.C., and who was the last great king of the empire. Upon his death Assyria began to disintegrate.

In 625 B.C. Nabopolassar, king of Babylon, declared the independence of Chaldea from her Assyrian lords, thus establishing an independent kingdom in Babylon. This led to war between Babylon and Nineveh. In 614 B.C. the Medes captured Ashur, a chief city of Assyria. Nebuchadnezzar, son of Nabopolassar and general of his army, led an attack against Nineveh. Assisted by the Medes, he was able to take the city and destroyed it completely in 612 B.C. This is an important date in history. The remnant of the Assyrian army fled west where it entrenched itself near Haran. After destroying Nineveh, Nebuchadnezzar reorganized his forces and followed the Assyrians to Haran where he attacked and destroyed the remaining forces of Assyrian power in 609 B.C. The last vestige of Assyrian supremacy was now gone. This left the Chaldean nation the undisputed master of the East.

Pharaoh-necho of Egypt determined to help Assyria at Haran by marching north with his army (609 B.C.). Josiah attempted to stop him at Megiddo by throwing his forces in the path of Necho. He succeeded in preventing the Egyptian army from reaching Haran, but he was killed in the battle. For four years Egypt dominated Judah, but in 605 B.C. Necho was defeated by Nebuchadnezzar at Carchemish, west of Haran. Nebuchadnezzar pursued the Egyptians as far south as the land of Judah, whose people he took under his own wing. Here is enacted one of the ironies of history. Judah, led by Josiah, had attempted to aid Chaldea by fighting against Egypt at Megiddo. The kingdom that gave its king in the struggle to aid Chaldea was now a vassal of the nation it had attempted to help. Later Judah was to be destroyed by Chaldea (Babylon). Learning of the death of his father Nabopolassar, Nebuchadnezzar made a rapid return to Babylon to claim the throne. As he returned to Babylon he carried hostages with him, among whom were Daniel and his three friends, chief characters of the Book of Daniel. It seems altogether possible that it was the rise of the Babylonian power and their westward threat that gave occasion for Zephaniah's prophecy.

c. **Religious and Moral.** As already pointed out, the sweeping reforms undertaken by Josiah reached their peak in the eighteenth year of his reign. The king was under prophetic influence most of his life: Jeremiah, Zephaniah, Nahum, and Habakkuk prophesied during his reign. It is interesting, however, to note that the prophet Zephaniah seems not to have been impressed with the reforms of Josiah, for he makes no reference to them. In spite of Josiah's reforms and his own good life, the people appear at this time to be nervous, cruel, and corrupt. Social injustice and moral corruption appear to be widespread; luxury and extravagance are seen on every hand. The baalim were still worshiped, and what worship was offered to Jehovah was little other than idolatry. The time was ripe for judgment.

4. Teaching and Lessons

a. **The Day of Jehovah.** Like his predecessor Joel, Zephaniah gives an emphasis to the day of Jehovah that should have struck terror in the hearts of the wicked, leading them to repentance. The day is "at hand" (1:7), "near" (1:14), a day of darkness and of terror (1:15, 16). It comes as a judgment against sin (1:17), accompanied by great convulsions of nature (1:15). It falls upon all creation—man and beast, Hebrews and the nations (1:2, 3; 2:1-15; 3:8). The day of Jehovah is a day of doom! The prophet sees it as a day of terror, imminent and falling upon all creation as a judgment for sin. Only a remnant will escape, but it is a day of deliverance for the faithful. George Adam Smith has well summarized its spirit when he writes, "No hotter book lies in all the Old Testament. Neither dew nor grass nor tree nor any blossom lives in it, but it is everywhere fire, smoke and darkness, drifting chaff, ruins, nettles, saltpits, and owls and ravens looking from the windows of desolate palaces" (*The Book of the Twelve Prophets*, Vol. II, p. 48). However, out of this grim picture of destruction would come redemption, which must not be overlooked nor minimized. The prophet does not indicate who would be the instruments of Jehovah's judgment.

b. **Universalism.** Jehovah is the God of the universe. The judgment falls upon all. The gods of the nations are non-entities; Jehovah alone is God. As terrors fall upon all alike, so also from among all will some be saved. As he looks beyond the doom and destruction of a world judgment, the prophet draws a sublime picture of the Messianic age (3:14-20), though he does not mention or describe the Messiah Himself. Whatever is accomplished either in judgment or salvation, Jehovah alone accomplishes it. The other prophets make clear that this redemptive work of Jehovah would be accomplished through the Messiah; but to Zephaniah it is Jehovah who will fulfill His purpose.

Outline of the Book

Title and Inscription, 1:1

I. Judgment upon the whole world—Judah in particular, 1:2-18.

    A. A world judgment, vv. 2-6.
        1. Prelude: judgment on the whole world, vv. 2-3.
        2. Judgment on Judah and Jerusalem for idolatry, vv. 4-6.

B. Judgment on sinners of every rank, vv. 7-13.
1. On princes, vv. 7-8.
2. On thieves (or idolaters), v. 9.
3. On traders, vv. 10-11.
4. On indifferent and wealthy, vv. 12-13.

C. The imminence and terrible nature of the judgment, vv. 14-18.
1. Imminent, v. 14.
2. A terribly dark day, vv. 15-17.
3. There will be no deliverance, v. 18.

II. Exhortation to repentance and perseverance, 2:1—3:8.

A. Call to repentance and to seek the Lord, that they may be hidden in the day of the Lord, 2:1-3.

B. Reason: God will judge the nations near and far, 2:4-15.
1. Judgment upon the nations that are near, vv. 4-11.
   a) Upon Philistia, vv. 4-7.
   b) Upon Moab and Ammon, vv. 8-10.
   c) Upon all the gods of earth, v. 11.
2. Judgment upon powerful nations afar, vv. 12-15.
   a) Upon Ethiopia, v. 12.
   b) Upon Assyria and Nineveh, vv. 13-15.

C. If God punishes the heathen, He will not spare Judah, 3:1-8.
1. Woe to the polluted city—classes of sinners and sin, vv. 1-7.
   a) Princes, judges, prophets, priests, vv. 1-4.
   b) Jehovah's constant reminder of His sovereignty, vv. 5-7.
2. God has called; they have refused—therefore, Woe! v. 8.

III. After the judgment, salvation and glorification for the remnant, 3:9-20.

A. From among the heathen will God's remnant come, vv. 9-10.

B. Israel restored will be cleansed and sanctified, vv. 11-13.

C. Israel comforted and exalted to honor, vv. 14-20.

Comments

Chapter 1

1:1 As pointed out in the introduction, in tracing back his ancestry through four generations, it is inferred that Zephaniah is the great-great-grandson of King Hezekiah. Although he prophesied in the days of Josiah's reform, he shows no interest in it. It is probable that the prophet knew it would end in failure, for it did not change the hearts of the people. Any reform that works permanent good must change the heart. A far-reaching judgment was on its way; out of it would come a change of heart and redemption by Jehovah.

> *1:2-6. Jehovah, the judge of all creation, declares a world judgment in which all will be affected. Judah and Jerusalem will receive a particular judgment. The idolaters, the idols, the idolatrous priests, the false-swearers and the apostates will fall under the wrath of Jehovah.*

1:2 The prophet announces a universal and all-consuming judgment. The declaration "saith Jehovah," "is the saying of Jehovah" or "oracle of Jehovah," indicates a weighty pronouncement. The judgment is portrayed as comparable to that of the great flood in *1:3* its universal scope. "I will consume": sweep away, make an end of man and beast, birds and fishes, stumblingblocks and the wicked who stumble over them. This all-embracing declaration is not to be explained away simply as hyperbole, for other proph-

ets had shown that the animal creation is affected by
man's sin (Joel 1:18; Hos. 4:3; Jer. 12:4). "Stumblingblocks" are the idols and incentives to sin that
accompany idolatry; all will be swept away. "I will
cut off man," for it is man who is responsible for the
condition that brings about the judgment. Judah and   *1:4*
Jerusalem are the objects of Jehovah's wrath, for they
had known better. "I will stretch out my hand" upon
the inhabitants of both. Observe the "I wills": "I will
utterly consume" (v. 2), "I will cut off" (v. 3), "I will
stretch out my hand" (v. 4). In stretching out His
hand He consumes and cuts off. The "remnant of
Baal" includes all who worship Baal, whether few or
many, who dwell in Jerusalem. Jerusalem will be
cleansed of these. "The Chemarim with the priests"
were to be cut off with the idols and idol worshipers.
The "Chemarim" were the idolatrous priests of the
baalim and high places who had been appointed by
the kings of Judah to serve these and to burn incense
to the hosts of heaven (II Kings 23:5, cf. margin
ASV, also Hosea 10:5). "With the priests": the legitimate priests of the temple who had been unfaithful
to Jehovah would share the same fate with the priests
of Baal. In verse 5 two classes of idolaters are intro-   *1:5*
duced: star worshipers and the false-swearers. The
star worshipers are those "that worship the host of
heaven." To worship is to bow down to or kiss the
hand toward. Worship of "the host of heaven" had
been specifically forbidden by Moses; it included the
sun, moon, and stars (Deut. 4:19). These had been
given to all people for service and not as objects of
worship. These were worshiped from "the housetops"
by burning incense on altars erected on the flat roofs.
From this vantage point they had a clearer view of
the stars and felt nearer to them. The second group of
false subjects to Jehovah were those "that swear to
Jehovah and swear by Malcam." These were of a
divided loyalty, swearing partly by Jehovah and partly by Malcam. The latter was one of the baalim,
whom they reckoned as their king—not an earthly
king, but a king among the deities. These claimed to
worship Jehovah but constantly had the names of the

1:6 baalim upon their lips. They did not give Jehovah their undivided heart and worship. A third class of worshipers is introduced, those "that are turned back from following Jehovah." These are utterly indifferent to Jehovah; they have turned back; they have not sought nor inquired after Him. They could not care less for His favor or disfavor.

> *1:7-13. Jehovah invites the nations to His sacrifice, which is the destruction decreed. All are to fall under the judgment: the princes and king's sons; thieves who steal for their masters; traders who have become "Canaanites" (traffickers); and the wealthy who have become indifferent, having "settled on their lees."*

1:7 Because Jehovah is to be present, silence is commanded as in Habakkuk 2:20. "Hold thy peace": a hushed awe. "The day of Jehovah" always refers to a day of judgment against the wicked. It "is at hand," nearby. The sacrifice to be offered is Judah; the invited and consecrated guests are the nations whom Jehovah has called to witness and execute His judg-

1:8 ment. Habakkuk points to the Chaldeans as the executors of the judgment. Members of the royal family are threatened; they are to share in a special way the knowledge of Jehovah's wrath, "in the day of Jehovah's sacrifice." "The princes," the offspring and descendants of former kings, and the sons of Josiah, although young at that time, will all come under the rod of judgment. These of royal blood are held responsible for the conditions in Jerusalem. Josiah, the king, is not named in the group to be judged as he was one of Judah's most God-fearing rulers. Those "clothed with foreign apparel" are the rulers, the wealthy, and the socially elite who by their dress indicated their leaning toward Egypt or Babylonia and the ways of those heathen nations. They had forsaken the customs of their own divinely appointed

1:9 kingdom and had adopted those of a heathen people. The clause "those that leap over the threshold" has been subject to a number of interpretations, chief among them being the following. One interpretation appeals to the custom of the priests of Dagon who would not tread on the threshold of Dagon's temple because he had fallen on the threshold and had been broken in pieces (I Sam. 5:4-5). It is thought that this superstition had somehow been introduced in Judah. There is no evidence for this conclusion; thus this interpretation is unlikely. It is more plausible that the expression had become a common term for violent burglary and thievery. "That fill their master's house with violence and deceit" may indicate that these were working under or for a chief or head of a gang. If "their master" refers to the king, then it would suggest that the servants of the king were becoming wealthy, which would reflect upon the king's rule. Though they did not fill his coffers with their wealth, they did bring reproach upon his rule by their violence. The second group denounced are the merchants. A great cry is heard from "the fish gate," thought to have been located somewhere in the northern wall, toward the east. This is the direction from which the destroyers would come. Mention is made of the fish gate in relation to Manasseh's building program (II Chron. 33:14), and by Nehemiah as the Jews rebuilt the walls of Jerusalem after their return from Babylon (Neh. 3:3; 12:39). Although the location is not certain, the "second quarter" or Mishneh, the "lower city" (Keil), or "New town, literally, second town" (J. M. P. Smith), was a section of the city thought to have been in the general vicinity of the fish gate. "And a great crashing from the hills" probably refers to the cries of men from various heights within the city, as their city is taken and their society is crashing about their heads in the destruction. This heightens the terror of the occasion. The part of the city identified as "the Mortar" or Maktesh is unknown; but, as indicated by the context, it was probably a section where the merchants plied their trade. "The people of Canaan" are not Canaanite or Phoenician merchants, but merchants of Judah who had become as Canaanites in the way they conducted

1:10

1:11

their business (cf. Hos. 12:7). They followed the unscrupulous practices and principles of the heathen traffickers. Both the merchants and the money changers, those "laden with silver," the bankers of that day, would be cut off. A third class, the depraved and indifferent, is next brought under the judgment. None should be spared, for Jehovah would search Jerusalem as one would take a lamp and search carefully and minutely through every corner of a small and darkened room. "To settle on the lees" is a metaphor from the treating of wine. In making the best wine the liquid is poured from vessel to vessel, separating the wine from dregs or settlings. If allowed to remain too long on its lees the wine became harsh and syrupy (cf. Jer. 48:11-12). In the stupidity of their hearts they ignored Jehovah and were indifferent to Him. They looked on Him as one would an idol who possessed power to do neither good nor bad. Because they had ignored God and lived in the lusts of their depraved hearts, God would demonstrate His divine power. Their wealth would become a spoil for others; their houses would be made desolate. Though they would build houses or plant vineyards, they would not dwell in the houses or drink the wine from the vineyard. These would be devoted to destruction, to the sacrifice determined by Jehovah.

1:12

1:13

1:14-18. The prophet declares the nearness of the day and emphasizes its terribleness: it will be a day of darkness and terror, of trumpet and bloodshed. There will be no deliverance from the terribleness of judgment, nor from the end determined.

1:14   Once more Zephaniah stresses the nearness of the day of Jehovah. It is hastening speedily toward its realization; it is nearer than the people realize. The day of Jehovah is the day of His "voice" as His judgment fell like mighty thunders and the roaring of the lion. It will be a bitter day, a day of such complete defeat that the strong men who have fought violently to defend their city and homeland will weep

bitterly at their failure. Zephaniah's description of   *1:15*
the day is vivid and electrifying. It is to be a day
overflowing with divine wrath which the prophet
stresses and emphasizes by five highly descriptive
couplets. These need little comment: they should be
read with all the feeling of the prophet's soul as he
sought to describe it and to warn the indifferent
nations by its terror. "That day is a day of wrath, a
day of trouble and distress, a day of wasteness and
desolation, a day of darkness and gloominess, a day
of clouds and thick darkness, a day of the trumpet   *1:16*
and alarm," which would be directed against the
fortified cities and battlements (the high corner
towers) of the city. The description makes one feel
that he is present, beholding the clouds of smoke as
they billow heavenward, hearing trumpet blasts from
various parts of the city, and seeing the utter desolation when it is all over. The distress is brought upon   *1:17*
them by Jehovah in consequence of their sins. They
would stagger as if blind, not knowing which way to
go. Their lifeblood would be poured out and destroyed as dust, and their flesh would be flung to the
soil as dung. Each would be worthless as the dust and
dung of the field. They would be unable to bribe the   *1:18*
enemy even with all the silver and gold they had
accumulated and laid up. The destruction had been
determined by Jehovah and there would be no
escaping the judgment against their sins. With a fresh
declaration of the complete destruction of the land
and the people, Zephaniah closes the description as
he had begun it (vv. 2 ff.). This destruction would be
accomplished by the fire of Jehovah's jealousy, for
He is a consuming fire. Jehovah's jealousy is His
righteous resentment and indignation at being supplanted in the affection of His people by empty idols
and having His righteousness exchanged for pagan
wickedness.

Chapter 2

*2:1-3. There is an urgent call from Jehovah to
His people to repent before the fierce anger of*

> *His indignation sweeps them away as chaff.*
> *Let the proud seek meekness and righteous-*
> *ness as the only avenue of escape.*

2:1   "Gather yourselves together . . . O nation that hath no shame." To whom is this call for repentance issued? J. M. P. Smith (*I.C.C.*) thinks it is to Philistia, introducing the specific directive of verses 4-7. But this is very doubtful; for the call fits better as a climax to 1:14-18, where the destruction against Judah and Jerusalem is described as a dark day of judgment. In His call to repentance Jehovah addresses His people as "O nation," the same term He uses of the heathen people. Judah had sunk to the level of the heathen, having "no shame," without a longing for anything better; therefore, it is repent or perish

2:2   with the surrounding idolatries. This repentance is to be manifested "before the decree bring forth," before the execution of the decree of judgment formerly issued; for after it falls it will be too late. The "chaff" indicates that the wicked nation will be scattered before the fierce anger of Jehovah, as chaff is scattered before the whirlwind. "The day of Jehovah's anger" is the day of His judgment. The exhortation to the people is to repent that this may be averted. The

2:3   call is for action on the part of the people; "*seek ye* Jehovah": let repentance be demonstrated by return- ing to Jehovah's way. But the call is to the meek, the humble, the lowly, and the submissive who bend their wills to a higher power. God includes "all" the meek of the earth, all the pious Israelites scattered through- out the world who "have kept his ordinances." This implies that somewhere the Lord still had His "seven thousand who had not bowed the knee to Baal." The directive is to Israel; but since the judgment was worldwide, there is no cause to think that Jehovah excluded from among the nations judged any who would recognize Him in righteousness and meekness. Righteousness and meekness are essentials of escape, but the prophet does not promise certain escape. Rather, "it may be ye will be hid"; for the wicked- ness is so great and the judgment so terrible that even these who seek righteousness and meekness may suffer vicariously for the sins of society. If there is to be any way of escape, Zephaniah offers the only possible hope for that escape in righteousness and meekness. The only hope for immunity is that one be hid under the shadow of the wings of the Almighty.

> *2:4-7. In this judgment no nation is going to escape. The prophet introduces the cities of Philistia and the judgment upon them. The judgment is to pave the way for ultimate salvation.*

The prophet begins with Philistia to the west, then directs his prophecy to Moab and Ammon representing the east, Ethiopia the south, and Assyria the north. The four cities of Philistia which are specified represent the whole of that nation. As in Amos 1:6-8 and Zechariah 9:5-7, Gath is not named among the group, although at one time it had been a city of prominence. As suggested in the comments on the Book of Amos, by this time Gath had either lost its prominence or had been destroyed. Gaza will be renounced, deserted; Ashkelon will become a desolation, wasted and forsaken; and they of Ashdod will be driven out at noon. The expression "drive out . . . at noonday" is subject to two interpretations: (1) the suddenness of the attack at noon, the hottest part of the day, when least expected; or (2) the shortness of the siege, driven out by noon; "it will be all over in half a day" (J. M. P. Smith). It is uncertain which is the correct view. The fourth city, Ekron, will be rooted up, leaving no sprout from which its former glory could be restored. The prophecy against Philistia is continued in the form of a "woe" that includes all the inhabitants of the seacoast nation. "The nation of the Cherethites" seems here to be used of the Philistines. Cherethites were among David's bodyguard (II Sam. 8:18; 20:23; I Chron. 18:17). They dwelt in the South or Negeb (I Sam. 30:14), and appear to have been either a tribe or branch of Philistia or Philistia itself (Ezek. 25:16). The Philis-

2:4

2:5

2:6

tines are said to have come from Caphtor (Amos 9:7; Jer. 47:4), which is thought to have been the isle of Crete. "I will destroy thee [land of the Philistines], that there shall be no inhabitant." In its complete destruction Philistia is to share the lot of all Canaan. The once heavily inhabited seacoast, where a strong nation of people dwelt, will become pasture land for shepherds. Instead will be "cottages"—"caves" (margin, ASV) is better: this indicates that where proud cities once stood there would be huts or "dugouts" in the ground for the protection of the shepherds and

2:7

their flocks. "And the coast shall be for the remnant," not the remnant of the Philistines, for they will have been destroyed (v. 5), but the remnant of Judah. In spite of the judgment about to come upon Judah, a remnant would be brought back from the captivity, possessing the hill country, the lowlands (Shephelah) and the South (Negeb), "subscribing deeds" to the land and carrying on regular business (Jer. 32:42-44). God never promised that it would be other than a remnant, a small number, who would return. Those of the remnant would use this land of the seacoast as pasture for their flocks, and they would "lie down" in the ruins of the "houses of Ashkelon." Ashkelon is probably used here to represent all the cities of Philistia. The prophecy concerning the land was fulfilled when the Jews returned from Babylon. However, Deane thinks that the complete fulfillment was to have been realized under the Messiah (*P.C.*). Only one of infinite foresight, such as that possessed by Jehovah, could have declared the return of a remnant from captivity and their possession of the land as here foretold.

2:8-11. From the cities of the west the prophet looks to the east and declares the judgment of Moab and Ammon. Perpetual desolation will be their reward for pride and idolatry.

2:8

The reproaches of Moab and the revilings of Ammon against God's people extend back to the time of Moses. When Israel came to the borders of Moab,

Balak sent to Mesopotamia for Balaam to come and curse the nation (Num. 22—24); and in the time of the judges both Moab and Ammon sought the destruction of Israel. In strong and clear language Amos announced the indignation and judgment of Jehovah upon each of these nations because of their cruelty toward others (Amos 1:13-15; 2:1-3). These few occasions by no means exhaust the expressions of contempt for God's people demonstrated by Moab and Ammon. The immediate sin before the prophet appears to have been efforts to diminish the territory of Judah, as they "magnified themselves against their border." "Therefore as I live, saith Jehovah of hosts, the God of Israel": as there is none higher by whom He could affirm His intentions, Jehovah swears by Himself that both nations would be completely destroyed, Moab as Sodom and Ammon as Gomorrah. Encrusted with saltpits, and productive of nettles only, these two would become the picture of utter desolation. Nelson Glueck, the famous Jewish archaeologist, has located hundreds of rock-strewn ruins of ancient villages and towns of Moab, Ammon, and Edom, which bear mute testimony to the prophet's inspiration. The prophet declares that though these two, Moab and Ammon, be destroyed, His people would continue and would build on the ruin of these heathen nations. As in the case of Edom (Obad. 3—4), the basis of the sin of Moab and Ammon was pride; and for this pride they would have utter desolation as their reward. Isaiah said of this trait that characterized them, "We have heard of the pride of Moab, that he is very proud; even of his arrogancy, and his pride, and his wrath" (16:6). Jeremiah says of Moab, "He magnified himself against Jehovah" (48:26), and then he quotes Isaiah, showing that Moab had not changed (48:29). In reproaching the people of God and in magnifying themselves above them, these descendants of Lot had reproached Israel's God and magnified themselves against Him. This conflict was between the pride and arrogance of two nations and the God of all the earth. Jehovah is terrible in His demonstration of anger against sin and

2:9

2:10

2:11

the worship of false deities; false worship lay at the root of sin and evil. In the fierce contest between Jehovah and the idols He would make clear who is supreme. These would be destroyed as those nations that worshiped them were brought to an end. Out of the conflict Jehovah would emerge as the recognized sole God of all the earth, who only is worthy of worship and homage. Men would see this glory and be constrained to worship Him. Those idols are long since gone, and today God rules in the hearts of millions. This rule stands as a monument to His eternal Godhood. "Isles of the nations" indicates "the remotest regions of the earth and their inhabitants" from among whom His worshipers are found.

2:12-15. Ethiopia to the south, representing all of Egypt, and Assyria to the north, the most powerful nation of earth, would all be brought to nothing. Assyria's destruction would be complete.

2:12   "Ye Ethiopians also": "also" indicates that as Jehovah would bring Ammon and Moab to an end, so also He would slay Ethiopia. Ethiopia was the most remote of the nations to the south known to the Jews. It was located south of the second cataract of the Nile and probably included the third and fourth and possibly the fifth cataract. For years Egypt had been under the rule of Ethiopian kings; therefore, when the prophet foretold the downfall of Ethiopia his prophecy would include Egypt as well. A few years later the fall of both powers is clearly declared by Ezekiel (30:4-5). "Ye . . . shall be slain by my sword" points to Jehovah as the one by whom the destruction would be accomplished. This sword of Jehovah was to have been put in the hand of Nebuchadnezzar, the executor of the judgment (Ezek. 30:24-25). The booty of these nations would be as wages from Jehovah to Nebuchadnezzar for the executing of His will against Tyre, who came under His wrath and judgment, and against these two great powers of the south (Ezek. 29:17-20). The prophet

turns his face from the south to the north as he   2:13
proclaims judgment against Assyria, which represented the most northerly nation bearing on the history of the period. There follows one of the most
vivid and expressive prophecies found in all Scripture.
Assyria was at the moment a powerful and flourishing
nation, dominating the world of that day. Only from
one under the influence of the divine Spirit could
such a prophecy originate. The picture is one of
complete destruction and desolation in spite of the
fact that it was uttered while the nation maintained
its power and influence in the world. God's hand
would stretch out to the north against Assyria to
destroy it, and against Nineveh, her capital, to make
it desolate, swallowed up as in the midst of a dry and
parched desert. Instead of mighty armies and a   2:14
swarming populace, herds of cattle and flocks of
sheep and goats would be found there, "all the beasts
of every kind" (margin, ASV). Unclean creatures such
as "the pelican and the porcupine," creatures that
inhabit desolate regions, would perch upon and bur-
row under and in the crevices of the crowns or carved
heads of the magnificent columns, now fallen to the
ground. The cries and songs of these animals and
birds, both doleful and otherwise, would proclaim to
the world the desolation of the once magnificent and
proud city. The hand of Jehovah would strip Nineveh   2:15
of its glory. Only rubble and rubbish would mark the
site of the once magnificent city that rejoiced in her
power and force, boasted of her cruelty and vaunted
the claim that she alone stood as mistress of the
world. What a contrast! The once proud and powerful
nation would now be an utter desolation, a place for
wild beasts to lie down, and an object of the sneering
contempt of all passersby. How the mighty are
brought low when Jehovah stretches forth His hand
against them! As if to comfort Pharaoh in the judgment and fall of Egypt, Ezekiel announced that when
in Sheol (the pit, the nether parts of the earth)—that
is, when his nation is destroyed—he will find Assyria
there also. Destruction and oblivion is to be the lot of
these nations, "all of them slain by the sword who

caused terror in the land of the living" (Ezek. 32:18-23).

Chapter 3

3:1-7. The prophet turns again to Jerusalem to warn her that since her inhabitants have acted as the heathen, so will be her judgment. The difference is, Jerusalem may be helped if only her subjects will fear Jehovah.

3:1   "Woe to her that is rebellious and polluted!" The prophet addresses Jerusalem. As Jehovah had pronounced woe upon the Philistines, so now He pronounces woe upon the city of His own people. That which follows makes clear that Jerusalem is under consideration. Jerusalem is described as rebellious against the will of God and polluted as a result of rebellion. "To the oppressing city": rebellion against God results in depravity, and depravity leads to cruelty and oppression of the poor. For this she stands 3:2   under the woe of Jehovah. Four charges are leveled against the rebellious city: (1) "She obeyed not the voice," the voice of Jehovah, as He had spoken through His law and His prophets; (2) "She received not correction" or instruction, either through the voice or through the chastenings sent upon her (cf. Amos 4:6 ff. to Israel); (3) "She trusted not in Jehovah," but put her trust in false gods, in her military power, and in alliances with foreign nations; such arms of flesh utterly fail; (4) "She drew not near to her God" in faith and supplication to find in Him the guiding hand when in need and the spiritual power so essential to life at all times. She had failed miserably to live up to her place in the favor of the 3:3   Lord. The four classes in Jerusalem to whom the people looked for guidance are now introduced and exposed as unfit for the high calling to which they had been appointed or chosen. (1) "Her princes," who ought to rule with dignity and equity, are instead "roaring lions" who seek to devour those they should protect. (2) "Her judges" did not judge fairly the cases brought before them, but rather "are evening wolves" that slink about in the twilight, greedily devouring all they can find, leaving "nothing till the morrow." They think only of themselves. (3) "Her prophets" are described as light, or empty and treacherous, deceiving the people by uttering their own will and pleasure instead of God's. This is the only mention Zephaniah makes of the false prophets who lead the people astray. (4) "Her priests," whose function was to interpret the law to the people and officiate at the altar with reverence, had acted in an opposite manner. They had profaned the whole temple service and had "done violence to the law" by treating its teaching as unholy. In the midst of a city filled with such wickedness and perversion of right, Jehovah can but act consistently with His own character and nature. He cannot deny Himself (II Tim. 2:13); He must do what is right; He must act in harmony with His own absolute Godhood. God will not do iniquity by violating any principle He has declared; He would not be just if He would pass over sins. He had not deceived them; for continuously, "morning by morning" (margin, ASV), He had brought to light and manifested His justice and righteousness before them in His treatment of both Israel and the heathen nations. Although filled with rebellion and sin, His people had recognized no wickedness on their part nor felt any shame for what they had done. Jehovah reminds Jerusalem that from the time of their entrance into Canaan to the present He had cut off the inhabitants of Canaan and brought them to nothing because of their iniquity and wickedness. The battlements, or corner towers of their walled cities, have been brought down. Their cities have been destroyed and left without inhabitants. Their streets have been made desolate, with none found walking on them. These judgments against the nations would serve as a reminder to the careless and rebellious city in which He had chosen to put His name. When He gave them the land of Canaan God had told the people that it was not because of their righteousness but because of the wickedness of the inhabitants

3:4

3:5

3:6

3:7 whom He was casting out (Deut. 9:4-5), and that if they would forget Him, He would likewise cast them out (Lev. 26; Deut. 28). What had He asked of Jerusalem? "Only fear thou me; receive instruction" (margin, ASV); give to Him the reverence and regard that are rightfully His and receive from Him correction when He would speak. If they would do what Jehovah had appointed for them, He had promised that Israel would endure permanently as a nation and her dwelling would "not be cut off." But instead of giving heed to the Lord, she had risen early to be about her wickedness as one who rises early to get to his work.

> *3:8. The pious are urged to wait patiently for Jehovah and for His judgment upon the nations.*

3:8 "Therefore," in the light of the woe and judgment of verses 1-7, "wait ye for me, saith Jehovah." Apparently Jehovah calls upon the pious few among the faithful, the people who seek Him (2:3), to "wait for" Him. The exhortation "wait for Jehovah" is a favorite with Isaiah, who uses it over and over. In his use of the expression one may best find a satisfactory explanation for it as he says, "They that wait for Jehovah shall renew their strength" (40:31); "the isles shall wait for his law" (42:4); "they that wait for me shall not be put to shame" (49:23); "neither hath eye seen a God besides thee, who worketh for him that waiteth for him" (64:4). To wait for Jehovah is to put one's trust in Him, not despairing, but allowing God to work out the future. They must wait, trust in Him, until the judgment is executed, and then will come the blessing. "Until the day that I rise up to the prey" points to that for which they wait. The "prey" seems to indicate the ones who become His, the converts who, out of the impending judgment, turn to Him. This interpretation is in harmony with the exhortation to wait for Jehovah, and with God's promise that the servant "shall divide the spoil with the strong" (Isa. 53:12), the prey being His part of

the divided spoil. The decision of Jehovah is to bring
a universal judgment upon the nations, "for my determination is to gather the nations." This judgment will
not be for utter extermination, but it will be of a
fiery and refining nature that out of it would come
His prey or portion. Jealous because He had been
supplanted in the affections of both His people and
the nations, Jehovah would make the judgment so
fierce that only the purest of metal would survive; the
dross would be consumed. The faithful few must look
beyond the judgment of the heathen nations for the
complete fulfilling of God's purpose and plan for
them.

> *3:9-13. After the impending judgment of
> both Judah and the nations, Jehovah would
> turn to Himself a people of purified lip and
> united heart. These would be selected from
> the humble and the poor. No unrighteousness
> would be found among them, and none would
> make them afraid.*

"For then," after the impending judgment,   *3:9*
Jehovah will "turn to the peoples a pure language" or
"lip." The lips that had been profaned by the names
and worship of idols would be purified so that they
may call in unison on the name of Jehovah, speaking
from purified hearts through cleansed lips (cf. Isa.
6:5, 7; Jer. 1:9; Dan. 10:16). Their service would be
with one consent or "shoulder," that is, with one
yoke. Yoked together in the Lord they strive together
in one great objective of service. This is a Messianic
hope, and looks to that time for its fulfillment (cf.
Heb. 13:15-16). "Ethiopia" indicated the extremely   *3:10*
remote region to the south; "beyond the rivers of
Ethiopia" would point to regions even beyond the
most remote. "The rivers" would be the Nile and
tributaries that flowed into it. But how will we treat
the remainder of the verse? If the translation of the
American Standard Version and King James Version
is accepted, Jehovah is saying that the redeemed from
among the scattered Jews will come as His suppliants,

and bring their supplications and offerings to Him. If the alternate translation of the American Standard Version marginal reading is accepted, "shall they bring my suppliants, even the daughter of my dispersed, for an offering unto me," we have an entirely different meaning. This would say that the converted Gentiles would turn their hand to convert and bring wayward Israel to Jehovah as an offering. On the basis of Isaiah 66:20, Keil strongly defends this latter position; and Deane and Laetsch lean toward it. If Zephaniah's statement is accepted as parallel to Isaiah's, then the dispersed Jews who would be brought to the Lord would be the offering. "In that

3:11 day," the day of the fulfilling of verses 9-10, the people of the Lord shall "not be put to shame." That which had brought the shame upon them will have been abolished, or will have given way to a nobler and purer condition. Sins will have been blotted out. The proud and the haughty will have been taken out from among them; there would be no place for pride and arrogance in God's "holy mountain," the new order of things. The meek of the earth who seek righteousness (2:3) will dwell in the holy mountain, God's new

3:12 spiritual Jerusalem. Instead of the haughty there will be an afflicted and poor people, but these will be rich and strong in their faith (cf. Mic. 4:7). Their confidence and strength will not be in themselves but in the name of Jehovah, in whose name they will take

3:13 refuge. Although poor and afflicted, this redeemed remnant would find power and glory in the purity of their character. They "shall not do iniquity," commit wickedness, as had their fathers; "nor speak lies," probably referring to the religious lies of idolatry and false prophets that had characterized those before them. They will not be guilty of "a deceitful tongue" that is intended to deceive others. They will feed on the truth and righteousness of their God and will lie down in the security of Jehovah's protection, for He will be about them as a wall of fire. In this security there will be none who can make them afraid. This is a glorious picture and promise of hope, given in the wake of the dark picture of judgment and wrath.

3:14-17. With judgments taken away and the enemy cast out, the people will rejoice. Jehovah will be in their midst; they will not fear; Jehovah will joy over them. This points to the Messianic time.

As the prophet had introduced the character of the redeemed remnant under the Messiah (vv. 9-13), he now describes their joy as he calls upon them to sing and rejoice in their salvation. "Sing": break out in exultation in songs of lively spirit. "O daughter of Zion" personifies as one the redeemed and purified Zion; "shout, O Israel," joins all the tribes together again into one as the new "daughter of Jerusalem," the spiritual people of the new spiritual nation (cf. Zech. 2:10; 9:9). Zion, Israel, and Jerusalem are again one, rejoicing in Jehovah. Zephaniah assigns the reason for rejoicing: "Jehovah hath taken away thy judgments" which had been brought upon them (cf. vv. 1-7), and had "cast out thine enemy" that had inflicted it. But the greatest cause of all for rejoicing is that "the King of Israel, even Jehovah" was in the midst of Zion. Should the next phrase be read, "thou shalt not *fear* evil any more," or "thou shalt not *see* evil any more"? Probably the latter is correct: "Thou shalt not see evil any more," in the sense of experiencing evil, or seeing it practiced among them; for Jehovah is in their midst. The Messiah is not specified, but it is evident that Jehovah would be in their midst in the person of the Messiah. This is clearly pointed out in the New Testament. "In that day," the day of singing because the judgments are taken away and Jehovah is in the midst of them, they will not see or experience evil any more; and they have nothing to fear. "Let not thy hands be slack." Slack or fallen hands are a symbol of despair; so now with Jehovah in their midst and with nothing to fear, let the fallen hands be lifted up (cf. Heb. 12:12). Jehovah is now in the midst of them as their King and God; therefore, their salvation is assured, for He is mighty to save to the uttermost. This is the real basis of courage and hope. When Jehovah's people become irredeemable

3:14

3:15

3:16

3:17

He withdraws Himself from them (cf. Ezek. 11:22-24; Matt. 23:38). This He had done, but now He has returned to them. Jehovah is described as rejoicing over them, resting or silent in His love, and joying over them with singing. Of the expression, "He will rest [Heb.: be silent] in his love," Deane offers the following suggestion, "For the very greatness of his love God rests, as it were, in quiet enjoyment of it" (*Pulpit Commentary*). The verse expresses the love and esteem of God for His redeemed.

> *3:18-20. The prophet closes with a renewal of the promise of Jehovah to gather what was driven away and make them a praise to Himself.*

3:18 Jehovah will demonstrate His love for the pious of Israel by gathering them together to Himself. But before this can be done, Judah must be scattered among the nations in the judgment at hand. Through this refining experience, those would be restored who sorrow for the assembly, who yearn for the presence of Jehovah, and to whom this scattering from the presence of the Lord was considered a great reproach.

3:19 God would deal with those who would afflict His people; they would not escape the fire of His wrath. The "lame" and the "driven away" indicate the state of the people in a hapless, helpless, and homeless condition. As He had promised to make of these a "strong nation" (Mic. 4:6-7), so now He will make of them "a praise" instead of the shame which they had been and which had been brought on them. With

3:20 some slight change in wording, Jehovah repeats the promise already made. This gives emphasis to the determination to accomplish His purpose. Note the use of the personal pronoun "I" in verses 18-20: "I will gather," "I will deal," "I will save," "I will make," "will I bring you in," "will I gather you," "I will make," "when I bring back your captivity before your eyes." While they are still a people He would so fulfill His promise that all would see it. The work of redemption will be the work of the Lord. The people had refused to give heed to Him when He had called; therefore, He had scattered them abroad. Now it would be He who would bring them back. In this assurance let them hope and rejoice!

8
NAHUM
"Consolation"

General Observations

1. The Man

a. **Name:** "Consolation" or "Consoler." In the words of another, the name "is in a sense symbolical of the message of the book, which was intended to comfort the oppressed and afflicted people of Judah" (Eiselen, *I.S.B.E.*, p. 2109).

b. **Home.** The prophet introduces himself as "Nahum the Elkoshite"; evidently he was from a place known as Elkosh. But where was Elkosh located? Some have suggested El-kosh, a town or village twenty-four miles north of Nineveh. But since the earliest suggestion for this place appears first in the sixteenth century A.D., this location is most doubtful. Others have concluded that since Capernaum means "village of Nahum," the town in Galilee bearing this name may have been the birthplace of the prophet, who migrated to Judah; but there is no solid foundation for this conclusion. A third suggestion has been that Elkosh was "Elkesie beyond the Jordan"; this is equally without foundation. It must be admitted that the location of the Elkosh of our author is unknown. Many modern writers look for the location to be found somewhere in Judah or southern Palestine.

c. **The Occupation** of the prophet is unknown.

d. **Characterization.** Most students of the prophets acclaim Nahum's writing to be one of the most poetic of them all. His book is described as a poem, "stately and impressive." As one reads it he feels himself carried from thought to thought at a rapid and highly excited pace. The style is forceful, brilliant, and lifelike. One feels that he is sharing with the prophet the excitement of the moment. As George A. Smith describes it, "His language is strong and brilliant; his rhythm rumbles and rolls, leaps and flashes, like the horsemen and chariots he describes" (Vol. II., p. 91).

The prophet says nothing of the internal conditions of Judah and Jerusalem; he leaves this to his contemporaries, Jeremiah, Habakkuk, and Zephaniah. He is a prophet of a single theme: the fall and destruction of Nineveh, that city of great and dreadful people. He has been described as an "enthusiastic, optimistic patriot" (J. M. P. Smith). His book is not the recording of personal glee over the fall of Nineveh, expressing the narrow hatred and prejudice of a single individual; but it is the fervent expression of the outraged conscience of mankind. "It is one great At Last!" (G. A. Smith). His cry is not only the cry of jubilation at the fall of an oppressive foe, but it is also the cry of faith in the sovereign rule of Jehovah and a vindication of confidence that He will avenge His elect when the time is ripe. The lesson of his beautifully worded yet dreadful prophecy is one to which the world could well give heed today. The prophet reveals the eternal principle of the omnipotent God that for a nation to survive it must be established upon and directed by principles of righteousness and truth. Wickedness will eventually turn a nation back to Sheol, the oblivion of the unseen, when it makes cruelty and wickedness the standard by which it lives.

2. Date: 663-612 B.C.

The earliest date identifiable in the book is the fall of No-amon, the Egyptian Thebes (3:8). The expedition alluded to was carried out by Ashurbanipal, king of Assyria, about the year 663 B.C. In the campaign Thebes was destroyed and a great store of booty carried into Assyria. Nineveh was destroyed by the combined forces of the Medes and Chaldeans, 612 B.C. Somewhere between these two dates Nahum announced the fall of Nineveh, the theme of his book. Most scholars narrow the date to the time between 630 and 612 B.C.

3. Background

Inasmuch as the prophet does not touch upon the internal conditions in Judah and Jerusalem, but deals with Nineveh, the capital of Assyria, only information concerning the background of Assyria and Nineveh will be considered. The Assyrian rulers from the beginning of Assyria's policy of westward conquest and world domination, and the dates of each, are as follows:

Tiglath-pileser III, 745-727 B.C. This monarch began a program of world conquest. He invaded the West and deported some of the inhabitants of northern Israel, removing them to an area north of Nineveh.

Shalmaneser V, 727-722 B.C. Shalmaneser began the siege of Samaria, 722 B.C., but died before the city fell.

Sargon II, 722-705 B.C. This king completed the siege of Samaria, 721 B.C., which had been begun by Shalmaneser. He was murdered 705 B.C.

Sennacherib, 705-681 B.C. Sennacherib boasted on his monuments that he had shut up Hezekiah in Jerusalem "as a bird in a cage." He was murdered by two of his sons in 681 B.C., who were then driven out by a younger son, Esarhaddon, who became king.

Esarhaddon, 681-668 B.C.

Ashurbanipal, 668-625 B.C. His campaign in Egypt resulted in the fall of No-amon (Nah. 3:8). Much booty was carried away by him into Assyria. According to the records this king was very cruel.

Assur-etil-ilani, 625-620 B.C.

Sin-shar-ishkeen (Esarhaddon II), 620-612 B.C. When Nineveh was being besieged by the Medes and Chaldeans, Esarhaddon II gathered his wives and children and wealth into the palace and set fire to it. He perished in the fire.

The native forces of Assyria were expended and exhausted by long and extensive wars. The population of her cities was never homogenous, but was made up of foreigners who were drawn to them by trade and the desire for wealth. With nothing more than trade and commerce to hold them together, the nation was bound to break up eventually. The character of the Assyrian rulers and people in general was that of excessive cruelty. Farrar gives a vivid and clear description of their general character:

> Judged from the vaunting inscriptions of her kings, no power more useless, more savage, more terrible, ever cast its gigantic shadow on the page of history as it passed on the way to ruin. The kings of Assyria tormented the miserable world. They exult to record how "space failed for corpses"; how unsparing a destroyer is their goddess Ishtar; how they flung away the bodies of soldiers like so much clay; how they made pyramids of human heads; how they burned cities; how they filled populous lands with death and devastation; how they reddened broad deserts with carnage of warriors; how they scattered whole countries with the corpses of their defenders as with chaff; how they impaled "heaps of men" on stakes, and strewed the mountains and choked rivers with dead bones; how they cut off the hands of kings and nailed them on the walls, and left their bodies to rot with bears and dogs on the entrance gates of cities; how they employed nations of captives in making brick in fetters; how they cut down warriors like weeds, or smote them like wild beasts in the forests, and covered pillars with the flayed skins of rival monarchs.
>
> (*The Minor Prophets*, pp. 147, 148)

The time had now come for divine judgment to fall upon such a nation, and the responsibility to make it known to the people of Judah and preserve it for all posterity fell upon Nahum!

Outline of the Book

Title: The prophet and his subject, v. 1.

I. Nineveh's doom—by the decree of Jehovah, ch. 1

    A. The goodness and severity of Jehovah, vv. 2-8.
       1. Vengeance and mercy of God, vv. 2-3.
       2. The terribleness of His anger against sin, vv. 4-6.
       3. The greatness of His mercy—a stronghold to the faithful, v. 7.
       4. The pursuer of His enemies, v. 8.

    B. The complete overthrow of Nineveh, vv. 9-15.

    1. God's faithfulness in the present crisis: affliction not again to come from Assyria (as in the past), vv. 9-11.

    2. Judah delivered from the yoke of Assyria by destruction of Nineveh's power, vv. 12-13.

    3. Destruction of Assyria, v. 14.

    4. Rejoicing in Zion, v. 15.

II. Siege and destruction of Nineveh—decreed by Jehovah, ch. 2.

    A. Assault upon Nineveh: doom of the city, vv. 1-7.

        1. Furious preparation for battle, vv. 1-4.

        2. Hopelessness of resistance, vv. 5-6.

        3. The city, as a queen, is captured and moans, v. 7.

    B. Flight of the people and sack of the city, vv. 8-13.

        1. The inhabitants flee, the city is plundered, vv. 8-10.

        2. The destruction is complete, vv. 11-13.

III. Nineveh's sins and her inevitable doom, ch. 3.

    A. Nineveh's fate brought upon herself as retribution for her crimes, vv. 1-7.

        1. The graphic description of the battle, vv. 1-3.

        2. The cause: her sins, v. 4.

        3. The uncovering of her shame is of Jehovah, vv. 5-7.

    B. The fate of No-amon is to be the fate of Nineveh, vv. 8-11.

    C. Inability of Nineveh's resources to save the city, vv. 12-19.

        1. Fall of the outlying strongholds, vv. 12-13.

        2. Siege and destruction of the city, vv. 14-19a.

        3. Universal exultation over the fall of Nineveh, v. 19b.

Comments

Chapter 1

"The burden of Nineveh. The book of the vision   *1:1*
of Nahum the Elkoshite." "Burden" literally means a
heavy load to be borne or to be lifted up. Here, and
in the writings of other prophets, it means to lift up
the voice in proclamation, an utterance or prophecy,
denouncing the sins of a people by pronouncing on
them or their place of habitation a heavy judgment. It
is also a vision in which Jehovah reveals in a vivid and
moving manner the destruction of Nineveh which is
soon to be accomplished. This destruction of Nineveh, the capital of Assyria, located on the Tigris
River, is the object of the prophecy. For "Elkoshite"
see the Introduction.

*1:2-8. The fierce wrath of Jehovah against His
enemies, before which none can stand, is
graphically described. Over against this wrath
is the mercy of the Lord, but only for them
who take refuge in Him.*

The burden of the prophet's message is empha-   *1:2*
sized by the fivefold use of "Jehovah" in verses 2-3.
"Jehovah is a jealous God and avengeth." Jehovah's
jealousy stems from His own honor and that of His
people. His jealousy may be compared to that of a
husband for his wife; He will brook no rival; He will
not be supplanted by another in the affection of His
people. "Jehovah avengeth and is full of wrath." His
avenging is not to be thought of as "getting even
with," but of vindicating His own righteousness by
inflicting a just judgment upon offenders. "Jehovah
taketh vengeance on his adversaries, and he reserveth
wrath for his enemies." Not only is Jehovah jealous
of His people, but He is also jealous for them; and He
expresses this jealousy by executing judgment upon
those who would destroy them or who would hinder
their service to Him. "Jehovah is slow to anger, and   *1:3*

great in power, and will by no means clear the guilty." Jehovah's slowness to anger is not an indication of weakness, but of His Godhood; He does not act impulsively, but exercises His great power with caution and reserve. Though He may be slow to anger, waiting until man has filled the cup of his iniquity, Jehovah will act; He will not clear or excuse the guilty. Punishment will come. "Jehovah hath his way in the whirlwind and in the storm, and the clouds are the dust of his feet." Jehovah's power is expressed in the tornado or the awesome storm as in its destructive force it sweeps away all that is in its path. So will the jealousy of the Lord's wrath sweep away as does the storm. Jehovah is here revealed as one of great might and majesty, coming to the defense and vindication of His people. In the storm of His presence the clouds are as the fine dust of His feet, boiling up as He strides on His way.

1:4   His power is further revealed in nature, for "he rebuketh the sea, and maketh it dry, and drieth up all the rivers." The sea and the rivers are under His control to be dried up at His beckoning. "Bashan languisheth, and Carmel." Bashan was the land east of the Sea of Galilee, north of the river Yarmuk. While enjoying only a limited rainfall, Bashan was a section of rich soil, noted for its grain and pasture. Carmel was the wooded mountain to the west that jutted into the Mediterranean Sea. "And the flower of Lebanon languisheth." Lebanon, noted for its majestic and valuable cedars, was located north of Galilee, west of the Jordan River. Although each of these was rich and productive in its own right, each was subject

1:5   to the expressed power of Jehovah. "The mountains quake at him, and the hills melt." The ancients considered the mountains to be the pillars of the earth and the symbols of strength and endurance. These tremble and collapse, and the hills melt like wax at the presence of One so mighty as Jehovah. "And the earth is upheaved at his presence, yea, the world, and all that dwell therein." The earth itself and the inhabited world, and man and the whole creation are thrown into convulsion by the presence of Jehovah.

If the whole earth and all forces of it are under   *1:6*
the immediate control of such an infinite power,
"who can stand before his indignation? and who can
abide the fierceness of his anger?" Even a power as
great as Assyria would be helpless before the wrath of
One so infinitely great. "His wrath is poured out like
fire, and the rocks are broken asunder by him." Like
the molten lava which no force can stay as it flows
down the mountainside, and like the rocks broken by
the mighty upheavals of the earth, so is the wrath of
Jehovah. But there is another side to the nature and   *1:7*
expressed power of this great and mighty God:
"Jehovah is good, a stronghold in the day of
trouble." This presents "God's other side." When
perilous times come and trouble like a mighty river
overflows, Jehovah is an impregnable stronghold to
all who will flee to Him. "And he knoweth them that
take refuge in him." In love and protective care, He
knows fully those that take refuge in Him. His power
is as great to protect as it is to destroy. This had been
demonstrated in the Assyrian invasion of Judah
when, through the intercessions of Isaiah and Hezekiah (Isa. 37:36-38), Jehovah had turned back the
overflowing Assyrian tide. "But with an over-running   *1:8*
flood he will make a full end of her place"; as a river
in flood time overruns its banks, carrying destruction
in its wake, so God "will make a full end of her
place." "Her" refers to Nineveh, introduced in verse
1. "And [he] will pursue his enemies into darkness."
The destruction of His enemies, the Assyrians, will be
complete (cf. Zeph. 2:13 ff.); the darkness of complete disappearance from the earth will be their end.
It will be by the controlling power and wrath of
Jehovah.

> *1:9-13. A full end of Nineveh is decreed;
> affliction from that source will not arise
> again. As a yoke upon Judah, that yoke will
> be completely broken off.*

This passage is admittedly difficult as indicated   *1:9*
by the various views taken by commentators. "What

do ye devise against Jehovah? he will make a full end; affliction shall not rise up the second time." Who is addressed, the Assyrians or the Jews? Some would address it to Judah, others to Assyria, and others to both. In all probability it is addressed to both: Assyria, what do you devise against Jehovah? And you, Judah, do you think that Jehovah is not able to handle the Assyrians? Jehovah's answer is that He will make a full end of the Assyrians; affliction will not again arise against you, Judah, as it did in the days of Ahaz and Hezekiah. Jehovah had promised the destruction of Assyria (Isa. 10:24-27), and now the time has come for the carrying out of the promise in the complete destruction of that nation. Further, Jehovah can and will accomplish His purpose. "For

1:10 entangled like thorns": as a thornhedge that is thought to be impregnable, which man cannot penetrate or pass through, so the Assyrian nation considered itself. "And drunken as with their drink" refers also to the Assyrians. In this self-confidence of their impregnable position and power, the nation was intoxicated on pride and the power of conquest. Jeremiah used the figure of intoxication when he indicated that Judah was filled with drunkenness in their pride (13:9, 13-14); and Habakkuk declared that the wine of the Babylonians, which was their own power on which they were intoxicated, was treacherous (2:5, margin, ASV). In this condition of drunkenness through pride and boastful defiance against Jehovah through their feeling of security, "they are consumed utterly as dry stubble." Jehovah will light the fire, and as dry thorns and stubble they will go up in smoke.

1:11 "There is one gone forth out of thee," out of Nineveh, "that deviseth evil against Jehovah, that counselleth wickedness." It is uncertain who this one was. The last real threat to Jerusalem from Nineveh had been Sennacherib (*ca.* 702-701 B.C.). If there was an immediate threat from that direction, the occasion is unknown. It is more probable that the prophet is speaking of the entire spirit and purpose of all Assyria toward Jehovah, which he here personifies as one

man. The counsel followed by Nineveh toward
Jehovah had been that of "Belial," or worthlessness,
for it would be brought to nothing. Jehovah directs   *1:12*
the next word concerning Nineveh to Judah:
"Though they be in full strength, and likewise many,
even so shall they be cut down, and he shall pass
away." Though Assyria still boasts her full strength
and outwardly appears to have control of the world
of her day, and though her nation is made up of
many people, they—the many—will be cut down.
"And he shall pass away." The "he" of this verse is
the "one gone forth out of thee," introduced in verse
11. If the "he" is an individual, he will pass away; if
"he" personifies the nation, then the nation will pass
away. In either case Assyria is doomed, and so also
are her counselors who had devised evil against
Jehovah. The determination expressed in verse 9,
"affliction shall not rise up the second time," is now
repeated: "Though I have afflicted thee"—Judah—"I
will afflict thee no more." Jehovah had used Assyria
to afflict Judah and Jerusalem (Isa. 10:5-21), but
Judah will never again experience affliction from that
source. "And now will I break his yoke from off thee,   *1:13*
and will burst thy bonds in sunder." This is addressed
to Judah. Jehovah will break the yoke of Nineveh
from off the neck of Judah; He will burst in sunder
the bonds of Nineveh under which Judah had been
held.

*1:14-15. Assyria's doom is determined; her
grave is made. A messenger is on his way
bringing these good tidings to Judah.*

"And Jehovah hath given commandment con-   *1:14*
cerning thee, that no more of thy name be sown."
This oracle is directed to Nineveh. The commandment given is from Jehovah with whom Nineveh will
deal, instead of dealing with the idol gods of other
nations as she had in the past. "Out of the house of
thy gods will I cut off the graven image and the
molten image." The graven and molten images, the
gods worshiped by the Assyrians (Ashur, Nabu, Anu,

Adad, the goddess Ishtar, and others), would be cut off out of the temples that had sheltered them. As Assyria had destroyed the idol gods of conquered peoples and had carried other images as booty to Nineveh, so now would her deities be destroyed or carried away. "I will make thy grave; for thou art vile." God would so completely bury Assyria the nation, and Nineveh the capital, that they would pass into oblivion. Weighed in the balance of God's scales of justice and righteousness, this great and powerful nation was found to be "vile," that is, light in weight. As the psalmist said of men of low and high degrees, "In the balance they will go up; they are together lighter than vanity" (Ps. 62:9), so now could it be said of Nineveh that in the balances they would go up.

1:15   The prophet looked beyond the vantage point on which he stood and pointed others to the herald of good tidings that Assyria had fallen. "Behold, upon the mountains the feet of him that bringeth good tidings, that publisheth peace!" Isaiah had used practically this same expression in a Messianic context, looking to the coming of the Saviour (40:9; 52:7). Nahum, who borrows Isaiah's language, speaks not of the Messiah, but of the herald of good tidings who brings the news that Nineveh has fallen. He sees the fall as having taken place, although as yet the city was still standing "in full strength." With the message of this good news the prophet urges, "Keep thy feasts, O Judah, perform thy vows; for the wicked one shall no more pass through thee; he is utterly cut off." Let Judah keep the feasts of thanksgiving to Jehovah and pay the vows made to Him, for His victory over the terrible enemy is complete and final. Though Judah may experience trouble from other sources, her oppression from Assyria will have come to an end; "for the wicked one shall no more pass through thee; he is utterly cut off." Praise God for His infinite power, and for the providence by which He exercises it.

Chapter 2

2:1-7. The destroyer of Nineveh is on his way! The prophet sees the destruction as accomplished. The destroyer draws nigh; excitement is high; Nineveh prepares for the siege. But it is all to no avail; the city is doomed.

"He that dasheth in pieces is come up against thee." "Dasher in pieces" (Keil), "Shatterer" (J. M. P. Smith), "Scatterer" (Laetsch)—all these sum up the character of the destroyer: one who shatters by dashing in pieces and scattering. The one coming is not named, but the annals of history point to the combined forces of Nebuchadnezzar of Babylon and the Medes as the destroyer. They will come "against thee," the Assyrians. "Keep the fortress, watch the way, make thy loins strong, fortify thy power mightily" is directed to the people of Nineveh. Make full and complete preparation to meet the invading force. The reason for this preparation is that Jehovah has determined the judgment against the Assyrian power. "For Jehovah restoreth the excellency of Jacob, as the excellency of Israel." Jacob and Israel are not used here in reference to Judah and the ten tribes separately, but to the whole nation of the twelve tribes. Jacob was the natural name and Israel was the name divinely given to the father of the nation. The "excellency" of the nation is that in which she should have been proud: her honor, self-respect, and glory which were given her by Jehovah and which should have grown out of her relation to Jehovah. "For the emptiers have emptied them out." These are not here named, but they would include all heathen people who had overrun and destroyed God's people; however, the prophecy points to the Assyrians in particular, who had emptied them out of their land. "And destroyed their vine-branches" points to the emptiers who had destroyed the Israelites, the families of the nation, God's vineyard.

The approaching "dasher in pieces" is now vividly described. "The shield of his mighty men is made

2:1

2:2

2:3

red," either by copper-overlay, which in the sunlight gave the appearance of being red, or by heavy leather over wood or wicker painted red. "The valiant men are in scarlet," which seems to have been the color of the garments worn by the Chaldean troops (see Ezek. 23:14). "The chariots flash with steel in the day of his preparation, and the cypress spears are brandished." There is no indication from the Babylonian monuments that their chariots were equipped with rotating blades on the wheels or with blades protruding from the sides of the chariots. The flashing of the chariots must therefore refer to the reflection of sunlight flashing from the steel armor or ornaments of the chariots as they rushed about in their preparation for attack. The cypress spears would be those made of cypress wood, brandished, and likewise flashing in the sunlight. "The chariots rage in the streets; they rush to and fro in the broad ways." The chariots rushing here and there about the streets of the cities entered by the foe, or of Nineveh as if already entered, have an air of madness about them. They dash here and there seeking out the prey, destroying the defenders. "The appearance of them is like torches; they run like the lightnings," as they are beheld from the walls of the city, rushing about in the suburbs or the countryside nearby. They appear as flashes of lightning in their dashing about. "He remembereth his nobles: they stumble in their march" is thought by some to refer to the oncoming destroyers. But others think the prophet refers to the king of Nineveh who rushes his nobles to their position of battle. The latter has a greater degree of probability. These stumble toward their position as men panic-stricken, weakened in their terror, stumbling and fumbling about in their effort to fight off the invaders. "They make haste to the wall thereof, and the mantelet is prepared." If this refers to the Assyrians stumbling toward their positions, which is the more probable view, then either they prepared a covering on the walls for themselves, or they saw the battering engines and coverings of the enemy coming into position outside their own walls. This latter best fits the

2:4

2:5

entire context. From the inscriptions on the monuments the mantelets seem to have been small towers, carried on four or six wheels, in which men were protected as they were brought to the walls of a city. Some were battering rams with covers under which men were protected.

"The gates of the rivers are opened, and the palace is dissolved." All efforts at defense are vain; the city is destined to destruction. The specific meaning of this verse is difficult to ascertain. An ancient historian (Diodorus Siculus) states that due to heavy rainfall and the rise of the rivers Khosr and Tigris, the floodgates were overrun and a section of the city wall dissolved, enabling the enemy to enter the city. On the basis of Diodorus's statement some have taken the language literally, implying a literal dissolving of the walls. A more likely interpretation is that the prophet is simply saying that God will open the gates and that the overflowing army will destroy the palace and rule of the Assyrians. For prophetic use of the expression "overflowing stream" or "flood," see Isaiah 28:2; 30:28; Jeremiah 47:2; and for Jehovah's opening doors or gates, see the prophecy of His going before Cyrus "to open the doors before him" (Isa. 45:1-2). This is the more probable meaning of Nahum's word. "And it is decreed: she [Heb.: *Huzzab*] is uncovered, she is carried away." It is determined by Jehovah that she, Nineveh, which has so long been the mistress of the world, should be brought to an end, dissolved, and carried away. "And her handmaids," the women of the profligate city who have lived in luxury, or a figurative expression for all Nineveh's inhabitants, "moan as with the voice of doves," a plaintive wail, "beating upon their breasts." The picture is one of deep anguish and sorrow as the proud city comes to an end.

2:6

2:7

2:8-13. With the fall of the city the people flee; they are in terror as the city is plundered. The lair of the old lions is invaded and a new experience is theirs—destruction!

2:8 "But Nineveh hath been from of old like a pool of water": whether an artificial pond or an oasis, she had been a central gathering place for the peoples of earth. "Yet they flee away": as her walls crumble and she becomes like a dry and parched lake, her people flee. She is no longer a gathering place, but rather is she now a place avoided. "Stand, stand, they cry; but none looketh back." In spite of the cry of one person to another to stand, and of the leaders to the people to remain and fight, they flee in desperation.

2:9 The prophecy is now directed to the invaders as Jehovah says, "Take ye the spoil of silver, take the spoil of gold." The plunder that had been gathered through the centuries by the plundering of the nations of the world now becomes the spoil of others. "For there is no end of the store, the glory [wealth] of all goodly furniture." The treasures of Nineveh were seemingly unlimited; they were the accumulation of centuries. The description of them by the

2:10 ancient writers borders on the fabulous. But now, how different! "She is empty, and void, and waste." These three Hebrew words yield an assonance that cannot be carried over into the English (J. M. P. Smith). The picture is one of utter desolation and destruction. The spirit of the people is described as matching the desolation of the city, "and the heart melteth, and the knees smite together, and anguish is in all loins, and the faces of them all are waxed pale." That which the cruel Assyrians had inflicted on nations for centuries has now become their own lot. The reaping of a harvest long sown is now their own experience; terror is on every side and anguish on every face. The heart, the knees, the loins, and the faces all combine in expressing the utter despair and terror of the moment.

2:11 As the prophet looks about for the capital of the once proud and cruel Assyrians, he asks, "Where is the den of the lions, and the feeding-place of the young lions?" The destruction of Nineveh was so complete that for centuries its original location was unknown. It was not until the turn of the nineteenth century that archaeologists were able with certainty to identify it. To describe the people of Nineveh and their disposition to crush and to tear, the prophet uses the lair of a lion family and the lion symbol found on their monuments to impress his lesson: "Where the lion and the lioness walked, the lion's whelp, and none made them afraid." All ages of the lion family are here used: the old lion, the lioness, the young lions, and the whelps. Some would apply these to the ruling family; but more likely the prophet includes all: the rulers and their wives, the fighting forces, and the people of Nineveh in general together with their young for whom they provided. "And none made them afraid." For centuries Assyria had been the dominant people of the world, ruling and controlling the nations without fear. But all of this was about to end. The figure of a lion is continued,   *2:12* "The lion did tear in pieces enough for his whelps, and strangled for his lionesses." The king of Nineveh had provided for his young by plundering the nations of the world, tearing them in pieces. But he was not content with this; he also "filled his caves with prey, and his dens with ravin." As the lion brings in the prey to his cave and young, so the rulers and the great of Nineveh had brought in the prey to their city and had filled the dens with "ravin." The word "ravin" is from a word that meant to tear, hence with that which had been torn from others, booty.

But the end is come, for Assyria is not now dealing   *2:13* with the nations of men, but with Jehovah. "Behold, I am against thee, saith Jehovah of hosts." Nineveh's end has been determined by the great God of the universe, who raises up nations to serve His purpose and then destroys them in their wickedness. "And I will burn her chariots in the smoke": the chariots of which she had been so proud and on which she had relied for her conquest of the world were now to be burned and destroyed. "And the sword shall devour thy young lions." The sword, that dreadful instrument which had wrought such destruction throughout the world, was now to bring Nineveh to an end. "And I will cut off thy prey from the earth": that with which she had filled her caves and dens was now to be dissipated throughout the world until it would cease to be. "And the voice of thy messengers shall no more be heard." No more would her emissaries be sent throughout the earth to command, compel submission, and extort tribute from her miserable subjugated nations.

Chapter 3

3:1-7. Nineveh's fate is brought upon herself as retribution for her crimes. A graphic picture of the battle is described. Her own sins are the cause. The uncovering of her shame is of Jehovah.

3:1   "Woe to the bloody city!" A miserable and sorrowful fate is to befall the city stained with blood. Not only were her hands stained with the ruthless shedding of blood of nations, but within her own walls blood had been shed without scruple. Her monuments abound with descriptions of her atrocities and destruction of life (see Introduction). "It is all full of lies and rapine" describes further the wickedness of the capital of the world. Indifferent to a moral standard and recognizing no right but might, she had not hesitated to break covenants or to attain her goal by falsehood. By "rapine," tearing in pieces, a figure taken from the lion (cf. 2:12), she had further contributed to the blood stain of her character. "The prey departeth not." Because of continued warfare and the rape of the nations, the store of booty had not been extinguished. There follows one of the most moving descriptions of the fierceness of a battle to be

3:2   found in any literature. These verses need little or no comment; one needs only an imagination and an ability to read the rumble and roll of the prophet's description. With the ears and eyes of this imagination one hears and sees the mighty struggle, "The noise of the whip, and the noise of the rattling of wheels, and prancing horses, and bounding chariots,

3:3   the horseman mounting, and the flashing sword, and the glittering spear, and a multitude of slain, and a great heap of corpses, and there is no end of the bodies; they stumble upon their bodies." The fierceness of the battle ends with the corpses of the dead scattered everywhere and with men stumbling over them in their rush from place to place as the battle waxes hot and fierce. With this breathless description, the prophet comes to a pause to lay in its proper place the blame for all this carnage. "Because of the multitude of the whoredoms of the well-favored harlot" reveals the cause of it all. In order to achieve her goal, Nineveh, as a harlot well favored, had used all the wiles and enticements of seduction known to men. Whoredom is at times used figuratively to describe idolatry; and in the name of her gods, worshiped for their cruelty and insatiable bloodthirsty character, Nineveh had waged her wars of conquest and plunder. The harlot is noted for her outward appearance of sensual and amorous affection. So Nineveh had feigned lovemaking in order to entice nations into her fold and to enrich her coffers through them. As "the mistress of witchcrafts," Nineveh was acquainted with every subtle means of achieving her goal. As one "that selleth nations through her whoredoms, and families through her witchcrafts" she had enticed, seduced, and led many to destruction. Like the immoral woman of Proverbs, "She is clamorous and wilful; her feet abide not in her house" (Prov. 7:11); and, "Her house is the way to Sheol, going down to the chambers of death" (Prov. 7:27). This was the story of Nineveh.

3:4

But the time of her judgment was come; no longer was she dealing with nations, but with God: "Behold, I am against thee, saith Jehovah of hosts." The nations of the world do not consider that it is with Jehovah, the God of battles, that they have to do. But this ignorance is to their own shame and destruction. To "uncover thy skirts upon thy face" would be to expose her nakedness to shame and contempt before the nations and kingdoms of earth. Further, "And I will cast abominable filth upon thee, and make thee vile." Like a vile and low woman, exposed to the world for what she is, and upon whom the

3:5

3:6

people cast disdain and reproach, so would be the lot of Nineveh. She will be set as a gazing stock for the nations upon which they cast their reproaches and slurs. With her grandeur gone and her shame exposed, she will become the object of the reviling of all mankind. The fall will be such "that all they that look upon thee shall flee from thee"; none will remain to behold lest they, too, suffer a kindred fate. Their wail will be, "Nineveh is laid waste"; and that waste was to be so complete that for centuries—indeed, over two millennia—men did not know with certainty where the site of ancient Nineveh was. There will be none to bemoan her, no comforters to give her consolation. The message of her fall would be glad tidings to the ears of the world that had suffered so severely at her hands.

3:7

3:8-11. The fate of No-amon is to be the fate of Nineveh.

3:8

"Art thou better than No-amon?" No-amon, the city of the god Amon, was the Thebes of upper Egypt and was located about 450 miles south of Cairo. For centuries Thebes, or No, had played an important role in the history of Egypt; but in 663 B.C. it had been destroyed by Ashurbanipal, ruler of Assyria. The prophet now asks if Nineveh is greater than No-amon, the great city that had been destroyed by Nineveh. The Nile, the moats about the city, and its series of canals had been her "sea" or wall of protection. At this point the two great cities had enjoyed similar likeness: both had been protected by a "sea" about it. "Ethiopia," to the south, and "Egypt," to the north, "were her strength, and it was infinite," unlimited. Added to this power and array of strength were Put and Lubim. The location of Put is uncertain; Lubim is probably the Libya to the west of Egypt.

3:9

"Yet was she carried away." In spite of this infinite or unlimited strength, Ashurbanipal had sacked the city and boasted of the great store of booty carried away to Nineveh. The description of No-amon's destruction is a perfect example of the character of the

3:10

Assyrians: "her young children also were dashed in pieces at the head of all the streets," and for the honorable men and the great men of the city they cast lots, sellihg them into bondage. Not all were carried away, but the city was left in such a state that it never recovered from the fall at the hands of Ashurbanipal. "Thou also shalt be drunken." The *3:11* "also" indicates that as No-amon had fallen like a drunken man, so will a like fate befall Nineveh. Whether intoxicated on her own pride, self-confidence, and strength, or intoxicated on the cup of Jehovah's wrath (cf. Obad. 16; Jer. 25:15 ff.), the end is the same. "Thou shalt be hid": as one that is hidden or brought to nothing and, therefore, cannot be found, so would Nineveh's dwelling place be lost to sight. As No-amon had sought a stronghold and hiding place from the enemy, so will Nineveh, for God is against her.

3:12-19. Nineveh's resources are unable to save the city. The prophet points to the fall of the outlying strongholds, to the siege and destruction of the city, and to the universal exultation over the fall of Nineveh.

Nineveh's outlying or frontier fortresses, and also *3:12* those that immediately defended the city, would "be like fig-trees with the first-ripe figs: if they be shaken, they fall into the mouth of the eater." After a winter with no fresh fruit, the first ripe fig is eagerly sought as a delicacy and falls readily into the mouth of the eater. So would her fortresses fall before the on-coming foe. The reason for the rapid fall of the *3:13* fortresses is the weakness of the people who occupied them: "Behold, thy people in the midst of thee are women." The Assyrians had been a brave people, and it can be said to their credit that the people of Nineveh made a courageous defense of their city. But the old fire and strength of other years was gone. "The gates of thy land are set wide open unto thine enemies: the fire hath devoured thy bars." As Nineveh had set fire to the bars and gates of cities she had conquered, so would her own be opened to the conquering enemy. The prophet probably alludes to the fact that God opened the gates and burned the bars as He gave victory to the destroyer of the city.

3:14   "Draw thee water for the siege." The prophet calls ironically upon the people of Nineveh to provide for the siege; for in spite of all she could do, destruction was inevitable. Water is an essential; therefore he would have them make ample provision either by filling the moats, directing the aqueducts into the city, or providing cisterns for a reserve. "Strengthen thy fortresses" by repairing the breaches in the walls and providing towers and bulwarks about them. "Go into the clay, and tread the mortar," in order to make the bricks necessary for the walls and the within-the-city protections. For this strengthening of her fortresses bricks almost beyond number would be required. The walls of the city are estimated to have been about eight miles in length, and one hundred feet in height; and the width is believed to have varied from fifty to one hundred feet (Diodorus). "Make strong the brickkiln." Some of the bricks were sun dried; others were baked. All the population of Nine-

3:15   veh is here pictured as engaged in the work of drudgery. But all this work will be in vain! "There shall the fire devour thee," as the bars are burned and her buildings are consumed in the devouring flame. It is said by ancient historians that as the siege drew toward the end, the king and his family withdrew into the palace and set fire to it, dying in the holocaust. "The sword shall cut thee off; it shall devour thee like the canker-worm." The swift devouring character of the cankerworm is revealed many times in Scripture; its destruction is complete. So will it be with Nineveh; a complete destruction by the sword is decreed as the swarms of enemy soldiers seek out the individuals for death. "Make thyself as the locust" is now directed to the people of Nineveh. As the invaders destroy like the cankerworm, the early stage of the locust, so now make yourselves as the locusts in multitude.

3:16   "Thou hast multiplied thy merchants above the

stars of heaven," but these cannot save her now. The trade routes from all parts of the world had converged at Nineveh, bringing into the city treasures and wealth untold, and at the same time keeping and carrying away the products of Nineveh. "The cankerworm ravageth, and fleeth away," or, "spreadeth himself." This seems to apply to the destroyers who conquer the city and flee with its spoil. "Thy princes are as the locusts." The word for "princes" is found only here and has been given many interpretations, but it is clear that the prophet is speaking of the high-ranking men of Nineveh. "Are as the locusts" indicates the multitude of these men of rank. "And thy marshals," found only here and in Jeremiah 51:27, is another word of uncertain meaning. It is sometimes translated "scribes," and is thought by some to have referred to a priestly rank. However, it may have had reference to a position in the military establishment. These likewise were many, "as the swarms of grasshoppers." The picture that follows is that of a cold day in which the wings of the locusts or grasshoppers become stiff, causing them to encamp in the hedges or on the wall. But when the sun breaks through the clouds and the insects are warmed by its rays, they fly away. So will the Assyrian army flee away, perish, and disappear for ever, leaving no trace of its having ever existed.

3:17

"Thy shepherds slumber, O king of Assyria." The long siege of some two or more years is now over. The "king" refers not simply to the last king, but personifies the rule of her line of kings; the line has come to an end. The "shepherds" are the many military leaders, counselors, and great men of the nation; they now "slumber" in death. Her "nobles are at rest"; these also are with the shepherds in the rest of death. "Thy people," those who had escaped the sword, "are scattered upon the mountains." As sheep without a fold and a shepherd to care for them, scatter and are left to the predators of nature, so those remaining of Assyria are left with "none to gather them" in. Scattered on the bleak heights, they are left to perish. "There is no assuaging of thy hurt," or

3:18

3:19

healing for the nation. The wound is such that it can never be repaired. It is unto death; it is final. "All that hear the report of thee clap their hands over thee." What a way to go! But worse, what a way to have lived that when the end comes there would be universal rejoicing. This rejoicing is not necessarily the expression of a selfish glee on the part of the world of that day, but rather it is the rejoicing over a vindication of righteousness: "for upon whom hath not thy wickedness passed continually?" The whole earth had felt the pain of Nineveh's destructive sword and unbounded cruelty, not once or twice, but continually. And now with the good tidings of her fall, the whole world rejoiced. The words of George Adam Smith, as quoted in the Introduction, well summarize the feeling of the prophet and the people of the world: it is one great "At Last!"

9
HABAKKUK
"Embrace"

General Observations

1. The Man

a. Name. Habakkuk means "embrace" or "ardent embrace." Farrar prefers "embraced" or "pressed to the heart." Geikie says, "His name, as Luther well puts it, speaks as one 'who took his nation to his heart, comforted it and held it up, as one embraces and presses to his bosom a poor weeping child, calming and consoling it with good hope—if God so will.' " (Cunningham Geikie, *Hours with the Bible*, Vol. V., pp. 353-4).

b. Home. The home of the prophet is unknown. The context of the book leads one to conclude that it was Jerusalem.

c. Occupation. Nothing is known of the prophet's occupation.

2. Date: 612-606 B.C.

Various dates from 630 B.C. to a date during the Babylonian captivity have been assigned for the activity of Habakkuk. The most probable is somewhere between 612-606 B.C. Ward (*I.C.C.*) argues that 1:12—2:20 was written after the captivity of the first group, 605 B.C. or possibly later; but he overlooks Habakkuk's statement, "I must wait quietly for the day of trouble, for the coming up of the people that invadeth us" (3:16). This places the date before the Chaldean invasion. Assyria fell to Babylon in the year 612 B.C. When Habakkuk spoke, Nebuchadnezzar was already pressing westward, but had not reached Jerusalem. The oppression of Judah and the carrying of the first group into Babylon, 605 B.C., had not yet taken place. It seems best, therefore, to assign the preaching of Habakkuk to a date shortly before 606 B.C., but after the beginning of Babylon's westward move for world conquest.

3. Background

For the background of the period in the east and in Judah, see *Background* in the Introduction to Zephaniah. To what is said there could be added an additional word concerning Judah. Upon the death of Josiah at Megiddo, Jehoahaz, his son, was made king at the age of twenty-three. His reign is summed up in a sentence, "And he did that which was evil in the sight of Jehovah, according to all that his fathers had done" (II Kings 23:32). The young king had reigned only three months when Pharaoh-necho deposed him and set his brother, Eliakim, on the throne. Pharaoh-necho changed Eliakim's name to Jehoiachim, the name by which he is usually known. He reigned for eleven years; his reign was equally as wicked as that of his brother, Jehoahaz.

4. Characterization

The Book of Habakkuk differs from other books of prophecy in one special aspect. Instead of taking Jehovah's message directly to the people, he takes the complaint of the people to Jehovah, representing them in the complaint. The lawlessness and injustice in Judah and Jerusalem and the rising power of Babylon, as it was ruthlessly sweeping everything before its mighty move for conquest, sent the prophet to Jehovah with his problem of faith.

The book opens with a cry to Jehovah because of the wickedness, injustice, and disregard for law in Judah. In response, Jehovah points to the rising Chaldean power as His instrument of judgment against Judah's sins. This only heightens the prophet's perplexity. How could Jehovah punish Judah by using a nation more wicked than it? Jehovah points out that the righteous man will live by his faith; and as Habakkuk and the few righteous live by their faith, they must wait for Jehovah. Jehovah then observes that whatever the people must suffer, the doom of the wicked is certain. This partially solves the prophet's problem. While waiting patiently for the nation to come up against them, he looks back over Israel's history and sees Jehovah coming to assist His people at all times of their need. His judgments are for the salvation of His people. With this realization in mind, he can now see that this judgment will also serve this purpose. The prophet's faith now reaches its peak as he breaks forth in one of the most beautiful expressions of faith found in the Old Testament. Though all avenues of life's sustaining food are cut off and taken away, yet he will joy in Jehovah; he will rejoice in the God of his salvation. The prophet has now learned the principle that God had spoken through him, "The righteous shall live by faith." The prophet has learned and announced to the world how God can permit and use tyranny to accomplish His divine purpose; but in the end the tyranny must be punished.

5. Lessons or Message

a. **The universal supremacy of Jehovah's judgment upon the wicked:** Jehovah used Chaldea against wicked Judah, but Chaldea would be destroyed because of its own wickedness. God may tolerate wickedness for a season, but ultimately it must reap its just recompense of reward. The destiny of all nations is in His hand. This lesson is outstanding and can answer many of today's questions.

b. **Faithfulness is the guarantee of permanence.** "For the righteous his integrity and fidelity constitute elements of permanency, they cannot perish, they will endure forever" (F. C. Eiselen, *Prophet Books of the Old Testament*, Vol. II., p. 524).

c. **Evil is self-destructive.** This fact is stressed by Habakkuk. The Lord points out this great principle to His prophet in the five woes pronounced upon a character such as the Chaldean conqueror. If the righteous will but be patient, he will survive the tyranny and arrogance of the tyrant.

d. **The fact of divine discipline.** In Job it is the suffering of the individual that is shown; in Habakkuk, it is the suffering of a nation. In both, suffering is disciplinary.

e. **"To solve the problem for his fellow-countrymen still faithful to Jehovah, is the great aim of his book"** (Geikie, *Hours with the Bible,* p. 354). The growth of faith from perplexity and doubt to the height of absolute trust is one of the beautiful aspects of the book. Its lesson is for all time.

Outline of the Book

Title and name of author, 1:1.

I. God's judgment upon Judah, the wicked people of God, through the Chaldeans, 1:2—2:3.

A. First perplexity, and Jehovah's reply, 1:2-11.
   1. The prophet's lamentation over the rule of wickedness and violence, vv. 2-4.
      Perplexity: How can Jehovah justify His indifference in the presence of wickedness and violence?
   2. Jehovah's reply: He is not indifferent; He will raise up the Chaldeans to execute His judgment, vv. 5-11.
      a. Their rise is of Jehovah, vv. 5-6.
      b. Their character is of themselves, vv. 7-11.

B. Second perplexity, and Jehovah's reply, 1:12—2:3.
   1. How can a holy God employ an impure and godless agent? 1:12-17.
      a. The confident hope that God's people will not perish, v. 12.
      b. The perplexity: God's use of so wicked a nation as Chaldea, vv. 13-17.
   2. Jehovah's reply: The judgment is sure, but not immediate, 2:1-3.
      a. The prophet's decision: wait, v. 1.
      b. The command: write plainly, for the promise is certain, vv. 2-3.

II. God's judgment upon the Chaldeans, the ungodly world power, 2:4-20.

    A. Fundamental principle in world government, vv. 4-5.
        1. The righteous—live by faith, v. 4.
        2. The wicked—drunken on pride, power, greed—will not continue, v. 5.

    B. Woes upon the Chaldeans: a taunt song, vv. 6-20.
        1. Woe upon lust of conquest and plunder, vv. 6-8.
        2. Woe upon effort to build a permanent empire through cruelty and godless gain, vv. 9-11.
        3. Woe upon the building of cities with blood, vv. 12-14.
        4. Woe upon cruelty in the treatment of conquered kings and nations, vv. 15-17.
        5. Woe upon idolatry, vv. 18-20.

III. Prayer for compassion in the midst of judgment, ch. 3.

    A. Petition, vv. 1-2.
        1. Title: author and melody, v. 1.
        2. Revive thy works, v. 2a.
        3. In wrath remember mercy, v. 2b.

    B. The mighty works of Jehovah in the past: judgment and salvation, vv. 3-15.
        1. Jehovah's terrible approach, vv. 3-7.
        2. Question: Why did Jehovah appear? vv. 8-12.
        3. Answer: For salvation of His people, vv. 13-15.

    C. Implicit confidence in Jehovah, the God of salvation, vv. 16-19.
        1. Fear and trembling at the tribulation, vv. 16-17.
        2. Joy and confident trust, vv. 18-19.

Comments

Chapter 1

1:1-4. The prophet brings to Jehovah his complaint of violence, destruction, strife, and contention which he finds in Judah.

1:1
1:2   For comments on "burden" see Nahum 1:1. In his first sentence Habakkuk identifies himself as a prophet. The prophet opens his oracle with a cry to Jehovah, "How long shall I cry, and thou wilt not hear?" This implies that the prophet has been calling to Jehovah for a long period of time, but with no response. To "hear" indicates a reply in action; Jehovah had not acted. "I cry out unto thee of violence": not the violence of an invading power, but the violence found among his own people, Judah and Jerusalem. "Violence" includes the wrongs exercised by men on their fellows. His complaint was that Jehovah would not save, but Jehovah does not violate the sovereign will of man by directly interfering. He appeals through the moral suasion of His law and the word of the prophets. When this fails He interferes by judgment. Why, then, does not God interfere with a judgment?

1:3   Instead of interference that would stop the violence, the prophet continues to behold "iniquity" and "perverseness" in the character and conduct of his people. The prophet's question is, How could God look on this condition without punishing it, thus bringing it to an end? "Destruction and violence" are exercised by those in whose hand was the power to destroy and run roughshod over the weak. "Strife
1:4   and contention" rise up on every hand. The quarrelsome and contentious nobles ignored the law; "therefore the law is slacked," because God has not interfered to bring an end to conditions that exist. "Justice doth never go forth"; it is constantly perverted. Right and just verdicts are not issued by the judges; there are verdicts that show partiality to favored groups. The "wicked doth compass about the righ-

teous," twist and distort what is right and control the righteous contrary to the law of God so that "justice goeth forth perverted."

1:5-11. Jehovah replies to the prophet by saying He is at work: He is raising up the Chaldeans for judgment. He then describes the character of the Chaldeans and the fierceness of their manners.

In the dialogue between Habakkuk and Jehovah, one of the most practical lessons of prophecy may be learned: Jehovah's use of the nations. God may tolerate wickedness to a point, but judgment is inevitable. The Lord uses a wicked nation to execute His judgment against wickedness. "Behold ye among the nations," for from among them God was choosing one for His work. Jehovah does not reply to the prophet alone, but to those with him, using the plural "ye." The Lord emphasizes His exhortation, "Behold, . . . look, . . . wonder marvelously"; for He was working a work which they will find hard to believe even when He tells them what He is doing. He was working a work in their (your) days, but it is always difficult for men to see what is at hand. One can see God's hand in history but not in the present. "For, lo, I raise up the Chaldeans, that bitter and hasty nation." This was His selection from among all the nations. Incredible! The Jew could see Jehovah at work in his own nation, but it was preposterous that He would raise up a nation so bitter and fierce as the Chaldeans. They are called "bitter" because of their fierce and cruel behavior toward their conquered, and "hasty" because of their impetuous decisions and rapid movements. The Chaldeans occupied the lower part of the Tigris-Euphrates Valley with Babylon as their capital. Babylon had played an important role in Eastern history since shortly after the beginning of the second millennium B.C. Its history had been characterized by periods of greatness and dejection. Under Nabopolassar it was rising to a new zenith of power and conquest. In their march nothing stopped

1:5

1:6

them; Nineveh, Haran, and later Carchemish, where Pharaoh-necho was defeated—all had fallen into his hand. And now the Chaldeans were being raised up and were on their way to punish Judah. Jehovah describes them: "They are terrible and dreadful," which depicts the fierce disposition of the conquerors. "Their judgment" and dignity proceed from themselves; they are a self-willed people who acknowledge no master. Their own will is their rule of right.

1:7

The Chaldeans are further described: "Their horses also are swifter than leopards," indicating the rapidity with which they strike. The horse and its rider are one, swift and "fierce [as] the evening wolves" that go out in the evening seeking prey which they voraciously devour. Another figure is added to that of the leopard and the evening wolves, "they fly as an eagle that hasteth to devour." They come from afar and swoop down as an eagle on the prey. In pride and arrogance they press on, taking all before them. They are a violent crowd; their whole being is set on violence, destruction, and conquest. Their faces are set forward; they do not look back. "They gather captives as the sand" indicates the multitude of their captives; they are innumerable. Babylon followed the practice of Assyria in transporting captive peoples from their own land to one afar off. This would discourage any spirit of nationalism and revolt.

1:8

1:9

The fierce spirit of this servant whom God is raising up is further described in his attitude toward all who stand in his way. "He scoffeth at kings, and princes are a derision unto him." He makes light of the kings and ridicules their leaders, making light of any opposition they make to his power. The mightiest of strongholds are likewise laughed at by him. He heaps up mounds, destroys the strongholds, and leaves them as heaps of rubble. He is like a terrible tornado that strikes a city, leaving it in shambles, then going on its way. But even the mightiest of tempests must eventually expend its force and fade away. So the Chaldeans will "sweep by as a wind, and shall pass over." Although Jehovah raised him up for

1:10

1:11

a work and used him as His instrument, the Chaldean
was nevertheless held guilty in the sight of the Lord;
for, he shall be guilty, even he whose "might is his
god." As God had used the Assyrian as the rod of His
anger and the staff of His indignation against Israel,
so because it was "in his heart to destroy and to cut
off nations not a few" (Isa. 10:7), He was able to use
the Chaldean against Judah. It was not the intent of
the Chaldean to serve Jehovah's purpose; but because
of his cruelty and fierceness, God was able to use
him, leaving him guilty of his deeds.

> *1:12-17. This response from Jehovah to the
> prophet's question only leaves him more per-
> plexed. The prophet presents his second com-
> plaint to Jehovah: How can Jehovah, a righ-
> teous God, use a wicked nation like the Chal-
> deans?*

The prophet begins his complaint to Jehovah by   *1:12*
recognizing and acknowledging two infinite characteristics of Jehovah. He is "from everlasting," the
eternal One, and He is absolutely holy, "my Holy
One." On the basis of this confidence that He cannot
die, and that in His holiness He will never do wrong
or deny Himself or His covenant, the prophet confesses his assurance, "We shall not die." As Jehovah
had addressed the faithful few in the plural "ye" (v.
5), so now the prophet speaks for the same group:
"*We* shall not die." We may be chastened, corrected,
and even carried away, but we will not perish. In the
confidence of God's eternal and absolute character,
the prophet bows to the inevitable conclusion, "Thou
hast ordained him for judgment . . . and hast established him for correction." "O Rock" is an acknowledgment of Jehovah as the foundation of their hope
and the fortress in whom alone refuge must be
sought. Although the prophet acknowledges this, his
perplexity yet remains at God's use of one so cruel.
The prophet has recognized the wickedness in Judah   *1:13*
and has made it the subject of his complaint to
Jehovah (vv. 2-4). He is in full harmony with the fact

that this wickedness should be punished. But how can One so holy as Jehovah, who cannot look upon evil and perverseness, look upon the Chaldean and use him as an instrument of judgment against His own people? Can Jehovah's use of a tyrant so wicked be harmonized with such absolute holiness? This becomes the prophet's problem and the cause of his perplexity. The Chaldean is in the prophet's mind as he speaks of "evil . . . perverseness . . . them that deal treacherously . . . and the wicked [who] swalloweth up the man that is more righteous than he." The Chaldean falls into each of these categories. "The wicked" denotes a depraved and godless one. His rapacious conduct has been described in verses 6-11. Does the prophet speak of the nation of Judah or of the faithful remnant when he speaks of "the more righteous than he"? In spite of the charge brought against Judah, it is possible that the prophet could be speaking of Judah in comparison to the Chaldeans; in the prophet's sight they would be more righteous than he. But God does not see as man sees. The greater one's opportunity to know and do right, the greater is his sin when he refuses both. It seems probable, however, that he has in mind the faithful among the ungodly Jews who will suffer along with them when the judgment comes. How can God allow this? The answer is that it is an invariable law of God that the righteous must suffer along with the guilty.

1:14   As a fisherman drops his net into the sea and takes everything before it, so the Chaldean has taken the peoples of the nations in his wild rampage of conquest. "The creeping things" are the swarms of smaller water creatures that, with the fishes, suffer at the hand of the netter. Neither the fishes nor creeping things have a king to whom they can look for protection. If God gives up His people to the Chaldeans then they, too, have no king and no protection, but

1:15   are equally helpless. All manner of fishing equipment is introduced by the prophet to describe the completeness of the Chaldeans' conquest: "the angle" or hook, "his net" or small casting net which is cast upon the water, and "his drag," the large net that is let down to the bottom of the water with floats on top. In the totality of his conquest "he rejoiceth and is glad." Because of his victories the invader worships— sacrifices and burns incense to his mighty power by thinking of it as the means of his victory. There is no indication in the monuments of the Chaldeans that they actually sacrificed to an army; the prophet uses the figure to indicate the disposition to worship their own power. His might is his god (v. 11). In their career of conquest, plundering and destroying, will they continue without interference from Jehovah? Will the spoiler empty his net of plunder to set out on a further expedition of rape and destruction? When will he be stopped? These are questions now contributing to the perplexity of the prophet and for which he seeks an answer. These are questions which through the centuries have been raised in the hearts of many as they beheld the ruthless destroyers riding roughshod over the weaker. God answers this question in the next chapter.

1:16

1:17

Chapter 2

2:1-3. The prophet determines to wait for an answer from Jehovah to his second complaint. He is not to wait long, for it seems that Jehovah responds immediately.

The prophet's second complaint (1:12-17) had been much longer than the first (1:2-4). What will God say to the perplexity caused by His using the Chaldean terror against Judah, and what will be His reply to the question of the Chaldeans' continued conquest and destruction of nations? What is to be the end of such a king and nation? The prophet decides to stand upon the "watch," and to set himself "upon the tower," and from there look for Jehovah's answer. Neither expression, "watch" nor "tower," is to be taken literally as one who would seek an eleva- tion or special watchtower alone from others; both terms are to be considered as figurative. The prophet will simply look to Jehovah to reveal the answer he

2:1

2:2   seeks and wait patiently for Jehovah's own time to
make known the revelation. Jehovah did not disap-
point His faithful servant; "Jehovah answered me,
and said, Write the vision." A "vision" is a revelation
from God made known by His Holy Spirit to His
chosen servant. The vision was to be written on
tablets, making the message plain, "that he may run
that readeth it." The tablets were plates or plaques
such as those used in public places where the passing
populace could read and be informed. The instruction
may have carried a deeper significance: write them on
the hearts of the faithful who will listen, that they
may hurry to others with the message. The reader's
running does not imply that the tablet was of modern
billboard size that one could read while running, but
that the message was such that one would hasten to
another with it, or hasten in preparation for what it
pointed to.

2:3   "For the vision is yet for the appointed time," a
time fixed in the mind of God. Because it is not to be
fulfilled immediately it must be written; when fulfilled, men will know that God spoke it, foretelling
what to expect. "It hasteth [Heb.: "panteth"]
toward the end." But what end is before the prophet?
Does he look to the end of the Babylonian power for
which the vision hastens or pants, or does he look
beyond the judgment and destruction wrought by the
Chaldeans to the coming of the Messiah, in whom all
Old Testament vision would find its ultimate realization? The answer is uncertain. But the prophet assures his hearers that the vision will not lie or fail,
urges them that "though it tarry, wait for it," and
concludes with the promise that "it will surely come,
it will not delay." The indication here is that he is
assuring the suffering few that God will bring them
through the ordeal at hand and destroy the destroyer.

*2:4-5. A basic fundamental between the un-
righteous and the righteous: one is puffed up,
living by pride, whereas the other lives by
faith.*

The Chaldean is first described, "His soul is puffed   *2:4*
up, it is not upright in him." His life is distorted by
pride; it is bloated out of proportion to its real worth.
It is not straightforward, honorable, standing straight
as it should. In contrast to the character of the proud,
and in the face of his swaggering arrogance, "the
righteous shall live by his faith." Although this is the
first time the principle is stated in these words, it is
not new; it is as old as God's dealing with man. The
righteous have always lived by their faith, and will
ever live by it. This principle stated by Habakkuk
became the foundation argument of Paul's gospel
against the Jewish contention of salvation by works
of the law (Rom. 1:17; Gal. 3:11). As the writer of
Hebrews saw the Roman invasion approaching, and
realized a parallel destruction of the Jewish order in
his day, he appealed to this passage. As in Habakkuk's
day, so in his, "the righteous should live by his faith"
(Heb. 10:37-39).

"Yea, moreover" introduces another characteristic   *2:5*
of the Chaldean. "Wine is treacherous," or better,
"And also because his wine is treacherous" (margin,
ASV), he stays not at home. Wine is described as "a
mocker" (Prov. 20:1) that brings sorrow, contention,
and wounds, and at last bites like a serpent, eventually taking away the reason (Prov. 23:29-35). It
leads to shame and destruction. It is said that the
Chaldeans were fond of drinking and excess, but here
the Chaldean's wine is his pride; he is intoxicated on
power and conquest, which are equally treacherous.
For a similar drunkenness, but not on literal wine, see
Isaiah 29:9 and 51:21. Instead of keeping at home
and building a noble government that would stand, he
strives to extend his power throughout the world. As
"Sheol" and "death" are never filled or satisfied but
eventually claim every descendant of Adam, so the
Chaldean's desires are equally insatiable. He "gather-
eth unto him all nations, and heapeth unto him all
peoples." This intoxication on power and utter greed
for conquest is exceedingly treacherous, and would
lead to his own destruction. This denunciation of the

wine of pride and conquest is followed by five woes
pronounced on such a character as the Chaldean. The
name of the Chaldean is not specified; therefore the
woes set forth principles of divine government against
any power that follows the pattern presented.

> *2:6-8. The first woe is pronounced against
> the lust of conquest and plunder. These will
> be plundered by the remnant of the con-
> quered.*

2:6 "All these"—the conquered nations who have been
heaped up, robbed, and plundered by the conqueror—shall "take up a parable against him." The
parable here signifies a terse and energetic song, and
in this case, pithy and derogatory. The "taunting
proverb," according to Delitzsch, is a clear and intelli-
gible speech, whose meaning the Chaldeans could not
miss. The clearly understood song is, "Woe to him
that increaseth that which is not his!" The woe is
upon any nation that, by conquest of lands to which
it has no moral right, continues to build its empire.
"How long?" is not answered; questions of time must
remain locked in the purpose and providence of God.
"And that ladeth himself with pledges!"; pledges
taken from the conquered nations are here indicated;
they became as so much "thick clay" (KJV). Even-

2:7 tually these arouse the down-trodden conquered who
"rise up suddenly" to bite and vex, "toss . . . to and
fro" (margin, ASV), the conqueror. Then that which
he has taken as plunder, the wealth and riches of
nations, will become booty to the oppressed. This
principle is seen at work in the present day just as it

2:8 has operated in ages past. The charge against the
Chaldeans is announced by the Lord. It is threefold:
(1) "Thou hast plundered many nations"; (2) "because of men's blood"; and (3) "for the violence done
to the land, to the city and to them that dwell
therein." The verdict is, "The remnant of the peoples
shall plunder thee." This was fulfilled against the
Chaldeans by Cyrus, ruler of the Medes and Persians,
who entered Babylon, October, 539 B.C., twenty-

three years after the death of Nebuchadnezzar (562 B.C.). The execution against nations of today is by those whom Jehovah raises up for the purpose.

2:9-11. The second woe is pronounced upon the disposition to build an empire through cruelty and godless gain.

"Woe to him that getteth an evil gain for his house"; he obtains his wealth and builds his empire by plundering other nations. The gain is evil because of the manner pursued in obtaining it. "His house" is either his family, which he seeks to establish, or his nation, which he seeks to secure. As an eagle sets its nest among the crags of the rock (Obad. 3-4), so the Chaldean has sought to make his stronghold impregnable. By this means he thinks to be delivered from destruction. In describing the city of Babylon it is said, "Nebuchadnezzar's Babylon, straddling the Euphrates, was protected by a huge wall more than eleven miles long and eighty-five feet thick" (Pfeiffer, *The Biblical World,* p. 127). However, all this effort to provide for his security only "devised shame" to his house. In "cutting off many peoples" to accomplish his end, he had sinned against his soul. God may use a ruler and nation to accomplish His purpose, but the man will be guilty of his cruel deeds, for he is responsible for the character he developed. "For the stone shall cry out of the wall," for by the blood of slave labor they have been built into the mighty wall and moat about the city. "The beam [the tie beam] out of the timber shall answer it." These bear witness to the crimes of the founder, and as Abel's blood cried out from the ground (Gen. 4:10), and as the mountains were called to witness Jehovah's charge against Judah (Mic. 6:1-2), so the stones and timbers cry out for a vindication of righteousness and testify against the guilty.

2:9

2:10

2:11

2:12-14. The third woe is a cry against men who build cities with slave labor, who hold

life cheap and ignore the misery of those
employed.

2:12   To "[build] a town with blood, and [establish] a
city by iniquity" is to build by the labor of conquered and subjugated peoples. It is to hold life cheap
and employ it in building and beautifying one's own
palace, city, and nation. The prophet sees the slaves
dying under the blows of cruel taskmasters or falling
from weariness and hunger as they are mercilessly
2:13   driven on in their tasks. There is no feeling of human
sympathy, only greed. "Is it not of Jehovah": has not
God decreed in His own eternal law that such cruelty
prompted by vanity is a "labor for the fire"? Vanity
demonstrated by the Chaldeans, or any nation that
follows their path, will eventually come to the fire of
its own destruction. This labor for the fire is to
2:14   "weary themselves for vanity." This destruction of
Babylon by the Medes is foretold by Jeremiah (ch.
51). As the prophecy is fulfilled and stands through
time as mute evidence to the fact that God had
foretold and then fulfilled the promise, the earth is
"filled with the knowledge of the glory of Jehovah, as
the waters cover the sea." Fulfilled prophecy is one
of the great witnesses of Jehovah's deity (II Peter
1:19-21). In His challenge to the idols, Jehovah rested
His claim to be the sole Deity of the universe on His
ability to foretell events and to declare the end from
the beginning (Isa. 41—48). This knowledge is accessible to all everywhere; its voice covers the earth as
waters cover the sea, for there is no place where
God's fulfilled prophecies are not to be found.

> 2:15-17. The fourth woe pronounces con-
> demnation of those who through intoxication
> on the wine of power and conquest mistreat
> and degrade conquered nations.

2:15   "Woe to him that giveth his neighbor drink" sets
before us the baseness of one who would intoxicate
his neighbor that he might look upon his nakedness
or strip him of his possessions. The Chaldean had

used his power to conquer, and having conquered he would use his rod of rule and influence to weaken and ultimately prostrate the conquered people before him. He would add his own deadly poison of promises of honor, aid, and riches, which deadened and destroyed the people, but were never kept. Eventually they found themselves stripped not only of their possessions, but also of their honor and dignity. The Chaldean power is by no means the last great power that has used his position and prestige to intoxicate, strip, and destroy honor and dignity. Instead of glory in such conduct, the Chaldean is "filled with shame." As he has prostrated others before him through conquest, plunder, and maltreatment, he, too, shall drink and fall down exposed before the world as one uncircumcised, not belonging to God. "Babylon hath been a golden cup in Jehovah's hand," said Jeremiah, "that hath made all the earth drunken: the nations have drunk of her wine; therefore the nations are mad" (51:7). Now the time has come for Babylon to drink of the cup of God's wrath; "the cup of Jehovah's right hand shall come round unto thee." Through Jehovah's cup of fury on Babylon "foul shame shall be upon thy glory"; his glory will be turned to utter disgrace; he will wallow in his own vomit. Should the expression "For the violence done to Lebanon . . . and the destruction of the beasts" be taken literally or symbolically? Some commentators think Jerusalem is in the prophet's mind; others consider the text to apply to Palestine in general; still others would apply it to the great of earth destroyed by the Chaldeans. The most probable explanation is that the prophet speaks of the general devastation of nature, and of the destruction of the forests of Lebanon in particular. The Chaldean had held the whole creation of God in contempt, considering it all his to be used to his own selfish ends. Forests, beasts, men's blood, the land, cities, and their inhabitants had all suffered at his hand. It is as wrong today to denude the world of God's natural resources, created for the good of man, as it was then. The same curse rests upon such conduct, for Habakkuk's woes are universal.

2:16

2:17

> *2:18-20. The fifth and final woe is upon the
> idolater. It is a condemnation of materialism
> in general and of its worship in particular.*

2:18   The prophet does not begin this final woe as he
had the first four with the woe itself; but in eloquent
irony he asks, "What profiteth the graven image . . .
[or] the molten image?" Like the nations of the
time, Chaldea was given over to idolatry, "for it is a
land of graven images, and they are mad over idols"
(Jer. 50:38). What, now, is this going to profit the
nation? The idol is a teacher of lies; it promises what
it can never produce; it leads away from Jehovah and
to destruction. The "graven image" was made of
wood, sometimes overlaid with gold or silver; the
"molten image" was one of metal, molded by the
craftsman. (For a classic in sarcasm against all idols
2:19   see Isa. 44:9-20.) "Woe unto him that" calls upon the
dumb idol to speak and upon the dead stone to
arise. In spite of the precious metals, silver and gold,
used to overlay it, there is no life in it. In vain do men
call upon such to arise and teach the right way. Only
intelligence that accompanies life can teach man what
2:20   he needs to know. At this point all the creations of
man are doomed to fall. In contrast to the dumb idols
that cannot awake, arise, or teach, "Jehovah is in his
holy temple"; not in the sanctuary at Jerusalem, but,
as the psalmist adds to this identical phrase, "Jehovah, his throne is in heaven" (Ps. 11:4). "Let all the
earth keep silence before him," silently submitting to
His divine rule and judgment, rejecting the dumb
idols that cannot answer or help. Zephaniah had
called for the same silent recognition of Jehovah's
presence, and more than a century later Zechariah
urged the same silence before Him (Zech. 2:13). This
verse is the final exclamation of the prophet in response to Jehovah's answer to his perplexity. With
this answer from Jehovah in his ears and heart he is
ready to wait for the enemy to come up against them,
and is prepared to meet him with "faith unto the
saving of the soul."

Chapter 3

*3:1-2. The title of the chapter: a prayer set
to music. In the midst of fear and judgment
the prophet prays for mercy.*

The prophet concludes his book with what is con- *3:1*
ceded by many writers to be one of the most beautiful psalms in the Bible. The Lord has answered his
complaints. He now understands that Judah and Jerusalem must be punished for their sins, that God is
going to use the Chaldeans for His work of judgment,
and that God will then punish the wicked Chaldean
nation who deified its power, going beyond the
bounds of all restraint. Realizing what he may expect
in the near future, the prophet prays to Jehovah. The
prayer takes the form of a dithyramb, a poem "after
the manner of a stormy, martial, and triumphant
ode." "Set to Shigionoth" is a word meaning to reel,
to stagger like a drunken man. Deane explains its use
here to mean, "in an impassioned or triumphal strain,
with rapid change of emotion, a dithyrambic song."
The word describes the poem as having been com- *3:2*
posed under strong emotional pressure. The whole
picture of what is about to take place wrings from the
prophet the confession, "O Jehovah, I have heard the
report of thee, and am afraid." The report makes the
prophet tremble, but his fear draws him closer to his
God. He calls upon Jehovah to revive His "work in
the midst of the years," to carry out His purpose now
as He has in the past. "In the midst of the years"
would be at the present time, the time between the
announcement of judgment and its execution. Out of
this fear comes the urgent plea of the prophet, "In
wrath remember mercy." As God, moved by His great
mercy and loving-kindness, had delivered His people
in the past, so let Him act now. This becomes the
burden of his plea to Jehovah.

*3:3-15. The poem takes the form of a
theophany: the prophet sees Jehovah coming*

for the salvation of His people as He had come in ancient times. Judgment against the enemies of God always brings salvation to the righteous.

3:3   The prophet glances back over the history of Israel's experiences from Egypt to Sinai to the present, and in this experience he sees Jehovah coming to help as He has in the past. God has been their hope of salvation from the beginning of Israel's existence. "God came from Teman, and the Holy One from Mount Paran." This is reminiscent of Deuteronomy 33:2, where Moses praised Jehovah in a similar strain. Some scholars translate in the present tense, "God cometh," and so throughout the poem, contending that this better suits the text. As God came in the past, so He comes now. Teman was located in Edom, east of the Arabah about midway between the south end of the Dead Sea and the north end of the Gulf of Aqabah. Paran was the mountain or plateau area west of Edom and northwest of Aqabah. Jehovah is depicted as a mighty radiance coming from these mountain areas. "The Holy One" is another name for God that lays stress on His absolute holiness. "Selah" is used three times in the poem; its definite meaning is uncertain. It is used only here and in the Book of Psalms. It is thought that the word indicated a pause in the singing, and possibly a crescendo in the music, the song being renewed after the pause. When God

3:4   comes, His glory covers the heavens and His praise fills the earth. "His brightness was [is] as the light," a celestial brilliance that transcends anything man can approach, which accompanies the presence of Jehovah. He had "rays" or "horns" (margin, ASV) "coming forth from his hand." The horns were rays of light. His hand simply designates the streaming forth of His light in both directions and from both sides. In this light so magnificent and wonderful "there was the hiding of his power." This splendor of absolute holiness covers the infinite power which He exercises.

3:5   The writings of other prophets reveal God's use of plagues and pestilence. These were used in Egypt, in the wilderness, and in the land of Canaan. They are pictured here as weapons of Jehovah, the pestilence going before Him and fiery bolts issuing from His feet. He uses the pestilence, the lightning, the hail, and the storm to achieve His end. What Jehovah has done in the past He does now. As His glory covers the heaven, so His presence fills the earth. As one would walk through and thereby measure a field, Jehovah walks through and measures the earth. "He beheld, and drove asunder the nations"; and in the confidence of His unchangeable Godhood, the prophet sees Him driving them asunder now. "The eternal mountains" and "the everlasting hills" bow before Him in the earthquake and in the floods of the storm. They burst and sink down at His presence. He is unchangeable, "His goings [are] as of old." What the faithful have known and seen of Jehovah in the past, they can expect in the future. From the expressions of terrifying power exerted among the inanimate creatures of nature, the prophet looks at the nations. Two are selected: "Cushan," a lengthened form of Cush, the land of Ethiopia, and "the curtains of the land of Midian," the people of Midia who dwelt east of the Gulf of Aqabah. These nations, hostile to Jehovah, are in affliction; they tremble at the presence of Jehovah. As Egypt had been judged and as the Midianites had been put to riot by Gideon and his three hundred, God is about to afflict and put to riot the heathen oppressors of His people.

3:6

3:7

The prophet interrupts his picture of Jehovah and the demonstration of His power to ask, "Was Jehovah displeased with the rivers" or the sea (the Nile, Red Sea, Jordan, Kishon or others), when He demonstrated His power by using them? The implied answer is No; they were instruments of His wrath against the wicked. He had come as the leader of a mighty host, riding "upon thy [His] horses, upon thy [His] chariots of salvation." God's actions and judgments had been for the salvation of His people. Psalm 77 presents a parallel picture of Jehovah's use of His power in the execution of His wrath. God's judgments are for the salvation of His own as He destroys the

3:8

3:9

ungodly. "Thy bow was made quite bare"; it was taken out of its sheath or bow case, which was either worn on the back of the warrior or carried on the side of his chariot. The bow had been taken from this and was ready for battle. "The oaths to the tribes were a sure word." The translation and interpretation of this are uncertain. Laetsch observes that Delitzsch has enumerated more than one hundred different interpretations of the passage. Keil translates it, "rods are sworn by words," signifying the oath of God and His use of rods put under oath in punishment. The prophet apparently has in mind God's promise to the tribes, "For I will lift up my hand to heaven, and say, as I live for ever . . . I will render vengeance to mine adversaries, and will recompense them that hate me. I will make mine arrows drunk with blood, and my sword shall devour flesh" (Deut. 32:40-42). This oath given through Moses will be "a sure word"; it will be kept even now against the Chaldeans. "Selah," coming at the end of the word of the oath as it does, and before "Thou didst cleave the earth with rivers," has led some to think that this latter should be a part of verse 10 instead of verse 9. The cleaving of the earth with rivers expresses the mighty power of God in His world, either at creation or in any upheaval

3:10   that causes a new river to be born. These could have come into being at the shaking of the mountains or upheavals that caused the waters to pass by. The entire verse is descriptive of nature's reaction to Jehovah's command and to the revelation of His great power. All obey Him: sun, moon, stars, mountains, storms, and rivers. The language used by the prophet is reminiscent of the great flood in the days of Noah.

3:11   "The sun and the moon stood still" looks back to the valley of Aijalon and Joshua's battle of the long day when God responded to his cry for additional time. These stood still as Jehovah fought for Israel. Also the sun and moon hid themselves many times as Jehovah's "arrows" sped as shafts into the hearts of His enemies, and at "the shining of his glittering spear" exposed in the day of judgment (cf. Isa. 13:9-13; Joel 2:1-2, 10; 3:14; Amos 8:9; etc.).

Jehovah had marched "through the land in indigna-   *3:12*
tion" and had threshed "the nations in anger." The
prophet looks to the past and to the future. What
God had done in delivering His people from their
enemies, He would do again. The upheaval and up-
roaring in nature express the power that can and will
be used to protect the righteous and thresh the
wicked who so cruelly devastate His world.

In all of God's actions there is purpose; never does   *3:13*
He act out of caprice or whim. The purpose of His
coming in the past is clearly expressed: "Thou
wentest forth [or, art come] for the salvation of thy
people." Judgment against one may be salvation for
another. "Of thine anointed" or "with thine
anointed" (margin, ASV) probably looks not at an
immediate king of the house of David, but to the
Messiah-King who would come. God is working out
His purpose in history. Through the remnant protected or saved He would bring the Anointed One of
His eternal plan. The prophets never lose sight of this
central theme of prophecy; God keeps it ever before
His people. "Thou woundest the head of the house
of the wicked man." The house of the wicked one
looks to his royal family where God wounds the head
and brings it to an end. The people would remember
Pharaoh's house and the death of his firstborn and
the kings of Canaan and neighboring kings whom
Jehovah subdued when Israel came into Canaan.
Here, however, the prophet has in mind the Chaldean
king and God's destruction of his house. He had laid
"bare the foundation even unto the neck," and will
do it again. In his poetic manner the prophet includes
the whole house: head, foundation, and neck, from
top to bottom, and all in between are brought to an
end by the judgment and power of Jehovah. "Selah":
pause, and let the sound of praise to Jehovah increase
to thundering tones.

"Thou didst pierce with his own staves the head of   *3:14*
his warriors." This had been exemplified many times
in history when nations had fallen out and fought
among themselves. Again God would "revive his
works" in the midst of the years. The Medes had

combined forces with the Chaldeans to attack and
destroy Nineveh. Jehovah would turn the Medes
against the Chaldeans to destroy them (Jer. 51:11,
28), thus piercing the heads of his warriors with his
own staves. The prophet identifies himself with the
people: "they came as a whirlwind to scatter me,"
the righteous, the people of God. "Their rejoicing"
was as that of robbers and plunderers who exulted in
their plans to overpower, take the possessions of the
helpless, and carry them away. "The poor" are the
unprotected, those at the mercy of others, upon

3:15   whom the Chaldeans had come as a whirlwind to
scatter and rob. But their rejoicing is premature; for
as Jehovah had splashed through the seas and parted
the rivers, riding upon His chariots of salvation in
coming to the aid of His own (vv. 8-12), so would He
now come. The people would remember the examples
of the Red Sea, the crossing of the Jordan, and the
overflowing of the River Kishon and find assurance.
His past actions were expressive of His character, and
they become pledges for present and future action.

> *3:16-19. In this assurance of Jehovah's care
> the prophet can look to the future with his
> fears alleviated. He can rest in the assurance
> of the principle he has announced, "the righ-
> teous shall live by his faith."*

3:16   At this point the poem takes on a change of
tempo. From an excited and agitated spirit of one
who can scarcely control himself, he now manifests a
spirit of calmness and faith born of a deep spiritual
experience. Although there was a sense of dread at
what he knew must come, he was no longer afraid.
Fear had been conquered by love and faith. "I heard,
and my body trembled, my lips quivered ... rottenness entereth into my bones." The prophet had
heard through the ears of a waiting servant; he had
seen through the eyes of an honest inquirer; he had
accepted and made known as a true prophet of God
who receives his message from Him, and he was now
ready for whatever may come. This reaction was not

that of one who would run away, but of one who "must wait quietly for the day of trouble." It was the emotion of an athlete as he waits that last hour before the contest or of the speaker who dreads the pressure to be generated by his speech. It is felt by the family huddled in a room or cellar just before the storm breaks or by the soldier before the order to "Charge!" He must wait quietly "for the coming up of the people that invadeth us." The battle of faith has been fought and won in the prophet's heart; the experience for which it was wrought is yet ahead. From perplexity and doubt he has passed through the school of God's revelation to him, and now he can look to whatever may come and meet it with quiet dignity and confidence.

There follows one of the greatest expressions of faith to be found anywhere. In this verse the prophet includes all means or resources of food and declares that though all fail, he will trust in Jehovah. The fruit trees on which the people of Palestine must depend are introduced. These produced staple foods for the Jews and were prolific and highly prized by them. Though the fig tree would not blossom or bear, and there would be no fruit on the vines and the labor of the olive fail, and though the various grains of the field would yield no food, the flock be cut off from the fold and the cattle be kept from the stalls, "yet," says the prophet, "I will rejoice in Jehovah, I will joy in the God of my salvation." The prophet has enumerated every avenue of food peculiar to the Jews; and though all be taken away by the invader, he will continue to put his trust in Jehovah and to joy in Him. Here the peak of faith is reached; here is the faith by which men live. "Jehovah, the Lord, is my strength"; upon this he has learned to depend. The "I Am That I Am" will not fail nor forsake him. "He maketh my feet like hinds' feet," swift and sure as the deer of the forests and mountains. He "will make me to walk upon my high places," a symbol of victory and triumph. As the deer is able to climb to the summit of the mountain peak, far above the fears and shadows of the valley below, so Jehovah will

3:17

3:18

3:19

make His faithful walk upon the high places, far above the doubts and despairs of the valley of shadows from which he has escaped. Faith is now victorious. The prophet's questions have been answered and he himself has come through his perplexities a complete conqueror. The faith by which he came through victorious is the faith by which all will triumph.

10
HAGGAI
"Festival"

General Observations

1. The Man

a. **The Name.** Haggai means "festival" or "festive." Robinson suggests that it may be a shortened form of Haggiah, meaning "festival of Jehovah." Our knowledge of the man himself is limited to Ezra 5:1-2; 6:14-16; and to the short book that bears his name. The Lord needed one who could take a message from Himself, convey it to the people, and get results. This the prophet achieved; he was the man of the hour. Some have inferred that he had seen the temple of Solomon in its glory before the destruction of Jerusalem, but this cannot be inferred from what is written in Ezra or Haggai's book. Did he live to see the temple completed and to worship in it with the faithful remnant? We could wish he did, but we are not told.

b. **Home and Occupation.** Of the home and occupation of Haggai we know nothing except that he returned from Babylon with the remnant under Zerubbabel. It is assumed that he lived in Jerusalem, but nothing is said of his occupation other than that he was a prophet.

2. Characterization

Haggai, like one of his predecessors, Nahum, was a man of a single idea: build the temple! He confined his work to this single theme; anything else said was built around this essential necessity. Without rebuilding the temple, that for which they had returned, Jehovah's favor could not be expected. This central place of devotion and worship was essential if the nation was to be held together and Jehovah's blessings were to be bestowed on the people. Jehovah raised him up and endowed him with His Spirit, the spirit of prophecy, for the purpose of arousing the people to action. The temple must be rebuilt!

The writing of Haggai is unlike that of his predecessors. Lacking in his work is the rhythm and rolling grandeur of Nahum, the poetry and charm of Habakkuk, or the fire of Amos. In comparison his work seems subdued and prosaic. But he was completely successful. Within three weeks and a few days after his first address to the people they began work on the project. He realized the immediate need, and he knew his people and how to reach them. Having this essential data and the Spirit of Jehovah, he was successful in moving them to action. Jehovah knew the kind of man needed for the task at hand and that Haggai was the man. The most striking feature in his message is the repeated appeal to Jehovah as the source of his word. In some form he uses the appeal "saith Jehovah," "the word of Jehovah of hosts," and similar expressions twenty-six times in the four short addresses of thirty-eight verses. This appeal to the divine origin of what he said stirred the people, moved their hearts, and got results.

3. Date

The prophet dates his work. He began to prophesy in the second year of the reign of Darius (1:1), which would be 520 B.C.

4. Background

Judah had been carried into Babylonian captivity by Nebuchadnezzar when Jerusalem and the temple were destroyed, 586 B.C. Daniel, who was carried into Babylon by Nebuchadnezzar after his first invasion of Judah, 605 B.C., spanned the entire period of the captivity. Ezekiel was taken to Babylon by the Chaldean king in 597 B.C. He prophesied until 572 or 570 B.C. In these two men Jehovah provided spiritual hope and guidance to the exiles.

Following Nebuchadnezzar's death (562 B.C.) Babylon had a series of weak rulers; there was not one who could continue the work of the great founder of the empire or who could hold it together. By 549 B.C. Cyrus, a Persian, had defeated the Median king and united the Medes and Persians under his own rule. In 539 B.C., while Nabonidas, king of Chaldea, was away and his son, Belshazzar, acted in his stead, Cyrus entered and took the city of Babylon. To rule over the city he appointed a "phantom king," known in the Bible as Darius the Mede. This man is not to be confused with Darius Hystaspes of Haggai's book. Darius the Mede was probably Gubaru (or Gabryas) of secular history.

Cyrus demonstrated an unusually benevolent spirit and attitude toward those he conquered. His disposition was to reverse the practice of the Assyrian and Babylonian conquerors who transplanted conquered peoples from their homeland into distant places and transported others from their land into the conquered land. Soon after his conquest of Babylonia Cyrus issued a decree that the various exiled peoples could return to their own lands, rebuild the temples to their deities, and call on their gods to act favorably toward him and his house. The account of the decree concerning the Jews is found in II Chronicles 36 and Ezra 1. The decree was issued some time in 538 B.C.; the first group of exiles returned under Zerubbabel in 536 B.C. Over 150 years before, Isaiah had prophesied that Jehovah would raise up one named Cyrus, whom He designated as His servant, who would allow a remnant to return (44:24—45:7). From this some have concluded that Cyrus was a monotheist, but such is not true; he sought the favor of all the gods. There is no evidence that he was a worshiper of Ahura Mazda, the Persian lord of light and goodness, whose attributes are said to have been life, truth, and righteousness. However, Ahura Mazda was the god of Darius I. In the Cyrus Cylinder, discovered *ca.* 1880, Cyrus claims that Marduk, god of the Chaldeans, looked through all the lands for one to lead the troops in delivering

Babylon, selected him, and accompanied the great general in his conquests.

Cyrus was succeeded by his son, Cambyses (529-522 B.C.), who had none of the greatness of heart of his father. Cambyses invaded Egypt with carefully laid plans for its conquest, but was called home by a rebellion in which the schemer Gomates posed as the brother of Cambyses. Secretly Cambyses had already put that brother to death. Unable to face the ignominy of having slain his own brother, there is strong evidence that Cambyses took his life while en route to Babylon.

The empire was thrown into a state of upheaval, convulsed by a series of revolts, especially in the east. Darius I, Hystaspes (522-486 B.C.), with the aid of his father, Hystaspes, an able general, and one or two others on whom he could depend, put down these revolts one by one. In his record he lists nine specific major revolts; there are others not listed. He is described as "an able administrator as well as a successful general" (Sayce). To him is ascribed the credit for organizing the empire into a homogeneous whole.

Upon their return to Jerusalem, 536 B.C., the Jews erected or restored the altar of sacrifices to Jehovah and laid the foundation of the temple. At this point they ceased work on the temple until the second year of Darius I, when Haggai and Zechariah were called to the work of arousing their fellow Jews to complete the work begun sixteen years earlier. The condition of the Jews seems to have been wretched and miserable. Things in Judea had not been as they had anticipated. The cities and houses lay in rubble, the walls were torn down, and the land had been neglected for fifty years. Food was scarce and the land had not produced as they had expected. Neighboring peoples were unfriendly and at times antagonistic to them. As a whole, the picture was quite discouraging.

5. The Message

As indicated above, Haggai was a man of one paramount idea. Without eloquence or flights of oratory, but in simple, earnest warning and urging, his message was—build the temple! The hope of blessing from Jehovah rested upon accomplishing this task for which they had returned. In his message he revived the Messianic hope, pointing out that the house would be filled with glory, a glory that would surpass anything previously seen. He likewise pointed to Zerubbabel as Jehovah's signet, an assurance that in Zerubbabel would the hope be realized.

6. Lessons

Several lessons may be learned from this brief book of only two chapters.

a. In Israel's condition the prophet sees faithfulness and material blessings directly connected.

b. "Discouragement however profound is not an adequate reason for neglecting duties, even when they seem to be encompassed with difficulty. 'Be strong and work' is a glorious motto for human life" (Farrar).

c. "When a good work is awaiting its accomplishment, the time to do it is *now*" (Farrar).

d. The basis of all successful preaching is "saith Jehovah." It got results then, and such preaching will get results today.

Outline of the Book

Title: The prophet and his commission, 1:1.

I. First message—Rebuke for religious indifference and admonition to build the temple, ch. 1.

   A. The message, vv. 2-11.
      1. The people's selfishness and unconcern, vv. 2-6.
         a) Their selfishness, vv. 2-4.
         b) Their ways and the result: curse, vv. 5-6.
      2. The divine displeasure and exhortation to resume the building operation, vv. 7-11.
         a) Consider your ways—get busy, vv. 7-8.
         b) The visitation from God, vv. 9-11.

II. Second message—Consolation to those in despair: the glory of the new temple, 2:1-9.

    A. Jehovah's presence with the builders, vv. 1-5.
    B. The temple's future glory, vv. 6-9.

III. Third message—Completion of the temple a guarantee of blessings of nature, 2:10-19.

    A. The people's uncleanness a result of their own conduct, vv. 10-14.
        1. Their punishment the result of their own uncleanness impressed by two questions, vv. 10-13.
            a) Question one: Communication of holiness by holy objects on contact, vv. 10-12.
            b) Question two: Communication of legal defilement by contact, v. 13.
        2. Application to Israel—the cause of their uncleanness, v. 14.

    B. Indifference has produced calamity; zeal will restore prosperity, vv. 15-19.

IV. Fourth message—Renewal of the promise of salvation: exaltation of Zerubbabel, 2:20-23.

    A. Overthrow of the nations, vv. 20-22.
    B. Messianic hope preserved in Zerubbabel, v. 23.

Comments

Chapter 1

1:1-6. The first message: The prophet rebukes the people for their religious indifference and admonishes them to build the temple.

1:1   The prophet dates the four speeches he delivered, a résumé of which he has preserved in the book bearing his name. "The second year of Darius the king" would be 520 B.C., the second year of the reign of Darius I (522-486 B.C.), son of Hystaspes. "The sixth month" would be the month Elul, equivalent to our

September/October. The remnant of the Jews had returned to their homeland in 536 B.C., had laid the foundation of the temple (Ezra 3:8), but had ceased work on it (Ezra 4:24). Sixteen years after their return from the captivity, Jehovah called forth Haggai and Zechariah to urge the people to complete the task for which they had been brought back. The prophet is not speaking from himself; it is "the word of Jehovah by Haggai." Twenty-six times in the short book of thirty-eight verses the prophet claims that it is God's word he is speaking. "By Haggai" indicates that Haggai is the instrument of Jehovah by which the word is announced. This first message is directed to Zerubbabel, the governor, and to Joshua, the high priest. They were the leaders of the people and should have considered themselves responsible for completing the temple and for the lack of enthusiasm that had been shown toward the task. A degree of confusion exists over the identity of Zerubbabel and Sheshbazzar (Ezra 1:8, 11; 5:14, 16). Some writers contend that these are two individuals and that Sheshbazzar dropped out of the picture soon after the remnant reached Jerusalem. Others conclude that the two names apply to Zerubbabel, Zerubbabel being his Hebrew name and Sheshbazzar his Chaldean name. The point is disputed; however, it seems from the use of the two names that they apply to one individual. In the context of Zerubbabel's return to "the house of God at Jerusalem" (Ezra 3:8), it is said that "the builders laid the foundation of the temple" (Ezra 3:10). Later it is said, "then came the same Sheshbazzar, and laid the foundation of the house of God" (5:16). However, the matter seems to be settled by Jehovah speaking through Zechariah who said, "The hands of Zerubbabel have laid the foundation of this house; his hands shall finish it" (Zech. 5:9). Sheshbazzar laid the foundation of the house; Zerubbabel laid the foundation. This confirms the identity of the two as one man.

Speaking through the prophet Jehovah charges, *1:2* "This people say" the time has not come to build the house. "This people," instead of "my people" or some other phrase identifying them as Jehovah's, may indicate Jehovah's attitude toward them and His reluctance to claim them as His own. This quibble of time should long since have been answered by the two leaders of the people, Zerubbabel and Joshua, to whom the prophet addresses his message (v. 1). Could it be that the people were using Jeremiah's seventy years (Jer. 25:11-12; 29:10) as excuse for their negligence, arguing that from 586 B.C. the seventy years were not yet elapsed? This would serve only as a subterfuge; the real reason is to be found somewhere

1:3   else. Haggai's ready response is from the Lord; it is He who speaks. The reply from the Lord is a rebuke and

1:4   an appeal to the conscience of the hearers. "Is it a time for you yourselves to dwell in your ceiled houses?" This gives a true insight into the real interest and labors of the people. "Ceiled houses" indicates a degree of luxury and concern for themselves as they lived comfortably in expensive wainscoted dwellings. It may have been excusable for the people to build comfortable and conveniently furnished houses if first they had built the house of God. The irony of the charge is that while they spent their energies and wealth, probably using the materials gathered for the house of the Lord, in their own dwellings, "this house lieth waste." By no means is this the last time the people of God have looked to the building of their own ceiled houses while the house of the Lord lay

1:5   waste. "Consider your ways"; literally, "set your heart on your ways," take a good look at yourselves and what you have done since your return from

1:6   Babylon. Their expectations had failed miserably because Jehovah's blessing had been meager. "Ye eat, but ye have not enough"; for the short harvests since their return had not been sufficient to satisfy their hunger. "Ye drink, but ye are not filled with drink" probably refers to the inadequate vineyard harvest. "Ye clothe you, but there is none warm" could refer to unusually rigorous winters for which their clothing was insufficient or to the lack of wool for the necessary cloth. Also the wages they earned seemed to evaporate and disappear like money put in a bag with holes, because of inflated prices. Nothing could be saved.

1:7-11. The rebuke is followed by a challenging charge, Get busy! The Lord makes clear the reason for His failure to bless them.

The Lord repeats the challenge of verse 5: "Consider your ways." This need for serious, heart searching reflection on the people's part merits a repetition of the challenge. A remedy for the condition of verse 6 is "build the house." "Go up to the mountain" ("hill-country," margin, ASV), is thought by some to indicate the mountains near Jerusalem (cf. Neh. 2:8), but by others to refer to the Lebanon mountains from where cedar wood would be brought (Ezra 3:7). The latter seems probably correct. Build the house and Jehovah "will take pleasure in it" and "be glorified," or glorify Himself in it by directing His good pleasure and blessings to the people. When the people had returned to their homeland, their expectation had run high; they had "looked for much, and, lo, it came to little; and when ye brought it home, I did blow upon it." The crops had been short (v. 6), and Jehovah blew upon what little they were able to harvest and bring in, causing it to disappear like chaff. They probably ascribed this to natural causes, observes Pusey, not seeing that it was Jehovah's doings. The Lord makes plain to them that the cause is, "Because of my house that lieth waste, while ye run every man to his own house." To be eagerly zealous for one's own material welfare and house, running enthusiastically to care for it but loitering negligently in his responsibility to the Lord, is to invite retributive consequences. "Therefore for your sake," or on account of your sin and in order to bring you to see this, the dew came not upon your growing plants, and the fruit of the earth was withheld. The heavy dews of Palestine were essential in the dry season if a harvest was to be reaped. They had failed to see that it was Jehovah who, for their sake, had withheld the dew. It was He who sent the drought upon them,

1:7

1:8

1:9

1:10

1:11

affecting all resources of food, which in turn affected both man and beast. Deane (*Pulpit Commentary*) points out a play on words that is lost in the translation, "As they had let the Lord's house lie 'waste' (*chareb*) (vv. 4, 9), so the Lord had punished them with a 'drought' (choreb)."

> *1:12-15. The reproof and exhortation got results! The people began work on the house of God.*

1:12 Results from the sermon were immediate. The governor, the high priest, "with all the remnant of the people, obeyed the voice of Jehovah their God, and the words of Haggai the prophet." It was Jehovah's voice through the mouth of Haggai. A prophet was a mouth (Exod. 4:16; 7:1) through which Jehovah spoke the word of His message (Deut. 18:18-19). "The remnant" refers to the small number of Jews who had returned from Babylon under Zerubbabel and Joshua. The prophets before the exile had repeatedly said that only a remnant would return from captivity (Isa. 10:21; Jer. 23:3; 31:7; Ezek. 6:8; 14:22; Joel 2:32; Mic. 2:12; 7:18; Zeph. 2:7, 9), and likewise that only a remnant would return to Him in the Messiah (Isa. 1:9; 10:21-22; Joel 2:32; Mic. 4:7; 5:2). The Lord never promised to redeem or bring back the whole people, only those that would return to Him with all their heart (Deut. 30:1-10; Jer. 24:7). This promise was fulfilled in the remnant that returned; four of the five books written after the exile make mention of the remnant whom Jehovah brought back to their land (Hag. 1:12, 14; 2:2; Zech. 8:6, 11, 12; Ezra 9:8, 13-15; Neh. 1:3). The promises of Jehovah to the Jews have been fulfilled: the land promise, for they possessed the land; the promise of a return from captivity to the land, for the remnant returned; the promises of the Messiah and His kingdom, for the Messiah has come and now rules over the kingdom of promise. God has nothing present or future for the Jews except the salvation now offered in Christ. If this salvation is rejected, there remains nothing future except the judgment and eternal destruction. When the people heard Haggai they "did fear before Jehovah" and demonstrated the fear by obeying the exhortation.

The next word is a word of encouragement and   *1:13*
assurance to the people, spoken by "Haggai Jehovah's messenger." The same designation, messenger, is used by Malachi of the priests (2:7). This is the only occasion that a prophet spoke of himself as a messenger; Haggai would impress the fact that he was sent by Jehovah with His word. The word was simple but assuring, "I am with you, saith Jehovah." This is   *1:14*
the assurance they needed; for through it Jehovah stirred the spirit of Zerubbabel, Joshua, and the people to begin work on the house. It took some time to make preparation for the work, but on the twenty-   *1:15*
fourth day of the month, just three and a half weeks later, they began the long neglected task of restoring that which for nearly seventy years had lain in ruins. in ruins.

Chapter 2

2:1-9. The second message: Consolation to those in despair. The message of consolation assures the disheartened laborers that "the latter glory of this house shall be greater than the former."

In the seventh month, Teshri (equivalent to our   *2:1*
October/November), three and a half weeks after work had begun on the house of God, a second message was received and delivered by the prophet. The first message had been delivered on the first day of the month, a minor festival day of the law (Num. 28:11-15); but the second one was received and announced on a major festival day, the last day of the Feast of Tabernacles, following the Day of Atonement (cf. Lev. 23:39 ff.). The word is addressed to   *2:2*
the governor, the high priest, and the people. The ones who had seen the house in its former glory, as   *2:3*
they had inherited it from the wealth of David's

accumulation and Solomon's genius, now saw it as nothing. The Lord refers to it as "this house." Whether the house built by Solomon but now in ruins, or the one erected by the returned exiles, or the one renovated by Herod, the Lord never had but one house in Jerusalem, "the house of the Lord." Fifteen years earlier when the foundation had been laid, some wept as others shouted for joy (Ezra 3:12). Some of these who had wept were yet alive, and what they saw now seemed so insignificant in comparison to the glory of Solomon's temple. Resources were scarce and times were hard, which added to their discouragement. They must realize that the glory of the former had vanished with the glory of the nation, and now they must build anew from the ground up.

2:4   Seeing their need for encouragement, the Lord speaks through His prophet to the governor and the high priest who, as leaders, should be examples, and to the people saying, "Yet now be strong . . . and work." Their strength, like that of God's saints today, is "in the Lord, and in the strength of his might" (Eph. 6:10). In this power through the strength of the Lord nothing that comes within the promise of God's will is impossible to His people. While God provides the strength, the believer must do his part; he must work. When strength through faith is combined with work, obstacles vanish. The urgent admonition, "and work," referred directly to the building of the house; this was the immediate task before the people. This exhortation is followed by the assuring promise, "for I am with you, saith Jehovah of hosts." They should be of good courage, for if Jehovah, the God of all forces, is for them, who can be against

2:5   them? The promise of His being with them was "according to the word that I covenanted with you when ye came out of Egypt." At Sinai Jehovah declared that Israel would be His own possession from among all peoples, "a kingdom of priests, and a holy nation" (Exod. 19:5-6). This relation of God and His people was cemented by a covenant dedicated with blood (Exod. 24:8). In the covenant God gave the solemn assurance, "And I will dwell among the children of

Israel, and will be their God" (Exod. 29:45). Jehovah would not break nor deny the word of this covenant. "And my Spirit abode among you"; the Spirit was given to Moses and from him to the elders who assisted him in judging the people (Num. 11:17, 25). The Spirit was in Joshua (Num. 27:18), upon Saul (I Sam. 10:6, 10), and "mightily upon David" (I Sam. 16:13). In the blessing pronounced by the Levites, they looked back to Sinai and were able to say, "Thou gavest also thy good Spirit to instruct them" (Neh. 9:20). This same Spirit would now be among the people giving them strength through the divine presence; therefore, "fear ye not."

The difficulty and multiplicity of interpretations of the following four verses (vv. 6-9) is indicated by the fact that Keil devotes almost thirteen pages to a discussion of them. When the remnant returned (536 B.C.), they brought with them for the house of God a rather liberal offering of gold and silver from their fellow Jews (Ezra 1:4), besides the gift of gold and silver vessels from Cyrus (Ezra 1:7-11). They also had a grant from Cyrus to go up and bring cedar trees from Lebanon (Ezra 3:7). These gifts and this grant seem to have been insufficient for the task, for the people were quite destitute at the time except for their own ceiled houses.

Jehovah encourages them by giving assurance of what He purposes to do and of what will be the future glory of the house. "Yet once, it is a little while," indicates that soon, in a short time or while, "I will shake the heavens, and the earth, and the sea, and the dry land." This is similar to the language of former prophets, who used these expressions to describe the upheavals among nations and their overthrow (cf. Isa. 13:10, 13; 24:18-20; Joel 2:10; etc.). Jehovah follows this description of upheavals among the forces and elements of nature with an additional word, "and I will shake all nations; and the precious things of all nations shall come; and I will fill this house with glory." This raises the question of the inclusion of this promise: Does it look to the immediate stirring of nations to bring offerings with which to

2:6

2:7

complete the house, or does it look to the judging of nations from their present point in history to the coming of the Messiah? God stirred Darius to give help in building the temple (Ezra 6:6-15); and He stirred Artaxerxes to supply gifts to Ezra when he and a contingent of Jews returned, 486 B.C. (Ezra 7:12-26). This seems entirely too limited to fit the promise. The shaking within the natural world and of the nations seems to point to the divinely decreed rise and fall of nations from that time to the coming of the Messiah. There would be warfare and constant disturbances among them which would begin soon, in "a little while." The Medo-Persian empire was shaken and so was Alexander's empire, as well as were Syria, Egypt, and finally Rome. This interpretation is further confirmed by Haggai's fourth speech (2:20-23). "And the precious things of all nations," all that is desirable and valuable among them, would be brought into the house of God (cf. the similarity of Isaiah's prophecy, 60:5, 11). This translation and interpretation is preferable to that of the King James Version, "the desire of all nations shall come," which Pusey defends, and interprets to be the Messiah. According to this view, Jehovah's further promise, "and I will fill this house with glory," is fulfilled when Jesus taught in Herod's temple during His personal ministry. This view is rejected on three counts: (1) the grammatical structure of the sentence: the word rendered "desire" is singular, and in this instance the verb "shall come" is plural; this is pointed out by a number of writers, and by Deane in particular; (2) none of the four evangelists quoted or referred to this word of Haggai in connection with Christ's teaching; (3) God has never had but one house. It may have taken different forms and degrees of glory, but always there was but one. The church of the New Testament is the house of God, filled with the glory of God to a far larger degree than ever was the house of Solomon, Zerubbabel, or Herod. The application of the passage made by the writer of Hebrews (12:26) confirms this view. As God shook the heaven and earth at the giving of the law at Sinai, so He shook the heathen nations, removing them; and now He has shaken and removed the Jewish economy that man could receive a kingdom that cannot be shaken (Heb. 12:28). It was this removing of the old order and the founding of a new one that was before Isaiah's mind when he wrote of old things being forgotten and the creation of new heavens and a new earth (65:16-17).

"The silver is mine, and the gold is mine"; all belongs to Him. If these are required to build the present house, Jehovah will provide them. If Jehovah promises that the Gentiles will bring their wealth into His more glorious house of these latter days, He is able to do it. "The latter glory of this house shall be greater than the former" has been touched upon already. The house is one, whether the one erected by Solomon or Zerubbabel or the one erected by Christ. This assurance answers the complaint of verse 3, for the latter glory surpasses that of Solomon's or Zerubbabel's. This is fulfilled in the temple built by Christ, the church, now filled with the glory of the divine presence. "In this place," the spiritual temple in the spiritual Zion to which all saints have come, God gives peace (cf. Isa. 9:6-7; Mic. 4:4; 5:5; Zech. 6:12-13; 9:9-10; Eph. 2:15-17; Phil. 4:7). *2:8*

2:9

> *2:10-14. The third message. The first half of the message is composed of two questions to the priests, their answers, and a conclusion: the people and their works are unclean.*

Exactly three months after work on the house had begun, Haggai received his third message from Jehovah. The ninth month, Chislev, is compared to our November/December. Blessings from Jehovah in response to their zeal and labor had not been as the people had hoped. Jehovah, through His prophet, propounds two questions to the priests, both of which they answered correctly. "Ask now the priests concerning the law." The questions were directed to the priests because they were to distinguish between the clean and the unclean and were to teach the law to the people (Lev. 10:8-10; Deut. 17:8-13; Mal. *2:10*

2:11

2:7). The first question dealt with a negative side, "If

2:12 one bear holy flesh in the skirt of his garment, and with his skirt do touch" articles of food, will that touched become holy? The "holy flesh" borne was the flesh of animals slain in sacrifice to Jehovah (cf. Jer. 11:15). The "skirt" was a wing or lappet of the priest's garment. If this skirt would touch any article of food, does this contact make the article holy? The answer was No, which is correct, for the garment made holy could not communicate holiness beyond

2:13 itself (see Lev. 6:27). Haggai responds with a second question that pertained to the positive aspect of the problem: "If one that is unclean by reason of a dead body touch any of these, shall it be unclean?" Again the priests answered correctly, "It shall be unclean." The law had been clear at this point. If a high priest or a priest (Lev. 21:1, 11), a Nazarite (Num. 6:6-8), or any from among the people (Num. 19:11-13) touched a dead body, he would be unclean, and everything touched by the unclean person became

2:14 unclean (Num. 19:22). The prophet makes a practical application to the remnant, "So is this people, and so is this nation before me, saith Jehovah." Although Israel represented both, one who would carry holy flesh in his garment, and yet was unclean by having touched the unclean, the prophet drops the first question to make an application of the answer to his second. "This people" and "this nation" (cf. 1:2) may indicate that Jehovah does not yet consider them in a right relation to Himself. The word "nation" is that usually used of the heathen peoples. Israel represented herself as one who would bear holy flesh, yet she was unclean by having touched what was unclean (cf. Hos. 9:3). "And so is every work of their hands; and that which they offer there is unclean." Neither the land to which they had returned nor the altar they had erected imparted holiness; they were yet unclean. "The work of your hands" is used in verse 17 of the produce of the land. In whatever way the people had defiled themselves, they had communicated their uncleanness to the products of the land so that what they offered in sacrifice on the

altar had been unclean. They were looking for
Jehovah's blessings prematurely; they must first
cleanse themselves of their defilement, and then they
could expect His presence among them and His blessings on them.

> *2:15-19. Their uncleanness and indifference
> had borne calamity. A right relation with God
> plus zeal for Him demonstrated in work will
> restore prosperity.*

The prophet bids them look back fourteen to six-   2:15
teen years to the time before a stone was laid upon
the foundation and then to the present. Throughout   2:16
those years, when they had come to a heap of un-
threshed wheat that should have produced twenty
measures, they found only ten. When they came to
the wine vat, the place of treading the grapes, ex-
pecting to draw fifty measures, they found even less   2:17
return; there were only twenty measures. Jehovah
explains this lack as a judgment upon them in an
effort to turn their hearts to Him. The smiting with
blasting, mildew, and hail, and their failure to return
to the Lord are reminiscent of Amos 4:9-11. (See
note on Amos 4:9 for blasting and mildew.) "The
work of your hands" refers to their agricultural pursuits. The prophet makes a second appeal for them to   2:18
look back from the present, the twenty-fourth day of
the ninth month, to the day the foundation was laid.
He asks them to give serious consideration to what
had happened to them during that time. This is the   2:19
same period considered in verse 15. "Is the seed yet
in the barn," the granary (cf. Joel 1:17)? The answer
would be No; for the fields had produced so little
that what had been produced had been eaten, and
what had been kept for planting had now been
planted. Likewise the fruit trees and the vines had
failed to produce, and this was in spite of all they
could do to induce a harvest. All production and
fruitfulness depends on Jehovah. But now this twenty-
fourth day of the ninth month will mark a turning

point in their fortunes; things will be different; "from this day I will bless you."

> *2:20-23. The fourth message: The Lord renews the promise of salvation. The kingdoms of the world will be shaken and the Messianic hope fulfilled.*

2:20   On the same day that Haggai received and delivered his third message, a message of hope and assurance, Jehovah speaks a second time through him. This time the promise looks beyond the material blessings to the fulfillment of the spiritual hope in Zerubbabel, the head of the nation and a descendant of David.

2:21   This speech is addressed "to Zerubbabel, governor of Judah," in whom was vested the oversight and rule of the small nation. "I will shake the heavens and the earth" refers to the promise in the second speech (2:6). This further explains what was said at that

2:22   time. Jehovah declares a complete overthrow of the heathen kingdoms, their thrones, and all the implements of war on which they depended. These will be destroyed as everyone is brought down "by the sword of his brother." As is repeatedly brought out in the prophets, Jehovah uses one heathen nation to destroy another, and then raises a third to destroy the former.

2:23   The Lord now bestows a signal honor on Zerubbabel. "In that day," the day when these heathen kingdoms and their thrones and strength will have been brought down, "will I take thee, O Zerubbabel, my servant . . . and will make thee as a signet." Zerubbabel is a faithful and true servant of Jehovah, on whom Jehovah is pleased to bestow honor. The signet, or seal, was a ring or cylinder engraved with the owner's name or some design. It was worn on the finger or on a cord about the neck, and was used to make an impression of ownership or authorship on clay tablets; or if papyrus was used, the impression was made on wax affixed to the material. The signet was considered precious because it was the authentic designation of the owner. The Shulamite had urged her beloved to set her as a seal on his heart, and on his arm, as a guarantee that she was his (Song of Sol. 8:6). Jehovah had declared of Coniah before the captivity that though he "were the signet upon my right hand, yet would I pluck thee hence" (Jer. 22:24). Coniah was cast out and carried into Babylon by Nebuchadnezzar, 597 B.C., "for no more shall a man of his seed prosper, sitting upon the throne of David, and ruling in Judah" (Jer. 22:30). The promise made to David (II Sam. 7:11-14) is now revived in Zerubbabel, a descendant of David through Coniah, and the one through whom the seed would come. "For I have chosen thee, saith Jehovah" gives validity and assurance to the promise. The people are now back in their homeland and Jehovah has assured them of temporal blessings, of the overthrow of the heathen, and of the fulfillment of the spiritual promise through Zerubbabel. The honor bestowed on Zerubbabel was not realized in him as a person, but in his office and lineage. Matthew confirms the fulfillment of this promise as he points out that Jesus is the heir to the throne of David through Coniah and Zerubbabel (1:12, 16).

11
ZECHARIAH
"Whom Jehovah Remembers"

General Observations

1. The Man

As indicated above, the name Zechariah means "whom Jehovah remembers." Zechariah was a popular name among the Hebrews; there are at least twenty-seven men bearing the name who are mentioned in the Old Testament. Zechariah identifies himself as "the son of Berechiah, the son of Iddo." Like Jeremiah and Ezekiel before him, he was of priestly descent, being of the group of priests who, under Zerubbabel's leadership, returned to Jerusalem from Babylon, 536 B.C. (Neh. 12:4, 16). Ezra identifies him only as "the son of Iddo" (Ezra 5:1; 6:14). The probable explanation for Ezra's omission of Berechiah is that the latter died shortly after the return from Babylon, leaving Zechariah next in line to his grandfather, Iddo. However, this is conjectural.

The author of the prophecy is not to be confused with Zechariah, also a priest, son of Jehoiada, who was slain in the house of Jehovah (II Chron. 24:20-22). It seems possible that it was to this Zechariah rather than the prophet that Jesus referred (Matt. 23:35). However, one is left with the need for an explanation of Matthew's use of Berechiah instead of Jehoiada, as in the Chronicles account. The explanation is that either a scribe confused the two names in transcribing Matthew's book, or else the prophet suffered a similar death to that of the son of Jehoiada. However, we have no account of this.

Zechariah, although a priest, was called to the office of prophet to assist Haggai in stirring the people to complete the temple. He began his prophetic ministry about two months after Haggai had begun his and about a month after work was begun on the house of God. His last dated prophecy was in the ninth month of the fourth year of Darius's reign, two years after Haggai's last recorded word to the people.

The book by Zechariah may be thought of as a sequel to Haggai. The temple was begun and constructed in the midst of conflict, but it would be completed. Zechariah looks beyond the immediate temple to the Messiah and the spiritual temple of God, and to the final consummation of God's purpose in the glory of the Messiah and His rule. This would be accomplished amid great opposition, but Jehovah would fight for His people and give them victory.

2. The Date

There is no controversy concerning the dating of chapters 1—8; all scholars agree that these prophecies were spoken in the years 520-518 B.C. But concerning chapters 9—14 there is great diversity of opinion as to both the date and the authorship; especially is this true among modern critics. Among the scholars who defend the unity of the book, affirming that chapters 9—14 were written by Zechariah some time after the first eight chapters, are Deane (*P.C.*), Geikie, Keil, Laetsch, Leupold, Pusey, Robinson, Schultz, and Young. Keil explains the omission of dating the last six chapters on the ground that the first section of the book was concerned with times in the days of Darius I, and that the latter section dealt with times future. After discussing the conditions during the days of Xerxes I and Esther (485-465 B.C.), Geikie suggests that under these circumstances "the prophet Zechariah, now an old man, once more came forward to cheer his contemporaries. His style of address had changed with the altered state of affairs" (Vol. VI., p. 462). For a detailed discussion of the evidence and defense of the unity of the book, consult any of the above writers.

Great diversity of opinion exists among scholars who reject the unity of authorship. For an extended table of dates, early and late, assumed by various authors, see Pusey, Vol. II., pp. 335-338. Among those who place chapters 9—14 before the exile is Farrar, who suggests that chapters 9—11 were written by a younger contemporary of Hosea in the earlier age of Isaiah, and that chapters 12—14 were written shortly after Habakkuk in the age of Jeremiah. Beecher thinks the evidence points to both sections having been written in the days of Hosea and Isaiah (p. 59). Driver says the six chapters were written not earlier than the battle of Issis, 333 B.C. Eiselen says they were not written earlier than 350 B.C., and perhaps they were written after the battle of Issis. Mitchell places the section after 333 B.C., probably between 247-217 B.C. Mitchell suggests so many writers for these chapters that one almost becomes dizzy trying to follow him. Pfeiffer dates them in the third century B.C., but before 200 B.C. G. A. Smith would place the section between 300-280 B.C. After considering the evidence for and against the unity of the book, one feels that Keil has well expressed the view of conservative scholarship when he said of the conclusions reached on the evidence brought against the integrity or unity of authorship of the entire book, "they are founded upon false interpretations and misunderstandings" (Vol. II., p. 222).

3. Background

For a discussion of the background of the period, see the Introduction to the Book of Haggai.

4. Characterization of the Book

The prophecy of Zechariah has several outstanding characteristics that make it unique among writings of the prophets.

a. It is the longest and most obscure of all the Minor Prophets and is the most difficult of any of the Old Testament books to interpret. When this is recognized, one should approach an interpretation of it with prayer and humility, acknowledging his own limitations and knowing that he cannot afford to be dogmatic.

b. In Robinson's judgment, Zechariah's book "is the most

Messianic, the most truly apocalyptic and eschatological, of all the writings of the O.T." (*I.S.B.E.*, p. 3136). From this view some might dissent. In its Messianic import the book compares with Isaiah; the two of them are outstanding in their revelation of the coming Messiah and His work.

c. Zechariah differs in three points from the prophets who preceded him: (1) He gives emphasis to visions as a means of divine communication. It is true that visions appear in the Book of Amos, but not in proportion to those in Zechariah. (2) Angelic mediation occupies an important place in his message. Angels are especially conspicuous in the first six chapters of the book. (3) Apocalyptic symbolism entering into the visions is another outstanding characteristic of this prophet's writings.

d. The Messiah is presented as "the Branch" or "Sprout" of David, a servant of Jehovah. He comes as a king, lowly in spirit, providing salvation for the people. He comes as a shepherd rejected, sold for the price of a wounded slave, and finally pierced for the sheep who would then be scattered. But He redeems a remnant, and through Him the divine sovereignty of Jehovah is restored. The kingdom will be one of glory, with everything pertaining to it consecrated to the Lord. The heathen forces who oppose Jehovah's work will be ingloriously defeated.

e. The prophet sees and emphasizes the truth that ultimate triumph is dependent on divine cooperation and on the submission of the people to God's divine will.

Outline of the Book

I. Visions, and messages of exhortation, consolation, and encouragement, chs. 1—8.

    A. Call to repentance, 1:1-6.

    B. Eight night visions and their interpretation, 1:7—6:8.
        1. The rider and horsemen among the myrtle trees, 1:7-17.
           a) The date, v. 7.
           b) The vision: the horsemen among the myrtles, vv. 8-11.

C. Symbolic crowning of the high priest, Joshua, 6:9-15.
1. Children of captivity provide the gold and silver for the crown, vv. 9-11.
2. Explanation: symbolic of the Branch, crowned king and priest, vv. 12-15.

II. The question of fasting, and Jehovah's answer, chs. 7—8.

A. The fast-days of Israel, and obedience to the word, 7:1-7.
1. The occasion of the prophecy, vv. 1-3.
2. Fasting not essential, but hearing is, vv. 4-7.

B. The first half of the Lord's answer to the question of fasting, 7:8-14.
1. What Jehovah had required of the fathers, vv. 8-10.
2. The refusal of the fathers to hearken—the lesson that should have been learned, vv. 11-14.

C. The second half of the Lord's answer—the promise of restoration to His favor, ch. 8.
1. The time of redemption draws nigh, vv. 1-8.
2. Message of encouragement and admonition, vv. 9-17.
3. Fasting to be changed into rejoicing, vv. 18-23.

III. World powers and the kingdom of God, chs. 9—14.

A. First oracle—judgment! Destruction of heathen powers over Israel, chs. 9—11.
1. Fall of the heathen world, and deliverance and glorification of Zion, chs. 9—10.
   a) Judgment—fall of heathen world, 9:1-7.
   b) The Messianic King and His reign, 9:8-10.
   c) Complete victory of the sons of God over the sons of Greece, 9:11-17.
   d) Complete redemption of the people of God, ch. 10.
2. Allegories of the good and foolish shepherds, ch. 11.

a) Lamentation of the humiliated land, vv. 1-3.
b) Allegory of the good shepherd, vv. 4-14.
   (1) The shepherd's loving care, vv. 4-6.
   (2) The people's lack of appreciation, vv. 7-8.
   (3) Withdrawal of the good shepherd, vv. 9-14.
c) Allegory of the foolish shepherd, vv. 15-17.
   (1) Conduct of the foolish shepherd, vv. 15-16.
   (2) Overthrow of the foolish shepherd, v. 17.

B. The future of the people of Jehovah; judgment by which sifted and refined, chs. 12—14.
  1. Israel's conflict and victory, conversion and sanctification, 12:1—13:6.
    a) Marvelous deliverance of Judah and Jerusalem, 12:1-9.
     (1) Conflict of nations and Jerusalem; destruction of the new nations, vv. 1-4.
     (2) Strength by which to overcome, vv. 5-9.
    b) Spirit of grace and of penitential lamentation, 12:10-14.
    c) A fountain of grace for salvation, 13:1-6.
  2. Judgment of refinement for Israel, and glorious end for Jerusalem, 13:7—14:21.
    a) Fate of the shepherd's flock by which refined, 13:7-9.
    b) Judgment and deliverance, 14:1-5.
    c) Complete salvation, 14:6-11.
    d) Destruction of enemy nations, 14:12-15.
    e) Conversion of the heathen nations, vv. 16-19.
    f) Everything unholy removed; all is holy to Jehovah, vv. 20-21.

Comments

Chapter 1

1:1-6. A call to repentance. The appeal for repentance is made on the ground that God spoke by the former prophets whose word

*was fulfilled. If these people again refuse His
word they will suffer similar consequences.*

When Haggai and Zechariah are compared, one   *1:1*
concludes that among those who returned from Babylon there were some who were completely dedicated
to the Lord, and others whose total commitment was
sorely lacking. Haggai moved the dedicated ones to
begin work on the temple immediately; Zechariah
called upon this second class to repent and join in the
work. "In the eighth month, in the second year of
Darius" would correspond to our October/November
in the year 520 B.C. This would have been two
months after Haggai had begun prophesying to the
people, and a week or two after Haggai's second
address. The rainy season was now at hand and possibly work had begun to lag. The prophet identifies
himself as "the son of Berechiah, the son of Iddo."
(See under *General Observations.*) Zechariah begins
by making an appeal to Jehovah as the source of his
message: "The word of Jehovah" came to him. In the
following five verses the prophet uses the expression
"saith Jehovah of hosts" four times—three times in
his appeal to the source of his message and once in
regard to the word of former prophets; also he uses
"saith Jehovah" once.

The prophet begins his call to repentance by   *1:2*
pointing back to the fathers who lived before the
exile: "Jehovah was sore displeased with your
fathers." That displeasure with the fathers caused the
Lord to send them into captivity. This now becomes
the ground of the prophet's appeal to the remnant
who returned from that captivity; therefore, be
warned by the fathers' experience. Zechariah's exhor-   *1:3*
tation is reminiscent of an earlier Zechariah's charge,
"Because ye have forsaken Jehovah, he hath also
forsaken you" (II Chron. 24:20). Now the Lord says,
"Return unto me . . . and I will return unto you."
The repetition of the expression "saith Jehovah of
hosts" gives emphasis to the charge and promise.
Both the chastisements and blessings of God are con-   *1:4*
ditional. All about the remnant there were constant

reminders of the fathers' rebellion; the city, the temple, and the villages were in ruins. Therefore, "Be not as your fathers" who had refused to hearken to the pleas of Jehovah through the preexilic prophets. The fathers had been urged to turn from their evil ways and from their evil doings; but "they did not hear, nor hearken unto me," said Jehovah. The experience of history should be one of the greatest teachers people have, but the teacher has dull students. Each new generation must learn for itself. This

1:5 accusation is followed by two questions, "Your fathers, where are they? and the prophets, do they live for ever?" Jehovah had risen up early and sent prophets to the fathers, but they had refused to heed His word through them. Where are they now? They have perished. Their death in an unclean land and the rubble of ruin in their own country stood all about them as a monument to Jehovah's righteousness and integrity. "And the prophets"—no, they do not live forever; those who had lived in the land and warned

1:6 the fathers were likewise dead. But the word of Jehovah had stood firm; the words and statutes of Jehovah had overtaken the people. The people had been forced to say, "Like as Jehovah of hosts thought to do unto us, according to our ways, and according to our doings, so hath he dealt with us." Here was a powerful argument to move the people to repent; the land had been destroyed, the people had died as Jehovah had said, and the word of God stood fulfilled. The same Jehovah is now saying through that same word by a new generation of prophets whom He has raised up, "Return," do that which Jehovah commands and act not as your fathers acted; for Jehovah changes not.

1:7-17. The first vision: the prophet is shown horsemen among the myrtle trees, and is given assurance by Jehovah that the temple will be built.

1:7 Exactly five months after work on the house had begun (Hag. 1:15), and two months after Haggai's last speech (Hag. 2:10, 20), a series of eight visions was shown Zechariah in one night. The prophet says that the word of Jehovah came unto him, then proceeds to say, "I saw in the night." The Lord was revealing His word in a vision. Visions differ from dreams in that dreams appeared while the individual was asleep, whereas visions appeared to the sight during one's waking hours. The prophet sees either with his physical eye or the eyes of the Spirit as he is wrapped in ecstasy, but he sees. In the night vision Zechariah saw a rider of a red horse standing among the myrtle trees. Behind him were other riders upon red, sorrel, and white horses. The scene takes place in a "bottom," or hollow, a "shady place," probably a low area which may suggest the low status of Israel at the time. The myrtle tree was a large flowering bush that still grows in Palestine. Some suggest that the colors of the horses—red (a brownish-red), sorrel (uncertain, some identify it as dappled or grizzled), and white—may signify war, famine, and victory; however, their true significance is uncertain. The prophet addresses the rider of the red horse, apparently the angel of Jehovah (v. 11), "O my lord, what are these?" Not "who" but "what"—what do they signify? The angel who replies is the interpreting angel, the angel who explains to the prophet what he sees and hears (cf. v. 13). He replies, "I will show thee what these are." The "man . . . among the myrtle trees," the angel of Jehovah (v. 11), explains that the riders of the various-colored horses are Jehovah's servants or messengers whom He has sent to keep watch over the earth, especially the nations of earth. There is diversity of opinion regarding the identity of the rider of the red horse and the "angel of Jehovah." Are they the same, or do they represent two different individuals? Keil defends the distinction, identifying them as two, the rider of the red horse being the leader of the riders who report to "the angel of Jehovah." However, the weightier evidence points to their identity as one; this view is held by most writers. Throughout Scripture Jehovah is represented by His angel, often called "the angel of Jehovah" (Gen. 22:11, 15-16;

1:8

1:9

1:10

etc.). It was he who redeemed Jacob (Gen. 48:15 ff.),
who went before Israel as a cloud by day and a fire
by night (Exod. 13:21; 14:19), and whom the people
were to obey (Exod. 23:20 ff.). He is referred to as
the "prince of the host of Jehovah" (Josh. 5:14), and
is called "the angel of his [Jehovah's] presence" (Isa.
63:9). In the light of the total evidence it seems more
likely that the chief of the riders is the angel of
1:11   Jehovah. The horsemen respond in chorus, which is
perfectly compatible with a vision scene, reporting to
the angel of Jehovah that they had walked to and fro
in the earth, and that the earth was still and at rest.
There had been many uprisings against Darius when
he assumed rule over the kingdom, but these had
been put down and his throne had been assured;
therefore, "all the earth sitteth still, and is at rest."
This was not as Haggai had promised (2:6-8). This
posed the question among the Jews, When will Jehovah carry out His promise to "shake the heavens, and
the earth . . . and all . . . the nations" (Hag. 2:6)?
While the small nation of Jehovah's people were in a
depressed state, the remainder of the world was at
rest. The depressed remnant was looking to Jehovah
to act.

1:12   The angel of Jehovah responds with a petition in
the form of a question to Jehovah, "How long"
before mercy is shown on Jerusalem and the cities of
Judah? How long before their misery will be brought
to an end? This is the longing cry of the people as the
great mediator presents it before Jehovah for them.
"These threescore and ten years" is the time foretold
by Jeremiah (25:11-12; 29:10). There were two periods of seventy years associated with Judah's captivity: the seventy years of bondage to Babylon,
606/605 B.C., the year Nebuchadnezzar had taken
Judah into his empire, to 536 B.C. when Babylon fell
to Cyrus; and the period from the destruction of the
temple, 586 B.C., till its completion, 516 B.C. This
latter period of seventy years was now almost com-
1:13   pleted. Jehovah's answer was given to the prophet
through the interpreting angel; the prophet was to
relay this answer to the people. The answer from

Jehovah was one of comfort and assurance. The
prophet is instructed to cry to the people, saying,   *1:14*
"Thus saith Jehovah of hosts: I am jealous for Jerusalem and for Zion with a great jealousy." The term
"jealousy" implies divine love which cannot be despised and Jehovah's refusal to be supplanted in affection by another. Jehovah has not forgotten His
people; He will avenge their plight. In fact, He has   *1:15*
already begun to answer their desire. In contrast to
His jealousy for His own city and people, He is "sore
displeased" with the nations "at ease" in their self-
sufficiency and proud self-security. Jehovah was a
"little displeased" with Jerusalem; and although "he
hath poured out his fierce anger" on Zion (Lam.
4:11), it was not for permanent destruction. "His
anger is but for a moment; His favor is for a lifetime"
(Ps. 30:5); "neither will he keep his anger for ever"
(Ps. 103:9). The nations "helped forward [promote
or execute] the affliction" by seeking the complete
and permanent destruction of the people. Jehovah
now answers clearly the question of verse 12; He has   *1:16*
"returned to Jerusalem with mercies" and will build
His house in it. This is the assurance the people so
sorely needed, and it indicates that the people had
returned to Him in response to the earlier call (v. 3).
"A line shall be stretched forth over Jerusalem,"
indicating the space Jerusalem was to occupy and the
general outlay of its arrangement.

This assurance does not exhaust the purpose of   *1:17*
Jehovah. The prophet is urged to cry again to the
people, in which cry Jehovah reveals a threefold
promise of blessings: (1) the "cities shall yet overflow
with prosperity," those round about Jerusalem; (2)
"Jehovah shall yet comfort Zion," the mount of His
presence among the people; and (3) He will "yet
choose Jerusalem" as the capital of His people. These
promises find a partial fulfillment in the building of
the temple by Zerubbabel and the walls of the city by
Nehemiah. God had made rich promises to His people
to be fulfilled upon their return to Him (Deut. 30:5;
Ezek. 36:11), but His blessings were conditional upon
the people's faithfulness to their God (Deut. 30:8-10;

Jer. 18:7-10; Ezek. 33:13). The people did not fulfill their part of the contract, as is indicated by the Book of Malachi; therefore, God could not bless them as He wished until the Messiah would come. The plan of Jehovah is here presented as a long-range plan; Jehovah's eye is upon both the heathen nations and His people; He will carry out His plan upon both.

1:18-21. The second vision: four horns and four smiths. The nations that scattered Judah, Israel, and Jerusalem are to be cast down. Their destruction is determined by Jehovah.

1:18   In the second vision the prophet sees four horns. Horns are symbols of power or strength (Amos 6:13). Daniel used "horns" to represent fullness of power (7:7, 8) and of kings' exerting power (7:24). Four is the complete world number: the four corners of the earth (Isa. 11:12); the four winds (Jer. 49:36; Dan. 11:4); four sore judgments (Ezek. 14:21); four beasts, which are four kings or kingdoms (Dan. 7:3,
1:19   17). In response to the prophet's question, "What are these?" the interpreting angel replies, "These are the horns [hostile powers] which have scattered Judah, Israel, and Jerusalem." The attempt to make these point to four specific kingdoms such as Assyria, Egypt, Babylon, and Medo-Persia, or to Babylon, Medo-Persia, Macedonia, and Rome is futile. The four stand for all world powers who have scattered God's people, sifting them among the nations (Amos 9:9). Judah, Israel, and Jerusalem seem to be used to include both nations and the capital city where Jehovah had recorded His name. However, Keil, following Hengstenberg, considers Israel to be the name for the covenant nation as then existing in Judah; it is an
1:20   honor name for Judah. Immediately, in the same context, Jehovah showed the prophet four smiths or carpenters, craftsmen. They probably represent what was formerly known in this country as "black-
1:21   smiths." As the prophet had asked the meaning of the horns, so now he asks concerning the smiths. The reply is that as the horns had scattered and humiliat-

ed Judah, so now the smiths had come to terrify the powers. The powers would be destroyed by instruments raised by Jehovah for this purpose. The power of their own destruction rests in the nations that destroy. This vision clearly teaches that Jehovah is the Judge of all and that every nation meets its match in Him.

Chapter 2

2:1-5. The third vision: the man with a measuring line. Jerusalem is to be inhabited as unwalled villages, suited for a multitude, for Jehovah will be her protection.

"And I lifted up mine eyes" indicates the introduction of a new vision. The prophet beheld "a man with a measuring line [a cord for measuring] in his hand." He proceeded to ask the man with the measuring line what he is about to do. In reply to the prophet's query the man answers, "To measure Jerusalem," to see what is its length and breadth. This raises the question, which Jerusalem is under consideration—the physical of that time or the spiritual of the future? This point is determined later (vv. 4-5). The interpreting angel went forth and met a second angel, making four characters before us: the "man" (v. 1), the prophet (Zechariah), the interpreting angel, "and another angel." This latter angel seems to possess superior authority over either "the man" or the interpreting angel. The second angel speaks to the interpreting angel saying, "Run, speak to this young man, saying, Jerusalem shall be inhabited as villages without walls, by reason of the multitude of men and cattle therein." Commentators are divided over the identity of "this young man" to whom the interpreting angel is to speak. Is he the "man with the measuring line" (v. 1), or is he the prophet? Without arraying a list of authorities or arguments on each side, it seems that the "young man" to be addressed is "the man" who was about to measure the city. In the vision he represents those among the Jews who

2:1

2:2

2:3

2:4

thought only of physical Jerusalem, who had little concept of the spiritual nature of what God was doing. But the Jerusalem of Jehovah's concern is not to be measured for its breadth and length and surrounded by walls, but is to be ever expanding as

2:5   villages without walls, capable of including growing multitudes and all their possessions. Jehovah further assures "the young man" and the prophet, and through him all the people, that Jehovah will be a wall of fire about His new Jerusalem. He will be her protection and the glory in her midst. This makes it clear that the vision is to assure the people that the Jerusalem of Jehovah's concern is not physical, but spiritual; it is not of the present, but of the future from their point of view.

2:6-13. The vision is followed by a call from Jehovah to His people to flee out of the world and come rejoicing to spiritual Zion, for there Jehovah will dwell in their midst.

2:6   Jehovah calls to His people to flee from Babel, the land of confusion. "Ho" is hortative: give heed! "Flee from the land of the north," Babylon; for though they were located to the east, Assyria and Babylon always invaded Judah from the north (cf. Jer. 1:14; 6:22; 10:22). "For I have spread you abroad as the four winds of the heavens, saith Jehovah." Some think the prophet is speaking in the *prophetic perfect,* which is to speak of something future as already accomplished (Keil, Laetsch, Leupold); therefore, He issues a call to leave Babel for a further scattering throughout the world, which scattering or spreading among the peoples of the world would be for the redeeming of the Gentiles. Others (Deane, Mitchell, Pusey) think the prophet speaks to the Jews yet in Babylon—not in the city only, but in the whole of Assyria-Babylonia. This is indicated by their having been spread abroad as "the four winds of the heavens." These Jews had become settled and were

2:7   imbibing the spirit of Babel. The latter seems more probable, although the speaker looks beyond the im-

mediate present to the Messianic age. This interpretation seems to be confirmed by the exhortation to
Zion, the people of God who dwelt with "the daughter of Babylon," Babylon's people, to escape, get out
and return to Jehovah's land; for Jehovah's land is
wherever Jehovah is. Again Jehovah speaks, but He   2:8
identifies Himself with the angel of Jehovah as His
messenger when He says, "After glory hath he
[Jehovah] sent me [the angel of Jehovah]." So,
whether the Lord or the angel speaks, it is the word
of Jehovah. The angel through whom Jehovah acts
has been sent "after glory," to get glory to God by
taking vengeance upon the nations "which plundered
you." In the light of the context, this seems preferable to the view held by some that it refers to glory
through converting the nations under the Messiah. It
is true that Jehovah got glory to Himself by their
conversion, but this seems not to be the thought of
this passage. To touch the people of God is to touch
"the apple of his eye." The apple or "gate" of the eye
is exceedingly delicate and capable of great pain when
touched or affected by an outside substance; for this
cause it is constantly protected and guarded. To
touch or afflict the people of God gives great pain to
Him. The nations had done this when they destroyed   2:9
and scattered Judah. "I will shake [wave] my hand
over them." The angel speaks for Jehovah. The
waving or shaking of the hand indicates the ease with
which Jehovah can and will destroy the enemy; He
can do this simply by a wave of His hand (cf. Isa.
11:15; 19:16). These over whom He waves His hand
will become a prey and "a spoil to those that served
them" (cf. Hab. 2:6-8). Through this avenging Himself
of His enemies, Jehovah vindicated His claim to deity
and procured glory to Himself. In the fulfillment of
Jehovah's word the claim of the angel to be Jehovah's
spokesman was verified and confirmed; Israel would
understand that God had spoken.

"Sing and rejoice" is addressed to the "daughter of   2:10
Zion," the true believers in Jehovah and His word.
Those who fled out of Babel, giving heed to Jehovah's
call, are the true Zion to whom He now says, "For,

lo, I come, and I will dwell in the midst of thee, saith Jehovah." This is the Jerusalem-Zion of verses 4-5, Jehovah's dwelling place, a city without walls, protected by His own divine presence. The message has looked from beyond the temporal Zion to the spiritu-

2:11 al. "And many nations shall join themselves to Jehovah in that day, and shall be my people." The Lord looks beyond the physical descendants of Israel to a nation that includes some from among all the nations, Gentiles as well as Jews. In the midst of such a people Jehovah will dwell. Therefore, the city could not have been measured, for its extent would be "from sea to sea, and from the River to the ends of the earth" (9:10; cf. 2:3-4). Again the angel says, "And thou [daughter of Zion] shalt know that Jehovah of hosts hath sent me unto thee." The destruction of the nations that scattered Zion, and the redemption of a remnant from Israel and the nations under Christ, stands as a monument to the divine inspiration of Scripture and to the integrity of the

2:12 messengers who spoke. "And Jehovah shall inherit Judah"; this shall be "his portion in the holy land." The "holy land" is wherever Jehovah dwells. The reference is not to be limited to Palestine as His holy land, for that land has been rejected; but it is "the mountain of Jehovah's house" unto which the nations shall flow (Isa. 2:2-4), the "mount Zion . . . the city of the living God, the heavenly Jerusalem" to which the redeemed have come (Heb. 12:22). The Jerusalem He would yet choose would be that above "which is our mother" (Gal. 4:26), "the heavenly."

2:13 "Be silent, all flesh, before Jehovah; for he is waked up out of his holy habitation." Here is a call similar to that of Habakkuk (2:20), for reverence in His presence. Things were about to change; the indifference indicated by the report of the horsemen (1:11) was to be altered. The heathen nations would be judged, Jehovah would build and inhabit the new Zion, and He would fulfill His promises concerning Jerusalem. This is Jehovah's answer to the Jews who could not see beyond the immediate physical temple and city and to those indifferent to His purpose.

Chapter 3

3:1-5. The fourth vision: the cleansing and restoration of the high priest. Joshua the high priest, representing the priesthood, is cleansed and restored by Jehovah in spite of Satan's accusations.

The vision now shown to the prophet does not involve just one man, Joshua the high priest, but must be thought of as including the entire priesthood, and through them the whole nation. Joshua stands for the priesthood, and the priesthood represented the people before Jehovah; therefore, Satan's charge is against all—the priesthood and the nation. The scene is one in which the prophet is shown Joshua, the high priest, standing before the angel of Jehovah with Satan at his right hand to accuse him. Satan, "the adversary" or accuser of men, would prevent Jehovah from accepting Joshua, and through him the nation would be denied favor with God because of sin. He would overthrow the throne of grace, leaving Jehovah as a God of judgment and condemnation only. (For further evidence of Satan's work see Job 1:6-12; 2:1-6; and for his defeat see Rev. 20:10). To the charge of Satan against Joshua, Jehovah replies (whether directly or through the angel of Jehovah makes no difference), "Jehovah rebuke thee, O Satan." Jehovah's rebuke of any opponent silences him and sweeps him awa. Satan may have felt confident in his charge against Joshua; for whatever the present accusation may have been, the priesthood had been guilty of making no distinction between the holy and the common and between the clean and the unclean (Ezek. 22:26). To a degree they had been responsible for the ignorance of the nation (Hos. 4:6) and had fed on the sins of the people (Hos. 4:8); they had taught for hire (Mic. 3:11) and had been further polluted by having been in an unclean land. But Satan misjudged the grace of God; he could not fathom a love that could and would forgive. For the third time Jehovah's choice of Jerusalem is repeated (cf. 1:17;

3:1

3:2

2:12), and He will not be thwarted in His choice and purpose. Joshua stood for "a brand plucked out of the fire," the fire of trials through which the nation had passed in its captivity. Jehovah had declared Himself to be the Saviour (Isa. 43:3; Hos. 13:4), that through His care as Saviour a remnant would return (Isa. 10:21), and that He would cleanse this remnant and give to the ones who returned a new heart and a new spirit (Ezek. 36:25 ff.). Joshua represented this people of Jehovah whom He would cleanse and make His own.

3:3   Bearing the sins of the priesthood and of the people, "Joshua was clothed with filthy garments" as he stood before the angel. The filthy garments represent the sins by which the priesthood and nation had become polluted. Instead of the beautiful and glorious garments of the priesthood, or "the beauty of holiness" with which the people of God should ever be adorned, he was in the condition of the people of other years as described by Isaiah, "For we are become as one that is unclean, and all our righteousnesses are as a polluted [filthy] garment" (Isa. 64:6).

3:4   Jehovah spoke to those that stood before Him, saying, "Take the filthy garments from off him." Those that stood before Him were apparently the attendant angels who waited upon Jehovah, ready to carry out His bidding. Then to Joshua it was said, "Behold, I have caused thine iniquity to pass from thee." The removal of the filthy garments was symbolic of the forgiving or taking away of the iniquity which they symbolized. This ability and willingness to forgive and remove sins lay within the province of the God who had been sinned against. "And I will clothe thee with rich apparel," costly raiment, festal robes, "holy array," or "the beauty of holiness" (cf. Ps. 96:9). This is Jehovah's answer to Satan's accusation.

3:5   At this point, caught up in the excitement of the moment and carried away by the intensity of his interest in what was taking place, the prophet broke in saying, "Let them set a clean mitre upon his head." The mitre or turban was the high priest's headpiece, upon which was carried a plate of pure gold bearing the inscription, "Holy to Jehovah" (Exod. 28:36-38). As suggested by Keil, the prayer was not superfluous, but pointed to the holiness that characterized the priestly office before the days of its degradation. "So they set a clean mitre upon his head, and clothed him with garments." Once more the priesthood, through its representative, the high priest, stood before Jehovah in an imputed holiness, prepared to serve Him and to represent the people before Him. It must not be forgotten that Joshua stood as representative of the whole people, for they were a holy nation and priests unto Jehovah (Exod. 19:6). As a priestly nation which had been unfit for service before the Lord, they are now cleansed and made fit by Jehovah's grace. "And the angel of Jehovah was standing by," evidently directing the whole procedure for Jehovah. He spoke and acted in the stead of Jehovah.

3:6-10. Jehovah now gives a solemn charge to Joshua and assures him that he will have access for the people. Joshua and those with him will be a sign of the Branch that was to come.

The angel of Jehovah continues to speak for the Lord, or to act as the one through whom Jehovah speaks. He "protested unto Joshua"; that is, he solemnly and earnestly charged or declared to him. The angel would impress in a most grave manner the charge about to be laid on the high priest. The charge is twofold, "If thou wilt walk in my ways, and if thou wilt keep my charge." This involved (1) the personal righteousness of the high priest, and (2) his faithfulness to his priestly duties; these he must solemnly observe. The charge is followed by a threefold promise involving serious responsibilities: (1) "Thou . . . shalt judge my house"—that is, he will rule and direct the affairs and worship of Jehovah's house; (2) "and [thou] shalt also keep my courts," which is closely related to the first charge, but involves keeping the

3:6

3:7

courts of Jehovah's house free from idols and all forms of idolatry; (3) "and I will give thee a place of access," access to Jehovah on behalf of the people whom the high priest represents. This place of access would be "among these that stand by," the angels of verse 4, but not on their behalf. Among the host of angels the people would have access to Jehovah through the newly cleansed and sanctified high priest; but this honor would be his on the conditions stipulated.

3:8   A fresh address to which he is to give earnest heed is directed to the high priest. It is emphasized by the opening words, "Hear now." The message is not to him only, but it is addressed to "thou and thy fellows that sit before thee," his colleagues in office. "For they are men that are a sign [wonder, or marvelous wonder]: for, behold, I will bring forth my servant the Branch [Shoot or Sprout]." What God had just done in assuring the priesthood a place of access to Him would find its full and ultimate realization in the Branch. These would be a sign or assurance of future completeness of access under the full and complete High Priest. The high priest and his fellows were typical of the righteous Branch to come. This is the first introduction of the Branch by Zechariah. Both Isaiah (4:2; 11:1-10) and Jeremiah (23:5; 33:15) had introduced the Branch who was to come. He would be a descendant of David and a servant of Jehovah. In Him the priesthood and kingship through Zerubbabel (Hag. 2:23) would be combined and made complete.

3:9   There is great diversity of opinion among commentators regarding the "stone . . . set before Joshua." Some are emphatic in their conclusion that the stone is the Messiah. Although He is referred to as a stone in both the Old and New Testaments, this interpretation seems here not to fit best. It is referred to as "the stone . . . one stone." It has been revealed to the prophet that Jehovah's servant, the Branch, would be brought forth, in whom is to be combined the office of king and priest (Zech. 6:12-13). It seems evident from the context that the stone is the kingdom of Jehovah. At that time it was a rough, unhewn stone, but it was to be complete with the engraving or sculpture of Jehovah. The "seven eyes" focused on the stone represent the completeness and fulness of God's watchful care over His people and His promise that He would bring forth a kingdom which should never be destroyed (Dan. 2:44), which would endure forever (Dan. 7:14) in spite of the opposition of all heathen powers (Dan. 7). This is further verified by the promise, "and I will remove the iniquity of that land in one day." "That land" is the land born in one day (Isa. 66:8), the land over which the Messiah would reign as the priestly King, which would be "from sea to sea, and from the River to the ends of the earth" (Zech. 9:10). The iniquity would be removed "in one day," the day of the Messiah's sacrifice and assumption of His priestly functions. "In that day," the day or time of the removal of iniquity from Jehovah's land, the day of the Messianic rule, "shall ye invite every man his neighbor under the vine and under the fig-tree." Under one's vine and fig tree was a symbol of peace enjoyed in the midst of safety and security (I Kings 4:24-25; Isa. 36:16), promised by Jehovah through Micah in the kingdom of the Messiah (4:4). The redeemed will invite their neighbors to share with them their blessedness in the kingdom of God. This is the assurance Jehovah gives to His discouraged and faltering people through the cleansing of the priesthood and declaration of the Branch who would come and through the promise of the kingdom over which He carefully watched.

3:10

Chapter 4

4:1-10. The fifth vision: the lampstand and the two olive trees. The prophet is shown a vision in which is symbolized the restored community through divine grace and power. All obstacles will be removed; Zerubbabel will complete the building of the temple.

Apparently the prophet had been so overcome by the four previous visions that he had fallen into a

4:1

sleeplike exhaustion, for the interpreting angel "came again, and waked me, as a man that is wakened out of his sleep." "Again" indicates this was not the first time during the night that the angel had aroused him, although it is the first mention of such action. A similar incident seems to have been experienced by the three apostles on the Mount of Transfiguration (Luke 9:32). Instead of the prophet relating what he saw, the interpreting angel focused his attention on the object of the vision by asking, "What seest thou?" The prophet responded by describing the objects before him; he sees a golden candlestick or lampstand and two olive trees, one on either side of the lampstand. The candelabrum or lampstand differs in three respects from the one made by Moses for the tabernacle, and from the ten that adorned the temple of Solomon which were carried away into Babylon (I Kings 7:49; Jer. 52:19): (1) this one had a bowl or reservoir on top; (2) it had pipes that fed oil to the lamps; (3) the oil was provided by two olive trees adjacent to the lampstand. Men have exercised their ingenuity and drawn on their imagination in an effort to construct a picture of the bowl and its relation to the lamps, but they have had little success. Some have suggested an arm that extended back from the central lamp on which the bowl rested; others have suggested there were three lamps on one side of the bowl and four on the other; but this would throw the stand out of balance, destroying its symmetry; others have thought the seven prongs of the lampstand were in a circular form about the central shaft with the bowl on top of the shaft, enabling the lamps to send their rays of light in all directions. However, until evidence is discovered from some extra-Biblical source, the matter will continue to be a mystery. Another difficulty in the vision is the number of pipes to each lamp. Were there "seven pipes to the seven lamps" (KJV), or "seven pipes to each of the lamps" (ASV)? Scholars are divided. Deane (*P.C.*) defends the view that there was one pipe to each lamp as indicated by the King James Version. Keil defends the view that there were seven pipes to each lamp, making a total

4:2

of forty-nine pipes in all. Laetsch, Leupold, Pusey, and others concur with this view. The problem of seven pipes to each bowl presents no difficulty in a vision. The idea expressed by the seven would be that an abundance of oil for the lamps is amply provided by Jehovah. Two olive trees stood by the lampstand, one on the right and one on the left of the bowl. The purpose of these, which was to provide oil for the lamps, is more fully revealed in verse 12. This accounts for their proximity to the bowl as indicated in this verse.

4:3

Although the vision was clear to the prophet, the meaning of what he saw was not. His question, "What are these, my lord?" was a simple request: "what do these mean?" He asks not only concerning the two olive trees, but also about all items thus far included in the vision. The answer of the angel indicates surprise at the prophet's question: "Knowest thou not what these are?" Although the prophet had never seen the candlestick of the tabernacle or one of the ten in Solomon's temple, he should have known something of the significance of its symbolism. To the angel's question Zechariah was forced to confess his ignorance as he replied, "No, my lord." In the angel's reply we have an explanation of the purpose of the vision: it is a message to the despairing Zerubbabel. No doubt as he viewed the task before him of rebuilding the temple and the temper and weakness of the people, he had become discouraged. A word of assurance from Jehovah would be his greatest need. The angel's response was, "This is the word of Jehovah unto Zerubbabel, saying, Not by might, nor by power, but by my Spirit, saith Jehovah of hosts." "Not by might," an army (margin, ASV); that is, not by human strength would Zerubbabel accomplish his task. "Nor by power" when combined with "might" indicates that neither by human force, strength, wealth, or prestige, on which man so often relies, would the work be done. "But by my Spirit," by divine omnipotence, the infinite power of God, will the task be accomplished. The lampstand supports the lamps; the Spirit of Jehovah provides the light. It

4:4

4:5

4:6

is only by the divine power provided by His Spirit that man can accomplish the purpose of the Almighty.

4:7 Zerubbabel is further encouraged by the assurance that all obstacles that stand in his way will be removed. "Who art thou, O great mountain? before Zerubbabel thou shalt become a plain." The "great mountain" is a figurative expression denoting all the obstacles that stand in the way, whether the power of world kingdom, or the obstacles within Judah, or both; but most probably the world power that always stood in opposition to God's work is emphasized. These mountains would be removed, becoming as a plain over which travel would be made easy. This would be accomplished by divine power. "And he [Zerubbabel] shall bring forth the top stone"—not the cornerstone, for it had already been laid, but the finishing stone, the last stone which would complete the temple's construction. He would bring it out of the place where it had been cut for the finishing touch. It would be brought forth with shoutings of "Grace, grace, unto it." As the last stone is properly placed and the building completed, the multitude gathered for the occasion will break forth in a jubilant prayer for God's favor to rest upon it. When completed, it will have been built by the grace of God; and the prayer would be that it would continue under the divine favor, never again to be destroyed.

4:8 The prophet receives a new message which is closely associated with that of verses 6-7. By whom is this "word of Jehovah" that came to him delivered? Is it from the interpreting angel or from "the angel of Jehovah," hence, from Jehovah Himself represented by His angel? In the light of 2:9 where it was said, "And ye shall know that Jehovah of hosts hath sent me" (cf. also v. 13; 2:11) and the repetition of this in 4:9, one concludes the speaker is the "angel of Jehovah." However, even if it cannot be certainly determined which, it will matter little; for both angels were from God and either one spoke from God. As

4:9 Zerubbabel had laid the foundation of the house, so "his hands shall also finish it." The completed temple at the hands of Zerubbabel by the power of God would be assurance that Jehovah had sent His angel to them. But more, it would be also a pledge that the greater spiritual house would be built according to divine promise and power; for Zerubbabel was made "as a signet," chosen by Jehovah (Hag. 2:23), a symbol of Him who was to come. His work was a foreshadowing of what the Messiah would accomplish.

Jehovah continues to speak through His angel: 4:10
"For who hath despised the day of small things?" When the foundation had been laid, the people who had returned from Babylon wept with a loud voice because of the insignificance of the temple then being constructed when compared with the temple of Solomon (Ezra 3:12); and even after Zerubbabel had begun the work of completing the building fifteen years later, it appeared in their eyes as nothing (Hag. 2:3). All the things done since returning from the exile to the coming and work of the Messiah were small in comparison to His work. But when the work is Jehovah's work, predetermined and carried out by Him, nothing is inconsequential; everything has its place in His plan. "These seven," the seven eyes of Jehovah (cf. 3:9), will rejoice as they behold the plummet, a plumb bob or plumb rule to put stones in proper alignment, in the hand of Zerubbabel, the builder. He plumbs the top stone in place; the building is complete, thereby giving assurance that Jehovah's work will be accomplished. The "seven eyes" that "run to and fro through the whole earth" symbolize the perfection of God's watch over His purpose and the carrying out of His plan (cf. II Chron. 16:9; Prov. 15:3).

4:11-14. The question of the prophet concerning the two olive trees, and the angel's explanation: Jehovah would accomplish His purpose through His anointed ones.

With the explanation given to the prophet con- 4:11
cerning the lampstand, and with the assurance given

4:12
to Zerubbabel that he would complete the work begun, there remained one more question: what is the significance of the two olive trees? What purpose do they have in the overall vision? Either the angel waits for a more specific phrasing of the question or the prophet hastens to alter his question, for the angel does not reply immediately. In his second question the prophet introduces an element of the vision until now not revealed, "What are these two olive-branches, which are beside the two golden spouts, that empty the golden oil out of themselves?" The branches simply suggest clusters of olive berries which supply a never ending abundance of golden oil, oil of a rich golden color. The oil flows through two pipes or spouts to the golden bowl or reservoir (v. 2), from which the lamps are copiously supplied by seven pipes to each. Truths can be revealed in a vision or dream that could never be found in actual life. Olive berries do not of themselves drop oil, but must be pressed. In a vision this is not necessary. The picture is one of the completeness of God's Spirit by which the light of truth would be shed abroad in His temple.

4:13
The angel seems to be amazed that the prophet had not understood this aspect of the vision and responds with a queston of his own, "Knowest thou not what these are?" To this second question of the angel (cf. v. 5) the prophet was again forced to confess his lack of understanding. Is the angel disappointed that the prophet makes no greater effort to search diligently on his own for an understanding? This question must remain unanswered, but should become a challenge to

4:14
all. The angel answers the prophet's question, "These are the two anointed ones," oiled ones, or sons of oil. But who are the anointed ones of whom the angel speaks? Under the Old Covenant there were two offices held by men who were anointed, thereby being set apart as holy to the Lord, specially appointed to serve His purpose: these were the office of high priest (Exod. 30:30; Lev. 8:30; 21:10) and king (I Sam. 10:1; II Kings 9:1-6). These two offices represented the religious or spiritual, and civil or temporal powers of the theocracy. These two anointed ones are

described as they "that stand by the Lord of the whole earth"; that is, they are near to do His bidding, to carry out His will. Evidently the offices of Joshua, the high priest, and of Zerubbabel, the governor, are indicated by the "anointed ones." The two offices would be ultimately united in the Messiah, the Priest-King to come. However, a discussion of this point would be premature just here, so the angel leaves this to be dealt with later (6:12-14).

Chapter 5

5:1-4. The sixth vision: the flying roll. The prophet is shown a flying roll with a curse against stealing written on one side, and a curse against false swearing on the other.

"Then again I lifted up mine eyes" indicates the introduction of a new vision. The object of the vision was a "flying roll." The ancient Hebrews wrote on leather or parchment which was rolled up on two sticks, one at each end of the material. The parchment was rolled from one stick or rod to the other as the reader progressed. The response of the prophet to the interpreting angel's question, "What seest thou?" indicates that the roll was open, unrolled. The prophet replied that he saw a flying roll; "the length thereof is twenty cubits, and the breadth thereof ten cubits," which would be about thirty feet by fifteen feet. The prophet recognized the size of it, but how he recognized it is not revealed. The size of the roll is the same as the porch Solomon built before the entrance of the temple (I Kings 6:3), and the size of the holy place or first section of the tabernacle built by Moses. The definite size of the roll as stated by the prophet must have some positive significance, but what it is we are not told. If the size is taken from the holy place of the tabernacle, then we may conclude that the roll indicates the demand for holiness upon all who draw nigh to God in His holy sanctuary. This is only a suggestion.

5:1

5:2

5:3 "This is the curse," written on the roll, "that goeth forth over the face of the whole land." "The whole land" indicates not the whole world or earth, but the land of God's people, wherever they may be, whether in the land of Canaan or the uttermost part of the earth. This seems evident from the antithetical use of Shinar, to which wickedness is conveyed (v. 11). The roll contains a twofold curse; on one side is a curse against stealing, and on the other side is the curse against false swearing (cf. v. 4). Stealing was an expression of covetousness and was to the injury of one's neighbor. False swearing dishonored Jehovah, for the oath was to be taken in His name and observed (Deut. 6:13); but false swearing profaned His name (Lev. 19:12). To be cut off "on the one side" and "on the other side" was to be cut off according to the curse of God, one written on one side and one

5:4 on the other side of the roll. "I will cause it [the curse] to go forth" and it would "enter into the house of the thief, and into the house of him that sweareth falsely." The thief violated the property right of others; this was condemned by law (Exod. 20:15). Because of disregard for God's law Israel had gone into Assyrian captivity (Hos. 4:2-3) and Judah had gone into Babylon (Mic. 2:2-3). As indicated above (v. 3), there is a legitimate taking of oath and a false taking of oath. It was sin to take the Lord's name in vain (Exod. 20:7), to swear lightly or falsely (Lev. 5:4), and to swear by the name of any other god (Josh. 23:7). It appears that the people who had returned from captivity had grown careless in enforcing the law of right relation to both man and God. The curse would enter into and abide in the midst of the house of either type of violator, "and shall consume it with the timber thereof and the stones thereof." The curse will be like a devouring fire; it will abide upon the house, the family of the transgressors, until the destruction is complete.

5:5-11. The seventh vision: the ephah and the woman. Following the curse upon the evil

*doers, the land is purged of wickedness, which
is transported to its own land.*

Some moments, during which the angel had been   *5:5*
apart from the prophet, seem to have elapsed
between the sixth and seventh visions. Apparently the
angel was among the company of angels previously
introduced. He now comes forth and introduces the
next vision by telling the prophet to lift up his eyes,
"and see what is this that goeth forth," presenting
itself as an object of attention. No doubt the prophet   *5:6*
recognized what he saw as a large basket or barrel;
but desiring to know the deeper significance of it, he
asked, "What is it?" The interpreting angel did not
reprove the prophet this time, but said, "This is the
ephah that goeth forth." Mitchell (*I.C.C.*) says that
according to latest evidence the ephah "contained
38.86 American quarts." The ephah of the vision
probably did not specify a measurement, but was
used to designate a large basket or barrellike container of sufficient size to enclose a woman. "This is
their appearance in all the land"; that is, the ephah
and its content represent the people of wickedness
throughout the land. They, together with their wickedness, will be removed out of the land. This statement of the prophet seems to anticipate what follows, and is explained by it. The container was covered   *5:7*
by a large "round" or "circle" of lead. The talent,
as a weight, was used only of gold and silver, never of
lead; therefore, "round of lead" is preferable, as the
Hebrew term used here is used of a circle (plain, or
circle, Gen. 13:10-12). The lead covering was lifted
up sufficiently to reveal a woman "sitting [or crouch-
ing] in the midst of the ephah." That a woman could
be crouching in the ephah indicates that it was larger
than a bushel basket; therefore the word was used
only to designate the shape of the container and not
its size. The angel explained the significance and   *5:8*
symbolism of the woman when he said, "This is
Wickedness." Earlier prophets had used the figure of
an immoral woman to signify the wickedness of

Judah (Isa. 1:21) and Israel (Hos. 2:5), and of the cities of Samaria and Jerusalem (Ezek. 23). The angel seems to have lifted the lid only that the prophet could see what was in the ephah, for immediately he cast the lead lid upon its mouth or opening. The wickedness symbolized by the woman would include more than that of stealing and false swearing (vv. 1-5); it symbolizes all the wickedness among the people.

5:9   The prophet's attention is drawn upward as he lifts his eyes; "and, behold, there came forth two women, and the wind was in their wings." Whether these two women were either good or bad is not indicated; they simply indicate the instrumentalities of God for the removal of wickedness from the land. The wind "in their wings" was a blast that aided them in lifting and swiftly conveying the woman in the ephah into her own land. Their "wings like the wings of a stork" indicate the strength that was theirs to fulfill their task, as the stork is a migratory bird with strong wings.

5:10   The prophet was concerned about the destiny of the two women and their cargo, and asked,

5:11   "Whither do these bear the ephah?" Immediately the angel responds, "To build her a house in the land of Shinar: and when it is prepared [or established], she shall be set there in her own place." It was "in the land of Shinar" that Nimrod founded the first world kingdom, out from which other kingdoms were established (Gen. 10:10-11). From the time of its establishment this kingdom had stood in rebellion against God and His way and will. In the vision Shinar is not to be thought of as a geographical country, but as a symbol of Satan's world government. When the place is prepared, Wickedness is set there "in her own place." The vision signifies the complete removal of wickedness from Jehovah's land to a kingdom of this world, suited for it; it symbolized a complete separation of the two. This is further symbolized in the Book of Revelation by the "harlot" and the "bride," by the "great city" and the "holy city," and by the beast out of the sea and the one hundred forty-four thousand on "the mount Zion." Wickedness must be completely removed from God's kingdom and His people, and the complete separateness must be maintained throughout time.

Chapter 6

6:1-8. The eighth vision: the four chariots. The final vision of that night portrayed four chariots drawn by horses of various colors. These were dispatched by Jehovah to various parts of the earth to serve His purpose.

This fresh and final vision was introduced by the prophet as others had been introduced: "And again I lifted up mine eyes and saw." What he saw were four chariots coming out from between two mountains. The two mountains were not geographical mountains, but were of "brass," or better, of copper or bronze. The brass or bronze denotes the enduring nature of the mountains. Numerous and varied have been men's efforts to explain what particular mountains were before the prophet in the vision. Because the chariots went out to the north country and to the south, some have concluded they were Zion and the Mount of Olives. However, it seems safer to consider them as two lofty elevations of the vision, which served as pillars that guard the exit of the station or enclosure between which the chariots must come as they are sent on their mission by Jehovah. This view seems to be confirmed by verse 5, where it is said that the chariots, as four winds, "go forth from standing before the Lord of all the earth."

6:1

The colors of the horses drawing the chariots are described, but commentators find it difficult to attach definite or positive significance to them. "In the first chariot were red horses." The chariots are not designated as war chariots; therefore the association of red with war and bloodshed is not conclusive. However, in John's vision on Patmos the rider of the red horse indicates persecution and bloodshed (Rev. 6:3-4). On this basis one may be warranted in concluding that red in this instance does indicate war and

6:2

blood. "And in the second chariot black horses"—which color is thought to symbolize grief and famine—carried a balance as does the rider of the black horse in John's vision; the picture there is one of

6:3 great scarcity (Rev. 6:5-6). "And in the third chariot white horses"; white is the festive color, or color of victory. The rider of the white horse in John's vision "came forth conquering, and to conquer" (Rev. 6:1-2). The robes given to the martyrs underneath the altar were white, indicating both victory and festivity; therefore, white may here indicate victory. The chariot drawn by the white horses followed that drawn by the black horses (v. 6), indicating that God's mission of the latter was victorious. "And in the fourth chariot grizzled strong horses"; these horses were gray, spotted, speckled, or variegated colors. These were strong, powerful horses, fully capable of carrying out the divine mission on which they were sent. In his prophecy against Jerusalem, Ezekiel spoke of "God's four sore judgments . . . the sword, and the famine, and the evil beasts, and the pestilence" (14:21; 5:16-17). The similarity between Ezekiel and Zechariah supports the conclusion that these chariots drawn by varicolored horses and sent forth by Jehovah to the heathen nations indicate His judgments of famine, pestilence, and sword, which were victorious in their mission.

6:4 The scene left the prophet wondering what the chariots and steeds meant; for he asked the angel that talked with him, "What are these, my lord?" Some have thought the chariots represented four world empires or kingdoms, but this view is wholly out of harmony with the context. Keil has so completely refuted this view that no modern commentator of repute has attempted to defend it. The angel replied,

6:5 "These are the four winds [or spirits] of heaven, which go forth from standing before the Lord of all the earth." "The four winds" of the text may provide a clue to understanding the vision. Jeremiah writes of the four winds as scattering winds, as through him Jehovah said, "Upon Elam will I bring the four winds from the four quarters of heaven, and will scatter them toward all those winds" (49:36). He spoke also of "a destroying wind" to be brought against Babylon (51:1). In the vision shown Daniel, "the four winds of heaven brake forth upon the great sea" (7:2), out of which came four beasts. These were winds of social upheaval which broke forth upon society, out of which emerged four world empires. The four winds of Zechariah's vision "go forth from standing before the Lord of all the earth." They are His messengers (cf. Ps. 104:4), sent anywhere throughout all the earth to accomplish His purpose of scattering, destroying, or stirring, depending on the need of the hour.

The chariot drawn by the black horses was sent "forth toward the north country." The north country was the area of the Assyria-Babylonia Empires, which at that time were no more, but whose former domain was under Persian rule. In the first vision (ch. 1) it was reported by the horsemen, "all the earth sitteth still, and is at rest." In response to this report Jehovah had said, "I am very sore displeased with the nations; for I was but a little displeased, and they helped forward the affliction" (1:15). In this concluding vision the condition described by the horsemen is going to be changed. Babylon had gone beyond all bounds of humanitarian conduct in the affliction of nations (Isa. 14:6; 47:6); and, although the nation had fallen, the whole spirit of heathen cruelty that had characterized Assyria and Babylon and which now lived in the Persian empire had not yet been sufficiently dealt with. The chariot drawn by the black horses was followed by the one drawn by the white, indicating the victory of God's purpose in sending famine and ultimate destruction upon the heathen. "The grizzled went forth toward the south country," which was Egypt, and possibly Edom and Ethiopia, all enemies of Jehovah's people. The speckled or spotted may indicate a multiform judgment by famine, pestilence, and death by sword which would come upon these ancient oppressors of the kingdom of God. The north and south indicate the whole of the heathen powers.

6:6

6:7   "And the strong went forth" with instruction to "walk to and fro through the earth." This instruction they obeyed, for the prophet concludes his part of the visions by saying, "So they walked to and fro through the earth." A question is raised at this point: Do we have a fifth chariot, or is this the chariot that went forth into the south country? Another alternative is sometimes offered that this chariot is the one drawn by the bay or red horses of verse 2. This last possibility may be dismissed, for "red" and "strong" are not synonymous. The "red" are not mentioned again after verse 2. No reason is given for this, but one may conclude that God holds in reserve a final judgment when others have failed. To the question as to whether there is a fifth chariot, answer may be made that the prophet is said to have seen "four chariots" (v. 1), and the fourth team is described as "grizzled strong horses." The most reasonable conclusion is that the chariot that went through the earth is the fourth chariot which went to the south country. This conclusion is justified by their (the strong) having "sought to go that they might walk to and fro through the earth." They seemed to be eager to go not only to the south country, but to render a larger service by going through the whole earth.

6:8   The mission of the two messengers sent toward the north country is said by Jehovah to "have quieted my spirit in the north country." In the vindication of Jehovah's righteousness through judgment is His Spirit quieted (cf. Ezek. 5:13; 16:42; 24:13). What had been achieved in the north country surely can be said of the others sent forth; all accomplished the mission on which they were sent. The chariots, therefore, have been the messengers that carry God's Spirit into all parts of the earth. They represent not only the spirit of avenging and judgment, of scattering and destruction, but also the spirit of mercy and redemption. God's judgments always look to the ultimate redemption of a people, as Isaiah said, "For when thy judgments are in the earth, the inhabitants of the world learn righteousness" (26:9).

The visions had begun with the condition of the

heathen; all was quiet. The second through the seventh dealt with the fortunes of Judah, God's people. God had said, "Yet once, it is a little while, I will shake the heavens, and the earth, and the sea, and the dry land" (Hag. 2:6). It is altogether fitting that the concluding vision would deal with the heathen and his being shaken, completing a circle of visions dealing with the heathen and with Jehovah's own.

6:9-15. The symbolic crowning of the high priest. A double-tiered crown of silver and gold is placed on Joshua, the high priest, signifying the double office of king and priest to be held by the Messiah, the Branch.

The amount of time that elapsed between the eight visions and the symbolic crowning of the high priest is not revealed. One is tempted to think that the crowning took place the day following. That this is not a ninth vision is clear from the different way the prophet introduces his subject. He no longer says, "I lifted up mine eyes and saw," but, "the word of Jehovah came unto me, saying." The instruction from Jehovah was for the prophet to go to the three men, Heldai, Tobijah, and Jedaiah, and take silver and gold from them with which to make a crown. These three men had recently come from those of the captivity in Babylon. "Come thou the same day" indicates he should go either the day these men had arrived, or the day in which the word of Jehovah came to the prophet; probably they are the same. These men were residing in the house of Josiah, the son of Zephaniah, who was showing hospitality to these brothers from afar. "Yea, take of them silver and gold" indicates that these men had come from Babylon to bring these offerings from the brothers there, that they could have further fellowship in building the temple. With the silver and gold Zechariah was to "make crowns, and set them upon the head of Joshua . . . the high priest." He was not to make a plurality of crowns, although the word "crowns" is plural. Rather, it was a crown of silver and gold woven together to form

6:9

6:10

6:11

what might be called a double-tiered crown which would signify the double office of priest and king. This was to be placed on the head of Joshua the high priest. Some claim that one crown was to be placed on Joshua's head and another on Zerubbabel's head; but this is not reasonable, for Zerubbabel is not in the picture at all. Although he was governor, of the royal seed of David and in the genealogy of Christ, he was not king. Joshua was the bona fide high priest. The crown was to be placed on only Joshua's head. Under the law the high priest had not worn a crown, but a

6:12 turban or mitre (cf. 3:5). As the high priest was crowned, the prophet was to declare the word of Jehovah of hosts, saying, "Behold, the man whose name is the Branch," or Shoot, or Sprout. The "Branch" had been introduced earlier, at the cleansing of the high priest. The high priest and his fellows were to be for a sign that God would fulfill their true significance in the Branch (3:8). Isaiah had introduced Him as "a shott out of the stock of Jesse" (11:1), as "the root of Jesse" unto whom the nations would seek (v. 10). Jeremiah had further identified Him as "a Branch of righteousness" who would "grow up unto David" and who would "execute justice and righteousness in the land" (33:15).

Jehovah declares five things concerning the "man whose name is the Branch":

1. "He shall grow up out of his place." He would grow up "as a root out of a dry ground," in the midst of a corrupt age (Isa. 53:2); for the house of David would be as a tent that had fallen into decay (Amos 9:11). He would grow up from among His own people in His own land; and from a lowly origin and state of rejection He would "be exalted and lifted up, and shall be very high" (Isa. 52:13).

6:13 2. "Even he shall build the temple of Jehovah; even he shall build the temple of Jehovah." The hands of Zerubbabel had laid the foundation of the material temple and his hands would complete it (4:9), but the Branch would build the spiritual temple of Jehovah. This temple is the church of the

Lord, made of "living stones" (I Pet. 2:5), "a holy temple in the Lord . . . a habitation of God in the Spirit" (Eph. 2:21 ff.), "whose house are we" (Heb. 3:6). The fact and assurance that He would build it is emphasized by the prophet's repetition of the promise.

3. "And he shall bear the glory"; He will be laden with honor and majesty and power. This glory is realized in His preeminent greatness and Kingship: "and he shall sit and rule upon his throne." The throne promised Him was the throne of David (II Sam. 7:11-14; Isa. 9:6-7), which was the throne of Jehovah (Ps. 2:6-7; 110:1); for David's throne of rule had been the throne of Jehovah (I Kings 2:12; I Chron. 29:23).

4. "And he shall be a priest upon his throne." In the throne of the Branch is combined both the kingly and priestly offices over God's people. In the historical Melchizedek these had been combined, for he was "king of Salem [peace] " and "priest of God Most High" (Gen. 14:18). Through David Jehovah had sworn that the King of His appointment would be "a priest for ever after the order of Melchizedek" (Ps. 110:4). In the man whose name is the Branch Jehovah now declares that this oath will be fulfilled. In the New Covenant this is abundantly confirmed: He was raised to sit on David's throne (Acts 2:29-31); He sat down on the right hand of God (Heb. 1:3), where He is to sit until all His enemies are made the footstool of His feet (Heb. 1:13). This is to be accomplished when the last enemy, death, is abolished, put under His feet (I Cor. 15:25-26). This will take place at the final judgment (Rev. 20:11-15). Further, He is a priest after the order of Melchizedek now (Heb. 5:9; 7:1-3), making intercession for all who come to God by Him (Heb. 7:25), and serving as the great King-Priest on the throne of God (Rev. 3:21). The fulfillment of Zechariah's prophecy in Christ at this present time forever refutes the claim of millenarians that Christ is to rule on earth for one thousand years at His return from heaven. He is coming; but it will be

to judge and then deliver the kingdom up to God the Father, that He (God) may be all in all (I Cor. 15:24-28).

5. "And the counsel of peace shall be between them both"; that is, peace will be provided by the Branch holding the twofold office of king and priest. His concern will be to provide peace for His people, as had been foretold by earlier prophets (Isa. 9:6-7; Mic. 5:5) and preached by the apostles who came after (Eph. 2:14, 17). In reconciling men to God and in ruling in their hearts, He provides the counsel of peace.

6:14   The crown would be to the three men who had come from Babylon "for a memorial in the temple of Jehovah." The crown would be a memorial to these three men who had come from afar and an assurance that those who were far off would be permitted to build in Messiah's temple (see v. 15). Heldai (v. 10) is here called "Helem." Whether this is a second name or a copyist's error is unknown, but the two names seem to point clearly to the same man. "And to Hen the son of Zephaniah," who is included with the three as sharing in "the memorial." Is "Hen" here used as a proper name, or is the alternate marginal reading (ASV) to be preferred? The alternate reading is, "for the kindness of the son of Zephaniah." Hebraists prefer the secondary reading, contending that "Hen" is not considered a proper name (Keil, Laetsch, Leupold, Rawlinson, et al.), but means "grace" or "favor." In this sense the crown would be for a memorial to these three men who had come from afar and for the hospitable favor shown them by Josiah the son of Zephaniah. The crown would be laid up in the temple, where it would be kept for a memorial of the persons and events of the occasion.

6:15   "And they that are far off shall come and build in the temple" points not to the Jews of foreign countries, but to the Gentiles who would be invited to come and build in Jehovah's glorious spiritual temple, ruled over by the King-Priest, the Messiah. Once more the angel of Jehovah points to the accomplishing of his promise as evidence that Jehovah had sent him (cf. 2:9, 11; 4:9). There is no greater evidence to the divine origin of the word, nor to the integrity of His messengers, than the fulfilled word which they spoke. The final word is to the Jews: if they obey the voice of Jehovah and rebel not at His instruction, they will build alongside the Gentiles in the new spiritual temple. The fulfilling of God's word is not conditioned on their obedience but on their participation in that which He promises in conditional; they must accept and obey His word of truth. The New Covenant clearly reveals that this is what the prophet means.

Chapter 7

7:1-7. The question of fasting and Jehovah's answer: Hear the words of the prophets!

It was in the fourth year of Darius's reign, 518 B.C., when Zechariah comes forth with another recorded message, almost two years since he had received the eight night visions. The building of the temple seems to have been progressing favorably, and the prosperity promised by Jehovah was being enjoyed (cf. Hag. 2:19; Zech. 8:10-13). The silence of Zechariah concerning his work during this period is not to imply that he had been idle, for surely the people had needed encouragement all along; and no doubt he had supplied it. "The fourth day of the ninth month, even in Chislev," corresponded to our December/January.

7:1

Beth-el was the ancient site of calf worship introduced by Jeroboam I (I Kings 12:28-29), whose idolatrous altar had been destroyed by Josiah (II Kings 23:15). On their return from Babylon certain Jews had rebuilt and inhabited Beth-el, now a village (Ezra 2:28; Neh. 7:32). The people of Beth-el sent Sharezer and Regem-melech, "and their men, to entreat the favor of Jehovah." "Sharezer" is thought to have been an Assyrian name, which suggests that he was a Jew who had been born in either Assyria or Babylon. The embassy had been sent "to entreat the

7:2

7:3

favor of Jehovah," requesting information from the priests and prophets concerning fasting. Their question was, "Should I weep in the fifth month, separating myself, as I have done these so many years?" The use of the first person singular is used to include the inhabitants of Beth-el; such use of the singular to represent the whole is not uncommon. Weeping and separating themselves indicates fasting, which had been practiced for nearly seventy years. Now that they were back in their homeland and the temple was being rebuilt, should they continue this practice? The fast of the fifth month was in memory of the destruction of the temple by Nebuchadnezzar (II Kings 25:8 ff.; Jer. 52:12).

7:4

7:5

The reply of Jehovah was through the prophet Zechariah, to whom the word of Jehovah came, although He could have spoken through Haggai, and probably Malachi. The reply was blunt and was directed to "all the people of the land, and to the priests." It was a message that all needed; for those of Beth-el, as well as others, had kept the fasts out of a selfish motive. For nearly seventy years they had fasted and mourned in the fifth and seventh months, but "did ye at all fast unto me, even to me?" asked Jehovah. Jehovah had authorized only one fast in all the law, that of the Day of Atonement, a day in which they should afflict their souls. This fast of atonement was to be observed in the seventh month (Lev. 23:27), but the fast of the atonement is not the one now being kept. The one referred to by the prophet was in commemoration of the death of Gedaliah, the governor appointed by Nebuchadnezzar (Jer. 41:1 ff.). Other fasts kept by the Jews were in the fourth month, when a breach had been made in the walls of Jerusalem by Nebuchadnezzar (Jer. 52:6-7), and in the tenth month, when the siege against Jerusalem had begun (II Kings 25:1; Jer. 52:4; cf. Zech. 8:18-19). These fasts had not been authorized by Jehovah, but had grown out of their own

7:6

self-pity rather than from a consciousness of sin.

Not only had they fasted unto themselves, but when they had eaten and drunk, they had done this also unto themselves. They needed to learn that men could not win the favor of God either by fasting or by eating and drinking; neither then nor now can favor be won in this way. Jehovah's next question brings the real issue clearly into focus: "Should ye not hear the words which Jehovah cried by the former prophets, when Jerusalem was inhabited and in prosperity?" The people could have found the answer to their question in the word of those prophets before the captivity, for the word of Jehovah was not to that generation only but it was for all generations. "The word of our God shall stand for ever" had been the emphatic declaration of Isaiah (40:8). Had their fathers listened to Jehovah's word when Jerusalem was inhabited and in prosperity, there would have been no occasion to fast now; for the city would never have been destroyed. The prophet includes both Jerusalem and the cities round about; he also includes the Negeb, the southern semiarid land of ancient Simeon, and the "lowland" or Shephelah, the rolling hill country between the hills of Judah and the plain of Philistia. All would have continued if the people had listened to the word of Jehovah sent to them by His servants, the prophets.

7:7

7:8-14. The people had rejected the Lord's call to righteousness by former prophets, which had led to the destruction of their city and to their captivity.

A fuller answer is now given by Jehovah to their question of fasting. The reply is made in a continued appeal to what had been said by former prophets (vv. 7, 12), "Thus *hath* Jehovah of hosts *spoken*" (past tense). As Jehovah was saying now, so had He spoken through prophets before the exile. "Execute true judgment" or justice (cf. Jer. 7:5; Ezek. 18:8-9; Mic. 6:8); "show kindness and compassion" (cf. Hos. 6:6; Mic. 6:8); "oppress not the widow," fatherless, sojourner, or the poor (cf. Jer. 7:6); "and let none of you devise evil against his brother in your heart" (cf. Isa. 32:7; Mic. 2:1). All that Jehovah required then

7:8

7:9

7:10

7:11 He requires now, and what He requires now He had required then. Neither Jehovah nor His word has changed; both remain immutable. But they who lived before the captivity had refused to hearken; "they pulled away the shoulder"; that is, they turned a stubborn shoulder of rebellion to God's will as an ox that refuses to yield to the yoke. They had stopped their ears so they could not hear, as Jehovah had said to Isaiah they would (6:9-10). Their history had been one of rejection of and rebellion against their God.

7:12 Those outward acts of rebellion, transgression, and rejection had been the symptoms and expressions of a perverse heart. The Lord comes now to the seat of their trouble: "They made their hearts as an adamant stone." In preparing Ezekiel to meet the stubbornness of the Jews in Babylon, He had said, "As an adamant harder than flint have I made thy forehead" (3:9). It is thought that by "adamant" Jehovah referred to the diamond, harder than flint, by which engravings are made on flint. The hearts of the fathers had been harder than flint; they had been as an adamant stone. Because of this they were not able to "hear the law" in the sense of accepting and obeying it, nor could they hear the words which He sent "by his Spirit by the former prophets." In this word Zechariah identifies the law and the prophets as being from Jehovah,—"by his Spirit." All Scripture is God-breathed (II Tim. 3:16). Because of this hardness of heart and rejection of the law and the former prophets "came great wrath from Jehovah of hosts," the destruction of Jerusalem and the temple.

7:13 "And it is come to pass": the present condition is the inevitable consequence of their refusal to hear when Jehovah had called; for He had told them over and over if they would not hear when He was calling, He would not hear when calamity would come and they would call upon Him (Isa. 1:15; 59:2; Jer. 7:16; 11:14; Ezek. 8:18). From the time of Moses Jehovah 7:14 had told His people that when they forsook Him He would forsake and scatter them (Deut. 4:27; 28:64). Jehovah had now fulfilled these things which He had before declared. They had been cast out of their land

and scattered throughout the earth; their cities and temple had been destroyed; "the pleasant land," the land of their desire, had been left desolate for the seventy years according to Jeremiah's prophecy (25:11-12; 29:10; II Chron. 36:21). This places on the shoulders of the people the responsibility for the land's desolation. Jehovah had further fulfilled His word by bringing back the aforepromised remnant. Therefore, why fast over Jerusalem's destruction? Instead, do the will of Jehovah, which is what He has always wanted.

Chapter 8

8:1-8. Jehovah has returned to Zion and will carry out His purpose. He will gather His people to Himself in truth and in righteousness.

Chapter 8 contains the second part of Jehovah's answer to the ambassage from Beth-el concerning fasting. In chapter 7 the Lord had looked to the past and pointed out the cause for their fasting; sin on the part of the fathers who had refused to hear Jehovah had been the cause. In chapter 8 He looks to the future and announces what Jehovah proposes to do in fulfilling His purpose.

Twice the prophet says, "The word of Jehovah of 8:1 hosts came to me" (vv. 1, 18); and he emphasizes it by the formula, "Thus saith Jehovah of hosts." This latter expression is used ten times in introducing new thoughts or promises. Four times he says, "Saith Jehovah," making sixteen times in this chapter that 8:2 he appeals to Jehovah as the source of his message. Jehovah declares His great jealousy for Zion, which indicates His ardent love for His people. He can endure no slight on their part and can brook no rival. He is jealous with great wrath or fury; He will restore His people, dwell in their midst, fulfill His promises to them, and judge their adversaries.

Jehovah declares He has "returned unto Zion," His 8:3 chosen people and the place where He had recorded

His name. When the Jews had rejected Him before the destruction of Jerusalem, Ezekiel had seen in a vision the withdrawing of Jehovah from the city (9:3; 10:4, 19; 11:23). Jerusalem had now been purged by the "blast of justice, and by the blast of burning" (Isa. 4:4, margin, ASV), so that Jehovah could now return and dwell in the midst of it. Jerusalem would be called "the city of truth," or faithfulness or fidelity. The people of Jerusalem would be His people "in truth," faithfulness (v. 8), and would "execute the judgment of truth and peace" (v. 16). The lies of idolatry and heathen principles will have been abolished and the city purged of their impurity. The mountain of Jehovah's Zion would be called "the holy mountain"; for, set apart to Him, His presence would make it holy. There can be no doubt that the word had an immediate application; for Jehovah says, "I am returned unto Zion." But there is also no doubt that it looked to a fuller and more glorious fulfillment in the present Messianic period; for Jehovah had described it in the third vision as "a city without walls," with Jehovah Himself dwelling in its midst and as a wall of fire about it. It would be of sufficient size for a large company of inhabitants and their possessions (see 2:4-5).

8:4   In the midst of whatever discouragement and uncertainty of the future that may have gripped the people, Jehovah gives them a strong word of assurance. He assures the people that old men and old women will walk and sit in the streets of Jerusalem, enjoying a security that would extend to old age, even the age of using a staff for support. This picture of security and happy old age stands in contrast to

8:5   the times that had been until now. This idyllic scene is further enhanced by the delightful picture of streets filled with boys and girls playing together, unmolested and unafraid. Such a joyous and peaceful state had long been absent from the cities of Judea. However, it must ever be borne in mind that the fulfilling of such glorious promises as this was conditioned on the people's faithfulness to Jehovah (Deut. 4:40; Jer. 18:7-10).

Another word is announced as coming from 8:6
Jehovah, "If it be marvellous in the eyes of the
remnant of this people"—that is, if the promise just
made seems incredible to the remnant, the people
returned from captivity (for discussion of "the remnant" see comments, Hag. 1:12), or beyond any
power to fulfill—let them remember that it is Jehovah
who promises. Is there anything beyond His power to
accomplish? "Should it also be marvellous [difficult
or impossible to be done] in mine eyes? saith
Jehovah of hosts." Unbelief on the part of their
fathers had caused the city to be destroyed and the
people to go into captivity. Will unbelief again thwart
the purpose of God, make it impossible for Him to do
for His people what He desires to do?

Jehovah speaks again, making a threefold promise. 8:7
(1) He declares He will save His people "from the east
country, and from the west country"; He will be
continuing to save them. The two directions here
used by Jehovah indicate the whole world (see Isa.
11:11-12). (2) Having saved them, He "will bring 8:8
them, and they shall dwell in the midst of Jerusalem." This promise further confirms the conclusion
suggested in the comments on verse 3 that the Jerusalem under discussion looks beyond the literal city
in Palestine to a greater fulfillment. The ultimate
realization would be in the spiritual Jerusalem under
the Messiah (cf. Heb. 12:22; Gal. 4:26). (3) "And
they shall be my people, and I will be their God, in
truth and in righteousness." The relationship of
Jehovah with His people would be sustained only on
a basis of truth and righteousness. He would deal with
them on this basis, and their relation to Him would
be on the same basis. God would keep His part of the
covenant; they must keep theirs.

> 8:9-13. Jehovah now points to the present-
> day prophets and urges the people to hear
> them. In contrast to past scarcity, Jehovah
> promises a rich outpouring of blessings.

This is the sixth time the prophet uses the formula 8:9
"Thus saith Jehovah of hosts" to introduce his sub-

ject; there follows the lengthiest discussion of the ten. In contrast to the conduct of the fathers, he urges these whom he addresses, "Let your hands be strong, ye that hear in these days." The exhortation is to listen to what the present prophets, Haggai and Zechariah (Ezra 5:1), have to say and to *build the temple*. It was now eighteen years since the foundation had been laid by Zerubbabel and two years since building had been resumed under the preaching of Haggai and Zechariah. "These days" distinguishes

8:10 these two from the preexilic prophets. The prophet reminds the people that prior to work on the building two years ago there had been no hire for man or beast. This had been due to poor crops and lack of funds with which to pay (cf. Hag. 1:6, 10, 11; 2:15-19). Added to the poverty of those days there was lack of peace among them, for Jehovah had set neighbor against neighbor. Want and adversity had dogged their steps. It was now time to forget the fasts over a destroyed city and temple and to listen to prophets of Jehovah, to be strong, and to complete

8:11 the work begun. Jehovah promises that He will not be toward the remnant, those who had returned, as He had been "in the former days," the days between the return and laying the foundation, and the days since they began the work of completing the building. The curse that had rested on them would now be removed; "from this day will I bless you" (Hag. 2:19).

8:12 In contrast to the condition described above, there was no peace "because of the adversary" (v. 10); Jehovah declares that now "there shall be the seed of peace." Keil and others identify peace with the vine, making the passage read, "But the seed of peace, the vine, shall yield its fruit" (Keil), contending that it required a time of peace in which to cultivate and tend the vine. It seems preferable to interpret the words in the light of God's promise through Moses, "If ye walk in my statutes, and keep my commandments, and do them," followed by a rich promise of plenty from the field, the orchard, and the vineyard, "I will give peace in the land" (Lev. 26:3-6). Now that the people are listening to the word of the present-day prophets (v. 9), Jehovah can restore or give the seed of peace in the land, making it to grow and flourish, and can make the vine to give its fruit, the field its harvest, and the heaven its dew. He can now make His people to inherit all the things promised by Him through Moses.

Both Judah and Israel had been a curse among the nations, so now Jehovah includes the twelve tribes, "O house of Judah and house of Israel," among those whom Jehovah would save. God had promised that He would return the captivity of Israel and Judah and cause both houses to return to their land (Jer. 30:3). He had now fulfilled that promise as some from both houses had returned and were recipients of His gracious redemption. They had been a curse among the nations, having been "tossed to and fro among all the kingdoms of the earth for evil" (Jer. 24:9), fulfilling the imprecation of Jehovah through Moses (Lev. 26; Deut. 28). They would now be a blessing; they would "be in the midst of many peoples as dew from Jehovah, as showers upon the grass" (Mic. 5:7), bringing spiritual refreshing to a sin-parched and weary world. In the face of these promises, "Fear not, but let your hands be strong." 8:13

8:14-17. As Jehovah had fulfilled His word of wrath, so now He would fulfill His word of good.

Again the prophet begins with his familiar formula of assurance that the word he speaks is from Jehovah. That which Jehovah had said He would do to the fathers when they provoked Him, except they turn from their wicked ways, He had done, fulfilling His word. In contrast to His wrath poured out on the fathers, He thought now "in these days to do good unto Jerusalem and to the house of Judah." On the ground of God's keeping His word in fulfilling His threat, the people could rest assured He would keep His promise to do good and bless them. Before the exile Jehovah had rested His claim to solitary deity on the ground of His unique ability to foretell (Isa. 8:14

8:15

41–48). The predictions of wrath had been fulfilled; on that basis they should now believe the promises of blessing. Therefore, "Fear ye not." The very things the fathers had refused to do (7:9-11), Jehovah calls upon the remnant of "these days" (v. 9) to do. He sets two positive requirements over against two negative demands: (1) "Speak ye every man the truth with his neighbor," for Jehovah hates "a lying tongue . . . a false witness . . . and he that soweth discord among brethren" (Prov. 6:16-19); (2) "Execute the judgment of truth and peace in your gates"; that is, let all judgments determined "in the gate," the halls of justice, between man and man, be according to truth and to the end of maintaining peace. In contrast: (1) "Let none of you devise evil in your hearts against his neighbor," for this disposition to practice such evils had led to the exile of Judah and Israel (Mic. 2:1-3; Hos. 4:1-3); (2) "Love no false oath," an oath taken in the name of a false deity, or an oath taken which one does not intend to honor. "For all these are things that I hate, saith Jehovah." The first positive seems to be set over against the second negative, and the second positive over against the first negative. It is interesting to compare these with the curse written on the flying roll (4:3).

8:16

8:17

> *8:18-23. The answer is finally given to the question of fasting: God will turn their fasts into occasions of joy. Through the influence of this joy the Gentiles will seek the religion of the Jews.*

8:18
8:19

Once again the word comes to the prophet. The four fasts the Jews have been keeping in memory of Nebuchadnezzar's coming against Jerusalem (tenth month), of the breach made in the wall (fourth month), of the burning of the house of Jehovah (fifth month), and of the murder of Gedaliah (seventh month) (see comments, 7:5), "shall be to the house of Judah joy and gladness, and cheerful feasts." This answer indicates that the fasts had been neither pleasing nor displeasing to the Lord; they had been a matter of indifference. The sins that brought on the judgment had been displeasing to Him, and the righteousness He now demands will be pleasing to Him. Therefore, love truth and peace; for it is on this basis that Jehovah will turn their sadness to joy and their fasts to feasts of gladness.

This joy and gladness will so impress peoples from heathen nations and cities that they will say one to another, "Let us go speedily to entreat the favor of Jehovah." The expression "let us go speedily" indicates eagerness from within, prompted by an earnest desire "to entreat the favor of Jehovah," that they, too, may enjoy His wonderful blessings. Those designated as coming (vv. 20-21) are further described as "many peoples and strong nations," peoples who are strong in their desire for a fuller and richer spiritual life than they had found in their empty heathen religion. *8:20* *8:21* *8:22*

"Ten men" indicates a full or complete number, a large number (cf. Gen. 31:7; Num. 14:22; Neh. 4:12; Job 19:3; Dan. 1:20). "Out of all the languages of the nations" indicates that diversity of languages, which hinders unity among men, will be overlooked as these press themselves upon "him that is a Jew," seeking to worship God with him. The Jew, once a curse, a byword and despised by all, would be sought after as a means of reaching God. *8:23*

One may ask, "When was this fulfilled?" It would be futile to point to any one time. More and more pagans came to recognize the emptiness of their idolatry and turned to Jehovah; Cornelius and his household are excellent examples (Acts 10–11). Paul found worthy subjects for the gospel among men of "understanding" (Acts 13:7), and "devout Greeks" and "chief women" who attended the synagogue (Acts 17:4). These had been prepared in heart to give a ready ear to the truth of the gospel. The seeking after the Lord by the people of all nations found its complete fulfillment in Christ.

Chapter 9

The third division of Zechariah (chs. 9—14) consists of two "burdens," chapters 9—11 and 12—14. Each is introduced by the title, "The burden of the word of Jehovah"; the first is pronounced upon the heathen and the second concerns Israel. It was suggested in the Introduction that trying times were probably upon the little community of Judea and that the prophet, now an old man, comes forth once more to comfort his people. There were probably disappointments in the events that followed the completion of the temple. Gentiles had not flocked to the remnant as they had hoped, and no doubt the later Persian rulers had not been so considerate of them as had Cyrus and Darius I. The people needed another word of encouragement, which Jehovah uses Zechariah to supply.

In the first part of this third division (chs. 9—11), the prophet deals with the fall of the heathen nations and the coming of the King who would rule in peace. But when He would come, He would be rejected as a shepherd despised and cast away, to be sold for the paltry price of a wounded slave.

The second part (chs 12—14) presents in further detail the rejection of the shepherd and the victory of the kingdom of God in spite of His having been refused. Zechariah points to the passing of the antiquated order, typified in the ancient city of Jerusalem, and to the holiness of all that would pertain to the new. Everything will be holiness to the Lord.

Both sections are interspersed with prophecies of the Messiah, which are quoted in the New Testament and applied to the Christ who came. In view of the admitted difficulty of these chapters, and in the light of Peter's claim that no prophecy of Scripture is of private interpretation, "For no prophecy ever came by the will of man: but men spake from God, being moved by the Holy Spirit" (II Pet. 1:20 ff.), it seems wise to build one's interpretation of these chapters around the passages that are quoted by Jesus and the New Testament writers. In following this policy one will avoid the pitfalls of speculation and some of the quagmires of error into which many have fallen. In the comments that follow, this policy of appealing to the use made of quotations from Zechariah by the Holy Spirit in the New Testament will be adhered to so far as is possible.

> *9:1-7. The "burden" of Jehovah is pronounced upon the heathen nations which were neighbors to Israel. These would be dispossessed by the Lord, but a remnant from among them would become His.*

For a discussion of the word "burden" see comments on Nahum 1:1. Hengstenberg says the word is "restricted to a denunciatory character" (*Christology*). "Hadrach," found only here in Scripture, is listed with Damascus. Older commentators found great difficulty with the word. Modern archaeologists identify it with the "Hatarikka" of the Assyrian inscriptions, against whom Assur-dan III made expeditions. It also appears in the inscriptions of Tiglath-pileser III. These inscriptions place it north of Lebanon (*I.S.B.E.,* p. 1316), but this is not yet definitely established. Keil concludes from the meaning of the word, "sharp-soft, or strong-tender," that it is used symbolically of the Medo-Persian Empire. This nation had been strong in conquest and in the building of the empire, but it became soft through its later effeminate rulers. Leupold concurs in this interpretation. If this is correct, then the places mentioned in the text would all share in the judgment announced upon the empire. From Hadrach the burden of Jehovah's wrath would light on Damascus and there it would settle permanently. It is well to bear in mind that when Jehovah announces a judgment against a world power, He is acting according to the principle of His divine character. One may therefore look for fuller or broader application of the judgment. If the text (ASV) is the correct translation, then the prophet is saying that the eye of both the heathen and Israel is looking with interest and amazement at what Jehovah does. But if

9:1

the alternate reading (margin, ASV), which is identical with Keil's translation, "Jehovah hath an eye upon men and upon all the tribes of Israel," is correct, then the prophet is saying that Jehovah watches over the heathen and the people of Israel and will fulfill His judgment upon one and His blessing upon the other. This appears more consistent with the

9:2   entire burden. Hamath, whose territory borders that of Damascus, was located on the Orontes; it had been the gate of entrance into Canaan by nations from the north. Tyre and Sidon, chief cities of Phoenicia, are also included in the oracle. Sidon was the older of the two cities, but Tyre had far outstripped her elder sister in importance, thereby becoming the capital of Phoenicia. Both were wise to the things of the world, but in spite of their wisdom they would both come under judgment.

9:3   Tyre had demonstrated her wisdom in building a stronghold on an island about a half mile offshore from the mainland city and in turning to the sea where she established herself as a great commercial power. She had "heaped up silver as the dust, and fine gold as the mire of the streets." This extravagant hyperbole suggests the magnitude of her wealth accumulated through the wisdom exercised in trade.

9:4   "Behold, the Lord will dispossess her," impoverish the nation represented by Tyre and bring to nothing her great wealth and power. Her power in the sea would be destroyed. Ezekiel pictures Tyre as a beautiful ship made of fir-wood planks with a mast from a cedar of Lebanon, sails of the linen of Egypt, and oars of the oaks of Bashan. The benches of the ship were of boxwood, inlaid with ivory; her wise men were her pilots and calkers, and the citizens of neighboring cities were the oarsmen. But the ship with all its glory and beauty would go down in the midst of the sea (Ezek. 27). Added to this destruction of power in the sea, the city would be burned with fire. Nebuchadnezzar had attempted the destruction of Tyre, but he had failed. After seventy years she had resumed her trade (Isa. 23:15-17). It was left for Alexander of Macedonia to complete the fulfillment of both Ezekiel's and Zechariah's prophecies. When the citizens of Tyre refused to yield to Alexander's demands to submit, he built a two hundred-foot-wide mole from the mainland to the island. The construction required seven months of hard labor under the most adverse circumstances; but when it was completed, Alexander's catapults and ship-borne battering rams were able to breach the south wall, gaining entrance into the city. Like others before it, the city fell to the Macedonians. The city never recovered from the Macedonian assault; it became a place for fishermen to dry their nets (Ezek. 26:5).

The prophet passes from the destruction of the *9:5* two chief cities of Phoenicia to the four cities of Philistia, the ancient enemy of Israel. With the fall of Tyre and Sidon, fear grips the inhabitants of Ashkelon; Gaza is sore pained at what she may expect, for her king will perish from her; no more will one of her own rule in the city. Ekron may expect to be put to shame as she is humbled before the conqueror. Ashkelon will come to an end; she will not be inhabited. Ashdod will lose its own native population; "a *9:6* bastard" will dwell there. The word is found only here and in Deuteronomy 23:2. It means a stranger, or one of illegitimate parentage, born out of wedlock or of an incestuous relation. The word may also indicate a rabble or those of a low station in society. Such a race would inhabit the site of this once proud city; the pride of the Philistines would now be cut off.

To "take away his blood out of his mouth, and his *9:7* abominations from between his teeth" would be to abolish completely the idolatry and its consequent worship practiced by the cities of Philistia. These would be completely rooted out. "And he," Ashdod, as he personified the people of all four cities, "shall be a remnant for our God." As from among Israel and Judah there would be a residue, so also from among the Philistines there would be a remnant unto Jehovah. By New Testament times or shortly thereafter, Philistia had lost its identity. "He shall be as a chieftain in Judah" seems to point to the Philistines' being accepted into the commonwealth of God's people, sharing the rule with them. "And Ekron as a Jebusite" points to the original inhabitants of Jerusalem; some of them, as Araunah, had become faithful citizens under David's rule (cf. II Sam. 24:23 ff.). The prophecy looks to the common lot shared by the Philistines and the dwellers in Jerusalem. A historical fulfillment of the prophecy is unknown. Although Alexander of Macedonia conquered these cities, there was no general turning by them to God or to the Jews. The fulfillment of the prediction may be looked for under the Messiah when the gospel was preached to all, and all stood on a common level before Jehovah.

> 9:8-10. Over against this judgment of the heathen, Jehovah will establish His kingdom and enthrone His King. Both the King and the nature of His rule will be in contrast to the heathen rulers.

9:8   While the judgment of Jehovah is being brought against the heathen nations and they are being brought to an end, Jehovah will protect His people. "My house" does not refer to the temple, but to Israel, His family. Egypt, Assyria, Chaldea, and Persia had all oppressed them. And now Alexander the Great would invade the land, conquer the people, and impose the Grecian culture, philosophy, and religion upon them; but Jehovah would encamp about His people and through them fulfill His purpose. Jehovah had seen with His own eyes the oppression of the great heathen powers; but now no more would such nations pass through to thwart His purpose; it would be fulfilled in the Messiah.

9:9   The "daughter of Zion" and "daughter of Jerusalem," which expressions personify the individuals faithful to Jehovah and hopeful of deliverance, are exhorted to "rejoice" and "shout." Let these exult, for their long expected King is coming to Zion. This can look only to the Messiah's coming; there is no individual whom the higher critics have been able even plausibly to substitute. "He is just" describes not only His personal character but also the character of His rule. He would be "one that ruleth righteously, that ruleth in the fear of God" (II Sam. 23:3; cf. also Isa. 11:1-5; Jer. 23:5-6; 33:15-16; and others). He would come bringing the full and complete salvation which Jehovah had promised so profusely through Isaiah. The King is further described as "lowly," whose lowliness is emphasized by His entering the city riding on an unbroken colt of an ass. This does not indicate the peaceful nature of His reign, but the lowliness of it in opposition to the pride and pomp of worldly kings. Since the days of Solomon, royal persons had ridden upon horses; but the character of the Messiah's kingship would be completely different. This difference in character would be demonstrated by His humble entrance upon His rule.

The character of the Messiah's rule and kingdom is   *9:10* next described. The cutting off of the chariot and the horse, and the breaking of the battle bow, indicate the complete rejection of all carnal means in securing and defending His government (see also Hos. 14:3; Mic. 5:10). It would not be established, defended, or extended by methods of force. "Ephraim," which personified the ten tribes, and "Jerusalem," the capital of Judah and originally of the complete nation, would now be one under the reign of the Messiah. His message would be one of "peace unto the nations," the heathen people, who would be included with Ephraim and Judah. This was the message of Christ through the gospel to both Jews and Gentiles (Eph. 2:17). The extent of His reign would not be limited to that of the ancient promise (Gen. 15:18-20; Num. 34:1-15); but it would be "from sea to sea, and from the River [the Euphrates] unto the ends of the earth" (Ps. 72:8; cf. also Amos 8:12 and Mic. 7:12), which would be from the sea to the other side of the world where the sea would begin again—that is to say, worldwide. All four Gospel writers include Jesus' entry into Jerusalem in the manner foretold by Zechariah (Matt. 21:1-11; Mark 11:1-10; Luke 19:29-38; John 12:13-19), although only Matthew and John refer specifically to the words of the prophet. This entry of Jesus into Jerusalem among the "hosannas" of the multitude marked the beginning of His passion, which culminated in His being crowned King over God's kingdom, to reign at His right hand till the end of time.

9:11-17. The people of Zion will be redeemed from the pit—captivity—and will war triumphantly against their enemies. They will attain to the highest peak of honor.

9:11   "As for thee also" is addressed to the daughter of Zion or Jerusalem (cf. v. 9), all of Israel, including Ephraim and Judah (cf. v. 10). Israel and Judah had been one when Jehovah made a covenant with them at Sinai and dedicated it with blood (Exod. 24:8). And now, "because of the blood of thy covenant," the covenant made with both, Jehovah would set free as one the prisoners of each branch of the family. The "prisoners" were those yet in foreign countries, apart from God and in bondage to foreigners and to their sins. The "pit" signifies their imprisonment as one put in an empty cistern, as were Joseph (Gen. 37:22) and Jeremiah (Jer. 38:6). These pits or cisterns were bottle shaped with small openings from which one could not free himself, but could be released only by **9:12**   the help of another. "Turn you to the stronghold" is an urgent exhortation to those separated from God to return to Zion, Jehovah's stronghold, wherein alone is safety and protection. "Ye prisoners of hope" were those yet separated from the stronghold but who continued to hold fast their hope in Jehovah and in the redemption He had promised. Pusey says this is the only place where "hope" has the article, "*the* hope"; therefore he identifies the hope with that preached by Paul (Acts 28:20; 26:6-7; etc.). However, the first interpretation is probably correct. The Lord declares that He "will render double unto thee," the remnant who returned to Zion. The expression "render double" is used by Isaiah of Jerusalem's sins and their punishment (40:2); instead of shame they would have a double portion of joy or blessing

(61:7). Most commentators think Isaiah and Zechariah speak of double blessing for the punishment or shame endured. But in the light of John's use of the same expression in Revelation (18:6-7a), it would seem more probable that the "double" indicates a balancing of the scales; their sins have received commensurate punishment, and the punishment would receive commensurate blessings. A pound on one side of the scale is balanced by a pound on the other, making the double.

Jehovah reveals Himself as a mighty warrior, using as weapons of His warfare Judah as His bow and Ephraim as His arrow. The figure does not indicate that the two branches of the family are separate, but that they are one as a bow and arrow are one. It seems clear that Jehovah here speaks of the Grecian invasion under Alexander and the conditions that followed in the days of the Maccabees and even in the time of the Messiah. Alexander was a devoted apostle of Greek culture and philosophy, and his zeal left an indelible impression on all the countries of his invasion and an impression of special significance on the Jews. Many younger Jews left the orthodox faith for Hellenism or for a compromise with it. God would stir up the sons of Zion "as the sword of a mighty man" against the sons of Greece. This religious, cultural, and social difference broke out in violent conflict under the Seleucids of Syria and the Maccabees of Judea. It was a conflict of ideologies and religion. Jehovah promised to be "seen over them," the sons of Zion, as a protecting cover. He would manifest Himself by giving them victory. In strong similes Jehovah speaks of His arrow going forth as the lightning (cf. Ps. 45:5; Hab. 3:9, 11), of Himself blowing the trumpet of war as He leads them into battle, and of His going forth with whirlwinds of the south. These fierce storms from the south, coming as tornados, swept everything before them with a violent destruction (cf. Isa. 21:1; Amos 1:14). "Jehovah of hosts," the God of battles, will defend them, the sons of Zion. Many of the victories achieved by the Maccabees seem almost to demand a divine providential

9:13

9:14

9:15

directing or intervention. As a lion, they would devour and destroy their enemies, "and shall tread down the sling-stones," either the spent missiles fired against them, which they trampled underfoot, or the sons of Greece themselves who were helpless against the sons of Zion. A stronger simile follows: "and they shall drink, and make a noise as through wine." They would, in a figure, drink the blood of the slain; and in their exuberance of victory they would shout as men stimulated by wine. As the bowls of the altar were filled with the blood of the sacrificed animal, to be splashed (sprinkled) against the sides of the altar, so they would be filled with the blood of victory. Deane suggests that this may indicate a sacred war and that these slain were as sacrifices to Jehovah. Primarily, it indicates a hard-fought but victorious war between the forces of Jehovah and those of the world.

9:16   Their salvation would be of Jehovah, for it was He who would save them as a shepherd rescues and saves his flock. In contrast to the sling-stones trodden underfoot (v. 15), Jehovah's "sons of Zion" would be as the stones of a crown, sparkling and glittering in the brilliance of their glory. This brilliance "over his land" must not be limited to the Maccabean victory and the land of Judea but must include the victory over the Greek philosophy and religion through the Messiah as He leads His faithful followers (9:9-10). This is indicated by what follows. The exclamation at the sight of "his goodness" (or prosperity, margin, 9:17   ASV) and beauty refers not to Jehovah but to the prosperous state of His people. The grain will give strength to the young men, and new wine will give beauty and charm to the young women. The picture is one of prosperity, plenty, and increase. Whether this was ever fulfilled materially is unknown, but it was gloriously fulfilled spiritually in the victorious kingdom of the Lord. Hellenistic philosophy and religion went down in an inglorious defeat under the King of Jehovah's coronation, and spiritual fulness and completeness have been abundantly provided to His people.

Chapter 10

*10:1-7. All blessings are of Jehovah; the idols
can lead only to falsehood and false hope.*

There seem to be no new promises in chapter 10,   *10:1*
but it appears that the chapter is an enlarging or
expounding of those in chapter 9. The prophet continues the concluding promise of prosperity and plenty (9:17) by an exhortation to the people of God to
ask Jehovah for the blessings needed and to pray to
Him. They should ask for "the latter rain," the spring
rains before harvest, so essential to the development
of the grain. Jehovah, "that maketh lightnings" which
accompany the rainfall, will give the showers that
make for a harvest for man and beast. Even though
God promises man his daily bread, prayer to the Lord
for all blessings is an acknowledgment on man's part
of his dependence on a higher power for all he receives. In contrast to Jehovah's disposition and power   *10:2*
to provide, the idols can neither promise nor provide
anything; they are utterly false. Although the remnant had returned from Babylon, where they were in
captivity as a result of idolatry, they were yet subject
to the temptation of lies. The prophet deals with
three sources of false guidance: (1) the "teraphim,"
thought to have been household gods ranging in size
from those small enough to be carried on one's person (Gen. 31:19, 34) to the size of a man (I Sam.
19:13), revealed nothing; (2) the "diviners" pre-
tended to reveal the future, but these likewise saw
only a lie; Jehovah "frustrateth the signs of the liars,
and maketh diviners mad" (Isa. 44:25); (3) the false
dreamers only added to the confusion; they comfort
in vain, for their dreams are not from Jehovah but
from themselves. Because they had hearkened to
these, Israel had gone into captivity, been afflicted,
and were as sheep without a shepherd; for their king
had been cast out. When they rejected Jehovah for
falsehood and lies they were left with neither a king
to whom they could look, nor with an almighty God
on whom they could lean.

10:3   With the rejection of Jehovah by the nation and His casting off their king, the people were left at the mercy of foreign rulers. Jehovah's anger is now "kindled against the shepherds," the kings of the nations; and He will "punish the he-goats," another name for the leading men or shepherds of the heathen oppressors. He is ready to visit His flock, "the house of Judah," which is not the temple, but the people of Judah and Israel whom He claims as His own. Jehovah will not only visit and deliver His people, but He will use the delivered flock "as his goodly horse in the battle." He had earlier referred to Judah and Ephraim as His bow and arrow, the weapons of His war against Greece (9:13); He now speaks of them as His goodly charger in the battle. (For a glowing and stirring description of the war horse, see Job 39:19-25.)

10:4   "From him" refers to Judah, not to Jehovah; for out from Judah would come the "corner-stone" of the new edifice Jehovah was to build. The cornerstone is a stone placed at the angle where two walls of a building meet or are joined together. Christ is spoken of as "the chief corner stone" in the foundation laid by the apostles and prophets (Eph. 2:20). The "nail" or preferably, peg, was driven into the wall of the house to hang household utensils or clothing on. It here indicates one who can be depended on to uphold and support the laws of the constitution (cf. Isa. 22:23-24). And from him will come "the battle bow," and "every ruler" or exactor, everything necessary to withstand all enemy attacks; these will be provided by Jehovah through Judah.

10:5   Thus thoroughly equipped, Judah and Ephraim, now one, will be as "mighty men, treading down their enemies in the mire of the streets in the battle." In the power of Jehovah they will overcome all enemies. The source of their strength is Jehovah, for "Jehovah is with them." The strongly equipped cavalry of their enemies, "the riders on horses," will be confounded; for they will find themselves defeated on every hand and in every conflict. Not only will the hand of Judah

10:6   be strengthened, but "the house of Joseph," Ephraim, who stood for the ten tribes of Israel, will share in the salvation and victories of Jehovah. Jehovah had repeatedly promised that both Judah and Israel would return from captivity to their land (Jer. 30:3; Ezek. 37:11, 16, 17-21), from which captivity some of Israel did return (Ezra 2:70; 6:17, 21). Although not a great number of the house of Joseph returned, it is said of those who did return that Jehovah would "cause them to dwell" (margin, ASV), make them to share as heroes with Judah; for they would share equally in the redemptive mercy. In this redemption Ephraim would be as if he had never been cut off, because Jehovah is their God as He is the God of Judah. Because of His mercy and because they had once been His, He would hear them when they called.

Although from Judah would be the cornerstone, the peg, the battle bow, and every ruler (v. 4), Jehovah gives Ephraim further assurance that they of the northern tribes would not be neglected. They, too, would "be like a mighty man," thoroughly capable of casting off and defeating their enemies. And as men exhilarated through wine, they would rejoice. They would cheerfully and courageously face battle, and this same courage would be shared by their children. Their victory and rejoicing would be through Jehovah. *10:7*

The question arises as to whether these promises are limited to the Maccabean struggle, or whether they have a more far-reaching implication. True, Jehovah gave some great victories to the people through the Maccabean leadership, but to limit the prophecies to that particular period is to do violence to the general nature of prophecy. Often the prophet is laying down general principles of God's divine government and leadership. Prophecies such as these have been carried out many times when the Lord's people would return to Him, look to Him for help, and in the strength of the Lord wage their battles. However, for the ultimate and complete fulfillment of the prophecy one must look to the Messianic age when Judah and Ephraim were joined together in a spiritual union, fighting a spiritual warfare.

10:8-12. Jehovah will call for His scattered people and from all directions will they return to Him. He will dry up the source of their affliction, and in the strength of their Lord will they be secure.

10:8
Ephraim is yet before the mind of Jehovah; He would allure them to Himself. "I will hiss," whistle or make a tinkling sound to them as when bees are allured to swarm or called to the hive; by this they will be drawn to Him. The same provision made for Judah's redemption will have been made for Ephraim's; both would be redeemed from their captors and both would be redeemed in the Messiah. Their response would be such "that they shall be as many as they ever have been" (Mitchell). As they had increased in Egypt, so would they increase again. Inasmuch as Ephraim (Israel) had become "not my people," and I, Jehovah, "not your God" (Hos. 1:9), it is thought by some that Ephraim may here represent the Gentiles or at least be used to include them. Not only would those brought back with Judah from the captivity be Jehovah's but from among distant nations He would call those both of the scattered ten tribes and of the Gentiles to Himself. Paul's use of Hosea to include the Gentiles may further indicate this (Rom. 9:24-26).

10:9
Jehovah's sowing Ephraim does not here indicate a further scattering of them, but a sowing or planting of them to Himself, as indicated by Hosea (2:23). Thus sown to Jehovah among the nations, the people would increase, remember Jehovah, and with their children return to Him and worship Him, thus becom-

10:10
ing a witness for the Lord. Jehovah will again bring them out of the land of Egypt and Assyria, each a type of Ephraim's captivity (see Hos. 9:3; 11:11). The lands of Gilead and Lebanon were the northern sections of the ten tribes' territory; Gilead was east of Jordan and Lebanon was west and north of Jordan. But as Egypt and Assyria symbolized the bondage and captivity of the people, so Gilead and Lebanon seem to symbolize the restoration to their proper

habitation; for the prophet continues, "and place shall not be found for them." Original Canaan would be inadequate for these, as Isaiah had earlier prophesied that the redeemed who returned to Zion would say, "The place is too strait for me; give me place that I may dwell" (Isa. 49:19-20).

Jehovah will pass "through the sea of affliction"— *10:11* that is, "the sea, which is affliction" (Deane). As He had passed through the sea with His people in delivering them from their bondage in Egypt, while their enemies had perished, so once again would He be with them. He would dry up "the Nile," the source of Egypt's life, which would bring to an end the sceptre of Egypt's power. At the same time He would bring down the pride of Assyria, bringing to an end the two powers, symbolic of all the powers which sought Ephraim's bondage and destruction. At the same time *10:12* that Jehovah destroys these two great world powers, emblematic of all world powers, He will strengthen the redeemed of Ephraim. These redeemed will live in the strength of Jehovah's name, whose name stands for all that He is.

Chapter 11

11:1-3. A lamentation over the humiliated and devastated land, for its glory is departed.

Lebanon is called upon to open its doors that the *11:1* fire may devour its cedars. Lebanon had long stood as the northern entrance to the land of Jehovah's people and the way through which the destroyers had come. The cedars of Lebanon had been prized by ancient kings for building palaces and temples. From there Solomon had imported material for his temple: cedar for the walls and fir (or cypress) for the floors (I Kings 6:8-9, 15). With the fall of the greater, the *11:2* cedars, the lesser, the fir-tree (or cypress), is called upon to wail. Likewise the majestic oaks of Bashan, east of the Jordan, also are to wail, for they will suffer the same fate. The "strong forest" is that of Lebanon, which Leupold translates, "the impenetrable forest"; the greatest and the great will be brought down.

11:3   A voice of wailing or howling is heard among the shepherds, "for their glory is destroyed." When fire devours the pasture land, gloom descends on the shepherds; so, with the destruction of that which is majestic and great in a land, the rulers lament and wail; for that wherein they gloried is taken away. "The pride of the Jordan" was the thickets or reeds which grew luxuriantly on the east and west sides of the Jordan south of Galilee. Lions, no longer found in the Jordan valley, inhabited these thickets in seemingly great numbers in ancient times. From Lebanon to Bashan to the Jordan, judgment and destruction would come.

There can be no denying that the picture of these three verses presents a devastating judgment upon a land. But upon what land was the judgment to come? Mitchell thinks the punishment of Syria and Egypt are represented by the cedars and oaks. Farrar, who considers the chapters to have been written before the captivity, suggests the invasion of Tiglath-pileser as the occasion. But in the light of the context— chapter 10 and the remainder of chapter 11— it seems that the prophet is looking to the complete destruction of the Jewish economy. Jehovah called to the people to return to Him and to their homeland. A remnant responded whom He blessed. However, the old order was to pass away. Therefore, when He sent His Shepherd to them (11:4 ff.) and they rejected Him, the Romans were brought against the land; and all that was lofty, great, and meaningful to the Jews was destroyed. The picture points to the final judgment upon the political and religious Jewish system effected by the Roman legions, A.D. 70.

11:4-14. The symbolic action of the shepherd: the shepherd was rejected and sold for the price of a wounded slave; whereupon the people were rejected by Jehovah.

Jehovah puts the prophet in the role of a shepherd   *11:4*
with the instruction, "Feed the flock of slaughter."
This poses the question as to whether this was a
vision or an action to be carried out by the prophet.
Illustrations of both abound in the prophets. Jeremiah was told to take the cup of the wine of Jehovah's wrath and make all the nations to drink of it
(25:15-17). This is considered to have been a vision
to the prophet. On the other hand, Ezekiel enacted
before the people many of Jehovah's instructions—
for example, eating food by weight and drinking
water by measure (4:10, 11), digging through the wall
of his house and departing into the night (12:4-6),
and others. In this instance Zechariah probably exercised some kind of action, symbolic of the message
taught. "The flock of slaughter" are the people being
destroyed by their "possessors" or masters, those
who ruled over them. These who oppressed the flock,   *11:5*
making themselves rich by their oppression, tried to
offset their wicked conduct and inhumane treatment
of the people by claiming that Jehovah had favored
them and that, therefore, they were not guilty. The
shepherds were the foreign rulers to whom the flock
of Israel were subject. These showed no pity on their
poor subjects; they were concerned only for their
own wealth.

"The inhabitants of the land" seems better to be   *11:6*
translated "the inhabitants of the earth"; for upon
these, the inhabitants of the earth, Jehovah would
show no pity. These of the earth will be delivered
into the hand of their heathen fellows; God will use
world powers to destroy world powers. He will not
deliver one power out of the hand of another. This
reciprocal destruction will be by Jehovah's direction.

The "flock of slaughter" was transferred to the   *11:7*
prophet's care; he carried out the instruction of verse
4, feeding them as a good shepherd. He fed not only
the average of the flock, but also the poor or more
wretched or small among them, those who most needed his care. The prophet provided for his use two
shepherd staves by which to feed them: one he called

"Beauty," "Graciousness," or "Favor," which indicated that Jehovah's favor would be bestowed upon them. The other he called "Bands" or "Binders," indicating the unity or brotherhood between Judah and Israel; this was something that had long been needed but was lacking.

11:8   "I cut off the three shepherds in one month" has occasioned no little trouble among expositors. Leupold says that at least forty different explanations have been offered. Whether these were kings, priests, and prophets of Israel (Laetsch), or "heathen liegelords of the covenant nation" (Keil), or burgers, sellers, and pitiless shepherds (v. 5) (Deane), or undershepherds of the prophets who failed to measure up to their duties (Leupold), we do not know. Leupold's suggestion is the most reasonable. The shepherd simply dismissed those who did not conform to his standard, and this he did in a brief space of time. According to the pragmatical construction of the clause, "for my soul was weary of them, and their soul also loathed me," it is claimed that the prophet refers not to the three shepherds, but to the people (Deane, Keil, Leupold, et al.). He was righteously disgusted with them, and they loathed him.

11:9   With this display of their attitude toward the prophet-shepherd, which constituted a rejection of what Jehovah was doing for them, the prophet gives them up to their fate. Three scourges by which they will be consumed are probably indicated: pestilence,

11:10   sword, and famine. As a sign of this the prophet broke the staff "Beauty" or "Graciousness," indicating that Jehovah's favor would be taken away. This He did that He could break the covenant He "had made with all the peoples." The "covenant" was the restriction God had laid on the nations that they should not hurt nor destroy His people. With this restriction removed and the graciousness of Jehovah taken away, the flock would be at the mercy of the nations. Although history has no record of a covenant made with the nations, in speaking of the earth and of the judgment coming upon its inhabitants Isaiah said, "They have transgressed the laws, violated the statutes, broken the everlasting covenant" (24:5). Such a covenant may be compared to Jehovah's "league with the stones of the field" (Job 5:23).

Jehovah's work was not completely in vain; for *11:11* when this staff was broken and Jehovah's favor taken from them, the poor of the flock who had given heed to the message knew that it was the word of Jehovah. The affliction of Israel was not by chance but had come by the chastening hand of the Lord in an effort to save His people. The great bulk of the nation gave no heed, but there were always a few who listened.

With this part of his work done, the shepherd seeks *11:12* an evaluation of the people's estimate of his work: "If ye think good, give me my hire; and if not, forbear." Unlike the false shepherds, this shepherd does not demand or threaten; he leaves the question of the value of his work for them to decide. As a token of their contempt for his service, they weighed for his hire thirty pieces of silver, the price of a servant gored by an ox! (Exod. 21:32). This was nothing short of willful and intentional insult. The insult was not simply to the shepherd; it was an insult *11:13* to Jehovah and an expression of contempt for all He had done for them. His graciousness had been despised. Jehovah takes the insult as personal, as their rejection of Him. "Cast it unto the potter" has been subjected to many interpretations, none of which has been completely satisfactory. The interpretation yielding the most likely explanation is that it was proverbial, indicating utter worthlessness,—"fling it away"—although there is no other instance of such use. Other expressions of similar nature are "give it to the dogs," and "cast it to the moles and to the bats," as found in Scripture. The Lord's contempt for their disposition is revealed in the strongly ironical word, "the *goodly* [splendid!] price that I was prized at by them." The prophet obeyed, casting it to the potter "in the house of Jehovah." The casting away of the paltry price at which Jehovah had been prized was done publicly, before the Lord, that both He and the people could be witness to the insult thrust on Him and that He could bring them to account for their deed.

11:14   A second symbolic act by Jehovah, the breaking of the staff, "Bands," leaves the people not only without His favor, but to be devoured from within without fraternal bands to hold them together. As they had rejected Him, He now rejects them. No longer will He seek to hold the nations united as one.

These acts of the prophet as a shepherd teach symbolically that Jehovah had led, fed, and cared for Israel, the sheep of His pasture, only to be rejected and insulted. He had been forced to take away from them His favor and to give them up to dissolution and destruction as a brotherhood; this was fulfilled through the years that followed. But equally as great was the prophetic instruction in these acts. When God sent His Son to the people, as "the good shepherd," bestowing the bountiful favor of God on them, they likewise rejected Him, placing on Him an equal value of thirty pieces of silver, the price of a gored slave. With this money, which Judas in remorse and grief cast at the feet of the priests, they bought a potter's field in which to bury strangers. Israel's contempt for Jehovah was repeated in the contempt of their children for His Son.

A word needs to be said about the prophecy's having been ascribed by Matthew to Jeremiah instead of Zechariah (Matt. 27:9). Various attempts have been made to explain why this name appears in Matthew's account. Two seem the most plausible: (1) The two names being similar in appearance, an early copyist of Matthew's Gospel transcribed the wrong word. (2) Another explanation accepted by many is that the Book of Zechariah was part of a roll headed by Jeremiah's work, which roll was referred to by the title "Jeremiah," and that the evangelist so referred to it. At the present there is no absolute answer to the problem. Believers in the inspiration of Scripture reject the theory that the use of Jeremiah instead of Zechariah was due to a lapse of memory on Matthew's part.

11:15-17. Having rejected the true shepherd, the house of Israel was given into the hand of a foolish or worthless shepherd. In the hand of such they have been ever since.

The prophet is instructed to take the instruments *11:15* of an evil shepherd, a foolish one who is selfish, seeking honors and glory to himself. The instruments of a shepherd were a staff and bag (I Sam. 17:40) and a pipe (Judg. 5:16). Whether there was any difference between those of the true shepherd and the foolish is unknown. The point here is that the shepherd was to act foolishly, play the part of a fool. Jehovah says He *11:16* will raise up a shepherd "in the land," who will not care for the sheep, but for himself. Opinions differ as to who this shepherd was. A few suggestions offered are that he was "the antichrist, the man of sin . . . the head of the Roman papacy" (Laetsch), "the Roman Empire into whose hand Israel was given up" (Keil), "the Anti-Christ" (Pusey), "probably Ptolemy IV (Philo-pater)" (Mitchell), "the native chiefs and rulers ('in the land') who arose in later times—monsters like Herod . . . hirelings who made merchandise of the flocks . . . and deceived the people to their own destruction" (Deane), "the type of leader Israel will have if they reject Jehovah" (Leupold). The ideas expressed by Deane and Leupold appear more consistent with the entire chapter. These will have no interest in the people to visit those cut off, seek the scattered, nor heal those who are wounded. They will not even look after the sound, those who require very little care. Instead, they will feed themselves at the expense of the sheep, even tearing their hoofs in pieces. This latter expresses either the tearing apart of the hoofs to get the last remnant of flesh (Leupold), or the tearing of them by driving them over sharp, rocky ground, not caring what may result (Deane). The picture is one of utter indifference for those under the shepherd, except for what he can get from them.

Through the prophet Jehovah pronounces a strong- *11:17* ly denunciatory woe upon such a character. As through Habakkuk Jehovah pronounced five woes upon the Chaldean invader and by them expressed a universal condemnation upon any such ruler, so now His woe upon the foolish shepherd states a principle applicable to all such overlords. The arm of the shepherd that should have been protecting the flock, but did not, will have the sword fall upon his own arm; it "shall be clean dried up." The eye that should have kept watch over the flock, but failed, will "be utterly darkened," blinded. It is an irrevocable law of Jehovah that indifference to stewardship entrusted to a person must invariably bring its own individual judgment.

Chapter 12

12:1-4. The burden concerning Israel. In the conflict between Jerusalem and the nations, the nations are defeated because Jehovah fights for Jerusalem.

12:1   In section one of part three (chs. 9—11) Jehovah had revealed through His prophet the judgment and complete destruction of the heathen nations and of fleshly Jacob and Israel as a nation. In contrast, He had revealed the spiritual nature of the restored remnant and His use of it in conflict with the Grecian philosophy and religion. In this second section of part three Jehovah reveals the holy and indestructible character of the new spiritual body. Section one had been introduced as "the burden of the word of Jehovah" upon the world powers (9:1); section two is introduced as "the burden . . . concerning Israel." For the meaning of "burden" see comments on Nahum 1:1 and Zechariah 9:1. "Israel" is the new people of God under the rule of the Messiah.

The mightiness of the word spoken and the certainty of its being carried out is emphasized by an appeal to Jehovah, the architect of the universe, as its source. He "stretcheth forth the heavens" (see Ps. 104:2-4; Isa. 40:22; 42:5; Amos 4:13; 5:8), not only in the original creation, but He continues to uphold them "by the word of his power" (Heb. 1:3; cf. Col.

1:17). "And [He] layeth the foundation of the earth," gives to the earth its firmness and solidity on which it continues to exist. "And formeth the spirit of man within him" denotes not Jehovah's one creative act at the beginning, "but denotes the continuous creative formation and guidance of the human spirit by the Spirit of God" (Keil). This living, eternal, creative, and controlling God is He who now speaks, making promises and giving assurances which only one like Himself can fulfill.

At that time Jerusalem was small and despised; but *12:2* God would make it "a cup of reeling," as a large bowl of wine which the nations thought they could drink, gulp down, with ease. But instead, it would be a basin filled with the wrath of Jehovah, to which they would put their lips only to stagger back, reel, fall, and be no more (cf. Obad. 16; Isa. 51:17; Jer. 25:15; 51:39, 57; Hab. 2:16). Jehovah does not imply that Judah would join the enemies against Jerusalem, but that Judah would be one with Jerusalem in the siege; Jehovah would "be seen over them" (9:14), giving victory to His whole people. Jerusalem would also be "a burdensome stone," a large stone which the *12:3* peoples would try to remove out of its place; but they would find it immovable. Those who would undertake such a burden would find themselves "sore wounded," torn and lacerated by the attempt. Wine intoxicates and makes one useless and helpless, and the stone tears and rends. All the heathen powers, the nations of the unregenerate, will be gathered against spiritual Jerusalem in attempts to destroy it, but Jehovah will fight for His people. He will smite the *12:4* horses with terror and the riders with madness. The Lord will have the enemies utterly confused and their weapons impotent. This spirit of militancy against the Lord's city and people will lead only to the violent destruction of the foes. The terror, madness, and blindness with which He will smite Israel's enemies is the same punishment Jehovah had threatened to inflict upon disobedient Israel (Deut. 28:28). Jehovah will open His eyes upon the house of Judah; He will watch over His faithful nation to protect it and to

defeat its enemies. The enemies of Jerusalem will be
made to stagger as drunken men, be lacerated as they
try to remove her out of her place, and be ingloriously defeated when they try to destroy her. Jehovah's
church was to have been made to stand, for He would
be its power.

> *12:5-9. In the Lord Jehovah is strength for
> victory. Through this strength Jehovah de-
> fends Jerusalem and through victory exalts
> Judah.*

12:5 As in verse 4 Jerusalem and Judah are one, the
people of God, so in this place are they one. "The
chieftains of Judah" are the rulers or overseers, the
spiritual leaders among the people, who will say in
their heart that the inhabitants of Jerusalem afford or
give strength to them, the leaders. But this strength
given to the inhabitants of Jerusalem is strength
which Jehovah their God provides for them. Therefore, the ultimate source of strength for all is Jehovah; He gives strength to the inhabitants who in turn
afford strength to the chieftains. All jealousy is removed; both leaders and citizens work together in the
strength of the Lord. While the enemies flounder
blindly in their attempt to destroy Jerusalem (v. 4),
the saints find abundant strength to meet the enemies; for they meet the enemy with a divine power.

12:6 "In that day" (vv. 3, 4, 6, 8, 9) identifies and binds
into one all that is transpiring and being done in this
section (vv. 1-9). In the strength of Jehovah and the
zeal of their service, the chieftains of Judah will be
"like a pan of fire among wood, and like a flaming
torch among sheaves." These "shall devour all the
peoples round about, on the right hand and on the
left"; none will be able to stand or escape. Jerusalem
is personified as a woman who will yet dwell "in her
[margin, ASV] own place," which place is Jerusalem,
the city. All attacks of the enemy leave her un-
scathed; she will ever stand as the city of God in the
midst of His people, unto whom all nations will come
(Isa. 2:2-4; Mic. 4:1-5; Gal. 4:26; Heb. 12:22-23).

In the redemption of His people Jehovah will leave   *12:7*
no place for boasting or glorying; none can glory over
another. The humble dwellers in tents of Judah, the
open country round about Jerusalem, will be given
first preference. In this those of "the house of
David," the royal family, and those of Jerusalem, the
illustrious city, cannot magnify themselves above the
poor, humble peasants of the field. All will stand on
an equal basis before God; "all have sinned" and all
will have been saved by the same salvation of grace;
therefore all ground for glorying will have been excluded (cf. I Cor. 1:31).

The prophet continues to identify situations and   *12:8*
events in the same dispensation, "in that day." At
that time Jehovah will defend the inhabitants of
Jerusalem; there will be no other source of protection
to whom appeal can be made. All people will be
either for the Lord or against Him (Matt. 12:30). In
the conflict with the enemies of righteousness even
the feeble, the ones who could stumble, will be as
bold and courageous as David, the great hero of
ancient times. This hero feared neither the bear nor
lion of the field, nor Goliath, the champion of the
Philistines; but in the strength of Jehovah he met
them all (I Sam. 17:34 ff.). At the same time "the
house of David shall be as God," not possessing the
weakness that the fleshly David showed when he
stumbled. But the house of David will be "as the
angel of Jehovah before them," the feeble. This
places the "angel of Jehovah" on the same level with
Jehovah Himself (see comments under 1:9). In this
period it will be the constant aim of Jehovah to   *12:9*
destroy all the nations that come against Jerusalem;
this will be ever before His eyes. It should be clear
that this does not refer to physical Jerusalem, as no
such confederacy of nations against Palestinian Jerusalem was ever formed. Throughout these verses the
Lord is speaking of His spiritual Jerusalem.

*12:10-14. Through their looking on Him
whom they pierced, and the outpouring of*

> *Jehovah's spirit of grace, the people will be*
> *brought to repentance.*

12:10   The strength through which Jehovah enables His
saints to overcome and defeat their enemies is provided through His grace and their turning to Him in
supplication. Therefore Jehovah promises to pour
upon both the house of David and the inhabitants of
Jerusalem the spirit of grace—divine unmerited
favor—which would cause them to seek that which
His grace provides. This spirit of grace would bring
them to repentance and turn them to Him in supplication. They had rejected Jehovah in the person of
the shepherd (ch. 11), and now they "pierce" Him in
the person of His Son. "They shall look unto *me*
whom they have pierced" is the authentic reading.
They could not pierce Jehovah in the sense of putting
Him to death; but they pierced Him through insult,
blasphemy, and rejection. Of this they would be led
to repent and to mourn as for an only son, even in
the bitterness of grief for one's firstborn. In this
repentance Judah wins a victory over her own self.
What they had done to Jehovah, their descendants
would do to His Son. John quoted and applied the
text to the Christ (John 19:37). In looking unto
"me" whom they pierced and in looking on the Son
whom they pierced, the two natures—that of Jehovah
and the Son—are identified as one.

12:11   Throughout the chapter "in that day" continues to
identify what follows with what precedes. In their
recognition of what they had done, there would be
great universal mourning in Jerusalem and throughout
the land. The reference to "Hadadrimmon in the
valley of Megiddon" is thought by most scholars to
refer to the death of Josiah, who was slain at Megiddo
in battle against Pharaoh's Egyptian forces (see II
Chron. 35:20-25). Tradition has it that Hadadrimmon
was a village a few miles southeast from Megiddo,
though the actual site is unknown. As the mourning
for Josiah had been universal in the land and city, so
would be that of the people for the one whom they
12:12   pierced. The mourning would be among all the fami-

lies of the people, from the royal to the most humble. The families of David and his son, Nathan, indicate the greater and the lesser. Nathan was David's son, through whom were descended Zerubbabel and the Christ (I Chron. 3:5; Luke 3:27, 31). The men and their wives apart probably indicates a custom among *12:13* the Jews. Two families from among the priestly family are mentioned, those of Levi and of Shimei, the son of Gershon, the son of Levi (Num. 3:17-18). *12:14* All the families apart from the royal and priestly families likewise mourned with these.

Chapter 13

13:1-6. A fountain for sin and uncleanness will be opened for all the people. At that time the falsehood of idols will cease, prophesying will be discontinued, and the unclean spirits will pass out of the land.

What follows is identified with what precedes it by *13:1* the prophet's familiar phrase, "in that day." In the context three great events are brought together as of equal importance and so interrelated as to produce and effect salvation mutually. These are the piercing of the Lord (12:10), the opening of the fountain for sin (13:1), and the smiting of the shepherd (13:7). In the piercing of Him unto whom they looked, a fountain was opened to all the people for sin and uncleanness. "A fountain" suggests an abundant provision for the forgiveness of sins. It had been impossible for the blood of bulls and goats to take away sin (Heb. 10:4). All these sacrifices had been a shadow of what was to come (Heb. 10:1); they looked to the sacrifice of the Son for their fulfillment (Heb. 9:15). "Sin" was the missing of the mark; "uncleanness" indicates the pollution and defilement, the consequence of sin. These are all blotted out in the blood of Christ, to be remembered no more (I John 1:7; Heb. 8:12). By this means Judah's true sanctification would be effected.

At the same time that Jehovah opens the fountain *13:2* for sin and for uncleanness, idolatry will perish out of the land. This does not say "out of the earth," for it yet continues; but the names of the idols will be cut off out of the land of Messiah's rule, the true spiritual Judah. That which had been the plague of ancient Judah would be unknown in the new. An apostate church could yield to forms of idolatry, but the true church would not. True prophets would pass out of the land but false prophets would not, for these may ever plague the church. True prophets would cease, for there would no longer be need for them. Prophets were inspired teachers, often identified in the New Testament with the apostles, assisting in the laying of the foundation of the church and the completing of revelation (Eph. 2:20; 3:5; 4:11). Once the foundation was laid and the new revelation was complete, the need for prophets would cease. Daniel indicates the same in a strong Messianic prophecy, when he said of the anointed one, the prince, that He would "bring in everlasting righteousness," and "seal up vision and prophecy [prophet, margin, ASV]." Likewise, unclean spirits, the antithesis of the prophets, would cease. In the conquest of Christ over Satan and his forces, unclean spirits have ceased to control men as they did in the time of the ministry of Christ and the apostles (cf. also Mic. 5:12-13).

13:3   In the time under consideration in these two chapters (clearly Messianic), when revelation would be complete and true prophecy would cease, anyone who would be so presumptuous as to claim the power of prophecy would be a false prophet. His father and mother would bear witness against him, believing him to be a speaker of lies and worthy of death. The father and mother of the speaker of lies "shall thrust him through when he prophesieth." This must not be interpreted to say that parents themselves should put their son to death. Even under the law, though they testified against a son so as to incur his death, they only made the charge against him; others stoned him (Deut. 21:18-21). Parents pronounce him worthy of death and reject any spiritual relation to him. The

13:4   prophet continues to identify the time of which he speaks; it was not the period before or after the exile, but that of the opened fountain, the period under Christ. Prophets of this era will be put to shame, for their prophecies will fail. No longer will there be special badges to distinguish them, such as the hairy mantle worn by ancient prophets like Elijah (I Kings 19:13, 19; II Kings 1:8, marginal reading, ASV). They will be unable to deceive any who will compare their teaching with divine revelation. When his teach- *13:5* ing proves itself false, the lying prophet will endeavor to cover his error by denying that he was a prophet at all; he was a farmer, a slave of the soil from his youth. When asked what are the wounds between his arms or *13:6* hands, on the breast (Deane), or in the palms of the hands (Keil), he replies that he received them in the house of his friends. The exact meaning of the reply is not clear. The reply apparently points to wounds he had received in the house of idols, as the false teacher may continue to wear the scars of his error through life. Some think the reply is an evasion and that the false prophet seeks to cover the real source of his wounds; but the first suggestion seems to be the correct interpretation.

13:7-9. The shepherd is smitten, two-thirds of the flock are given up to death, and the remaining third is refined and purified.

The Lord calls upon the sword to become active, *13:7* to bestir itself. This does not mean that the shepherd was to be slain by the sword; the sword and smiting simply stand for his death through any instrument. The shepherd is "the good shepherd" who was willing to lay down His life for the sheep. "The man that is my fellow, saith Jehovah" indicates that though the shepherd is a man, He is "one united by community of nature" with Jehovah (Pusey). He is of the very essence of God and is identical in purpose with Him. The command "smite the shepherd" points out that which was done was "by the determinate counsel and foreknowledge of God" (Acts 2:23). Upon the smit- ing of the shepherd the sheep were scattered. Jesus quoted this and applied it to Himself and the scattering of His disciples (Matt. 26:31-32; Mark 14:27); therefore, like 11:4 ff. and 12:10, this prophecy can look only to the Messiah for its fulfillment, and can find it in none other. The turning of His "hand upon the little ones" indicated His gathering the scattered ones together and His protecting the weak.

13:8   Judgment and refining will follow the smiting of the shepherd. Two parts, which indicates a major portion of the people, would "be cut off and die."

13:9   The other part, the remaining third, will continue. This lesser part will be separated from the others and will pass through the fire of trials and afflictions. Through these trials they will be tested, refined, and purified as are silver and gold. Peter could have had this passage in mind as he encourages the saints by assuring them that in their manifold trials they will find the proof of their faith, "being more precious than gold that perisheth though it is proved by fire" (I Peter 1:6-7; 4:12; etc.). In the midst of their trials those being proved will call on the name of the Lord and He will respond to their cry. He will say, "It is my people"; and the people will claim Him as their only trust as they respond, "Jehovah is my God." In this Jehovah's promise through Hosea, "And I will say to them that were not my people, Thou art my people; and they shall say, Thou art my God," will be fulfilled (Hos. 2:1, 23; cf. Rom. 9:25-26; I Peter 2:9-10).

Chapter 14

14:1-8. The testing of Jerusalem: all nations will be brought against the city, but Jehovah fights for it. Through Him deliverance is provided.

14:1   The refining and purging introduced by the prophet, in which the larger portion were cut off (13:8-9), is continued under the general picture of Jerusalem's assault. "A day of Jehovah cometh," a day in which the Lord will manifest Himself to His people in a special way. The prophecy is addressed to Jerusalem, when her spoil will be divided among the enemies brought against her. "For I will gather all nations   *14:2* against Jerusalem to battle." Outrage upon outrage will befall the city. But which Jerusalem is the prophet speaking of? Some have concluded that he speaks of physical Jerusalem and its destruction by the Romans, A.D. 70. But this interpretation is made untenable by the assurance, "and the residue of the people shall *not* be cut off from the city." Of Jerusalem's destruction by the Romans Josephus says, "Now as soon as the army had no more people to slay or to plunder, because there remained none to be the objects of their fury . . . Caesar gave orders that they should now demolish the entire city and temple" (*Wars,* Book VII., 1:1). Others have concluded that this is a prophecy of the papal assault on the church of the Lord, which resulted in the Roman Catholic hierarchy and that church's captivity of so many of the saints. The more probable explanation is that the Lord is here pointing to the spiritual Jerusalem as the capital of His spiritual kingdom (cf. Heb. 12:22; Gal. 4:26) and of the assault upon it by the world. Daniel described such an attack on the saints by the "little horn" of the fourth world power, in which the saints were given into his hand (7:21). In his vision on Patmos John saw this fulfilled in the persecution of the saints by imperial Rome (Rev. 13:7). This does not exhaust Zechariah's prophecy, for his description is that of the conflict which would come time after time. "The residue," which is used of Jehovah's remnant (Mic. 5:3; Zeph. 2:9), would never be cut off from spiritual Jerusalem.

This attack by the world on His spiritual citadel   *14:3* affords Jehovah an opportunity to go forth and fight against those nations and in defense of His own city and people. "As when he fought in the day of battle" looks back to the time after time when Jehovah had come to the rescue of His oppressed saints (cf. Hab. 3). As Jehovah had fought for them in ancient times, so would He fight again. The presence of Jehovah is   *14:4* indicated by His standing "in that day," the day in which He fights against the enemy nations, "upon the

Mount of Olives, which is before Jerusalem." The purpose of His standing upon the Mount of Olives is that the Lord may provide a means of salvation for

14:5 His saints. Half the mountain will remove toward the north and half toward the south. By this great valley the people of the besieged city may flee. "The valley of my mountains" is the valley provided by the two halves of the mountain, the northern and southern. Here the besieged saints would find security. The identity of Azel is now lost. Some have identified it with the Beth-ezel of Micah 1:11, a village near Jerusalem; but this is uncertain. The earthquake in the days of Uzziah is mentioned by Amos (1:1), but other than these two references we know nothing of it. It must have been of unusual severity for it to have been remembered all these years. In their flight Jehovah will come with His holy angels to fight for them. Jehovah stood by His saints as they were scattered from Jerusalem (Acts 8); He brought Jerusalem to an end by the Romans (Matt. 24:30-31); He cast the beast, the Roman Empire, and the false prophet, paganism, into the lake of fire (Rev. 19:11-21). These incidents are only a few that illustrate the Lord's fulfilling of the prophecy.

14:6 The description which follows is clearly that of a day of distress: "there shall not be light; the bright ones shall withdraw themselves." Earlier prophets had spoken of days of distress as "a day of darkness and gloominess, a day of clouds and thick darkness, as the dawn spread upon the mountains" (Joel 2:2, 10); "For the stars of heaven and the constellations thereof shall not give their light; the sun shall be darkened in its going forth, and the moon shall not cause its

14:7 light to shine" (Isa. 13:10). It will be "a unique day, unparalleled" (Deane), but known to Jehovah. "Not day, and not night": not complete light, for there will be distress; and not complete darkness, for there will be hope in its midst. "At evening time there shall be light": help comes from the Lord when distress threatens to become despair; "I will not leave you desolate: I come unto you" (John 14:18); "For him-

self hath said, I will in no wise fail thee, neither will I
in any wise forsake thee" (Heb. 13:5).

"In that day" identifies what follows with what   *14:8*
has been said. In the unique day (v. 7), "living waters
shall go out from Jerusalem," the center of the kingdom of God. These living waters symbolize the fresh,
pure, life-sustaining waters of salvation, which would
go forth from the house of Jehovah (cf. Joel 3:18;
Ezek. 47:1-12), provided by Jesus, the Saviour (John
7:37-38). This living water would flow "toward the
eastern sea," the Dead Sea, sweetening its brackish
waters and making it sustain life, and "toward the
western sea," the Mediterranean. The supply would
never be diminished, but would flow perennially
through summer and winter.

In the midst of attacks from the world on God's
spiritual Jerusalem under the Messiah, Jehovah will be
near (v. 4); He will provide an avenue of escape (v. 5;
I Cor. 10:13; II Peter 2:9). When the day seems at its
darkest, His light will be present to guide and direct
(v. 7). In the midst of all opposition, His water of
salvation will never fail (v. 8).

*14:9-11. In that day Jehovah will reign as
King over the earth; His name will be one, and
under His rule Jerusalem will dwell safely.*

Jehovah's rule as King over all the earth would be   *14:9*
in the Messiah. He would be King, whose dominion
would be "from sea to sea and from the River to the
ends of the earth" (Zech. 9:9-10). This rule is ever
before the prophet and should be remembered by the
reader. The names of the idols will have been cut off
out of the land (13:2); therefore would "Jehovah be
one, and his name one." Jesus claimed this oneness
with the Father (John 10:30), and John recognized
"the Name" as all-embracing (III John 7). Like his
predecessors Isaiah (2:2-4) and Micah (4:1-4), Zecha-
riah saw the land about Jerusalem as a plain, "like the   *14:10*
Arabah," and the city exalted above all its surround-
ing territory. The Arabah was the Jordan valley, a

valley of varying widths which extended from the region north of the Dead Sea to the Gulf of Aqabah. "From Geba to Rimmon" would include the limits of Judah from Geba (I Kings 15:22), six miles north of Jerusalem, to Rimmon, which seems to have been the southern boundary, near the wilderness (Josh. 15:32; 19:7). From having been beaten down as in the past, Jerusalem would be lifted up, occupying her rightful position. "Benjamin's gate" was in the north wall, leading from Jerusalem to the territory of Benjamin and Ephraim. The "first gate" and "corner gate" seem to have been the gates at the northeast and northwest corners of the wall extending east and west. "From the tower of Hananel unto the king's wine-presses" seems to be the northeast to southeast ends of the eastern wall. The various locations seem to indicate the full length of the walls from east to west, and from north to south, although many of the ancient locations are no longer clearly definite. Men

14:11 will dwell in the city free from fear of being cast out as in ancient times. In the assurance of Jehovah's protection there will be no fear of a curse, for Jerusalem the ideal will dwell safely.

14:12-15. Instead of a curse upon Jerusalem, the curse will be upon those who war against the holy city.

14:12 Jehovah announces the plague that will fall upon the peoples who war against Jerusalem. They will experience a living death as their flesh rots away while they stand upon their feet; they are dead while they live. Their eyes, which spied out the land for destruction and sought to look on the nakedness of its inhabitants, "shall consume away in their sockets." And their tongue, which was used to blaspheme the honorable name and to curse God's elect, "shall consume away in their mouth." The curse of Jehovah will rest upon those who would curse His own. "In

14:13 that day" there will be a great tumult or discomfiture among the enemies of the Lord's people. God will turn the hand of every man against his fellow and against his neighbor (cf. 11:6). The condition that existed in national Israel (Mic. 7:2-6) will now rest upon the enemies of Jerusalem and God's Israel.

The people of God will be united; the people of 14:14 Judah and those from afar will fight for Jerusalem at her gates. The glory of the nations' wealth will be at 14:15 the disposal of Jerusalem and her children. Further, the plague will rest upon all the beasts of the enemy; all that is used against Jehovah will perish. Here is a strong rhetorical description of the victory of Jehovah's church and the defeat of all that would unite to fight against her. All the enemies of God's camp will go down in defeat.

14:16-19. The remnant of the nations will turn to the Lord in thanksgiving; those who do not will suffer under the plague of Jehovah.

Out of the judgment of Jehovah upon the heathen 14:16 who tried to destroy Jerusalem, the apple of His eye, a remnant will turn to Jehovah. These will "keep the feast of tabernacles" as they "go up from year to year to worship the King." This can only mean that under the Messiah the converted Gentiles will be one with the converted Jews, and that both will worship the Lord according to His prescribed service. The feast of tabernacles, held in the seventh month, was the festival of rejoicing and thanksgiving. It followed in the wake of the annual atonement, at which time all dwelt in booths in memory of Jehovah's deliverance from bondage and of His care for the people (Lev. 23:39-44). The use here of this festival indicates the rejoicing and thanksgiving of the combined remnants. Upon those families of earth who go not up to 14:17 Jerusalem to worship the King, Jehovah, "upon them there shall be no rain." These will live in a perpetual spiritual desert, for in Christ and in Him only is found "every spiritual blessing" (Eph. 1:3).

Egypt had long symbolized the great enemy of 14:18 God's people and had been a synonym for bondage and captivity. Jehovah had promised that He would

provide a highway out of Egypt and that she would be a third with Israel and Assyria; all would stand as equals before Him (Isa. 19:23-25). If Egypt refused to go up there would be no rain upon it; instead, Jehovah would smite her with the plague pronounced upon the nations that reject His offer and go not up
14:19 to the feasts. This will be the fate not only of Egypt, but of all nations who follow her example and refuse to keep the feast of thanksgiving to Jehovah. This is in full and complete harmony with the word of earlier prophets (see Isa. 60:12; Mic. 5:15).

14:20-21. In that day everything will be holy to Jehovah; all will have been sanctified to Him.

14:20 In that day everything that pertains to the kingdom of God will be holy to Him. The war horses will have been cut off from Jerusalem (9:10); therefore, the figure here is that instead of these being for war, they will be holy to the Lord, consecrated to a nobler service. These would bear a similar relation to Jehovah as did the sacred priesthood of old, for "Holy to Jehovah" was the engraving on their breastplate of gold (Exod. 28:36-38). The pots and bowls alike would be equally holy before the Lord; none would be considered common or unclean. All distinctions
14:21 between instruments and ministries of service would be abolished. Nor would there be a Canaanite, one who is unclean and thereby devoted to destruction, found in the house of Jehovah.

These wonderful and glorious promises are realized in the church of today. Every individual and every principle of worship and service has been cleansed and dedicated by the blood of Christ (Matt. 26:28). In Christ there is no distinction; all have sinned and all have been redeemed by Him (Rom. 3:21-26). The church thus cleansed and sanctified is going to be presented to Himself "a glorious church, not having spot or wrinkle or any such thing; but that it should be holy and without blemish" (Eph. 5:26-27).

12

MALACHI

"My Messenger"

General Observations

1. Name

The name Malachi is not found in this form anywhere else in the Bible. The word signifies "my messenger"; George L. Robinson suggests that it "may reasonably be regarded as an abbreviation of *Malakhiyah,* meaning 'messenger of Jehovah'" (*The Twelve Minor Prophets,* p. 157). There is division of opinion among scholars as to whether Malachi is a proper name or whether it is used anonymously for an unknown writer. Since no other prophet spoke or wrote anonymously, it is highly reasonable to conclude that this is the name of Jehovah's last literary prophet who is His final Old Testament messenger to the people. Of the prophet himself nothing is known other than that revealed in his book.

2. Date

Some writers have defended an early date, *ca.* 470 B.C., and others have suggested a time just before the Maccabees, *ca.* 200 B.C. Inasmuch as the content of the prophecy fits well into the conditions described by Nehemiah, the most acceptable date for the prophecy is the period 445-432 B.C.

402 / A COMMENTARY ON THE MINOR PROPHETS

3. Background

The first contingent of exiles had returned during 536 B.C., under the leadership of Zerubbabel the governor and Joshua the high priest. Encouraged by the preaching of Haggai and Zechariah, the people rebuilt the temple between 520 and 516 B.C. Ezra had returned with a second group of exiles in 458 B.C., and it is thought that Zechariah had encouraged the remnant with the message of Zechariah 9—14 sometime between these two dates.

Ezra's work had been to restore knowledge of the law and respect for it. Artaxerxes I (465-425 B.C.; Payne places the end of his rule at 424 B.C., Free at 423 B.C.) had permitted Nehemiah to return to Jerusalem to rebuild the walls of the city. Payne places the date of Nehemiah's first governorship in Jerusalem during the years 444-433 B.C., and the period of his second term as governor, *ca.* 430-425 B.C. (*An Outline of Hebrew History,* pp. 167, 169). For a full picture of the conditons in Judea during this period one should read Ezra 7—10 and the complete Book of Nehemiah. The conditions of the people as revealed in Nehemiah and the bold and courageous attack of Malachi against the problems which the latter sets forth in his book point clearly to the contemporary dates of the two.

4. Style of the Book

In Malachi we meet a new style of address known as the didactic-dialectic method of speaking. In this type of teaching an assertion or charge is made, a fancied objection is raised by the hearers, and a refutation to the objection is presented by the speaker. In the style of Malachi we have the beginning of a method of teaching that later became universal in the Jewish schools and in the synagogue. Earlier prophets had usually followed the rhetorical development of ideas, but no doubt the prophet of this book found the didactic-dialectic method better suited for the conditions and needs of his day.

Ten times the prophet presents the people as interrupting with an objection by putting the words "ye say" in their mouth: "yet ye say" four times (1:2; 2:14, 17; 3:17), "and ye say" twice (1:6, 7), "but ye say" twice (3:7, 8), "in that ye say" once (1:12), and "ye say also" once (1:13).

Another characteristic of Malachi (which reminds us of Haggai), is his appeal to Jehovah as the source of his message. He begins, "saith Jehovah" (1:2), then uses the same expression twice more. He uses "saith Jehovah of hosts" twenty-one times, and "saith Jehovah, the God of Israel" once, using this reference to Jehovah a total of twenty-five times. This appeal to Jehovah as the spokesman, and the prophet's own vigorous presentation of truth, give to his message a spirit of authority and conviction that reached the hearts of some of his listeners, producing results, though they probably were not phenomenal.

5. Message or Lessons

a. Indifference to both the moral and ceremonial aspects of the divine law now characterized the people of God. The exiles had been back in Judea from Babylon for over one hundred years; but instead of becoming better, they had become worse. The people could say that the promises of Jehovah to His people before and since the captivity were not being fulfilled. Why? The answer is that the promises had been conditional and the people were not living up to the conditions stipulated. God had fulfilled His part of the promises; He had done all He could. He had chastised by the captivity; He had brought back a remnant and had settled them in their land; He had graciously forgiven their sins; He had shown His ability and disposition to keep His glorious promises to them. There was nothing more to be done or said by the Lord until they would show a different disposition toward Him. Therefore, with the close of the Book of Malachi no word more could be said until the coming of Him whom God had promised and through whom God's final word would be spoken.

b. Worship was in a state of decay; the priesthood had allowed it to degenerate to the point of accepting the refuse of the flocks and herds as sacrifices. Further, the people had failed to bring in the tithes, thus robbing God. Malachi teaches that although ritual may be important in religion, it is not an end in itself. Ritual is only of value when it expresses a deep and sincere spiritual worship unto God.

c. The Jews were divorcing their wives and marrying heathen women. The prophet makes it clear that such flagrant disregard for God's law can only result in thwarting the divine purpose in securing a pure people unto Jehovah.

d. The book teaches "that there is eternal discipline in the law" (Robinson).

Outline of the Book

Title: Author and subject of prophecy: 1:1.

I. Condemnation of the priests' faithlessness, 1:2—2:9.

    A. Jehovah's love for Israel, 1:2-5.
        1. The divine love asserted, v. 2.
        2. The divine love demonstrated, vv. 3-5.

    B. Rebuke of the faithless priests and people, 1:6-14.
        1. Worthlessness of the people's sacrifices, vv. 6-8.
        2. Better to close the temple, vv. 9-10.
        3. A superior service rendered among the Gentiles, vv. 11-13.
        4. The curse of Jehovah, v. 14.

    C. Curse pronounced upon the faithless priests, 2:1-9.
        1. Immediate reformation the only way of escape, vv. 1-4.
        2. Covenant with Levi and the ideal priest, vv. 5-7.
        3. The apostate priests and their disgrace, vv. 8-9.

II. Condemnation of divorce and mixed marriages, 2:10-16.

III. Day of the Lord—Condemnation of religious indifference and skepticism, 2:17—4:6.

    A. Jehovah's approach in judgment, 2:17—3:6.
        1. Their question, "Where is the God of justice?" 2:17.
        2. Jehovah's appearance as a refining fire, 3:1-2.
        3. Purification of priests and people, 3:3-5.
        4. Jehovah's unchangeableness, 3:6.

   B. Wrongful withholding of tithes and offerings, 3:7-12.
      1. The people's fickleness and Jehovah's curse, vv. 7-9.
      2. Jehovah's bountiful reward for their respect and faithful discharge of duty, vv. 10-12.

   C. New defense of Jehovah's justice, 3:13–4:3.
      1. Complaint: the wicked prosper, the righteous suffer, 3:13-15.
      2. Separation of the pious from the wicked, 3:16-18.
      3. Utter destruction of the wicked, 4:1.
      4. Exaltation and glorification of the righteous, 4:2-3.

   D. Closing admonitions, 4:4-6.
      1. Exhortation to faithful observance of the law, v. 4.
      2. Elijah the messenger and his work of preparation, vv. 5-6.

Comments

Chapter 1

"The burden of the word of Jehovah" is used   *1:1*
only here and in Zechariah 9:1; 12:1. "Burden" or
"oracle of Jehovah" is used many times, but only in
these passages is "burden" followed by "of the
word." For comments on "burden" see Nahum 1:1.
"To Israel" is used of the whole nation with whom
Jehovah had made His covenant (Exod. 24:1-8), and
to whom He now addresses His message. Malachi,
"my messenger," is the name of the prophet, and is
not used of an anonymous speaker sent simply as a
messenger (see under *Name* in General Observations).

*1:2-5. Introduction and foundation of the
book. Jehovah affirms His love for Jacob,*

*confirming the claim by pointing to the dif-
ference He had shown between Jacob and
Esau.*

1:2   Jehovah declares His love for the people, and by
this love He seeks to bring home to the hearts of His
hearers their own ingratitude and lack of devotion
toward Him. In his characteristic way the prophet
puts an objection in the mouth of the people in the
form of a question, "Wherein hast thou loved us?"
This question reveals the inward doubt of the people
toward Jehovah's love for them. The conditions
round about and their own state of mind had led
them to the conclusion that the Lord did not love
them; otherwise things would have been different.
God's answer points to a positive refutation of their
charge; Esau was Jacob's brother, yet Jehovah had

1:3   loved Jacob, "but Esau I hated." God is not speaking
of the two men but of the two nations, Israel and
Edom (see v. 4). Before the birth of the two brothers,
as they struggled in the womb of Rebekah, Jehovah
had chosen the younger above the elder and had said,
"The elder shall serve the younger." But this was said
of the "two nations" and "two peoples": "And the
one people shall be stronger than the other people"
(Gen. 25:23). Paul appeals to this as proof that God
does not select according to the flesh, but according
to His own purpose and will (Rom. 9:8-13). Nor does
Jehovah act capriciously; He must not be charged
with acting from an arbitrary impulse. His choice of
Jacob was to show He was not controlled by human
concepts of action, but His hatred for the nation grew
out of His own immutable and absolutely holy character and Edom's unholy character and disposition
toward Him. Keil warns that the word "hate" is not
to be watered down to a simple "love less," but that
it is the opposite of love. With the same intensity that
Jehovah loves the right and good, He hates the evil
and bad. His attitude toward Edom had been demonstrated by His giving Edom into the hand of Nebuchadnezzar (Jer. 49:7 ff.; 25:9, 21) and not restoring
them to their land as He had Jacob. Their land was

becoming more desolate while Israel's was being culti-
vated. To give it to the jackals was to allow it to
return to its primitive state, a habitation for wild
animals.

Edom's boast that though beaten down, they   *1:4*
would return and build again the waste places was
having an impressive effect on Judah. Judah would be
saying, Edom has been beaten down before and has
come back. Jehovah's response to Edom's boast and
Judah's fear is, "They shall build, but I will throw
down." Edom's destiny is not in their own hands, but
in the hands of God. Edom had received a blow
already from which they would never recover. Two
epithets should be applied to the fallen people: men
shall call them "The border [or country] of
wickedness, and The people against whom Jehovah
hath indignation for ever." History has verified the
prophecy. After the Chaldeans came, the Nabataeans
drove them out. Then they were conquered by the
Maccabees, and finally the Romans drove them into
the eastern desert. "And your eyes shall see." Jacob   *1:5*
will continue as a people and will see the fulfillment
of this word in Edom's complete destruction. In
Jehovah's favor toward Jacob and His casting down of
Edom, He would be magnified in the eyes of the
world. His fulfilled prophecies in the nations of history magnify Him even today.

> *1:6-9. The ingratitude of Israel toward
> Jehovah was demonstrated in the sacrifices
> being offered. Jehovah holds the priests re-
> sponsible for this and sternly rebukes them
> for it.*

Jehovah begins His rebuke of the priests and   *1:6*
people by an appeal to a long established principle
among the Semitic race and His own people in particular. He speaks of the honor of a son for his father and
a servant for his master. The law had been specific
concerning the son and his father (Exod. 20:12), and
had carried the penalty of death for certain in-
fractions (Exod. 21:15, 17; Deut. 21:18-21). It was

likewise a generally accepted principle that a servant should respect his master. If honor and respect on the part of sons and servants for their father and master was accepted among them as a fundamental of society, where then was their honor and fear of Jehovah? From of old He had claimed them as His sons and daughters (see Exod. 4:22; Hos. 11:1; Isa. 43:6; etc.); Moses had spoken of God as Israel's Father who had bought the nation (Deut. 32:6), and Isaiah had called upon Him as the Father and Redeemer of the people (63:16). Therefore, by their own standard He was entitled to proper respect from them. But instead of honor, the priests had despised His name, that name which stood for all that Jehovah was, and the glory that attended His majestic person.

1:7   In response to their question, "Wherein have we despised thy name?" Jehovah charges the priests, who were responsible for the sacrifices, with having offered polluted bread on His altar. The bread does not refer to the show-bread, but to the sacrifices offered, "the offerings of Jehovah made by fire, the bread of their God" (Lev. 21:6), "my bread, the fat and the blood" (Ezek. 44:7). The priests are ready with another question, "Wherein have we polluted *thee*?" They refuse to recognize that to despise Jehovah's name and to profane His worship is to reflect directly on Himself. "The table of Jehovah" is the altar upon which the sacrifices were offered. Not by word, but by their action in what they offered, they were saying that the whole of Jehovah's worship was
1:8   contemptible. The Lord becomes specific in His charge of their contempt for Him and His worship. They were offering the blind, the lame, and the sick from among the flocks and herds and were saying, "It is no evil!" The law required that all sacrifices be perfect and without blemish and that only the best be offered to the Lord (Lev. 22:17 ff.; Deut. 15:21; etc.). If to offer such a worthless gift even to a governor, a political ruler, would be an insult, how much more of an insult it is to offer such to the God of heaven!
1:9   The exhortation of this verse is one of irony, as

indicated by verse 10. If the governor will not be pleased with your offering, how may one expect God to be pleased with it and to respond with gracious favor? "This hath been by your means": your priests are responsible for an attitude that is so bad toward God and His worship that He will not hear and answer your prayers. In your present state of indifference to His divine majesty, will He accept any of you or your offerings? The implied answer is No, for your disposition makes it impossible.

1:10-14. The prophet contrasts the present contempt of the priests' offering with what the Gentiles will offer in every place.

The words "Oh, that there were one among you that would shut the doors" express a wish that there could be found one among them with sufficient jealousy for the Lord and His altar to close the doors against such profane worship. It is better to lock up and stay at home than be guilty of their practices. No worship at all is better than one that rejects the divine honor and insults God with contempt. The doors were those of the inner court where the great altar was located. The fire was that of the altar which consumed the sacrifices. To light it in vain was to offer empty sacrifices which God would not receive. God found no pleasure in priests of such character, and no pleasure in that wherein He should have found delight. *1:10*

In contrast to His people's offerings, which should have been expressive of faith, devotion, and love, but which were an abomination to Jehovah, the Gentiles would offer a pure and acceptable worship. A question must be raised here as to whether the declaration of Jehovah concerning the Gentiles is in the present tense or future. Grammatically, it can be either; but there is no evidence that among the Gentiles Jehovah's name was held in this degree of greatness, or that incense and a pure offering of praise were being made by them to Jehovah. Such an idea is at variance with Paul's description of the Gentiles in *1:11*

Romans 1:18-32, and with his declaration, "There is none righteous, no, not one" (Rom. 3:10). The prophecy looks to that time when, under the Messiah, not in any one locality, but from one end of the earth to the other, God's name would be great among Gentiles. The "incense" offered are the prayers of the saints (Rev. 5:8), and the "pure offering" is the sacrifice of praise, the fruit of lips, and the doing of good in a holy life (Heb. 13:15-16). Through the gospel of the Messiah Jehovah's name would be reverenced as great.

1:12   The Jews, the people of God in the midst of the heathen nations, who should have been a living example of faith in Jehovah and of devotion to Him in worship, were actually making a mockery and scandal of their exalted responsibility. This was their reaction to Jehovah's love; they held both the altar and offerings in contempt. This lesson should be indelibly stamped upon worshipers of today who perfunctorily offer a meaningless religious service to God. Another

1:13   charge is laid against them, "Ye say also, what a weariness is it." Their function at the altar had become a burden to the priests. Instead of their worship being one of joy growing out of gratitude for the Lord's having chosen them to such an exalted honor, they found their work a boresome chore. Here might be found a lesson for preachers, elders, and teachers of the Lord's service in the present dispensation. "Ye have snuffed at it"—the altar and all that pertained to it. We would probably say, "You have turned up your nose at it." To the lame and the sick introduced earlier (v. 8), is added, "that which was taken by violence": that which was stolen or unjustly taken. As Jehovah had condemned stealing, certainly He would not accept an offering that had been stolen! Again the Lord asks, "Should I accept this at your hand?" To think He should is to miss completely the character and will of the Almighty One.

1:14   "Cursed be the deceiver," the cheater or dishonest individual, who vows to God and pays the vow with a blemished animal. The vow was made voluntarily, but it was being redeemed by passing over the best and offering to Jehovah that of less value. "When thou vowest a vow unto God, defer not to pay it; for he hath no pleasure in fools: pay that which thou vowest. Better is it that thou shouldest not vow, than that thou shouldest vow and not pay" (Eccl. 5:4, 5). The condemnation is for redeeming a vow with less than the vow demanded. The curse grows out of the greatness of Him with whom Israel had to do: "For I am a great King," the King of kings; and His name is feared and respected among the Gentiles.

Chapter 2

2:1-4. Because they are derelict in their duty, the priests are threatened with a curse from Jehovah.

The "commandment" given to the priests is not   2:1
instruction or admonition enjoined on them, but it points to the threat of verses 2-3. It is a commandment because the fulfillment of it will be brought on them by Jehovah. As Jehovah commands His blessings on them (Lev. 25:21), so now He commands His curse (cf. Nah. 1:14). The commandment or curse   2:2
will be carried out against the priests only "if ye will not hear, and if ye will not lay it to heart." The double condition is for emphasis. They had insulted the name of Jehovah and had brought it into disrepute; now they must give glory to it or suffer the consequence of Jehovah's curse, demonstrated in the outpouring of His wrath. Jehovah had chosen the priests to bless in His name (Deut. 10:8; 21:5; Num. 6:21-27). As He had turned the curses of Balaam into blessings (Neh. 13:1-2), so now He would turn the blessing pronounced by the priests into a curse. Yes, the curse was already at work on the priests and their blessings because they had not laid to heart God's honor and their responsibility.

"Your seed" which Jehovah threatens to rebuke   2:3
seems not to be the seed which the priests plant (Laetsch), for the Levites, which included the priests, were supported by the tithe (Num. 18:21-32). Orelli

considers the "seed" in the sense of offspring (Deane). J. M. P. Smith (*I.C.C.*) translates (as the marginal reading, ASV) "arm," and applies it to the priestly arm extended in blessing. Deane and Keil translate, "I will rebuke your arm," and interpret it to mean that God will neutralize or take away their power for performing their official duties. The meaning seems to lie between that suggested by Smith and that defended by Keil and Deane. According to the law the dung of sacrifices was to be burned "without the camp" (Exod. 29:14; Lev. 4:11-12; 16:27), but Jehovah says He will spread it on the faces of the priests, "even the dung of your feasts." The Lord refuses to recognize the feasts as His, but rather, they are "your feasts." To speak of spreading dung on the faces of the priests is strong language, indeed! It indicates an ignominious humiliation in which the priests are treated as dung, making them unfit for the service of the Lord, and fit only to be carried away without the camp from His presence. The priests will

2:4   be swept away as dung. The carrying out of the threat, the "commandment" (v. 1), will be the priests' assurance that it was from Jehovah. Jehovah had made the covenant or agreement with the tribe of Levi that they should minister at His altar and to His holy service. God expected this covenant to be respected and observed by them so that it could continue with them. But it could do so only if they kept themselves fit for the service.

> 2:5-9. *The ideal and the real. In the ideal of the covenant made with Levi Jehovah had found uprightness, but in the reality of the present Jehovah finds only corruption of the covenant.*

2:5   The covenant Jehovah had made with Levi, whose name here stands for the whole priestly class, had been one of "life and peace." Smith (*I.C.C.*) translates, "life and welfare," which he interprets to represent "a complex of ideas, viz., peace, quiet, protection, and health." Jehovah had said of Phinehas, who represented Levi, "Behold, I give him my covenant of peace: and it shall be unto him and to his seed after him, the covenant of an everlasting priesthood" (Num. 25:12 ff.). In the blessing of his closing speech to Israel, Moses summarized the responsibility of Levi to keep the covenant, teach the law, observe the sacrifices, and bless in and by their faithfulness (Deut. 33:8-11). Levi's response to Jehovah's covenant of peace was to fear Jehovah. He was not to be afraid, but to reverence and respect the God of the covenant and the duties laid on him. For an illustration of the priests of old standing in awe of Jehovah see Numbers 25:6-13. Probably the prophet points to no particular *2:6* time or period when "the law of truth was in his mouth," but to the realizing of the ideal at various points in their history. The "law of truth" was the whole of God's will as it had been revealed, for "the sum of thy word is truth" (Ps. 119:160). When the priesthood kept the covenant, when the law of truth was in his mouth, "and unrighteousness was not found in his lips," he found the true peace which God had promised, "and turned many away from iniquity." This was no more than God expected of them, but it demonstrates what tremendous results can be realized when responsibility is truly met. The knowl- *2:7* edge of God and of His will should be ever in the heart and on the lips of the priest. This could be maintained only by a constant study of the law and meditation on it. The priests were to fear Jehovah (v. 5), for "The fear of Jehovah is the beginning of wisdom; and the knowledge of the Holy One is understanding" (Prov. 9:10). The people "should seek the law at his mouth," for the priest was both a teacher of the law (Lev. 10:11) and a judge between the people concerning differences which were to be decided by the law (Deut. 17:8-13). "For he [the priest] is the messenger [angel] of Jehovah of hosts." Only here is a priest called a messenger or angel of Jehovah, as only in Haggai is the prophet designated as Jehovah's messenger or angel (1:13). Both priests and prophets were Jehovah's messengers.

But instead of finding the faithful ideal among the *2:8*

priests, Jehovah makes three solemn charges of corruption and faithlessness: (1) "Ye are turned out of the way" of duty and from the way of truth; (2) "Ye have caused many to stumble in the law"; that is, you have so failed in your duties that you have made the law a stumblingblock to the people instead of the light it should have been to guide them aright; (3) "Ye have corrupted the covenant of Levi," the covenant made with him at Moab (see under v. 5). They had lightly esteemed the covenant and had ignored it, manifesting a spirit of disregard and disrespect for it.

2:9 "Therefore" introduces the consequence brought on them by Jehovah. They had corrupted it by failing to keep their part of it; therefore Jehovah was not bound to keep His part. Instead of the honor and high esteem in which they should have been held in the sight of men, Jehovah had made them "contemptible and base before all the people." They had lost all sense of prestige before the people and must now continue without it. Not only had they not kept Jehovah's ways of truth and righteousness, but in their judging of matters among brothers, they had shown "respect of persons in the law." They had shown favor for one against another. It was almost as it had been before the captivity (cf. Mic. 3:11; Zeph. 3:4; Ezek. 22:26).

2:10-16. Divorce of Jewish wives and marriage of heathen women is strongly denounced. Jehovah hates putting away.

2:10 The prophet is not speaking of a universal Fatherhood of God and brotherhood of man when He says, "Have we not all one father? hath not one God created us?" He speaks rather of God as the Father of the covenant people (1:6), and of His creation of them as His special nation and family. In their sinning through the divorce of their wives and marrying foreign women (v. 11), they were dealing treacherously against their brothers in a common faith. They were profaning the covenant Jehovah had made with them at Sinai (Exod. 19:5-6; 24:8) and by which they had been made sons and daughters of Jehovah, whom He had created (see Isa. 43:6-7). Jehovah now specifies the sin in which the people had dealt treacherously. Judah, Israel, and Jerusalem had been scattered (Zech. 1:19); and a remnant of Judah and Israel had been returned to their land (Zech. 8:11-12), with Jehovah dwelling in their midst in Jerusalem (Zech. 8:3). All three of these—Judah, Israel, and Jerusalem—are now indicted. Judah is here used of the nation, acting through her inhabitants, who had acted treacherously in breaking the faith on which they had been brought from exile. "An abomination," comparable to witchcraft, idolatry, and other grievous sins (cf. Deut. 18:9-14), was committed in Israel. The term *Israel* is used here as the sacred covenant name, posing a contrast between what the people were and what they should have been. Israel was to have been to Jehovah a "holy nation" (Exod. 19:6), worshiping Him "in the beauty of holiness" (I Chron. 16:29); but they had profaned this by marrying "the daughter of a foreign god." "The daughter of a foreign god" is used of a woman who is an idolatress, the worshiper of a heathen deity. Intermarriage with these had been specifically forbidden in the covenant (Exod. 34:16). Solomon's violation of this law had opened the door for idolatry to enter into Judah (I Kings 11:1-2; Neh. 13:23-27). Will the same sin now lead to a new apostasy?

2:11

Jehovah will punish this sin by cutting off every man who commits it. "Him that waketh and him that answereth, out of the tents of Jacob" is considered by many commentators to have been a proverbial expression. Explanations of the phrase are many and varied. Pusey explains it as "a proverbial saying apparently, in which the two corresponding classes comprise the whole." The comprising classes are the active watcher who calls and the passive hearer who is roused. This embraces the whole—every waker and every awakened soul. The same punishment will be meted to him who, under such circumstances, offers an offering to Jehovah. Such families would be practically exterminated.

2:12

2:13   Another heinous sin or transgression is introduced by the phrase "And this again [a second time, margin, ASV] ye do," in putting away their Hebrew wives. Not only had they married foreign wives, but they had put away their faithful companions, rejecting the covanant of their youth. The covering of the altar with their tears is thought by Smith (*I.C.C.*) to indicate the intensity of zeal with which they seek Jehovah's favor, for Jehovah was not responding to their cries. But verses 14-16 indicate a more probable explanation: the expression is a metaphor in which the rejected wives were covering the altar with their tears, weeping and sighing to such a degree that the fire was extinguished and the sacrifices were never received but rather rejected by Jehovah. The tears of these mistreated wives stood as an impenetrable barrier between the worshipers and Jehovah. The people

2:14   respond with their usual question, "Why is God displeased with us?" Jehovah's answer is, because Jehovah had been witness to the covenant made between the man and his wife in the day of their youth when love was pure and in full blossom. Likewise, He had been witness to the treacherous conduct of the men in putting away their wives and marrying foreign women, thus breaking the heart of their wives and causing them to weep before Him, figuratively extinguishing the fires of the sacrificial altar. The wife who had been the companion of a sacred covenant, who had borne children to her husband and who had shared his joys and sorrows, his hardships and days of darkness, now was being rejected for a heathen woman, a worshiper of foreign deities.

2:15   The following verse is admitted by both translators and interpreters to be difficult. The alternate reading of the American Standard Version seems to give the clearer sense, "not one has done so who had a residue of the spirit." Not one with a remnant of the spirit of respect for the law of God and of feeling for his mate would do as you have done. "Or what? is there one that seeketh a godly seed?" Anyone desiring to have a godly or holy posterity, which Jehovah desires, would not have put away his Hebrew wife and married a heathen woman. This practice would exclude one and his posterity from the covenant family of God. "Therefore take heed to your spirit": beware, lest you completely lose sight of that spirit of righteousness toward God and decency toward one's wife. Let none deal treacherously against the wife of his youth. Age does not change the relationship of youth's love and pledge.

The Lord emphasizes what He has been saying by an emphatic declaration, "For I hate putting away." From the dawn of creation and the beginning of man's existence, Jehovah has intended that there should be but one woman for one man; He intended that these should be one, divisible only by death (Gen. 2:24). He also hates "him that covereth his garment with violence"; the man who puts away his wife, willfully ignoring her tears and her deeply wounded feelings, covers his garment, himself, his character, with the violence of iniquity. The Lord closes with the same exhortation of verse 15, "Therefore take heed to your spirit, that ye deal not treacherously." Such a vigorous warning and exhortation from the Lord in a former decadent and permissive age should not be silenced; its principle should be heralded to the ends of the earth in our own time. *2:16*

2:17. This verse is an introduction to the remainder of the book. A faithless and murmuring people have sorely wearied Jehovah.

The remainder of the book is introduced by this verse. The faithless multitude of the people had worn Jehovah's patience thin by their skeptical attitude toward Him. The address is not to any one class in particular but to the large majority who had lost their faith in God; however, there was a remnant who were ready to hear (3:16). In response to their self-righteous query, Jehovah makes two charges against them: (1) The people challenged the moral government of Jehovah. They called into question the righteousness and holiness of His judgments and ways by charging, "Every one that doeth evil is good" in *2:17*

Jehovah's sight, and that "He delighteth in them." (2) They ask, "Where is the God of justice?" Instead of bringing the enemies to judgment, He acts in their behalf. Surely, unbelief and skepticism take some curious twists!

Chapter 3

3:1-6. The day of judgment is on its way! It will be preceded by Jehovah's messenger of the covenant.

3:1   Jehovah's response to their question, "Where is the God of justice?" (2:17), is that He Himself will come, and suddenly. But before He comes He will send His messenger to prepare the way before Him. This promise of a messenger rests on the prophecy of Isaiah (40:3-5); this messenger is the Elijah of 4:5. It is strange that there should be any dispute over who this messenger is, but many theories have been advanced by expositors. There is no prophecy more clearly established than that the "voice" of Isaiah (40:3) and the Elijah of Malachi (4:5) is John the Baptist; all four of the Gospels affirm this (Matt. 3:3; Mark 1:3; Luke 3:4; John 1:23). The angel of the Lord explained this coming of Elijah when he said of John the Baptist, "He shall go before his face in the spirit and power of Elijah" (Luke 1:17). This messenger would go before and prepare the way for the Lord's coming. Further, we have the testimony of Jesus Himself that the prophecy of Malachi was fulfilled in John the Baptist (Matt. 11:10), and that John the Baptist is the Elijah that was to come (Matt. 11:14). Jesus seemed amazed and disappointed that the disciples should ask Him further about the Elijah who was to come, and He declared emphatically, "Elijah is come already." They then understood that He spoke to them of John the Baptist (Matt. 17:12 ff.). The Lord whose coming they thought they desired would "suddenly come to his temple." To come suddenly did not mean immediately, but at once, instantaneously, unannounced. The temple to which He would come was not the temple built by Herod, but the temple of Jehovah, the spiritual temple. "The messenger [angel] of the covenant" is here identified with the Lord, not as one person, but as one in deity and Godhood. This establishes the fact that Christ, who came as the "messenger of the covenant," was divine, of the essence of Jehovah. Jehovah had promised that He, the Messiah, would be "for a covenant of the people"—that is, for a personal bond between Jehovah and His people (Isa. 42:6; 49:8). Jesus is the mediator of that New Covenant, the covenant of peace (Heb. 9:15; 13:20), and the bond that binds God's people to Himself.

However, the coming of Jehovah will not be as they had expected; for He will not come simply as a judge of the heathen, but as a judge of His own as well. The unbelieving skeptics will not be able to stand under the judgment which will include them, for "he is like a refiner's fire, and like fullers' soap." The double figure has not two meanings but one. The Lord will not come simply as a fire, but as a smelter, purging the dross from the silver. He will come as a "fuller," one who washes and thickens cloth, who will cleanse as with a strong lye soap. He will sit as a judge purifying and cleansing, but not necessarily as a destroyer. The special objects of His purifying and purging operation will be "the sons of Levi," the priests, who had been brought under such severe condemnation (1:6–2:9). When this is done, the purified priesthood would "offer unto Jehovah offerings in righteousness"; but an offering in righteousness could be offered only from a heart that is holy and righteous. This new refined priesthood is the spiritual priesthood under the New Covenant (I Pet. 2:5, 9), whose sacrifices are those of praise and thanksgiving. They are the fruit of lips that make confession to His name, a confession and praise that flows from a pure heart (Heb. 13:15-16). Under these conditions the offering of Judah, the new nation, and Jerusalem, the new city unto which the redeemed and purified have come (Heb. 12:22, 24), will be pleasant and acceptable to Jehovah. "As in the days of old, and as in

3:2

3:3

3:4

ancient years" does not intend to suggest that the same offerings would be made; but the phrase looks to those days when "Israel was holiness unto Jehovah," probably in the early days in the wilderness and possibly in the days of David and Solomon.

3:5 The Lord now comes to the heart of His reply to their question (2:17). Not only will He come in judgment against the priests, but He will come also against all the wicked among the people. From the beginning of their history the people had been plagued with sorcery and witchcraft, practices controlled by evil. The law specified death as the penalty for sorcery (Lev. 20:27). Adultery was being practiced in their marrying the heathen women; the penalty for adultery was also death (Lev. 20:10). False swearing violates the law (Lev. 19:12; see under Zech. 5:4), as did the suppressing of the wages due a laborer (Lev. 19:13). To oppress "the widow, and the fatherless" and to refuse the sojourner who dwelt among them were all condemned by Jehovah's law (Exod. 22:21-24). Jehovah would judge these moral and ethical sins. The root of their actions was clear: they did not fear Jehovah. When this respect for Jehovah is

3:6 gone, there is no restraining force against evil. Here is declared an immutable principle on which man can depend in all ages and generations: "I, Jehovah, change not." In Him is no shadow cast by turning (James 1:17). His infinite love, which is basic to His immutable character, will provide mercy that they be not completely consumed; but His eternal hatred for sin will consume with the fire of His everlasting justice those who are His adversaries (cf. Ps. 89:14 ff.; 97:2 ff.).

> 3:7-12. A charge and a challenge: The people had robbed God of tithes and offerings. Bring these in and prove Jehovah if He will not pour out blessings beyond imagination.

3:7 "From the days of your fathers" looks back, not simply to the previous generation or two, but to time immemorial, from the day they came out of Egypt (cf. Jer. 7:25 ff.). God's promise of blessings had always been conditional (Lev. 26; Deut. 28). Man must cooperate by doing his part; this they had not done. Jehovah's returning to them is conditioned on their returning to Him. In the spirit of their self-righteous Pharisaism, they respond to Jehovah's gracious invitation by asking, "Wherein shall we return?" Calloused and hardened by rebellion and sin, they seemed to have no consciousness of wrong doing. Jehovah responds with a question, "Will a man rob God?" To rob one's fellow man is a great sin, but to rob God should be unthinkable. Wherein had they robbed God? "In tithes and offerings." The tithe had been holy to Jehovah (Lev. 27:30-33); Jehovah had laid claim to "the heaven and the heaven of heavens, the earth, with all that is therein" (Deut. 10:14). Tithes and offerings freely given are acknowledgments of that ownership and of man's stewardship. Because of this refusal to acknowledge Jehovah's claim and of their disposition to rob Him, they had been cursed with the curse (cf. 2:2; Hag. 1:6; 2:15-17). Not just isolated individuals, but rather the whole nation is brought under the charge.

3:8

3:9

This charge is followed by an earnest exhortation and challenge: "Bring ye the whole tithe"—not just a part of it which would further defraud the Lord, but all of it—"into the store-house, that there may be food" in Jehovah's house for those for whom it was intended (Num. 18:24). "And prove me": you do your part and see if I will not fulfill mine, is Jehovah's summons and challenge to measure faith with deeds. To "open you the windows of heaven, and pour you out a blessing, that there shall not be room enough to receive it," is as when the floodgates of heaven are opened and rain descends in torrents. So will God pour out His blessings on them. If they will but return to Jehovah and fulfill their obligations to Him, Jehovah will fulfill the rich promises made through Moses and Ezekiel that He would bless them above their fathers (Deut. 30:5; Ezek. 36:11). Not only would Jehovah bless them so richly, but also He would destroy "the devourer," the locust and hail,

3:10

3:11

the blasting and mildew (cf. Amos 4:9; Hag. 2:17).

3:12 As the recipients of Jehovah's favor and His gracious beneficence, they would enjoy the praises of the nations, for their land would be a delightful land.

> *3:13-18. The impatient and impious among them murmur against Jehovah, while the faithful few fear Him and hearken.*

3:13 The Lord had laid before them the reason for withholding His blessings. He now proceeds to make another charge against them: "Your words have been stout against me." The adjective "stout" means hard, harsh, violent. In their conversations one with another they had said strong things against the Lord.

3:14 In reply to their characteristic question, Jehovah gives them a specimen of their harsh words; they had questioned God's moral government among men. They had said, "It is vain"—useless, unprofitable, to no advantage—to serve God. "And what profit is it that we have kept his charge," His commands? It is as if they were serving the Lord for hire and as if He were indebted to them for their service. They had walked mournfully, "in mourning apparel" (margin ASV), in fasting before Jehovah. Whether their mourning disposition before Jehovah was sincere or feigned is not a point at issue; the point is that they had put their confidence in the outward fasting which was of no worth before Jehovah. This question had been clearly settled by Zechariah (chs. 7—8). Because

3:15 they were not blessed immediately with favors from Jehovah for having "kept his charge" and having "walked mournfully before" him, they were prone to call the arrogant sinners a happy lot; for they appeared to prosper and to get great enjoyment from life. The murmurers further charged that the proud who worked wickedness were built up by Jehovah and that, though they tempted Jehovah, they escaped from judgment. Both their concept of Jehovah and of moral values was badly warped. Their thinking brought them under the woe of Isaiah (Isa. 5:20).

There is never a time when Jehovah does not have His "seven thousand in Israel" whose knees "have not bowed unto Baal" (I Kings 19:18). Even now, in contrast to the murmurers who questioned the moral government of Jehovah, there were some who feared Him. As they listened to the words of the unbelievers and to Jehovah's rebuke of them, those who were concerned conversed among themselves. What they said is not recorded, but their words were pleasing to Jehovah, who heard and hearkened to them. "A book of remembrance was written before him," that it could lie open before Him at all times and that at all times He could recall their pious words and faithful disposition toward Him. This indicates that the words, deeds, and disposition of Jehovah's own are ever before Him. The thought of Jehovah's keeping a book of remembrance is common to both Old and New Covenants (see Exod. 32:32 ff.; Ps. 56:8; 69:28; 139:16; Ezek. 13:9; Dan. 7:10; 12:1; Phil. 4:3; Rev. 20:12). The remembrance is of the life, deeds, and needs of "them that feared Jehovah, and that thought upon his name." These would be those who held His name in reverence and who kept Him in their thoughts.

3:16

These who are faithful will sustain a most intimate relation to Jehovah; they will be His own personal possession. "In the day that I make" is a day of judgment, such as Jehovah had introduced in 3:2 (cf. Amos 9:8 ff.). Jehovah's "day of judgment" is not to be confined to the final judgment, for He is continuously coming in judgment against wicked societies and nations. In such days Jehovah will be mindful of those who serve Him, and whose names are written in the book that lies before Him. He will be mindful of them as a father is mindful of his only son who serves and obeys him. In contrast to the judgment and destruction of the wicked, these will be delivered. Throughout their history the Jews had had opportunity to see the difference in results from serving God and not serving Him. But when "the day" comes and they see afresh the consequence that comes to

3:17

3:18

each, they will be able to see clearly the distinction between the righteous and the wicked, and between serving God and not serving Him.

Chapter 4

4:1-6. The prophet closes with a description of the ultimate, complete destruction of the wicked and the triumph of the righteous.

4:1   The reference to the coming of the day of judgment as a devouring fire was often used by former prophets (e.g., Amos 1:4, 7; Zeph. 1:18; 3:8). It will burn as a furnace in which the wicked and proud will be as the dry stubble of the wheat field. As a tree dug up by the roots is burned, roots and branches, so will be Jehovah's destruction of the wicked: total and complete. Although the prophet writes of many such days that have come upon the wicked of earth, especially the destruction of the Jews and of Jerusalem, a final day of complete destruction of the wicked from the face of the Lord will be at Christ's coming. At that time all the wicked will be eternally destroyed 4:2   from Jehovah's presence (II Thess. 1:9). To those that fear Jehovah's name, "the sun of righteousness [will] rise with healing in its [beams.]" It is certainly true that Christ came bringing to light the righteousness of God, but it is quite doubtful that the prophet here speaks of Him in person. Instead, the thought is that righteousness itself is the sun that will arise with healing in its rays or beams. This divine righteousness will be as accessible to all as is the light from the rays of the sun. Those who fear Jehovah and bask in the light of His provided righteousness will go forth from their confinement and frolic as calves turned out of a 4:3   stall into the green pasture. To "tread down the wicked" indicates the complete victory of the righteous and righteousness over the wicked and wickedness. Then reduced to destruction by the fire of Jehovah's judgment, the wicked will be as ashes under their feet. Whatever may be the lot of the proud or of the meek at given times, the ultimate victory of the righteous and the defeat of the wicked is abundantly assured by the Lord.

The prophet closes with an admonition, a final 4:4 promise, and a threat. The admonition is, "Remember ye the law of Moses." To meet the judgment of God in confidence the true Israelite must respect and keep the law. Malachi, the prophet with whom Jehovah closed His Old Covenant, affirms the Mosaic authorship of the Pentateuch. "My servant" indicates that Moses simply served as Jehovah's minister who wrote it; the source of the law was Jehovah Himself. Liberal theologians have divided the origin of the law among many sources and authors, but Malachi stamps the lie on all such intellectual nonsense—it is of Jehovah through Moses! Horeb is another name for Sinai, where among scenes of awe, terror, and wonder, Jehovah made known His law. This was not just the ten commandments, but the whole law: the ten commandments, the statutes, and the ordinances, which include all moral, ceremonial, and legal enactments. Before the great and terrible day of judgment, refin- 4:5 ing, and purifying will come, Jehovah promises to send Elijah the prophet. As the David whom Jehovah will raise up to be king and shepherd over His people (Jer. 30:9; Ezek. 34:23 ff.; 37:24; Hos. 3:5) is not David in person, but fulfilled in Christ, so the Elijah here is not to be thought of as Elijah in person, but his spirit in another. John denied that he was Elijah in person (John 1:21), yet Jesus said he was the Elijah of promise (Matt. 17:11-13). The promise was ful- filled in John the Baptist, sent to prepare the way for Christ (see comments under 3:1). The mission of this 4:6 Elijah, the forerunner of the Messiah, was to turn the affections of the people back to God and His divine law. He was to restore a right relation between par- ents and children and to turn the hearts of the chil- dren to the ancestral religion of their fathers. In this condition of heart they would be ready to receive the Messiah, for they would see in Him the fulfillment of all God's wondrous promises and the glorious hope of their fathers. Elijah had preached repentance and a return to Jehovah; this also was the preaching of John the Baptist. A return to Jehovah was the only way to avert destruction. Some hearkened, most did not. Consequently, Jehovah destroyed their city and their land. When Jesus left their temple desolate (Matt. 23:38), it was left a carcass, fit only for the vultures (Matt. 24:28). The vultures or eagles came and the carcass was devoured, A.D. 70.

The Book of Malachi serves as a fitting close to God's ancient revelation to His people. A final appeal is made to the people to purge out the wickedness found among them and to render to Jehovah an acceptable service. A final warning is given of inevitable judgment upon the wicked. And a final promise is made of Jehovah's righteousness to be provided in Him who would be the personal bond of unity between Jehovah and His people. There was no more that Jehovah could say or do; therefore no word was heard from Him until the silence was broken by the messenger who would introduce the Messiah. This messenger's call to repent was followed by the words of grace spoken by Him in whom God was doing His work and revealing Himself and His will.

BIBLIOGRAPHY

Introductions

Driver, S. R. *An Introduction to the Literature of the Old Testament.* Reprint. New York: The Meridian Library, 1956.

Eiselen, Frederick Carl. *Prophecy and the Prophets.* New York: Methodist Book Concern, 1909.

———. *The Prophetic Books of the Old Testament,* 2 vols. New York: Methodist Book Concern, 1923.

Pfeiffer, Robert H. *Introduction to the Old Testament.* New York: Harper and Brothers, 1948.

Robinson, George L. *The Twelve Minor Prophets.* Reprint. Grand Rapids: Baker Book House, 1952.

Unger, Merrill F. *Guide to the Old Testament.* Grand Rapids: Zondervan, 1956.

Young, Edward J. *An Introduction to the Old Testament.* Grand Rapids: Wm. B. Eerdmans, 1956.

Commentaries

Briggs, Driver, Plummer, (eds.). *The International Critical Commentary.* Minor Prophets: Julius A. Bewer, Wm. R. Harper, H. G. Mitchell, W. H. Ward. New York: Charles Scribner's Sons, 1905.

Cook, F. C. *The Holy Bible Commentary,* Vol. VI. Minor Prophets: Samuel Clark, F. C. Cook, W. Drake, R. Gandell, E. Huxtable, F. Meyrick. New York: Charles Scribner's Sons, n.d.

Farrar, F. W. *The Minor Prophets.* New York: Fleming H. Revell Co., n.d.

Geikie, Cunningham. *Hours with the Bible,* 3 vols. New York: James A. Pott and Co., 1889.

Keil, Carl and Delitzsch, Franz. *Biblical Commentary on the Old Testament,* 25 vols. Keil, "The Twelve Minor Prophets" (Vols. 24, 25). Reprint. Grand Rapids: Wm. B. Eerdmans, 1949.

Laetsch, Theo. *The Minor Prophets.* St. Louis: Concordia Publishing House, 1956.

Leupold, H. C. *Zechariah.* Reprint. Grand Rapids: Baker Book House, 1971.

Pusey, E. B. *The Minor Prophets,* 2 vols. Reprint. Grand Rapids: Baker Book House, 1950.

Smith, George Adam. *The Book of the Twelve Prophets,* 2 vols. New York: A. C. Armstrong and Son, 1898.

Spence, H. D. M., and Exell, Joseph. *The Pulpit Commentary.* W. J. Deane, commentator: The Minor Prophets. New York: Funk & Wagnalls Co., n.d.

Atlases

Pfeiffer, Chas. F. *Baker's Bible Atlas*. Grand Rapids: Baker Book House, 1961.
Wright and Fulson. *Westminster Historical Atlas of the Bible*. Philadelphia: The Westminster Press, 1956.

Dictionaries and Encyclopedias

Davis, John D. *A Dictionary of the Bible*. Reprint. Grand Rapids: Baker Book House, 1954.
Harrison, Everett F. *Baker's Dictionary of Theology*. Grand Rapids: Baker Book House, 1960.
Orr, James (ed.). *International Standard Bible Encyclopedia*, 5 vols. Grand Rapids: Wm. B. Eerdmans, 1949.

General Works

Baer, Dallas C. *The Messages of the Prophets*. Great Neck: Pulpit Digest, 1940.
Beecher, Willis J. *The Prophets and the Promise*. Reprint. Grand Rapids: Baker Book House, 1963.
Copass, B. A. *The Message of Hosea*. Philadelphia: American Baptist Publication Society, 1906.
Fairbairn, Patrick. *Prophecy*. New York: Carlton and Porter, 1866.
Fowler, Henry T. *The Prophets as Statesmen and Preachers*. Boston: The Pilgrim Press, 1904.
Knudson, Albert C. *The Beacon Lights of Prophecy*. New York: Eaton and Mains, 1914.
———. *The Prophetic Movement in Israel*. New York: Abingdon-Cokesbury Press, 1921.
Payne, J. Barton. *An Outline of Hebrew History*. Grand Rapids: Baker Book House, 1954.
Pfeiffer, Chas. F. *The Biblical World*. Grand Rapids: Baker Book House, 1966.
Robinson, George L. *Twelve Minor Prophets*. Reprint. Grand Rapids: Baker Book House, 1952.
Sampey, John R. *The Heart of the Old Testament*. Nashville: Broadman Press, 1922.
Sayce, A. H. *Ezra, Nehemiah, and Esther*. London: The Religious Tract Society, 1885.
Schwantes, Siegfried J. *A Short History of the Ancient Near East*. Grand Rapids: Baker Book House, 1965.
Shultz, Samuel J. *The Old Testament Speaks*. New York: Harper and Row, 1960.
Thiele, Edwin R. *The Mysterious Numbers of the Hebrew Kings*. Grand Rapids: Wm. B. Eerdmans, 1965.
Urquhart, John. *The Wonders of Prophecy*. New York: Christian Alliance Publishing Co., n.d.
Wallace, Foy E. *God's Prophetic Word*. Revised. Oklahoma City: Foy E. Wallace, Jr., Publications, 1960.
Yates, Kyle M. *Preaching from the Prophets*. New York: Harper Bros., 1942.
Young, Edward J. *My Servants the Prophets*. Grand Rapids: Wm. B. Eerdmans, 1952.